Transitions for Young Children

Transitions for Young Children
Creating Connections Across Early Childhood Systems

edited by

Sharon Lynn Kagan, Ed.D.

and

Kate Tarrant, M.P.A.

National Center for Children and Families
Teachers College
Columbia University

·P A U L·H·
BROOKES
PUBLISHING C?. ®

Baltimore • London • Sydney

Paul H. Brookes Publishing Co.
Post Office Box 10624
Baltimore, Maryland 21285-0624
USA

www.brookespublishing.com

"Paul H. Brookes Publishing Co." is a registered trademark of
Paul H. Brookes Publishing Co., Inc.

Typeset by Aptara, Inc., Falls Church, Virginia.
Manufactured in the United States of America by
Sheridan Books, Inc., Chelsea, Michigan.

The case studies described herein are based on actual people and actual circumstances. Real names and identifying details are used with permission.

Library of Congress Cataloging-in-Publication Data

Kagan, Sharon Lynn.
 Transitions for young children: creating connections across early childhood systems /
Sharon Lynn Kagan, Kate Tarrant.
   p.   cm.
 Includes bibliographical references and index.
 ISBN-13: 978-1-59857-083-0
 ISBN-10: 1-59857-083-8
 1. Early childhood education—United States. 2. Early childhood education—Curricula—
United States. 3. Child development—United States I. Tarrant, Kate. II. Title.
LB1139.25.K348 2010
372.21—dc22   2010022938

British Library Cataloguing in Publication data are available from the British Library.

2014   2013   2012   2011   2010

10   9   8   7   6   5   4   3   2   1

Contents

III Programmatic Perspective

IV Policy Perspective

V Integrating Pedagogy, Programs, and Policy

About the Editors

Sharon Lynn Kagan, Ed.D., Virginia and Leonard Marx Professor of Early Childhood and Family Policy and Co-Director, National Center for Children and Families, Teachers College, Columbia University, 525 West 120th Street, Box 226, New York, New York 10027

Dr. Kagan is the Virginia and Leonard Marx Professor of Early Childhood and Family Policy and Co-Director of the National Center for Children and Families (NCCF), Teachers College, Columbia University, and Professor Adjunct at Yale University's Child Study Center. Dr. Kagan, recognized nationally and internationally for her work related to the care and education of young children and their families, is a frequent consultant to the White House; Congress; the National Governors' Association; the U.S. Departments of Education and Health and Human Services; and numerous states, foundations, corporations, and professional associations; and serves on more than 40 national boards or panels. She has been the president of the National Association for the Education of Young Children, the cochair of the National Education Goals Panel on Goal One, chair of the Family Support America's Board of Directors, a member of President Clinton's education transition team, and National Commissions on Head Start and Chapter 1. She is dedicated to early childhood education, having been a Head Start teacher and director, as well as an administrator in the public schools and director of the New York City Mayor's Office of Early Childhood Education.

In addition to these contributions, Dr. Kagan is globally recognized for her unique scholarship. In more than 250 publications including 13 volumes, Dr. Kagan's analytic work has helped the field define school readiness, the early childhood system, dimensions of collaboration, and leadership in early care and education. With scores of grants from America's leading foundations and the federal government, she has researched early childhood pedagogy, strategies for service integration, and the evaluation of social programs. She is currently working around the globe with UNICEF to establish early learning standards in Armenia, Bolivia, Brazil, Cambodia, Chile, China, Georgia, Ghana, Jordan, Kazakhstan, Lesotho, Malawi, Moldova, Mongolia, Paraguay, Tajikistan, Thailand, Turkmenistan, Uzbekistan, and Viet Nam. Perhaps most important, however, Dr. Kagan may be best known as the only woman in the history of American education to be recognized for these contributions with its most prestigious awards: the 2004 Distinguished Service Award from the Council of Chief State School Officers, the 2005 James Bryant Conant Award for Lifetime Service to Education from the Education Commission of the States, and the Harold W. McGraw, Jr. Prize in Education.

Kate Tarrant, M.P.A., Graduate Research Fellow, National Center for Children and Families, Teachers College, Columbia University, 525 West 120th Street, Box 226, New York, New York 10027

Kate Tarrant is a doctoral candidate in Curriculum and Teaching, concentrating on early childhood policy. As a graduate research fellow at the National Center for Children and Families (NCCF), Teachers College, Columbia University, Ms. Tarrant works on the National and International Transitions analysis and the Policy Matters Project. In addition, she worked on the Early Care and Education Workforce Initiative and previously served as the Assessment Coordinator for the NCCF project with New York City's Administration for Children's Services to develop, field test, and evaluate a unified quality assessment tool for early care and education programs in New York City. Her research interests include the application of early care and education policy to practice in different types of early learning settings. She is also interested in the development of comprehensive and inclusive early childhood systems. Ms. Tarrant earned her master's degree in public administration at Columbia University's School of International and Public Affairs, with a concentration in social policy. She has been a consultant for New York City's Administration for Children's Services Division of Child Care and Head Start. Previously, she worked as the public policy specialist for Good Beginnings Alliance–Hawaii, an early childhood intermediary organization.

Contributors

Caroline Arnold, M.A.
Codirector, Education Programmes
Aga Khan Foundation
Avenue de la Paix 1-3
Geneva, Switzerland 1201

Kathy Bartlett, Ph.D.
Codirector, Education Programmes
Aga Khan Foundation
Avenue de la Paix 1-3
Geneva, Switzerland 1201

Anthony Berkley, Ph.D.
Deputy Director, Education & Learning
W. K. Kellogg Foundation
One Michigan Avenue East
Battle Creek, MI 49017

Kimber Bogard, Ph.D.
Associate Director
Institute of Human Development
    and Social Change
246 Greene Street
New York, NY 10003

Sue Bredekamp, Ph.D.
Early Childhood Education Consultant
2608 Crest Avenue
Cheverly, MD 20785

Jeanne Brooks-Gunn, Ph.D.
Virginia and Leonard Marx Professor of
    Child Development and Education
Teachers College, Columbia University
525 West 120th Street, Box 39
New York, NY 10027

Mary Beth Bruder, Ph.D.
Director
A.J. Pappanikou Center for Excellence in
    Developmental Disabilities
University of Connecticut
263 Farmington Avenue MC6222
Farmington, CT 06030

Richard M. Clifford, Ph.D.
Senior Scientist
FPG Child Development Institute
University of North Carolina
Campus Box 8040
Chapel Hill, NC 27599

Carolyn T. Cobb, Ph.D.
Consultant
North Carolina Ready Schools Initiative
Carolyn Cobb Consulting LLC
4701 Metcalf Drive
Raleigh, NC 27612

Alejandra Cortazar, M.A.
Psychologist
Teachers College, Columbia University
525 West 120th Street, Box 39
New York, NY 10027

Gisele M. Crawford, M.A.A.
Research Specialist
FPG Child Development Institute
University of North Carolina
Campus Box 8040
Chapel Hill, NC 27599

Carol Brunson Day, Ph.D.
President and CEO
National Black Child Development Institute
1313 L Street NW #110
Washington, D.C. 20005

Jocelyn Friedlander
Research Assistant
Teachers College, Columbia University
525 West 120th Street, Box 226
New York, NY 10027

Eugene E. Garcia, Ph.D.
Professor
Arizona State University
14421 South Canyon Drive
Phoenix, AZ 85048

Saima Gowani, Ed.M.
Monitoring, Evaluation, and
    Research Officer
Aga Khan Foundation
Avenue de la Paix 1-3
Geneva, Switzerland 1201

Aleksandra Holod, M.P.P.
Graduate Research Fellow
National Center for Children and Families
525 West 120th Street, Box 39
New York, NY 10027

Romilla Karnati, Ph.D.
Consultant, National Center for
    Children and Families
525 West 120th Street, Box 226
New York, NY 10027

Kristie A. Kauerz, Ed.D.
Project Director, PreK-3rd Education
Harvard Graduate School of Education
44R Brattle Street
Cambridge, MA 02138

Judy Langford, M.S.Ed.
Senior Fellow
Center for the Study of Social Policy
901 Forest Avenue
Evanston, IL 60202

William W. Malloy, Ed.D.
Associate Professor, Emeritus
University of North Carolina
Chapel Hill, NC 27599

Robert C. Pianta, Ph.D.
Dean, Curry School of Education
University of Virginia
405 Emmet Street South
Charlottesville, VA 22903

Craig T. Ramey, Ph.D.
Distinguished Professor and Director
Center on Health and Education
Georgetown University
3700 Reservoir Road
Washington, D.C. 20057

Sharon Landesman Ramey, Ph.D.
Susan H. Mayer Professor of Child and
    Family Services
Director, Georgetown University Center on
    Health and Education
3700 Reservoir Road
Washington, D.C. 20057

Jeanne L. Reid, M.P.A.
Graduate Research Fellow
National Center for Children and Families,
    Teachers College, Columbia University
371 Grace Dodge Hall
New York, NY 10027

Sharon Ritchie, Ed.D.
Senior Scientist
FPG Child Development Institute
517 South Greensboro Street
Carrboro, NC 27510

Susan D. Russell, M.S.
President, Child Care Services Association
1829 East Franklin Street, Suite 1000
Chapel Hill, NC 27514

Thomas Schultz, Ph.D.
Project Director
Early Education Accountability
Pew Charitable Trusts
1025 F Street NW, 9th Floor
Washington, D.C. 20004

Catherine Scott-Little, Ph.D.
Assistant Professor
University of North Carolina at Greensboro
248 Stone Building
Greensboro, NC 27402

Caroline Segal
Brown University, Rhode Island
7 Puritan Road
Rye, NY 10580

Sadaf Shallwani, M.S.W.
Education Associate
Aga Khan Foundation
Avenue de la Paix 1-3
Geneva, Switzerland 1201

Acknowledgments

We are grateful for the work of numerous individuals who have contributed to this volume. To begin with, we acknowledge the W.K. Kellogg Foundation and our program officer, Tony Berkley, for his steadfast support for this project. He pushed us to think comprehensively and practically, marrying research and theory with the real-world experience of individuals who work with young children and families. We also thank the contributing authors for their provocative chapters. In addition, we would like to acknowledge those who shared their experience with us to inform the case studies that populate this volume. Their insights enliven this body of work and illustrate its relevance for children and families. We also acknowledge Astrid Zuckerman and Julie Chavez at Paul H. Brookes Publishing Co., Inc., for their patience and support. Finally, we gratefully appreciate our colleagues Penina Braffman, Jennifer DeSantis, Jocelyn Friedlander, Rebecca Gomez, Saima Gowami, Ali Hill, Romilla Karnati, and Jodi Moss, who provided editorial and research support throughout the development of this project. Thank you.

For
Thomas Lawrence Kagan, Anne Louisa Kagan, and Darwin James Moneyhon
whose world and lives will be filled with transitions.
May our work, this volume, and the love we have for them make their journeys joyous.

Transitions for Young Children

I

Background and Context

1

Seeing Transition Through a New Prism

Pedagogical, Programmatic, and Policy Alignment

Sharon Lynn Kagan

INTRODUCTION

This volume is about a transcendent yet ephemeral construct. It is about an idea as common as air and as complex as the molecules that compose it. It is about a reality and a vision and about a single word with many interpretations. This book is about transition in the field of early childhood education, an evolving construct whose meaning has perplexed, and continues to perplex, researchers and educators today.

Conventionally, within the early childhood context, *transition* has referred to the movement that children make as they leave the preschool years and enter kindergarten. Most commonly, and with a nod to Piaget (Rabusicova, 2007), *transition* has referred to the assimilations and accommodations that children, families, preschools, and schools make to support children as they navigate the often quite disparate worlds of preschool and primary school. This first conception of transition evoked the development of activities to support children as they traversed the preschool-to-school gap, including preschoolers' visits to kindergartens, the transfer of preschool records to receiving schools, and meetings to help parents anticipate the demands of their children's formal schooling.

Over time, ideas about transition have expanded in scope and complexity. A second, two-dimensional conception has emerged. It posits both vertical and horizontal transitions. *Vertical* transitions are the transitions that children make as they advance chronologically through the periods of their lives—for instance, from infancy to toddlerhood and from toddlerhood to the preschool years. By contrast, *horizontal* transitions encompass the many spheres or settings that children experience simultaneously; they may, for example, move from home to child care to preschool over the course of a single day (Kagan, 1991). Others have written about transition from an ecological perspective, describing how "links among child, home, school, peer, and neighborhood factors create a dynamic network of relationships that influence children's transition to school both directly and indirectly" (Rimm-Kaufman & Pianta, 2000, p. 492).

3

As these ideas about transition took hold, so did new efforts associated with them. Moving from simple, often one-time activities, transition and transition-inspired efforts assumed many forms. Transition efforts expanded *vertically*, extending well beyond the original preschool-to-school linkage that spanned roughly the 4- to 6-year-old period, to embrace transitions for children from birth through age 8. They also expanded *horizontally*, shifting from creating transitions for one child, one program, or one school to creating transitions for the multiple institutions that support children's full range of development, including health, social services, and other community institutions. Because so many institutions were involved, creating effective linkages among them necessitated the building of collaborations, interagency agreements, joint councils, and common administrative entities. In essence, then, the idea of promoting effective vertical and horizontal transitions for children became associated with establishing linkages within and among diverse organizations and institutions. As this occurred, the focus expanded from an individual orientation to embrace an institutional change agenda.

Under the mantra of transition or institutional change, some efforts sought to transform entire schools; others attempted to reform primary education so that it more closely resembled the child-centered approach fostered by many early educators. Projects, councils, and schools of thought surrounding prekindergarten (pre-K) to Grade 3 and even pre-K to age 20 have been established under the rubric of transition. Bearing different names—*whole-school reform, community schools, developmental continuity, follow-through, child-friendly schools*, and *ready schools*, to name a few—these efforts dot the landscape. Although they differ in important ways, they similarly embrace a broadened approach to the transition challenge, seeking to ease transitions for individual young children and their families and to promote institutional change simultaneously.

Despite—and perhaps because of—the abundance of new ideas and efforts to support transitions, confusion about transition continues to persist today. Such confusion takes many forms. First, definitional ambiguity prevails. Multiple, related terms (*transition, alignment, continuity, linkage*) are used with little clarity regarding their similarities and differences. This cacophony of terms begs for distinction. Second, there are practical ambiguities. Scores of disjointed programs and services are being mounted under the diverse mantras, reflecting increased domestic and global interest in young children. As with the terms used to describe these efforts, there is often little discussion of what binds and conversely distinguishes these efforts. What, for example, are the real differences among a ready school, a child-friendly school, and a pre-K–3 school? Third, in a reflection of the previous two conditions, there is no overarching conceptual paradigm to guide the abundant work of so many dedicated pioneers. Transition projects emerge, flourish, and then often fade into oblivion, leaving a bare legacy that has not succeeded in appreciably altering early and primary education. Because of these ambiguities, the impressive work to advance smooth transitions has not yielded durable continuity for children, families, and communities.

To that end, the editors of and contributors to this volume take their place in the litany of strugglers who have attempted to define, categorize, implement, and evaluate early childhood transitions. By creating this volume and bringing together contributions from leading scholars, practitioners, and thinkers from around the globe, the editors seek to contribute a new conceptual approach to advancing transitions work. Such an approach must be informed by careful analysis of the factors that have inhibited durable structural transitions from taking hold in the past. Moreover, a fresh approach must review and build on existing research, fully absorbing lessons related to successes and failures. Finally, a new approach must proffer a clear framework that both explicates the concept and provides some guidance for its enrichment.

This chapter establishes the base for the volume. First, it examines transitions from a holistic perspective. It suggests that to understand why transition has been so challenging, we must look at the structure of early childhood itself. By so doing, we will see that multiple, unique, and trenchant fissures characterize early education. These structural fissures are more than simple discontinuities that could be ameliorated by one-time activities, and they demand structural responses. When we examine these fissures, we see that they are widespread and span time, disciplines, institutions, and settings. Discussed in this chapter as temporal, disciplinary, institutional, and contextual challenges, respectively, they collectively paint a clear picture of the depth and breadth of the challenge and provide a poignant rationale for why the field so desperately needs to adopt a fresh conceptual approach to transition.

Understanding these challenges is a necessary but insufficient prelude to fostering change. We also must understand the lineage of efforts that have taken place to address transition in early childhood education. Although this topic is discussed in detail elsewhere, the second section of this chapter takes a fresh look at what we have—and have not—learned from the myriad of transition studies. We also examine their relevance for today's children, schools, society, and understandings of transition.

Finally, armed with new understandings about the history and complexity of the transition challenge and a fresh perspective on the research, the author presents a new, more systemic way to think about transitions. Detailed in the third section of this chapter, the framework also guides the organization of the volume. Stated most simply, the new framework accepts the expanded ecological perspective on transition, one that embraces new vertical and horizontal approaches to transitions; furthermore, it suggests that a third approach—a structural approach—be added.

What is meant by a structural approach? Contemporary early education has three linked components that frame the structural approach to transition: 1) the pedagogical component (i.e., the nature and content of the learning exchange that takes place among children, their parents, and their teachers, irrespective of the early childhood setting); 2) the programmatic component (i.e., the array of nonpedagogical services provided by programs to foster children's full development, including health and outreach services); and 3) the policy component (i.e., the regulations and laws that allow best practices to be established, funded, monitored, and sustained).

This structural approach suggests that in order for meaningful transitions to take place, we must attend to the content of transitions—the *what* that we are attempting to alter, notably three components—*pedagogies, programs,* and *policies*. Simultaneously, we also must attend to *how* we foster transition, by supporting a process that transcends the superficial and works toward embedded *alignment*. Taken as a whole, then, the structural approach to transition suggests that we deepen conventional ideas and actions about both transition content (pedagogies, programs, and policies) and transition processes (alignment). Combining this focus on content and process, the structural approach embraces 1) pedagogical alignment, 2) programmatic alignment, and 3) policy alignment. Moreover, it posits that without attention to all three types of alignment, transition efforts will not be sufficient to override the deep fissures that frame the field.

Far from eliminating considerations of vertical and horizontal approaches to transition, this conceptual frame embraces and adds to them. Metaphorically, we might regard this approach as a prism. A prism has multiple sides; so does this conception of transition—vertical, horizontal, and structural. Further, in a prism, all sides are linked to make the prism whole. To be effective, transitions must be linked vertically, horizontally, and structurally. Moreover, as light bounces in and through a prism, it touches—and perhaps changes—the way we see each side. The structural approach that is described in this volume does so as well. When we focus on pedagogical alignment, programmatic alignment, and policy alignment, we are likely to alter horizontal and vertical approaches to transition and enrich them. Finally, a prism refracts and casts light: It is hoped that this volume will help shed light by providing a new conceptual and practical approach to transition.

UNDERSTANDING THE TRANSITION CHALLENGE: THE NATURE OF EARLY CHILDHOOD EDUCATION

To understand transitions in a contemporary light, we need to step back and tease apart the nature of early childhood education. More than simply a review of transition efforts, this analysis suggests that the very nature of the early childhood enterprise itself necessitates attention to transition. Four framing variables that are deeply embedded within the field both constitute the backbone of early education and predict its need to focus on transitions. These framing variables are *temporal*, *disciplinary*, *institutional*, and *contextual*.

Temporal Variables

Early childhood—generally considered the period from birth to age 8—is a special time; it embraces the period when the human organism undergoes its most rapid and remarkable physical, mental, and social growth (Hart & Risley, 1995; National Research Council and Institute of Medicine, 2000). As a result, early education is required to facilitate many transitions that young children naturally experience as they navigate this period of their lives. The early years are a time when everything is new and challenging, a time when young minds are fully vital, absorbing information from every experience. It is also the time in human development when change has the most impact and demands the most attention and support. Mindful of the rapid pace and the unique and evolving learning styles of young children, early educators notice children's transitions at every turn. How does Juan cope with change? Will Corrine be able to fit that peg into its appropriate hole? What new surprise will Anna master today that she couldn't handle yesterday? Precisely because very young children experience transitions—biological, intellectual, and physical—at every turn, early educators cannot escape dealing with transitions. Indeed, supporting children as they manage these natural temporal transitions is one of early educators' primary functions and a defining characteristic of this field.

Disciplinary Variables

In part because of the importance of the temporal variables just described, early childhood education spans disciplines. Children grow physically, mentally, emotionally, and cognitively simultaneously. Thus, however structurally inconvenient it may be, early education is grounded in diverse disciplines—health and mental health; developmental, cognitive, organizational, and community psychology; and educational theory and pedagogy (Beatty, 1995). Borrowing from each of these disciplines, early childhood education must then create linkages among them, negotiating the traditions, vocabularies, and epistemologies associated with each. Within academia, this interdisciplinary nature of the field is manifest in the lack of a consistent academic home or department. Early childhood education may be found within departments as diverse as home economics, family and community psychology, curriculum and instruction, and health and behavior studies. Moreover, early childhood's status as a hybrid discipline has resulted in the division of its funding, programs, and mechanisms for regulation and accountability among congressional committees and administrative entities that deal with health, education, social welfare, women's affairs, and community development (Kagan, Goffin, Golub, & Pritchard, 1995). Early education, then, is deeply hallmarked by disciplinary and corresponding jurisdictional divisions that necessitate transitions and alignment at virtually every turn: in what and how we teach children, in the nature of the programs that serve them, and in the public policies that are created to advance their development.

Institutional Variables

Institutional variables have also been critical in shaping the nature of early education and the corresponding need for educators to attend to transitions. Given that early education focuses on young children whose ties with families and communities are and must be strong, it is closely identified with supporting the transitions that children make as they move between the two most important institutions in their early lives—from the warmth and familiarity of the home and family to the more complex social worlds of child care programs, preschools, schools, and communities. Practically, it seems fairly simple: Early education is the bridge that spans the environments of the home and the school. Rather than being an add-on or politically correct endeavor, forging links between home and formal settings is the very essence of early education. It is why quality early education programs visibly manifest a commitment to families and to family engagement. It is why, conventionally, early education has been associated with parenting education, home visits, family support, and two-generation child and adult literacy programs. It is also the reason that early education is not firmly associated with one institutional structure, the way schools are for education or hospitals are for health. Rather, early education spans myriad program types and services, including but not limited to family child care, group home care, preschools, Head Start, for-profit child care, pre-K programs, kindergarten, and primary schools. Early education may be found in homes, church buildings, schools, parks, and community centers.

These institutional variables demand and have been accorded attention by early educators. But they also harbor deeper, more transcendent issues. In order to span the transition between the institutions of home and school, we tacitly span differences between the culture and language of the home, with its intimacies and nuances, and the culture of the mainstream society. Sociocultural negotiations that are sometimes in concert but other times in conflict play out over the course of a child's transitions among early care and education settings (Doucet & Tudge, 2007; Vogler, Crivello, & Woodhead, 2008). Early childhood, then, marks the starting point of the fusion between the privacy of the home and the public sphere of the larger society. Not only is it the first absorber of these adjustments at an individual level, but it also functions as an institutional mirror reflecting society's values. De facto, at its core, early childhood education forges transitions among institutions and values.

Contextual Variables

Finally, at the broadest glance, early childhood education sits at the confluence of a rapidly changing context in which technological, communication, information, and accountability advances are altering life globally. These reforms have changed early education, forcing it to transition from a field that is relatively remote from policy to one that has become central to discussions of intellectual, social, and economic advancement (Knudsen, Heckman, Cameron, & Shonkoff, 2006). This change has been propelled in part by neuroscience research that has clearly demonstrated the importance of early brain development to success later in life (National Research Council and Institute of Medicine, 2000). The world's majority populations, which often live in developing countries, are positioning early learning and development as a central policy cornerstone for social and economic growth (Clifford & Crawford, 2009), as are countries in the developed world.

But this was not always the case. Until as recently as the 1960s, young children were not the major subjects of public policy in the United States. Rather, they were sequestered from it by a national ethos that accorded hegemony to the primacy and privacy of the family. Of course, children and their behaviors were inherently intriguing, and they gradually made their way into emerging professional fields of child and developmental psychology. Fueled by this interest and supported by funding from several seminal foundations, a child study movement emerged. It was followed by the launching of the Children's Bureau by the U.S. government (Beatty, 1995). Despite these advances, however, children remained remote from the policy agenda, except in times of personal or national crisis. The Social Security Act of 1935 (PL 74-271) sanctioned services to orphans or otherwise destitute youngsters. National crises—World War I, the Great Depression, and World War II—triggered short-lived federal policies that provided child care so that mothers could work. But with the exception of these events, a hands-off policy stance prevailed until America's Head Start program was formed as part of a response to another national crisis, the War on Poverty. In the 45 years since Head Start's founding, early childhood education has transitioned from a back-burner policy issue to one that is front and center. Early childhood education is no longer simply the domain of academics but has become a matter of national economic, political, and social concern. It is the poster child for a field that has contextually transitioned, if not transformed, itself.

As defining elements for the early childhood field, these four types of framing variables— temporal, disciplinary, institutional, and contextual—have not been neutral. They have left a legacy that shapes the daily lives of those who inhabit, think about, and strive for the advancement of early education globally. Taken together, they have bequeathed a fragmented landscape for young children, their families, and the myriad institutions that serve them. Because of their limited cogency, the practices and policies that have evolved have done little to smooth these fissures. In their wake, a legacy of inconsistency and incoherence remains the transcendent challenge of the field and the rationale for this volume.

LESSONS FROM RESEARCH ON TRANSITIONS

Because efforts to facilitate transition are couched in a field that is characterized by the temporal, disciplinary, institutional, and contextual variables we have just discussed, it is not surprising that such efforts are not new to the early childhood agenda. Indeed, theorists and practitioners have long grappled with forging transitions during the early years.

Looking at Transitions from Theoretical Perspectives

Early childhood's founding fathers and mothers—the theorists whose work guided the development of the field—each emphasized transitions in young children's lives. Early on, developmental and learning theorists, including Pestalozzi and Froebel, noted the importance of easing the burdens of transition and ensuring continuity for young children. Writing at the turn of the 19th century, Pestalozzi advocated for strong links between the home and school. In order for education to be engaging and meaningful, he argued, it must be aligned with the culture and values of a child's home and community; school-based learning must enrich the practical and moral spheres of an individual's life (Green, 1969). He emphasized the role of parents as teachers, as well as the teacher's duty to "weave his accessory work into that of the parents' as a weaver works a flower into a whole piece of cloth" (Green, p. 79). This early conception of transition, then, reflected concern for the child's experience as well as beliefs about the ultimate purpose of education.

Froebel, Pestalozzi's student, similarly stressed the need for durable links between the home and school (Froebel, 1826/1974). Froebel also emphasized the importance of temporal continuity for young children: "It is highly pernicious," he wrote, "to consider the stages of human development—infant, child, boy or girl, youth or maiden, man or woman . . . as really distinct, and not, as life shows them, as continuous in themselves in unbroken transitions" (p. 27). He promoted a child-centered approach to pedagogy, one that would facilitate young children's natural intellectual and spiritual development. Arbitrary interruptions to this organic process, he warned, would be "destructive in their influence" (p. 27). As he initially conceived it, the child-centered kindergarten model served as a transitional year for children as they moved from informal early care to more academic settings.

Later theorists, from Piaget to Montessori, advanced more nuanced understandings of the relationship between learning and transitions, often offering new approaches to and rationales for practice. Piaget's claim that preoperational children experience and interpret the world through a single frame of reference, assimilating new information to self-centered cognitive schema (Gholson & Beilin, 1979), underscored the need to maximize continuity in their lives. Distress around transitions between home and school, the theory implies, may be reduced by aligning the two environments—all the way from their spatial configurations to the quality of adult–child interactions (Silvern, 1988).

Similarly, the Montessori model emphasized the importance of routine and predictability for young children, even while it advanced a uniquely individualized approach to pedagogy. Although children in Montessori schools have the freedom to select activities based on their interests, this freedom flows within the bounds of extremely organized classrooms and around precisely choreographed microroutines (Lillard, 2005). The underlying theory guiding Montessori's approach is that routines provide children with a stable basis that they need in order to assimilate new information and successfully navigate transitions.

Vygotsky's sociocultural theory of development offered yet another perspective on transitions. According to the theory, social experience serves as a catalyst for cognitive growth, particularly when young children are guided to act at the boundaries of their current development. From this view, transitions can serve as important opportunities for learning, as long as adults provide thoughtful scaffolding to help children adjust to new circumstances (Carlton & Winsler, 1999). Approaching the social dimension of transitions from another angle, attachment theory underscored the importance of stable relationships for young children's healthy social and emotional development (Ainsworth, Blehar, Waters, & Wall, 1978).

Therefore, over nearly 2 centuries, theorists have provided a variety of orientations to transitions: pedagogical, cognitive, and social. In so doing, each in his or her own way, with his or her own words, has underscored the importance of fostering continuity in young children's lives.

Applying Theoretical Conceptions of Transitions to Practice

Building on theorists' views, the idea of transition gained currency in public practice. Perhaps the first large-scale recognition of the importance of transition was the emergence of the kindergarten movement. Although kindergartens are acknowledged to have emerged over time and to have somewhat differing philosophical roots (Beatty, 1995; Chung & Walsh, 2000), kindergarten was always premised on the belief that children needed time to make the transition from the world of the home to the world of the school.

Froebel, who heavily influenced the emergence of kindergarten, saw early childhood as part of a continuous developmental trajectory toward unity, a state of intellectual and spiritual fullness (Chung & Walsh, 2000). Froebel's ideas were adopted by Elizabeth Peabody, whose conception of kindergarten embraced a moralistic stance that sustained the primacy of the family. She described the role of the kindergarten teacher in maternal terms, emphasizing the need to nurture innocence and guide moral development (Chung & Walsh, 2000).

Later, in 1873, William Harris and Susan Blow led the establishment of the first public kindergarten in St. Louis, reframing it as an important stage in the "transition between the life of the Family and the severe discipline of the School" (in Beatty, 1995, p. 66). In their view, kindergarten was less about sustaining the morality and intimacy of the home and more about preparing children for the institutional and social realities of the schools. Later, concerned that kindergarten's incorporation into the public school system had led to an overly academic focus, a new generation of developmentalists—who still advocated for kindergarten as a transitional year—returned to a truly child-centered approach (Chung & Walsh, 2000). Their scientific reinterpretation of Froebel's developmental theory characterized 20th-century research and thinking about kindergarten and transitions more broadly. From the origin of child study with the research of Stanley Hall to the progressive education movement and the work of John Dewey, psychological understandings of child development became central to the debate over transitions in early childhood (Beatty, 1995). Furthermore, the increasing prominence of the science of early childhood placed developmentalists at the center of policy debates. First advocating for White House conferences, then for the Children's Bureau, these thinkers were highly influential in contouring a commitment to developmental continuity that set the groundwork for the establishment of Head Start and the series of rich transition efforts surrounding it.

Head Start in particular raised the transition ante. To justify its existence, Head Start was called on not only to produce gains for children while they were in the program but also to ensure that such gains were sustained over time as children moved to and through the primary years of schooling. President Lyndon Johnson was concerned about disappointing results (Holmes & Holmes, 1966; Rivlin & Timpane, 1975)—dubbed *fade-out*—and he quickly launched a major national program, Follow Through, in 1967. This program represented the beginning of federal engagement in transition and had the goal of supporting children as they moved from Head Start to school. Although it was somewhat short-lived, Follow Through evolved into Head Start Planned Variation, an effort designed to discern whether different curricular approaches differentially affected the outcomes of Head Start children as they moved through the early years of schooling.

These efforts are noteworthy on two counts. First, they tilted the transition frame squarely in the direction of pedagogical continuity. Second, despite the investment and hopes that were lodged in them, the efforts did not result in clearly evident benefits of transition. Sustaining the gains remained a somewhat elusive goal, causing the then Office of Child Development to launch an impressive series of transition efforts over the next decade: Project Developmental Continuity (PDC; 1974), the Head Start Transition Project (1986), the National Transition Study (1988), and the National Head Start/Public School Early Childhood Transition Demonstration Study (1990).

Studying Transitions in Action

Launched in 1974 by the Office of Child Development, now called the Administration for Children, Youth and Families (ACYF), PDC moved beyond its predecessors in targeting children's transitions (Kagan & Neuman, 1998). The program linked Head Start and other early childhood programs to the public schools by providing guidelines that addressed the major aspects of transition that needed attention: administrative coordination; curriculum, preservice, and in-service training; developmental support services; parent involvement; and services for handicapped, bilingual, and multicultural children. The program suggested two models for implementing the guidelines: 1) creating new administrative bodies in communities where Head Start and schools existed under separate auspices, or 2) establishing Head Start Programs under the governance of public schools. Yet despite its comprehensive approach, PDC research did not produce particularly encouraging outcomes. Results of the program were inconclusive and showed no statistically significant differences between children who had participated in PDC and children in control groups who had not. Undermining the study's design were confounding factors such as poor implementation of PDC in treatment sites and transition efforts occurring at control sites (Bond, 1982).

The national Head Start office launched a similar experimental assessment of transition efforts, the Head Start Transition Project, in 1986. All Head Start programs were encouraged to develop transition activities, and ACYF provided additional funding for 15 programs to implement more comprehensive transition models. An analysis of treatment and control sites for this program did find a correlation between the frequency of teachers' participation in transition activities and higher ratings of children's school readiness, as well as reduced stress levels among children during the first month of school. Children from the intervention programs also demonstrated higher levels of resilience at the beginning of school (Hubbell, Plantz, Condelli, & Barrett, 1987). These encouraging outcomes were associated with particular transition strategies, including ongoing transition activities, visits to kindergartens by Head Start children, training for parents regarding their rights within the school system, parent support groups, and suggestions for parents of activities that they could do with their children (Hubbell et al., 1987).

In 1988, the U.S. Department of Education began the National Transition Study, an investigation of the efforts that public elementary schools were making to sustain the gains made by disadvantaged children in early intervention programs. The study was not an evaluation of these efforts, but an inventory of current practices. As it turned out, transition programs were not being widely implemented. Only 47% of schools had parent visitation programs (Love, Logue, Trudeau, & Thayer, 1992). Furthermore, only 10% of schools made efforts to communicate with children's previous teachers or caregivers, and only 12% had curricula that were aligned with those used in preschools. The study also revealed differences in practices between low- and high-poverty schools; transition activities in low-poverty schools tended to emphasize links between schools and early care and education programs, whereas high-poverty schools tended to emphasize family involvement as a way of easing transitions. The National Transition Study underscored the diversity of approaches that schools pursued to improve transitions but also made it clear that more transition activities were needed.

Two years later, Congress authorized the National Head Start/Public School Early Childhood Transition Demonstration Study to support low-income children and families in the transition from Head Start to school. Federal grants were issued to local programs under the condition that they provide support services for Head Start children and families through third grade. Although ACYF provided national guidelines for these services, their implementation was left to grantees so they could address local needs (Kagan & Neuman, 1998). Overall, 31 demonstration projects involving more than 450 public schools implemented programs to enhance parental involvement; developmentally appropriate practices; and educational continuity, social support, and health services (Ramey et al., 2000). An analysis of the project, which was conducted from the 1991–1992 school year to the 1997–1998 school year, revealed a variety of encouraging results, although not all were statistically significant. For example, teachers in demonstration classrooms reported increased communication with former teachers regarding curricula and individual children compared with teachers in controlled classrooms, but the improvement was not statistically significant; the same was true concerning communication between schools and preschools. In terms of child outcomes, children from demonstration and comparison sites fared similarly over the course of their transition to kindergarten and the first years of elementary school.

This brief overview of work that is detailed well elsewhere (Kagan & Neuman, 1998) indicates that there has been no paucity of effort to launch innovative approaches to transition and to evaluate them. Indeed, efforts have spanned the gamut from those which focused primarily on curriculum (Follow Through, Head Start Planned Variation), to those which envisioned transition more broadly (Project Developmental Continuity), to those which sought to chronicle existing efforts (National Transition Study), to those which sought to evaluate transition practices (National Head Start & Public School Early Childhood Transition Demonstration Study).

Irrespective of their locus (federal, state, or local) or their sponsorship (public or private), overall the efforts did not achieve their intended gains. Some of them cited methodological challenges (Bond, 1982); others said that the implementation was never fully realized (Bond, 1982; Hodges & Cooper, 1981). Still others noted that a 1-year inoculation model, even with the best transition efforts, could not be held accountable for children's long-term gains (Barnett, 1993). Whatever the rationale the programs proffered, transition remained a noble but elusive construct, and the vast majority of the nation's early childhood programs and schools failed to engage in its realization (Love et al., 1992).

Recognizing the dilemma of such limited transition uptake, scholars, practitioners, policy makers, and foundations set out to right the situation. Thoughtful essays and books emerged, as did diverse speculations on new ways to think about transition. Some experts suggested that transition efforts had been too narrowly construed as short-term, end-of-the-year activities; they called for sustained, year-long, non–Band-Aid approaches to preparing children for school and schools for children (Sameroff & Haith, 1996). Others noted that transition efforts were often too narrowly conceptualized, focusing on particular classrooms or schools; they suggested that to be effective, transition efforts needed to embrace families, schools, and communities as partners (Powell, 1989; Zigler & Kagan, 1982). Some scholars suggested that as important as transition efforts are, they often ignore the realities of theoretically inconsistent and pedagogically mis-aligned expectations, curricula, and assessments (Kagan, Carroll, Comer, & Scott-Little, 2006; Pianta, Cox, & Snow, 2007). Finally, others contended that transition and continuity might be false premises, as the pace of the world's change necessitates framing early education efforts in terms of the metrics of adaptation and change.

MOVING FORWARD

With the above issues framing transition efforts of the past, a stage was set for the current epoch during which transition efforts have also commanded much attention. They have, however, taken a different twist and, as such, evoke new ways of thinking about and enacting transitions.

Recent Major Efforts

Recently, major foundations have invested in transition and pre-K–3 agendas. The W.K. Kellogg Foundation, for example, has supported innovative transition initiatives across the country. Its Supporting Partnerships to Assure Ready Kids (SPARK) Initiative has grantees in seven states and the District of Columbia (W.K. Kellogg Foundation, 2008). SPARK programs have taken a variety of approaches to smoothing transitions, including training parents to be advocates, build-ing school transition teams, developing public–private partnerships, and linking early learning standards to those of the K–12 system. In addition, the Foundation for Child Development, which runs a PreK–3rd Initiative, has made a 10-year commitment to support efforts to align standards, curriculum, instruction, and assessment from pre-K through the first few years of elementary school. The Foundation provides grants to programs conducting basic and applied research in the area and supports policy development, advocacy, and communications strategies that are related to its pre-K–3rd vision (Foundation for Child Development, 2009).

The current interest in transition also has been reflected in the recent publication of several books on the topic. Two of them—*School Readiness and the Transition to Kindergarten in the Era of Accountability*, edited by Pianta, Cox, and Snow (2007); and *Tools for Transition in Early*

Childhood, by Rous and Hallam (2006)—stand out as examples of contemporary work on both the theoretical and practical dimensions of transitions.

In addition, there has been considerable interest in transition internationally. The Bernard van Leer Foundation, for example, supports interventions around the world to improve transitions for children who are under 8 years of age. The Foundation has focused on three areas that it sees as integral to children's transitions: access to early education, language development, and children's rights. It also has identified important avenues through which to address these looming issues: peer support, intergenerational support, curriculum and pedagogy, children's agency, and leadership and supervision (Bernard van Leer Foundation, 2009).

A New Approach

In reviewing the theoretical and practical work that has emerged over the decades, we have seen that the word *transition* has embraced numerous efforts, strategies, and approaches. Indeed, the term is dense in meaning, causing muddied understandings and actions. To that end, we offer a new approach for consideration. The approach suggests 1) a new *way of thinking* about transition and its relationship to early education, 2) a shift in the *zeitgeist* around transition, and 3) a new *definition* of transition. Each aspect of the approach is discussed in the remainder of this section.

Historically, the understanding of transition in early education was that transitions for young children were not easy or continuous, and the existing discontinuities needed to be overcome. Furthermore, transitions were not fully integrated into the early childhood routine but needed to be planned and added on to daily activities. If, however, one accepts the stance offered herein, a different view emerges. The stance notes first that the temporal, disciplinary, institutional, and contextual variables that characterize early education will not go away. Second, it suggests that these variables have led to fissures that, if not addressed, are harmful to children's development. Consequently, it suggests that the need to create transitions among disciplines, institutions, and times in early education is also durable. By (re)definition, early childhood is and will remain an inherently bridge-spanning endeavor. Transition, according to this perspective, is not an optional add-on; rather, it is fundamental and central to the practice of early education. Moreover, rather than regarding transition as a weakness to be eradicated, this volume regards transition as an opportunity to advance development.

Such a shift in thinking needs to be accompanied by a shift in the general zeitgeist if positive change is to take hold. *Zeitgeist* refers to the "spirit of an age" or "the trend in thought and feeling in a period." The paradigm shift that we suggest positions transition to permeate early childhood education and to be regarded as central to the overall field as play. As such, transition must become not simply part of the mindset, but part of the culture of early education, infiltrating its practices and policies. The transition zeitgeist must change so that transitions will be generally regarded as normative.

Such a zeitgeist will not emerge without some general consensus regarding the definition of and images associated with transition, the third element of the paradigm shift. Earlier, we suggested a prism as a graphic image of transition. The multiple sides of the prism reflect three approaches to transition—vertical, horizontal, and structural. In adding the third approach—the structural—this volume both acknowledges the importance of the first two approaches and suggests that all three are integrated. Moreover, it defines the structural approach as having three components: pedagogical alignment, programmatic alignment, and policy alignment. Elaborated next, each of these is actionable and involves durable structural alterations.

Pedagogical Alignment   The first type of alignment includes efforts targeted at what and how children learn and how teachers learn and teach. Pedagogical alignment is concerned with both the content and process of the educational exchange. It focuses on the alignment of standards, curricula, assessments, and philosophical orientations toward teaching as children move from their earliest years through primary school. *Pedagogical alignment* refers to the way that teachers conceptualize childhood and children (miniature adults vs. continually curious children), how they approach teaching (didactic vs. emergent), what they teach (subject areas vs. developmental domains), and what values they espouse (how they view parents, home culture, and language). Pedagogical alignment also focuses on the linkages between our expectations for children and how and what teachers are taught in their teacher preparation programs and in-service supports. Because it involves the intimate nature of the interactions between children and the caregivers in their lives, pedagogical alignment lies at the heart of transitions and has been the focus of transition work for decades.

Programmatic Alignment   The second type of alignment moves beyond the child and teacher in the classroom setting to embrace the nature of the services that children and families experience as they move between and among child-serving settings—from family child care to center-based child care, from Early Head Start to Head Start, from pre-K programs to kindergarten, or from kindergarten programs to primary school. Programmatic alignment addresses 1) the degree and nature of parental engagement; 2) the ways in which health, mental health, nutrition, and other services are incorporated into the conceptualization of the program or service; 3) the nature of community outreach and engagement; and 4) efforts to promote a culture of respect and engagement in all program elements. Programmatic alignment focuses on the congruence among program components that take place outside the classroom. It seeks to influence the programmatic nature of the institutions that touch young children's lives, including family engagement, school climate, and community support services.

Policy Alignment   The third type of alignment relates to policy. Taking a systematic view of transitions, the policy component moves well beyond the classroom or the program and embraces the laws and regulations that govern or affect services to young children. Policy alignment transcends the direct services that young children receive and seeks to establish a durable infrastructure where public expenditures for preschool-age children are comparable to those for primary school children; where preschool teachers are compensated at rates similar to those of primary school teachers; where federal and state policies support continuity in the pedagogical and programmatic areas; and where the durability, fiscal authority, and accountability that accompany policies for older children are accorded to policies for young children.

Pedagogical, programmatic, and policy efforts are not either–or types of alignment. They *must* be pursued *in concert* in order to alter the transition zeitgeist for young children and their families. Each side of the prism is necessary to make it whole and remains insufficient on its own.

The New Approach as a Platform for Reform: Transcending Band-Aids

This structural approach did not emerge from thin air. To the contrary, it emerged after a review of hundreds of domestic and international transition efforts. Those that were successful, as indicated either by formal evaluations or by recommender commentary, all shared some important qualities. They had a vision that transcended the Band-Aids. That is, inspired by teams or individuals of remarkable vision, they all assiduously went beyond a one-time, one-place activity.

Putting on a Band-Aid to temporarily cover a deep fissure is not the answer. Educators who were involved in successful programs understood that to overcome the chasms that characterize the disciplines and institutions that frame early childhood, they needed to probe deeper and achieve structural change at the pedagogical, programmatic, or policy level.

In some cases, programs worked at all three levels simultaneously; more often, however, they elected to focus on one or two of the alignment types. Sometimes their pedagogical work consisted only of vertically linking one preschool with a primary school or creating an integrated preschool-and-primary-school institution. In other cases, they revised entire state standards and curricula to promote developmental continuity among domains and disciplines from birth to age 8. In some cases, one policy was altered; in other cases, many policies were changed simultaneously. Whatever strategy was used, the programs include stunning examples, domestically and internationally, of how each of the three alignment approaches has been achieved.

To design this volume, we built on our review of these exemplary transition strategies and adopted a reform mindset. That is, using the prism concept we have described, we asked authors to present different perspectives on transition. Section I contains critical historical and contemporary perspectives, including chapters on transitions for children with disabilities and dual language learners. The volume then turns to conceptual chapters, with a section devoted to each of the three components of structural alignment that has been outlined. Following each conceptual chapter, two case studies—one domestic and one international—enliven the discussion. The volume acknowledges that many alignment lessons may be learned from both developed and developing nations; it also seeks to provide tangible examples of our conceptual framework. Real-world examples of the framework in action suggest that this new way of thinking about transitions can and should transcend temporal, disciplinary, institutional, and geographic borders. Finally, the volume concludes with a chapter that seeks to integrate the lessons that can be learned from these initiatives and that suggests concrete practice and policy strategies for using the framework.

REFERENCES

Ainsworth, M.D., Blehar, M.C., Waters, E., & Wall, S. (1978). *Patterns of attachment: A psychological study of the strange situation.* Mahwah, NJ: Lawrence Erlbaum Associates.

Barnett, W.S. (1993). Benefit–cost analysis of preschool education: Findings from a 25-year follow-up. *American Journal of Orthopsychiatry, 63*(4), 500–508.

Beatty, B. (1995). *Preschool education in America.* New Haven, CT: Yale University Press.

Bernard van Leer Foundation. (2009). *Successful transitions: The continuum from home to school.* Retrieved from http://www.bernardvanleer.org/partners/transitions

Bond, J.T. (1982). *Project Developmental Continuity evaluation: Final report. Outcomes of the PDC intervention* (Vol. 1). Ypsilanti, MI: HighScope Educational Research Foundation.

Carlton, M.P., & Winsler, A. (1999). School readiness: The need for a paradigm shift. *School Psychology Review, 28*(3), 338–352.

Chung, S., & Walsh, D.J. (2000). Unpacking child-centeredness: A history of meanings. *Journal of Curriculum Studies, 32*(2), 215–234.

Clifford, R.M., & Crawford, G.M. (Eds.). (2009). *Beginning school: U.S. policies in an international perspective.* New York: Teachers College Press.

Doucet, F., & Tudge, J. (2007). Co-constructing the transition to school: Reframing the novice versus expert roles of children, parents, and teachers from a cultural perspective. In R.C. Pianta, M.J. Cox, & K.L. Snow (Eds.), *School readiness and the transition to kindergarten in the era of accountability* (pp. 307–328). Baltimore: Paul H. Brookes Publishing Co.

Foundation for Child Development. (2009). *PreKindergarten–3rd Grade: A new beginning for american education.* Retrieved from http://www.fcd-us.org/initiatives/initiatives_show.htm?doc_id=447080

Froebel, F. (1974). *The education of man* (Rev. ed.). (W. N. Hailmann, Trans.). Clifton, NJ: Augustus M. Kelley. (Original work published 1826)

Gholson, B., & Beilin, H. (1979). A developmental model of human learning. In H.W. Reese & L.P. Lipsitt (Eds.), *Advances in child development and behavior* (Vol. 13). New York: Academic Press.

Green, J.A. (1969). *The educational ideas of Pestalozzi.* New York: Greenwood Press.

Hart, B., & Risley, T.R. (1995). *Meaningful differences in the everyday experience of young American children.* Baltimore: Paul H. Brookes Publishing Co.

Hodges, W., & Cooper, M. (1981). Head Start and Follow Through: Influences on intellectual development. *Journal of Special Education, 15*(2), 212–238.

Holmes, D., & Holmes, M.B. (1966). *Evaluation of two associated YM–YWCA Head Start programs of New York City: Final report.* New York: Associated YM–YWCAs of New York City.

Hubbell, R., Plantz, R., Condelli, L., & Barrett, B. (1987). *The transition of Head Start children into public school: Final report* (Vol. 1). Alexandria, VA: CSR, Inc.

Kagan, S.L. (1991). Moving from here to there: Rethinking continuity and transitions in early care and education. In B. Spodek & O. Saracho (Eds.), *Yearbook in early childhood education* (Vol. 2, pp. 132–151). New York: Teachers College Press.

Kagan, S.L., Carroll, J., Comer, J., & Scott-Little, C. (2006). Alignment: A missing link in early childhood transitions? *Young Children, 61*(5), 26–32.

Kagan, S.L., Goffin, S., Golub, S., & Pritchard, E. (1995). *Toward systemic reform: Service integration for young children and their families.* Falls Church, VA: National Center for Service Integration.

Kagan, S.L., & Neuman, M.J. (1998). Lessons from three decades of transition research. *The Elementary School Journal, 98*(4), 365–379.

Knudsen, E.I., Heckman, J.J., Cameron, J.L., & Shonkoff, J.P. (2006). Economic, neurobiological, and behavioral perspectives on building America's future workforce. *Proceedings of the National Academy of Sciences of the United States of America, 106*(44), 10155–10162.

Lillard, A.S. (2005). *Montessori: The science behind the genius.* New York: Oxford University Press.

Love, J.M., Logue, M.E., Trudeau, J.V., & Thayer, K. (1992). *Transitions to kindergarten in American schools. Final report of the National Transition Study.* Portsmouth, NH: RMC Research Corp.

Shonkoff, J.P., & Phillips, D.A. (Eds). (2000). *From neurons to neighborhoods: The science of early childhood development.* Board on Children, Youth, and Families, Commission on Behavioral and Social Sciences and Education. Washington, DC: National Academies Press.

National Research Council and Institute of Medicine. (2000). *From neurons to neighborhoods: The science of early childhood development.* Committee on Integrating the Science of Early Childhood Development. J.P. Shonkoff & D.A. Phillips (Eds.), Board on Children, Youth, and Families, Commission on Behavioral and Social Sciences and Education. Washington, DC: National Academies Press.

Pianta, R.C., Cox, M.J., & Snow, K.L. (Eds.). (2007). *School readiness and the transition to kindergarten in the era of accountability.* Baltimore: Paul H. Brookes Publishing Co.

Powell, D. (1989). *Families and early childhood programs* (Research Monograph No. 3). Washington, DC: National Association for the Education of Young Children.

Rabusicova, M. (2007). *Experience and views of adults and children on transition to school.* Prague, Czech Republic: European Early Childhood Education Research Association.

Ramey, S.L., Ramey, C.T., Phillips, M.M., Lanzi, R.G., Brezausek, C., Katholi, C.R., et al. (2000). *Head Start children's entry into public school: A report on the National Head Start/Public School Early Childhood Transition Demonstration Study.* Birmingham, AL: Civitan. Retrieved from http://www.acf.hhs.gov/programs/opre/hs/ch_trans/reports/transition_study/transition_study.pdf

Rimm-Kaufman, S.E., & Pianta, R.C. (2000). An ecological perspective on the transition to kindergarten: A theoretical framework to guide empirical research. *Journal of Applied Developmental Psychology, 21*(5), 491–511.

Rivlin, A.M., & Timpane, P.M. (1975). Planned variation in education: An assessment. In A.M. Rivlin & P.M. Timpane (Eds.), *Planned variation in education: Should we give up or try harder?* (pp. 1–21). Washington, DC: Brookings Institution.

Rous, B.S., & Hallam, R.A. (2006). *Tools for transition in early childhood: A step-by-step guide for agencies, teachers, & families.* Baltimore: Paul H. Brookes Publishing Co.

Sameroff, A., & Haith, M. (Eds.). (1996). *The five to seven year shift: The age of reason and responsibility.* Chicago: University of Chicago Press.

Silvern, S.B. (1988). Continuity/discontinuity between home and early childhood education environments. *The Elementary School Journal, 89*(2), 147–159.

Social Security Act of 1935, PL 74–271, 42 U.S.C. §§ 301 *et seq.*

Vogler, P., Crivello, G., & Woodhead, M. (2008). *Early childhood transitions research: A review of concepts, theory, and practice* (Working Paper No. 48.). The Hague, The Netherlands: Bernard van Leer Foundation.

W.K. Kellogg Foundation. (2008). *Linking early learning and the early grades to assure that children are ready for school and schools are ready for children—a SPARK legacy* (SPARK Working Paper). Retrieved from http://ww2.wkkf.org/DesktopModules/WKF.00_DmaSupport/ViewDoc.aspx?fld=PDFFile&CID=0&ListID=28&ItemID=5000542&LanguageID=0

Zigler, E., & Kagan, S.L. (1982). Child development knowledge and educational practice: Using what we know. In A. Lieberman & M. McLaughlin (Eds.), *Policy making in education. Eighty-first yearbook of the National Society for the Study of Education* (pp. 80–104). IL: University of Chicago Press.

2

The Transition to School

Concepts, Practices, and Needed Research

Craig T. Ramey and Sharon Landesman Ramey

SUMMARY

Children's successful transitions to school represent a balance of expectations and actions among children, parents, educators, and the community. It is important that all children get off to a good start as they begin learning the academic and social skills that are essential for their participation in our society and economy. Many children come to school without adequate preparation, which threatens their well-being and that of their families, schools, communities, and the nation. Concerted and sustained action, coupled with an understanding of the factors that contribute to school readiness, is essential to "improving the odds" for individual children and their contribution to society.

We begin this chapter by noting that we construe the transition to school as a multi-year, multiperson, multiple resource process that is directly relevant to a child's success in school and later life, as well as to community well-being. This perspective has replaced earlier notions of school readiness that focused primarily on the child's level of development and the extent to which families prepared their children for school. This shift represents a consensus that there are many factors, including school preparedness, that codetermine children's adjustment to, and benefit from, formal schooling. In essence, it embraces a social perspective that, as a nation of diverse communities, we share responsibility for the mutual well-being of our citizens. We selectively highlight scientific findings concerning the effects of early interventions to improve transition to school; the relationship between school readiness and subsequent school performance; and the associations among parenting, family, home variables, and children's school progress. We then identify specific gaps in knowledge and discuss research that is needed to increase the likelihood that children will make successful transitions to school.

INTRODUCTION

Starting school is nothing new—unless you are a child or the parent of a child going to school for the first time. Entering the world of formal school is a major, highly valued, and memorable life transition. The transition preparation begins long before the first day of kindergarten and is far from over at the end of the first day, week, month, or year of school. The transition to school is a time of remarkable opportunity that sets the stage for many years of formal education in a society that is constantly changing. What is new about the transition to school is how educators, developmental scientists, policy makers, and society are viewing this life event.

Current academic thinking construes a child's successful transition to school as a complex balance of expectations, values, and interactions among children, parents, educators, and communities. The goal is to ensure that all children have a good start as they begin learning the academic and social skills that are essential for success in school and life. There is increasing concern that many children do not come to school adequately prepared. Many teachers and schools lack the knowledge and resources to meet the diverse needs of the children and families they serve. This lack of preparation especially hinders children who enter school with below-average skills, special educational or health needs, and linguistic and cultural differences, as well as those from multirisk or deeply troubled families. The evolving conceptualization of the transition to school underscores the importance of cooperation, collaboration, communication, and a shared vision for what successful education can and should be—from the very first day of school and beyond.

A Definition of the Transition to School

We define the transition to school as a process that starts when families, educators, and communities engage in activities to prepare for children's school entry and ends when the child, family, teachers, and other key individuals perceive that a steady positive state has been achieved—when they have a mutual agreement regarding expectations, roles, and actions to ensure that a given child will make good progress in the school setting. For many families, the anticipation of the transition-to-school process begins at birth or even earlier. More typically, the transition process starts when a child is somewhere between 3 and 5 years old and school entry is perceived to be imminent. According to the preceding definition, the beginning of the transition to school cannot be delineated simply on the basis of a child's chronological age or enrollment in kindergarten. Similarly, the end of the transition process cannot be equated with a child's age or grade in school. This definition of transition thus emphasizes two points: 1) that there is individual variation in the transition-to-school experience and 2) that the processes of family and community adjustment and accommodation are essential to the positive outcome of this major life transition.

On a practical note, we recognize the usefulness of identifying a general timeframe that captures the transition process for the majority of children, families, and schools. The period from age 3 through 8 years captures the transition-to-school process for most children, corresponding to the 2 years prior to kindergarten entry through the end of the second grade, at which point basic mastery of reading is expected to have occurred.

A historical perspective on the transition to school may be helpful. Years ago, kindergarten itself was viewed as a year of preparation for school—and first grade was identified as the beginning of formal education. This has changed. Today, kindergarten has assumed a more academic role in a child's education, and attendance has become close to universal. More than 98% of all children attend at least a year of kindergarten before entering first grade (Zill, Collins, West, & Germino-Hausken, 1995). As a result, families, educators, and communities have become more actively engaged in preparing children for kindergarten itself and are more likely to identify kindergarten as the year of entry into "real school" (Crnic, 1994; Kagan, 1991, 1994; Ramey & Ramey, 1998).

Each year in school beyond kindergarten represents a new set of expectations that have corresponding curriculum goals, objectives, and procedures. Although each school year is accompanied by new and increasing challenges, these annual changes are not uniform across schools or school districts, and may not even be comparable within the same school or school district when they are viewed at the classroom level. A reasonable question, then, is, why should we demarcate the transition to school years as distinct from the annual transitions that occur throughout elementary school? Is there a strong rationale for viewing the earliest of the elementary school years as unique or especially important in the course of a child's schooling and life?

The research evidence supports the conclusion that there are important distinctions in both the magnitude and the type of adjustments that occur in the first major transition to school relative to subsequent yearly transitions (Pianta & Cox, 1999). The identification of an initial transition-to-school period in no way diminishes, however, the value of other transitions or of conducting longitudinal research that extends beyond the initial transition period. Rather, its identification serves to focus inquiry on specific activities and processes that occur during the early school years and the extent to which these have immediate and long-term consequences.

Three prominent features distinguish the transition to school from the general adjustment to school thereafter. *First, formal, public school itself represents a new culture that is not the same as that of the family, nonpublic preschool programs such as Head Start, or private child care programs.* School thus represents a major new organized force in a child's life—with new and consequential expectations that will be part of the child's everyday life for many years to come. Although there will be variations over the years in the school experience, children learn many of the essential features of the public school culture during the initial transition phase.

Second, given a diverse society and student body, there is a very high need for children, families, and schools to become acquainted, exchange information, and reach consensus about how best to promote children's learning and adjustment to school. In many ways, all transitions throughout life are characterized by an increase in uncertainty, the need for information, the need to acquire new skills, and the possibility of failure in the new situation. The transition to school, however, is the first *universal* transition in our society; therefore, much importance should be attached to its success.

Third, transitions to school are thought to be important because early experiences often set the stage for and significantly influence subsequent events. That is, what occurs during the transition to school is likely not only to affect what occurs in the first few years of elementary school, but to set in motion forces that may enhance or hinder a child's ultimate educational achievements and success in life. This is not to say that transitions are wholly deterministic, only that they can be very influential. Undeniably, extremely negative early experiences may contribute to a pattern of altered expectations, attitudes, behavior, and critical decisions that some children may find difficult to overcome.

The Social and Political Context of the Transition to School

The scientific and policy interest in the topic of transition to school derives, in large part, from concerns over social justice or equity. The first concern relates to changes in our country's demography and how these changes affect the culture of schools. The heterogeneity of children and families who are served by schools is arguably greater today than at any time in our country's history. More languages, countries of origin, religions, races, and socioeconomic strata are represented in the United States than ever before. A school superintendent recently said that kindergarten children in Florida come to school collectively speaking more than 200 different languages. This heterogeneity presents many practical challenges and often demands an increased level of public and educational resources, including teacher skills, relative to earlier eras when children mostly spoke the same language, came predominately from intact married families, had mothers who typically were not employed outside the home, and had parents who often had grown up in the same Judeo-Christian communities and attended the same schools as their children did.

The second concern relates to our schools' mandate to serve all children, including those who have disabilities. One example of this universal principle is the national mandate in 1975 to include children with disabilities in mainstreamed or inclusive educational settings. The transition to school for these children and their families represents almost unimaginable hurdles compared with those faced by typically developing children. The presence of children who have major health, behavioral, and intellectual differences in regular educational classrooms also represents a frightening and exhausting challenge to many teachers.

Many other legislative and judicial mandates concerning issues of equity in education have affected school transition. Issues related to busing and school redistricting, for example, continue to challenge many school districts, as do pending lawsuits about the distribution of educational resources, which can severely challenge school districts (e.g., *Abbott v. Burke,* 1994, 1997). Busing has removed the familiarity of neighborhood rituals and values and exposed children to greater diversity early in school life. The school setting has become, in many ways, a more public and visible part of society—and the mandate to educate has expanded far beyond the time-heralded original goal to teach "reading, writing, and arithmetic." That is, schools have been asked via legislation and judicial decree to help provide more services to meet children's developmental needs, to be instruments for racial and ethnic integration, and to correct economic disparities that have marginalized large groups of individuals by providing them with an inferior and segregated education. These external factors have made schools and communities more aware than ever before of the transition process—simply because the children who come to school and who are expected to stay in school and show progress represent a larger and more diverse group than ever before. These children's parents may better understand their children's rights and entitlement than did parents in decades past.

A third major factor relates to the shifting paradigms in early childhood education and developmental psychology. Historically, most theories about child success in school have been child centered, endorsing the dual assumptions that 1) development progresses in an orderly, stage-like manner, dependent largely on a child's individual maturation; and 2) a child's school readiness is determined mostly by his or her own intellectual and social skills. Within these traditional views of child development, much of the research on elementary school–age children concentrated on identifying variables associated with individual differences in performance on standardized tests of achievement, as well as the degree to which children's early academic and social competence predicts their subsequent school performance and later educational attainment. The current predominant theoretical perspectives on human development, in general, and early childhood in particular, emphasize the codetermination of multiple influences on developmental outcomes and the need for individuals, families, and schools to accommodate one another.

Probably the most influential shift in conceptualizing children's development is associated with the development of the perspective of social ecology (Bronfenbrenner, 1979). Social ecology places the child within a social context that can be evaluated at multiple levels, ranging from the child's everyday transactional encounters to more distal influences that affect other systems or ecologies and, in turn, influence what does or does not occur at the child's experiential level. Social ecology is especially informative in analyzing and understanding the complex process of change in schools, which is attributable to influences at many levels, such as teacher–child interactions, dynamics among school personnel, dynamics between school personnel and other constituencies; schools' interactions with families, and the overall community and political context in which schools exist. Much of the enthusiasm about studying the transition to school relies on the hope that the many diverse literatures about children, families, schools, and communities—historically quite separate literatures—can be brought together in practically useful ways to understand variation in school transitions and to test intervention programs that are designed to improve transition outcomes. The perspectives from elementary and early childhood education, neurobiology, sociology, psychology, economics, anthropology, pediatrics, and child psychiatry, to name a few, all have information that is relevant to creating and sustaining more successful transitions for children.

Another major contextual factor concerning the understanding of the transition to school has been an expansion in the techniques that are available to study this transition and new ways of estimating children's gains and adaptation. These methods include tools for measuring children's own opinions about schools (Ramey, Gaines, Phillips, & Ramey, 1998), tools for measuring their perceptions of their competencies in academic and other situations, qualitative ways of reviewing children's school accomplishment and achievements, and strategies for measuring the school climate from the perspectives of children, teachers, parents, and principals (Schmitt, Sacco, Ramey, Ramey, & Chan, 1999). In addition, there are new observational techniques for documenting classroom practices (Pianta, La Paro, & Hamre, 2007) and new rating tools for measuring developmentally appropriate practices (e.g., the Early Language and Literacy Classroom Observation Tool, described in Smith, Brady, & Clark-Chiarelli, 2008).

What Are Successful Transitions to School?

One of the problems in education is the absence of a strong consensus about intended outcomes and about the measurement of educational goal attainment. To define the transition to school only in terms of a multiperson, multiyear process of adjustment would be, in our opinion, a very limited perspective. What is needed is a more specified delineation of what factors create a "successful" transition to school. This is a challenge—in large part because ideas about what schools should be teaching children and what role they should play as social institutions are changing and are laden with defining values and controversy. The specific methods that are used to judge positive school adjustment at different times during elementary school may vary considerably among children, parents, educators, and communities. Nevertheless, we offer a general perspective on successful transitions and propose that it be considered for use in future research.

We propose that there are five key features of a successful transition to school (Ramey, Ramey, & Lanzi, 2006). These features are summarized in Table 2.1.

Table 2.1.   Key features of successful transitions to school

---

1. Children have positive attitudes toward school and learning and are motivated to do well in school.

2. Children maintain and enhance their academic and social skills via their school experiences.

3. Parents and other key adults show positive attitudes toward the school and learning in general and act as partners in their children's learning.

4. Teachers and other school personnel recognize and value children's individual and cultural differences and provide developmentally appropriate school experiences.

5. Schools, families, and communities are linked together in positive and mutually supportive relationships to enhance young children's well-being and education.

From Ramey, C.T., Ramey S.L., & Lanzi, R.G. (2006) Children's health and education. In I. Sigel & A. Renninger (Eds.) *The handbook of child psychology* (Vol 4, pp. 864–892). Hoboken, NJ; Wiley & Sons; adapted by permission.

This perspective includes a combination of types of outcomes, from attitudinal and social to more conventional measures of academic progress. It allows for local variation in what is judged to be a good working relationship and what constitutes mutual respect for individual and cultural differences. This definition of successful transitions underscores the need to consider multiple perspectives and the dynamic transactions that contribute to sustained supports for children's learning.

Examples of Interventions to Improve the Transition to School

Concerns about promoting a successful transition to school have a long history in the United States, dating to research that led to the creation of Head Start programs in the 1960s. It has been shown repeatedly that children from poor and undereducated families start school developmentally behind their peers and frequently fall further behind children from more resourceful families in key academic skills, including reading and mathematics, during the elementary years (Sirin, 2005). Various school readiness and transition-to-school intervention strategies have been and continue to be evaluated in efforts to give disadvantaged children an even chance at being successful in school, with the hope that school will serve as a gateway to a more contributory economic and social life (see Pianta & Howes, 2009; Zaslow & Martinez-Beck, 2005; Zigler & Styfco, 2004).

We have been involved as principal investigators and program developers in a series of randomized controlled trials (RCTs) and in population-based, large-scale statewide and county prekindergarten (pre-K) programs for high-risk children. Table 2.2 summarizes the key programs that form the basis for this section of the chapter. The table also provides references for supporting details for some of the observations that we will make in this section.

No single study listed in Table 2.2 has all of the components of our Successful Transitions Model. Nevertheless, if we think about the five major domains, we can make some potentially useful generalizations on the basis of the 40 years of work that are represented in these five projects, which included more than 54,000 high-risk children and their families as participants. We will organize our observations using the five domains and provide key references where the interested reader can find more detailed information.

1. *Children have positive attitudes toward school and learning and are motivated to do well in school.* The vast majority of high-risk children (93%) enter kindergarten with very positive attitudes toward school and only after not doing well in the early elementary grades come to dislike it (Ramey et al., 1998). When children report not liking school even in kindergarten, they are aware of it even before their parents or teachers are. Not surprisingly, they report that they and their parents do not value doing well in school. These children who have less-positive school perceptions are significantly more likely to be boys and to have lower receptive language skills than children who have more positive perceptions.

    High-risk children who have had pre-K early intervention are also more likely to have a greater internal locus of control concerning school performance (but not life in general) than comparable high-risk children who did not attend a preschool program (Walden & Ramey, 1983).

2. *Children maintain and enhance their academic and social skills via their school experiences.* Children who attended high-quality preschool programs in all five of the projects summarized here were more likely than control group participants to display greater school readiness on the basis of cognitive assessments; moreover, these gains are sustained in terms

Table 2.2. Salient findings of the various projects that are directly germane to our key features of successful transition to school

---

The Abecedarian Project (N = 111)

A two-phase randomized controlled trial (RCT) that compared three transition intervention strategies with a control condition that was composed of augmented health care, nutrition, and family support social services. The three intervention conditions were

- A birth-to-5 preschool program plus a K–2 home and school resource program
- A birth-to-5 preschool program without a K–2 program
- A K–2 home and school resource program

(Campbell et al., 2008; Pungello et al., 2010; Ramey & Campbell, 1992; Ramey et al., 2000; Ramey & Ramey, 2006; Ramey, Yeates, & Short, 1984)

Project CARE (N = 83)

An RCT comparison of two intervention strategies to a control condition that included augmented health care, nutrition, and family support services. The two intervention conditions consisted of

- A birth-to-5 preschool program (same as Abecedarian), plus a home visit birth-to-5 component, plus a K through 2nd-grade home and school resource program
- A birth-to-5 home visit program plus a K–2 home and school resource program

(Campbell et al., 2008; Ramey & Ramey, 1998; Wasik, Ramey, Bryant, & Sparling, 1990)

The Infant Health and Development Program (N = 985)

An eight-site RCT for low-birth weight children with a control condition of pediatric follow-up and referral and a treatment condition that consisted of

A birth-to-3 home visit program with a preschool program that replicated the Abecedarian and CARE preschool from 12 to 36 months of age

(Blair, Ramey, & Hardin, 1995; Ramey, 1990; Ramey et al., 1992)

The Head Start/Public School Transition Program (N = 8,400)

A 31-site RCT that compared control group children with transition treatment groups that received K through 3rd-grade services that included

- A developmentally appropriate curriculum
- Health services
- Parent involvement family support and home visits
- Social services

(Ramey et al., 1998; Ramey & Ramey, 1999; Robinson, Lanzi, Weinberg, Ramey, & Ramey, 2002)

The Louisiana Pre-K Program (LA-4, N = 44,815 to date)

A phased-in multiple cohort statewide program that was

- Implemented in classrooms in public elementary schools
- Created to serve 4-year-old-children, with a priority on serving high-risk families (indexed primarily by family income)
- Staffed by 1) a certified teacher in each classroom, with the requirement that the teacher hold a bachelor's or master's degree and specialization in early childhood and 2) a qualified teacher's assistant or paraeducator
- Staffed by teachers who received wages and benefits comparable to those of other public school teachers
- Staffed by teachers who received professional development, typically exceeding 18 hours per year
- Limited to 20 students per classroom
- Characterized by a specified pre-K curriculum with an explicit focus on language and early literacy
- Intended to meet statewide learning standards and benchmarks for children's progress, with classroom teachers themselves measuring children's progress at least twice a year and adjusting classroom instructional activities accordingly
- Supported by a full range of the additional supports available to elementary school classrooms, including specialists in reading, language, special education, and English language learning
- Organized to involve collaboration and coordination with other needed services and supports, such as health and mental health, child care (wraparound services), and social services

(Ramey, Ramey, & Stokes, 2009)

---

of greater K–3 performance in reading and mathematics achievement. High-risk children who attended preschool programs were also consistently less likely to be retained or placed in special education (Campbell et al., 2008; Campbell, Pungello, Burchinal, & Ramey, 2001; Ramey & Ramey, 2006; Ramey et al., 2009). Higher levels of participation in the preschool programs were associated with greater cognitive outcomes in the Infant Health and Development Program during program implementation (Blair et al., 1995) and at follow-up in grade school (Hill, Waldfogel, & Brooks-Gunn, 2002).

3. *Parents and other key adults show positive attitudes toward the school and learning in general and act as partners in their children's learning.* Many parents of high-risk students have reported in interviews that they found school very challenging themselves. This difficulty was exemplified by the fact that many of the parents had not graduated from high school when their first child was born. For example, the average last grade completed by the mothers in the Abecedarian Project and Project CARE was the 10th grade. Consequently, they were typically wary of school contacts but hoped that their children would do better in school than they had. They really didn't know how to support their children because they had not experienced such support from their parents when they were students. Nevertheless, they hoped that their children would succeed.

The K–2 Home/School Resource Program in the Abecedarian Project and Project CARE was designed to help parents become more effectively involved in their children's education. The premise in those programs was to keep parents fully informed of the curriculum that their children were experiencing and to suggest specific activities and positive behavior strategies that the parents could use at home that would be directly relevant to children's success in the classroom. When children and families received these services in the context of RCTs, the children's performance in reading and math was enhanced (Ramey & Ramey, 2006). This same rationale undergirds the Parent Involvement component of Head Start.

In the Head Start Transition Program, the Parent Involvement Strategy focused on trying to involve the parents in the school more broadly (e.g., getting them to serve on governing councils or volunteer at school) rather than encouraging them to get directly involved in their children's academic work. This strategy, however, yielded no measurable benefits in either parent involvement or children's academic achievement (Ramey, Ramey, & Lanzi, 2006).

4. *Teachers and other school personnel recognize and value children's individual and cultural differences and provide developmentally appropriate school experiences.* The Abecedarian Project, Project CARE, and the Infant Health and Development Program all emphasized an individually paced pre-K curriculum that was based on the child's level of progress in 27 key developmental domains (Sparling, Lewis, Ramey, & Neuwirth, 1995).

Each of these programs produced enhanced cognitive, language, and social benefits that were documented during the programs and sustained into adulthood (Campbell et al., 2008; Hill et al., 2002). These findings clearly further the premise that educational individualization is associated with developmental enhancement. Thus, individualization seems to be pedagogically sound. We know of no similar experiments on individualization or cultural variation, although such work could be of enormous importance.

5. *Schools, families, and communities are linked together in positive and mutually supportive relationships to enhance young children's well-being and education.* Although this premise is widely shared among educators, families, and policy makers, it is not, to our knowledge, addressed by systematic developmental research. A first step in addressing this issue would

be to document such linkages (or lack thereof) in a diverse sampling of schools and then to correlate variations in these attributes to measures of children's well-being and educational progress. This descriptive work could then be followed up with RCTs to test hypothesized causal relationships. This seems like an exciting area of research and one that has theoretical implications, particularly within a developmental social ecological perspective.

Gaps in Current Knowledge and High-Priority Research Directions

Inevitably, there are numerous gaps in a relatively new field of inquiry. As we mentioned earlier, there are very few studies of the transition to school per se as a multiyear, multiperson process. Our Successful Transitions Model identifies the elements that we consider to be promising for understanding what factors contribute to more successful transitions. In this section, we identify promising and potentially powerful strategies to close these gaps in knowledge so that future practice might be more firmly grounded on a scientific basis.

We propose that there are four critical questions which must be addressed in order to obtain a holistic, integrated, and contextual understanding of the transition to school. We have framed these questions in terms of known principles of human behavior and offer suggestions for relevant research designs, methods, and analyses.

Question 1: What particular aspects of transition have predictive value for subsequent school performance, and to which children do they apply?

Vast amounts of scientific data endorse the principle of the primacy of early experiences. The extent to which children's actual daily experiences directly influence their later school experiences and academic performance is, however, undocumented. This documentation is particularly needed for the diverse groups of children who are considered to be at risk for poor school adjustment and outcomes. Do children's early transition to school behaviors and experiences strongly predict their later experiences? This question cannot be adequately answered by relying solely on children's performance on routinely administered, nationally standardized tests of achievement and administrative information about classrooms and schools (e.g., classroom size, per-pupil expenditures, teacher credentials). This issue needs to be addressed in terms of children's attitudes toward school and learning, their engagement in learning activities within the school context and outside school (at home, in the community), their academic gains, and their social-emotional well-being.

There are a number of recommended research approaches. For example, research in this area may benefit from large-scale, population-based, prospective longitudinal studies of diverse groups of children, families, schools, and communities. Research also may be well informed by studies of targeted groups of children, families, schools, or communities with particular combinations of risk factors. Short-term, prospective, longitudinal studies that closely document the variations in early transition to school experiences and relate these variations to child outcomes are essential. The methodologies appropriate to these studies include participant observation, systematic classroom and family observations, and frequent interviews with all participants, including the children themselves.

Question 2: Can nonoptimal classroom and school environments during transition be significantly changed if an affordable investment of resources is made? If so, to what extent do these changes improve children's performance?

A large descriptive literature identifies many kindergarten and elementary school classroom and school practices and policies that are associated with differential student outcomes. The relative efficacy of these various practices and policies must be studied carefully using high-quality research designs that can provide definitive answers. Typically, this means conducting RCTs in which a set of promising practices and policies is implemented and compared with reasonable alternatives. Careful, unbiased documentation of what actually occurs at the level of the individual child, the family, the classroom, and the school is essential to test the efficacy of these changes. There is no adequate substitute for randomized, controlled designs that are well executed. These designs ensure, within the limits of sampling theory, that the results are attributable to the manipulations, rather than to extraneous factors such as initial inequality between the groups being studied (e.g., children, teachers, schools), failure to implement the treatment(s) as intended (i.e., treatment fidelity), differential attrition during and after treatment(s), or biased assessment of outcomes (e.g., those involved in giving the treatment also being the only ones to measure its outcome). Such research will be most useful if cost data and practical implementation concerns are routinely gathered, analyzed, and reported, so that the context of the trial may be adequately understood by other researchers, practitioners, and policy makers.

The question of ethics is often raised by individuals who are not familiar with scientific research designs. In fact, the vast majority of educational reforms are experiments that are being implemented in an uncontrolled and unsystematic manner and that can never be scientifically evaluated. This is why there is so much heated debate and lack of resolution about what is truly best for young children and their families. Educational research does not ever require that any children be kept in poor conditions that are known to be harmful to them. Rather, alternative strategies to improve educational outcomes should be compared in a value-added, systematic, and fair manner. Thus, there is no discrimination: The equal likelihood that children will be exposed to a better education renders the experiment equitable.

Question 3: To what extent can existing databases (historical, administrative, and research) provide useful information to educators, decision makers, and the public about effective educational practices and how to promote successful transitions to school?

The principle of historical change informs us that all societal institutions are evolving. Just as families' structures, functions, and values and goals for their children are changing, so early childhood programs and schools are in a state of change. We cannot assume that lessons from studying transition in one historical period will necessarily apply to all others. This situation necessitates a critical and thoughtful reanalysis and reinterpretation of findings from cohorts that were studied 50, 20, 10, or even 5 years ago. It also reminds us of the value of placing a present-day study within its full context, considering historical, geographical, economic, and political factors. All too often, educational and developmental research concerning children's school adjustment has glossed over where the study occurred, when it occurred, and what major societal forces could have influenced who was studied, what was happening in their lives, and the degree to which certain findings were obtained or not. This additional demand that research be placed within a historical and contextual perspective is not for the sake of mere academic completeness, nor is it to appease certain political or social movements. Rather, asking questions about the extent to which certain findings are conditioned by or transcend different periods and contexts is crucial in order for us to understand the meaning and consequences of school transitions in the lives of children, families, schools, and communities.

We must be certain that our research takes into account current issues. Some issues address practices or problems that plague particular communities, such as the now-popular tendency among upper middle-class families to have their children enter kindergarten a year later (referred to as "academic red-shirting") so that they will be at an advantage relative to peers, or the converse tendency among Head Start–eligible families to have children enter school at the earliest age possible, because there are no community educational alternatives for them. In communities where Head Start children and upper middle-class children share the same kindergarten classrooms, these tendencies create a divergence in the skill level of the children that is vastly greater than the disparity that is observed when children are the same chronological age. Other variables include mandated teacher-to-student ratios and dramatically differing policies about grade retention (from those which highly favor it to those which prohibit it), assessment and grading practices, and placement of children with significantly delayed language and reading skills in special education during their first few years in elementary school. We include these examples to illustrate the importance of being aware of community and other contextual factors that may affect what happens in classrooms and schools during a study.

There are complex, compelling social forces affecting school districts everywhere. It is vital for information that will help superintendents, school boards, principals, teachers, and families make informed decisions to be readily available, but right now it is rarely available at a practical level. Direct study of how existing information systems may be analyzed and enhanced to yield timelier, more relevant data about effective and ineffective practices and policies should be routine. Such research itself could be contextualized to consider the knowledge and beliefs held by decision makers at various levels as well as in the community at large. Technical assistance to schools and school districts would need to be an integral part of such research, along with adequate resources to develop the capacity to conduct timely and useful analyses and, of course, maintain privacy and confidentiality standards.

Question 4: To what extent can parents of at-risk children learn and sustain new behavior patterns and parenting practices that will increase the probability that their children will thrive as they transition to school?

Educators and developmental scientists affirm that there are powerful early influences on a child's development and readiness to learn. Parents are widely acknowledged to be the child's first and foremost teachers. Family factors—from demography to literacy—have always been strongly correlated with observed competency differences among children. What has been overlooked in most empirical research is the codetermination that undergirds children's learning. Typically, studies of effective schools and best classroom practices have ignored the family factors that contribute to the children's success; similarly, studies of family influences and the value of family participation in children's schooling often fail to consider what is happening in the classroom or at the level of the school and school district. Narrow study of only a few factors influencing children's progress is unlikely to result in substantial gains in knowledge. Such narrow approaches are counter to the emerging appreciation that is captured by a developmental social ecology perspective.

Randomized control trials that seek to improve parenting practices and parental involvement in children's learning are vitally needed. So far, such trials typically have addressed the correction of specific behavior problems or have occurred in the preschool years. These parenting interventions, just like the classroom and school interventions, must take into account factors such as cost and practical implementation on a large scale. Increasingly, it is necessary to consider parental language and literacy factors in the design and implementation of such programs, as well as cultural acceptability and endorsement. This is a topic that also could be complemented by more ethnographic and observational studies that explore parental perceptions of what is expected of them, how school personnel relate to them, and how they can best help and monitor their children's school progress. Many of the studies on these topics are outdated and may have little applicability to the diverse families in some school districts today. Interventions that are intended to be implemented at the whole school or school district levels are especially needed, as well as interventions that are intended to be multiyear.

Investigators studying transitions need access to rich and current databases about the transition to school. In addition, new longitudinal research of population-based samples representing different school and community ecologies is needed—with an explicit focus on the mechanisms that are responsible for more or less successful transitions.

CONCLUSION

The transition to school is the first universal cultural experience for children and families in our country (beyond the celebration of a child's birth). Further, this transition is almost universally highly anticipated by children, parents, and educators and viewed as important in determining a child's later success in school and life. Early experiences are sometimes encoded vividly in memory and often serve to set the stage for subsequent decisions, opportunities, and patterns of behavior.

Our schools and families are experiencing demands that seem unprecedented in our country, in terms of the challenge of providing continuous, high-quality support to all children for their learning and social development. Reports that many children arrive at school "not ready to learn" are alarming—and perhaps misleading. Such reports blame children and families and may be invoked to absolve schools and communities of their responsibility. Surveys of kindergarten teachers and parents confirm that children appear eager to learn and capable of learning when they come to school. What is a more accurate depiction of the crisis in early childhood education is that schools are being asked to address a vast range of competencies. Accordingly, more rigorous study of effective ways to prepare for children's successful transitions (by preparing not just children, but families, schools, and communities) and to provide positive supports during the transition process (including the study of how to "treat" or improve poor transitions when they occur) is needed. The good news is that the educational and developmental research communities are ready—with powerful new theories and analytic methods to address these important issues.

REFERENCES

Abbott v. Burke III, 136 N.J. 444, 643 A.2d 575 (1994).

Abbott v. Burke IV, 149 N.J. 145, 693 A.2d 417 (1997).

Blair, C., Ramey, C.T., & Hardin, M. (1995). Early intervention for low birth weight premature infants: Participation and intellectual development. *American Journal on Mental Retardation, 99,* 542–554.

Bronfenbrenner, U. (1979). *The ecology of human development.* Cambridge, MA: Harvard University Press.

Campbell, F.A., Pungello, E., Burchinal, M., & Ramey, C.T. (2001). The development of cognitive and academic abilities: Growth curves from an early childhood educational experiment. *Developmental Psychology, 37,* 231–242.

Campbell, F.A., Wasik, B.H., Pungello, E., Burchinal, M., Barbarin, O., Kainz, K., et al. (2008). Young adult outcomes from the Abecedarian and CARE early childhood educational interventions. *Early Childhood Research Quarterly, 23,* 452–466.

Crnic, K.A. (1994). Reconsidering school readiness: Conceptual and applied perspectives. *Early Education and Development, 5,* 91–105.

Hill, J., Waldfogel, J., & Brooks-Gunn, J. (2002). Assessing differential impacts: The effects of high-quality child care on children's cognitive development. *Journal of Policy Analysis and Management, 21*(4), 601–628.

Kagan, S.L. (1991). Moving from here to there: Re-thinking continuity and transitions in early care and education. In B. Spodek & O. Saracho (Eds.), *Yearbook in early childhood education* (Vol. 2, pp. 132–151). New York: Teachers College Press.

Kagan, S.L. (1994). Readying schools for young children: Polemics and priorities. *Phi Delta Kappan, 76,* 226–233.

Pianta, R., & Cox, M.J. (1999). *The transition to kindergarten.* New York: Brooks-Cole.

Pianta, R., & Howes, C. (2009). *The promise of pre-K.* Baltimore: Paul H. Brookes Publishing Co.

Pianta, R., La Paro, K., & Hamre, B. (2007). *Classroom scoring assessment system (CLASS): K–3.* Baltimore: Paul H. Brookes Publishing Co.

Pungello et al. (2010). Early educational intervention, early cumulative risk, and the early home environment as predictors of young adult outcomes within a high-risk sample. *Child Development, 81,* 410–426.

Ramey, C.T. (1990). The infant health and development program. Enhancing the outcomes of low birthweight, premature infants. *Journal of the American Medical Association, 263,* 3035–3042.

Ramey, C.T., Bryant, D.M., Wasik, B.H., Sparling, J.J., Fendt, K.H., & LaVange, L.M. (1992). Infant health and development program for low birth weight, premature infants: Program elements, family participation, and child intelligence. *Pediatrics, 89,* 454–465.

Ramey, C.T., & Campbell, F.A. (1992). Poverty, early childhood education, and academic competence: The Abecedarian experiment. In A. Huston (Ed.), *Children in poverty* (pp. 190–221). New York: Cambridge University Press.

Ramey, C.T., Campbell, F.A., Burchinal, M., Skinner, M.L., Gardner, D.M., & Ramey, S.L. (2000). Persistent effects of early childhood education on high-risk children and their mothers. *Applied Developmental Science, 4,* 2–14.

Ramey, C.T., & Ramey, S.L. (1998). Early intervention and early experience. *American Psychologist, 53,* 109–120.

Ramey, C.T., & Ramey, S.L. (1999). Beginning school for children at risk. In R.C. Pianta & M.J. Cox (Eds.), *The transition to kindergarten* (pp. 217–251). Baltimore: Paul H. Brookes Publishing Co.

Ramey, C.T., & Ramey S.L. (2006). Early learning and school readiness: Can early intervention make a difference? In N.F. Watt, C.C. Ayoub, R.H. Bradley, J.E. Puma, & W.A. Lebeouf (Eds.), *The crisis in youth mental health: Critical issues and effective programs: Early intervention programs and policies* (Vol. 4, pp. 291–317). Westport, CT: Praeger Press.

Ramey, C.T., Ramey, S.L., & Lanzi, R.G. (2006). Children's health and education. In I. Sigel & A. Renninger (Eds.), *The handbook of child psychology* (Vol. 4, pp. 864–892). Hoboken, NJ: Wiley & Sons.

Ramey, C.T., Ramey, S.L., & Stokes, B.R. (2009). Research evidence about program dosage and student achievement: Effective public prekindergarten programs in Maryland and Louisiana. In R. Pianta & C. Howes (Ed.), *The promise of pre-K* (pp. 79–105). Baltimore: Paul H. Brookes Publishing Co.

Ramey, C.T., Yeates, K.O., & Short, E.J. (1984). The plasticity of intellectual development: Insights from preventive intervention. *Child Development, 55,* 1913–1925.

Ramey, S.L., Gaines, R., Phillips, M., & Ramey, C.T. (1998). Perspectives of former Head Start children and their parents on school and the transition to school. *Elementary School Journal, 98,* 311–328.

Ramey, S.L., & Ramey, C.T. (2006). *Foundations for early learning.* Evanston, IL: Robert Leslie Publishing.

Ramey, S.L., Ramey, C.T., & Lanzi, R.G. (2004). The transition to school: Building on preschool foundations and preparing for lifelong learning. In E. Zigler & S.J. Styfco (Eds.), *The Head Start debates* (pp. 397–413). Baltimore: Paul H. Brookes Publishing Co.

Robinson, N.M., Lanzi, R.G., Weinberg, R.A., Ramey, S.L., & Ramey, C.T. (2002). Family factors associated with high academic competence in former Head Start children at third grade. *Gifted Child Quarterly, 46,* 278–290.

Schmitt, N., Sacco, J.M., Ramey, S., Ramey, C., & Chan, D. (1999). Parental employment, school climate, and children's academic and social development. *Journal of Applied Psychology, 84,* 737–753.

Sirin, S.R. (2005). Socioeconomic status and academic achievement: A meta-analytic review of research 1990–2000. *Review of Educational Research, 75*(3), 417–453.

Smith, M.W., Brady, J.P., & Clark-Chiarelli, N. (2008). *Early Language and Literacy Classroom Observation Tool, K–3 (ELLCO K–3).* Baltimore: Paul H. Brookes Publishing Co.

Sparling, J., Lewis, I., Ramey, C., & Neuwirth, S. (1995). *Early partners for low birthweight infants.* Lewisville, NC: Kaplan Press.

Walden, T., & Ramey, C.T. (1983). Locus of control and academic achievement: Results from a preschool intervention program. *Journal of Educational Psychology, 75,* 347–358.

Wasik, B.H., Ramey, C.T., Bryant, D.M., & Sparling, J.J. (1990). A longitudinal study of two early intervention strategies: Project CARE. *Child Development, 61,* 1682–1696.

Zaslow, M., & Martinez-Beck, I. (2005). *Critical issues in early childhood professional development.* Baltimore: Paul H. Brookes Publishing Co.

Zigler, E., & Styfco, S. (2004). *The Head Start debates.* Baltimore: Paul H. Brookes Publishing Co.

Zill, N., Collins, M., West, J., & Germino-Hausken, E. (1995). *Approaching kindergarten: A look at preschoolers in the United States* (NCES 95–280). Washington, DC: U.S. Department of Education, National Center for Education Statistics.

3

Going to School in the United States

The Shifting Ecology of Transition

Robert C. Pianta

INTRODUCTION

Young children are exposed to a loosely organized system of opportunities for learning and development in child care, state-funded pre-K classrooms, Head Start programs, and a host of other settings, including their homes. Many experts view this system as a point of leverage for addressing low levels of K–12 achievement and closing gaps in such achievement. During the 2008 presidential campaign, nearly every gubinatorial race, big-city mayoral campaign, and federal education initiative noted that these early learning and educational experiences contribute to achievement and success in school and presented them as a political as well as an economic and social good. In recent years, one of the most prominent education initiatives at the federal level was the Bush Administration's "Early Reading First" program, a national effort to deliver effective reading instruction to young children. President Obama has said that expanding and improving the quality and impact of early education is one of his top priorities.

But early education has not always received this kind of attention. These examples are evidence of a rapidly changing policy context surrounding the pathways from which children begin school in the United States. These pathways, which include the people, places, and resources that are key to fostering successful child development, are themselves a context—a *transition ecology* (Pianta & Rimm-Kaufman, 2006).

This ecology is as real as any other context for child development and may be identified in any local community or elementary school in the United States. It is a system of interactions and

The research reported here was supported in part by the National Center for Research in Early Childhood Education, the Institute of Education Sciences, U.S. Department of Education, through Grant R305A060021 to the University of Virginia. The opinions expressed are those of the authors and do not represent views of the U.S. Department of Education.

Correspondence should be addressed to Robert C. Pianta, University of Virginia, P.O. Box 400260, Charlottesville, VA 22904-4260.

transactions among persons (parents, teachers, and children), settings (homes, schools, and child care settings), and institutions (community and government facilities) that are oriented to support the developmental progress of young children prior to the start of their formal schooling and as they enter elementary school. A transition ecology is composed of clearly identifiable processes and procedures, such as kindergarten registration and the records that are transmitted between educational settings, and of "softer" elements, such as parents' feelings of belonging in a preschool or teachers' comfort level calling parents into meetings. The totality of these interactions and relationships is a context that can play a determining role in fostering the success of a child in elementary school.

However, for the most part, policy and practice in early education ignore the transition ecology as a developmental asset or treat it as a matter of chance. Rather than being part of an explicit and intentional transition ecology, the transition to kindergarten is most typically addressed solely in terms of the child's skills (i.e., "Is the child ready?").

It is the central argument of this chapter that 1) policies and practices must more actively engage the transition ecology as a distinct entity that operates to support (rather than inhibit) child competence over time, and 2) the extent to which this ecology may be harnessed to support child development is challenged both by the fragmentation of the ecology itself and by demographic pressures on it. In the discussion that follows, this chapter outlines some trends in the expansion of early education and care opportunities in the United States, explains their impacts on child development, and presents the challenges that are posed by the fragmentation of educational opportunity and demography.

EXPANSION OF EARLY CARE AND EDUCATION

The long-term effects of early gaps in achievement and social functioning are so pronounced that effective and efficient interventions targeted toward these gaps in the preschool period are essential not only to the developmental success of children but also to the economic and social health of whole communities (Heckman & Masterov, 2007; Magnuson, Ruhm, & Waldfogel, 2007). Compelling evidence documents the long-term costs and developmental consequences of readiness skills gaps that occur among children at the start of school. In response to these findings, policy makers have promoted a rapid expansion of preschool services for young children, mostly targeted toward 3- and 4-year-olds from low socioeconomic groups (Barnett, Hustedt, Friedman, Boyd, & Ainsworth, 2007).

This trend began in 1965 with the establishment of the Head Start program. Over the next four decades, the federal government and most states invested heavily in public preschool programs for 3- and 4- year-old children. By 2004–2005, 38 states offered one or more state-funded programs that served approximately 800,000 children across the nation and cost over 2.8 billion dollars (Barnett et al., 2007). Coinciding with the expansion of public preschool programs has been a fourfold increase over the past 40 years in the number of 4-year-olds who attend preschool, with attendance rising from 17% in 1965 to 66% in 2002 (Barnett & Yarosz, 2004). The combination of increased enrollment, expansion of publicly funded preschool programs, and recognition that early education experiences play a unique role in later academic success has led to the current standard in which school, for all intents and purposes, starts for the vast majority of children in the United States at age 3 (Pianta, 2005).

In terms of innovation and reform, in many ways early childhood education is outstripping K–12 in its efforts to improve program quality and the impacts of educational opportunities. Early childhood education is leading the way on observational assessments of teacher performance, systems for linking program and classroom inputs to professional development and financial investments (i.e., quality rating and improvement systems), and alignment of inputs to teachers with children's learning (Zaslow, in press). Yet even as the nation and states work to improve their strat-egies in early education and child care, these early learning and development opportunities remain a jumble of different programs, funding streams, credentialing and certification mechanisms, instructional approaches and curricula, and competing regulations and entities. It is simply not possible, in any community in the country, to point to that community's early education and care *program,* much less identify the ways in which such a program might align with K–12 programs and resources in that community (Kagan, 2009). Thus, although there is a real and potentially pow-erful ecology of transition, it is in large part idiographic—tied to each individual child's specific set of experiences, settings, and relationships—and invisible in any given community. In fact, a mark of communities in which early education and care outcomes have improved over time is more explicit public attention to the transition ecology and its elements (e.g., meetings to align curricula across preschool and kindergarten programs, longitudinal record keeping of children's developmental status and exposures). In these communities there is less idiosyncrasy in experience; that is, more children travel similar pathways through this ecology (Pianta & Kraft-Sayre, 2003).

THE TRANSITION ECOLOGY AS A DEVELOPMENTAL ASSET

Despite the significant investments that have been made in early childhood education over the past decade, the promise of early education as a scaled-up asset for fostering learning and development of young children in the United States is not yet being realized. Too many children, particularly poor children, continue to enter kindergarten far behind their peers (Jacobson-Chernoff, Flanagan, McPhee, & Park, 2007; National Center for Education Statistics, 2000). The wide-ranging and diverse set of experiences in the preschool years are not, in aggregate, producing the level and rate of skill gains that are required for children to be ready when they enter school (see Howes et al., 2008). As a result, some scholars contend that more comprehensive and intensive efforts are required to close skill gaps and that policy and program development should focus on reinventing the entry portal into public education. In other words, rather than assuming that skill gaps can be closed through exposure to a concatenation of 1-year, short-term experiences in highly varied and fragmented settings (even if the quality of the experiences is high), we must improve the consis-tency and coherence of these programs. This goal may be accomplished by aligning and integrating curricula, standards for teachers and programs, assessments, professional development, and even physical settings over time in an explicit effort to recognize the value of consistency and coherence of experience for developmental progress. One example of this effort is the FirstSchool integration of pre-K programs into elementary school settings (Ritchie, Maxwell, & Clifford, 2007).

The contemporary reinvention of the nonsystem of early education and care opportunities traces an arc over more than 3 decades, from a focus primarily on child care and socialization to a focus on intentional and desired contributions to achievement and competence that extends far beyond the elementary years. The "transition to school" does not happen when a child first gets on the bus for kindergarten; rather, it extends from birth through the early elementary years, a period during which attention increasingly is focused on ensuring that programs and practices support school-age learning outcomes and third-grade academic proficiency. Rimm-Kaufman and Pianta (2000) argued that one must understand the transition to school in terms of developmental pro-cesses that take place within the transition ecology: It is a system of interactions and transactions among persons, settings, and institutions that are oriented to support progress of children. Thus, rather than understanding a child's transition solely in terms of the child's skills or the influences on those skills at any given time, this perspective emphasizes the organization of assets within a social ecology, how this organization emerges, and how it supports (or inhibits) child competence over time.

One of the first federal initiatives to reflect the developmental/ecological model was the National Education Goals Panel (NEGP). Its contribution to Goal 1 (the school readiness goal) involved conceptualizing and defining ready schools and producing a guide for state and local policy makers that outlined key features of ready schools, nearly all of which were concerned with the ecology of school transition. In *Ready Schools,* the initiative outlined 10 keys to ready schools (National Education Goals Panel, 1998, p. 5), several of which directly called attention to the importance of the transition ecology (Pianta & Walsh, 1996; Rimm-Kaufman & Pianta, 2000). For example, school readiness was linked to a smooth transition between home and school and to continuity between early care and education programs and elementary schools. Although the NEGP's target date for having all children ready to learn when they enter school has passed, the ready schools principles and framework have had enormous influence. They are present in initiatives supported by the HighScope Foundation, in the Pathways Mapping Initiative (http://www.cssp.org/major_initiatives/pathways.html) of the Project on Effective Interventions at Harvard University, in the National Governors Association Task Force on School Readiness (National Governors Association Center for Best Practices, 2004), and in the Foundation for Child Development's Pre-K–3rd Initiative. They are also part of contemporary work in, among other states, Ohio (Miller & Close, 2009), Connecticut (Gruendel & McQuillan, 2009), and Pennsylvania (National Institute for School Leadership, 2009). Moreover, the ready-school principles (Kagan, 2009) have penetrated local communities across the country, fostering countless efforts to align and integrate K–12 education, child care, families, and formal preschool education. In a very real sense, there is momentum toward addressing the critical concerns of this transition period—alignment of curricula, standards, assessments, professional development, and parental engagement across years and settings—which encourages us to think that the American nonsystem of early education and care will begin to function more effectively and efficiently as a developmental asset.

In fact, one might have concluded from communities' and governments' unprecedented level of attention to early education and care, the infusion of new resources, and the focus on alignment at nearly all levels of program planning that it was simply a matter of time before a coherent, aligned, and efficient *system* of early education and care was in place for the majority of U.S. children. Indeed, the momentum in that direction is evident in the tremendous progress noted in recent state and local reports (see Kagan, 2009) and is foreshadowed in policy recommendations that are likely to influence reauthorization of federal education law (Kauerz & Howard, 2009; National Association for the Education of Young Children, 2009). In the very near-term and certainly the long-range future, the pace and shape of this evolution toward a transition ecology that is explicit, coherent, and functional as a detectable asset for development will be influenced dramatically by two realities: 1) the continued fragmentation of the constellation of early learning opportunities and the structures that support them and 2) socioeconomic and demographic shifts in the makeup of the population of young children. The remainder of this chapter outlines some of those realities and concludes with thoughts about future directions.

THE STRUCTURE AND QUALITY OF EARLY LEARNING AND CARE OPPORTUNITIES IN THE UNITED STATES

One of the first things that one notices about the transition to school, seen through an ecologically and developmentally informed lens, is that the features of transition ecology differ as much as children do. Discrepant K–12 and early childhood policies, fragmented workforce characteristics, and uneven quality of early education and care learning opportunities converge to create a vulnerable nonsystem that needs serious attention.

Fragmented Policies Create Fragmented Experience

As just one example of policy fragmentation, consider the policies that regulate access to K–12 education. Kindergarten attendance is mandatory in some states and optional in others (Vecchiotti, 2003); the starting age for compulsory school attendance in the United States ranges from 5 to 8 years (Education Commission of the States, 2003); kindergarten lasts 2.5 hours in some states and 6–7 hours in others (Vecchiotti); and state-funded pre-K programs are as short as 2.5 hours per day to as long as 10 hours per day (Bryant et al., 2004). If there is no such thing as universal full-day kindergarten, then how do we conceptualize and design a system of early education and care that is aligned with it?

The situation is far worse with regard to the balkanization and fragmentation of programs for younger children, where the term *preschool* encompasses a diverse array of programs under a variety of names. There are three broad types of programs serving children ages 3 and 4: private child care centers, Head Start programs, and pre-K programs that are linked to public education. Among 3-year-olds, private programs predominate and serve 1.4 million children, whereas Head Start serves about 320,000 children and state-funded pre-K programs serve only about 150,000 children. Enrollment of 4-year-olds is split roughly 50:50 between public programs (including special education) and private programs such as child care, with about 1.6 million 4-year-olds in each group. Many children in private programs also receive public services. Head Start serves about 450,000 4-year-olds, whereas state-funded pre-K programs serve nearly 1 million children, about a quarter of the country's population of children this age.

These age trends in enrollment reflect a larger pattern that extends backward toward birth: Younger children are more likely to be enrolled in home-based or informal settings for care. As children age, they tend to move into more formalized settings. This pattern is borne out in cross-sectional survey work and in prospective cohort studies, such as those carried out by the National Institute of Child Health and Human Development Study of Early Child Care and Youth Development (NICHD SECCYD). The point is that even if we focus only on a narrow "slice" of the transition ecology, in this case, opportunities for 3- and 4-year-olds, we see little to no evidence of consistency in policy or in programmatic initiatives that create the templates for local opportunities for children and families. In thousands of communities across the country, children, particularly the most vulnerable ones, are funneled into one program at age 3, shuffled to another at age 4, and sent to yet another at age 5—assuming that these options even exist.

Inconsistency in Workforce Qualifications

The attributes and skills of the adults who staff elementary school and preschool educational settings also vary with stunning regularity. At the kindergarten level, nearly all states require teachers to possess a bachelor's degree and some level of specialized training in education, and in practice this standard is achieved by over 95% of kindergarten teachers. However, preschool teachers vary widely in their level of training and, on average, possess less training and education than their elementary school counterparts (Early et al., 2007). The education level required to teach pre-K varies widely by state. Minimum requirements range from a Child Development Associate (CDA) certificate to a bachelor's degree (Bryant et al., 2004). Furthermore, some states require that the 2- or 4-year degree be in early childhood education or child development, while others do not specify a field of study.

The National Center for Early Development and Learning (NCEDL) Multi-State Study of Pre-Kindergarten (Clifford et al., 2003) showed that in the late 1990s preschool teachers had lower levels of education than elementary school teachers. Only 70% of pre-K teachers had at least a bachelor's degree, 15% had a 2-year degree, and 16% had no formal degree past high school. This study estimated that about half (51%) of pre-K teachers had attained a bachelor's degree *and* certification to teach 4-year-olds, a substantially lower statistic than the parallel figure combining education and training for elementary school teachers. Over 99% of kindergarten teachers have a bachelor's degree and over 75% have at least some training or experience in teaching 5-year-olds (National Center for Education Statistics, 1999). Thus, there is substantial variance in the preparation and qualifications deemed necessary for the workforce in the two fairly well regulated domains of state-funded pre-K programs and kindergarten, a reality that seems indefensible given the similar developmental needs of 4- and 5-year-olds. How could fostering early literacy for a 5-year-old require such a different set of training and qualification experiences than fostering literacy in a 4-year-old?

Children who do not receive early education services in pre-K programs but who are enrolled in the less regulated environments of family- or center-based child care have even lower exposure to credentialed or degreed staff (Helburn, 1995; Cryer, Phillipsen, & Howes, 1995; National Institute of Child Health and Human Development Study of Early Child Care and Youth Development, 2002). In addition, the inconsistencies across settings that these children experience are as dramatic as they are for pre-K and kindergarten, particularly considering that a very large number of 4-year-olds' preschool experiences take place in informal family-based or community child care.

The National Association for Regulatory Administration (2007) conducted one of the more recent and comprehensive studies of the child care workforce. Data gathered from 49 states and the District of Columbia showed that in the vast majority of states (42), directors of child care centers are required to have some occupational/vocational training, some higher education credit hours in early childhood education, or a CDA credential. Only one state requires that directors of child care centers hold a bachelor's degree. Forty states required teachers in licensed child care centers to possess some combination of a high-school degree and experience. Ten states required these teachers to have some vocational program degree, certificate, or CDA, and 13 states had no requisite educational qualification for child care teachers.

Head Start has national standards for program structure, operation, and teacher credentials, but as of spring 2010 it did not require all of its teachers to have college degrees. Starting in the 2011 school year, all Head Start teachers will be required to have at least an associate's degree with a specialization in early childhood, and all education coordinators will have to have at least a bachelor's degree with a specialization in early childhood. The education requirements for teachers escalate over time. By 2013, 50% of Head Start teachers will be required to have at least a bachelor's degree.

Clearly, there is no consensus on the minimum qualifications for teachers of young children, whether the teaching takes place in community child care, Head Start, or public pre-K programs. Moreover, there is little agreement on the performance standards for teachers, the metrics for those standards, or the preparation and support experiences that should align with such performance standards. In short, although teachers play an essential role in the transition ecology, there is a stunning level of variation in even the most basic qualifications of teachers from year to year and setting to setting.

VARIED AND MINIMAL ACCESS TO, AND QUALITY OF, PRESCHOOL EXPERIENCES

Access to programs, the length of programs, and attributes of program staff often reflect policy decisions that shape opportunities for children during the transition period. Such opportunities appear to be more restricted or of lower quality for children of color or children in poverty. Who gets access to resources also varies across states. Preschool-age Latino children are the least likely of any ethnic or racial group to enroll in preschool or child care in the United States

(Espinosa, 2007). Across all racial groups, 47% of California's children ages 3–5 years are enrolled in preschool or child care, whereas only 37% of Latinos ages 3–5 years are similarly enrolled (Lopez & de Cos, 2004). If Latino children live in a household where no one over the age of 14 years speaks English fluently, they are even less likely to be enrolled. Not surprisingly, pre-K and kindergarten children are much more likely to be African American or Latino than are their teachers (Clifford et al., 2003; National Center for Education Statistics, 1999), and they are far more likely than other children to speak a language that is different from their teacher's language (Clifford et al.). Thus, although in many ways preschool programs are explicitly intended to foster the early school success of children from highly varied minority backgrounds and to reduce the transition stress and strain that those children and their families experience, such programs are not widely available and often do not reach these constituencies. As we will point out later in this chapter, the population growth rate of these groups will place considerably greater pressure on early education programs and is a major force in the transition ecology.

Finally, nearly every single piece of state legislation that provides support for the implementation and expansion of educational programs for young children, from preschool to postkindergarten, emphasizes that such programs should be of *high quality* and should use appropriate practices (e.g., Bryant et al., 2002; Clifford et al., 2003; NCES, 2003; NEGP, 1995; Ripple, Gilliam, Chanana, & Zigler, 1999). A well-aligned and developmentally supportive transition ecology would be marked by consistent exposure of children to high-quality experiences with adults across time and settings. Several large-scale research efforts have observed the quality of classroom experiences in pre-K, kindergarten, and first grade. These projects observed approximately 1,000 children in first grade in over 25 states (National Institute of Child Health and Human Development Study of Early Child Care and Youth Development, 2002); 240 pre-K classrooms in six states that are part of the National Center for Early Development and Learning's Multi-State Pre-Kindergarten Study (Bryant et al.); and 223 kindergarten classrooms involved in the NICHD SECCYD in three states (Pianta, La Paro, Payne, Cox, & Bradley, 2002). In addition, observations of global quality have been conducted in Head Start settings that are part of the Family and Child Experiences Survey (FACES) and Head Start Transition studies (Administration on Children, Youth and Families, 1999, 2000, 2001, 2002). As a set, these results capture the best data that we have of the transition ecology in the classroom sector in America.

Two main conclusions may be drawn from this work. First, although there is variation from study to study, the quality of the typical early education setting is mediocre with regard to the kind of interactions and stimulation that are known to produce developmental gains for children (Mashburn et al., 2008; NICHD SECCYD, 2002, 2005). Second, there is tremendous variation in the quality of programs offered to children from time to time or setting to setting. At times this variation is systematically related to factors such as family income or teacher characteristics, and at times there is little or no relationship between the quality of the program and the parameters that are used to regulate or influence it (see Hamre, Bridges, & Fuller, 2003; NICHD SECCYD, 2002; Pianta et al., 2002). It is important to note that when we examine the same children's experiences over time, variation in classroom quality and experience remain the rule rather than the exception. The association between, for example, having a sensitive teacher prior to starting kindergarten and having one who is rated as sensitive in kindergarten, first grade, or third grade is barely significant (NICHD SECCYD, 2004, 2005). Furthermore, the same child moving through the early grades is not likely to receive similar levels of exposure to instructional activities in reading or math from year to year (Pianta, Belsky, Houts, Morrison, & National Institute of Child

Health and Human Development Early Child Care Research Network, 2007). So what does this tell us about transition? It says a great deal about the inconsistency of the learning environment.

In sum, the features of the transition ecology, including aspects that are tightly regulated by policy (such as entry age or eligibility) and aspects that are more subject to local constraints and circumstances (such as quality of classroom interactions), are stunningly variable across settings and across time. There is reasonable evidence that these features also vary as a function of family background factors. The resulting picture is one of too many children and families falling through too many cracks at too many levels. Thus, even in a policy and program development context where early education is valued and prominent and where there is increasing recognition of the need to close gaps and seal seams, the realities suggest that many of our most fragile and vulnerable citizens are passing through a fragile and vulnerable nonsystem.

THE CHANGING CHARACTERISTICS OF THE CHILDREN AND FAMILIES SERVED BY EARLY EDUCATION

The transition ecology we have described arose by accident, not design. Yet it currently is tasked to serve a highly vulnerable population and in fact to accelerate development in that group to help them "catch up" to their more buffered peers. This nonsystem will soon be asked to respond to the needs of children and families that vary even more widely than the ones that it presently serves. For these children, the chasms between home, the early childhood education setting, and elementary school are particularly deep due to barriers that arise from cultural and linguistic variation as well as from inadequate family resources. The remainder of this section outlines just a few of the characteristics of the children and families that will soon enter this transition ecology, raising questions about the capacity of that ecology to sustain and foster developmental progress.

Racial and ethnic minorities are rapidly becoming the majority population. This change will become a reality first among young children and is well described by Hernandez, Denton, and Macartney (2007). Moreover, young racial or ethnic minority children are 2–4 times as likely as whites to be officially poor. Thus, the very groups that are growing demographically in the United States are those whose achievement gaps are pronounced and difficult to ameliorate.

In a nationally representative study of more than 22,000 children who entered kindergarten in 1998, the Early Childhood Longitudinal Study of Kindergarten Children (ECLS-K), 68% of the children were classified as English speaking and 18.1% were classified as language minority children (Espinosa, Laffey, Whittaker, & Sheng, 2006). Almost 13% of the total sample were Spanish speaking. More recent estimates suggest that this and other groups of language minority children are growing rapidly (Hernandez et al., 2007). The majority of the language minority children in the ECLS-K were in the lowest two quintiles for household socioeconomic status (52%), as were 80% of the Spanish speakers who were judged to be the least fluent in English (Espinosa et al.). This means that Spanish-speaking children who are learning English as a second language during the preschool years are the most likely of all preschool children to live in poverty with an adult who lacks a high-school education. Other studies show that non–English-proficient children are about twice as likely to live in poverty as English-proficient children in grades K–5, and only about 50% of children who are not proficient in English have parents with a high-school education (Capps, Fix, Ost, Reardon-Anderson, & Passel, 2004). These dramatic increases in linguistic diversity during the early childhood years are intersecting with the features of the transition ecology previously described.

The proportion of young children who are white and non-Hispanic is projected by the U.S. Census Bureau to fall steadily and to drop below 50% within 25 years. The corresponding rise of the new American majority does not, however, reflect the emergence of a single numerically dominant group, but instead reflects a mosaic of diverse racial and ethnic groups from around the world (see Hernandez et al., 2007). By 2030, 26% of children are projected to be Hispanic; 16% black; 5% Asian; and 4% Native American, Hawaiian, or other Pacific Islander. Between 1990 and 1997 alone, the number of children in immigrant families grew by 47%, while the number of U.S.-born children with U.S.-born parents grew by only 7% (Hernandez & Charney, 1998). Thus, by 2000, 1 of every 5 children lived in an immigrant family.

Immigrant parents often have high educational aspirations for their children (Hernandez & Charney, 1998; Rumbaut, 1999), but they may have little knowledge about the U.S. educational system, particularly if they themselves have completed only a few years of school. Parents who have limited English skills, a characteristic often found in immigrant Spanish-speaking families, are less likely to find well-paid full-time, year-round employment than are English-fluent parents, and, because they frequently have a limited education, they may be less able to help their children with school subjects that are taught in English.

Children who live in households with poverty-level incomes often lack sufficient housing, food, clothing, books, educational resources, quality child care or early education, and health care. Consequently, they tend to experience a variety of negative developmental outcomes (Duncan & Brooks-Gunn, 1997; Sewell & Hauser, 1975). Although the official poverty level is commonly used to assess economic need in the United States, this index has been criticized because it has not been updated and does not take into account the local cost of living, which varies greatly across the country (Citro & Michael, 1995; Hernandez et al., 2007). Hernandez et al. presented estimates of poverty that were adjusted for inflation and actual cost of living, which tends to increase the gaps between whites and most other groups and to raise poverty estimates considerably. For example, their readjusted rate suggests that about 31% of young native white children are impoverished, taking into account the cost of child care or early childhood education and health care, while the rates for most native racial and ethnic minority groups and immigrant groups are in the range of 48%–82%.

Clearly, demographic shifts will place tremendous pressure on early education and care in the United States in the coming decades, a trend that is well underway in many states such as California and Texas. The consequences for program eligibility and enrollment, available slots, preparation and support of staff, and program resources such as curricula are enormous. The data describing contemporary realities and forecasting future circumstances make it abundantly evident that the features of transition ecology—connections between child care, preschool, and schools; links between families and the adults who teach their children; the capacity of the "system" to foster positive development in children who increasingly vary by race, culture, language, and economic background—will undergo tremendous strain. The pressure imposed on this context and these relationships by the sheer variability of the children and families will itself be a considerable threat to the viability of its capacity to promote positive developmental change.

SUMMARY, CONCLUSIONS, AND FUTURE DIRECTIONS

The transition to school occurs during the period from birth to age 8. Focusing a lens on the developmental and ecological aspects of that transition highlights not only the structural and process features of the shifting settings that children traverse in that period but also the characteristics and needs of the children and families who pass through the transition. It has been amply demonstrated that this is a period of shifts, seams, and cracks in an ecology that is being asked to serve an increasingly varied and vulnerable population. There have been many efforts to improve the carrying capacity of this nonsystem (Gruendel & McQuillan, 2009; Miller & Close, 2009; National Institute for School Leadership, 2009), and a set of policy recommendations has been set forth that would undoubtedly heal many cracks and seams (Kagan, 2009; Kauerz & Howard, 2009). Yet, at the same time that policy and resources are racing to strengthen what exists today, the changing demographics of the United States looms as a challenge that threatens to overwhelm a vulnerable and fragile support system for young children and families. Thus, although this chapter started with a discussion of the unprecedented attention and resources that are being devoted to early education and care and that are strengthening the ecology of school transition, it is not unjustified to suggest that a much more concerted and well-resourced effort must be mounted soon.

Current public policies for child care, Head Start, and state pre-K fail to ensure that most American children attend effective preschool education programs. Some children attend no program at all, and too many attend educationally weak programs. Increased provision of child care subsidies under current federal and state policies is particularly unlikely to produce any meaningful improvements in children's learning and development and could have mild negative consequences. Although increased public investment in effective preschool education programs (universal or targeted) can produce substantial educational, social, and economic benefits, it is clear that such programs need considerable regulation and resource-intensive efforts in order to be most effective (Mashburn et al., 2008). And 1 year of effective preschool education is not a panacea. Programs that start earlier and have longer duration do appear to produce better results.

Issues that need resolution very soon include appropriate standards (and accompanying assessments) for children's learning, programs, and teachers; a stable flow of public investments at levels that can ensure gap-closing gains in learning; models for community-based efforts that can, at a local level, integrate and align features of the transition ecology; and an aggressive model of charter schools or other innovative educational structures that span birth to age 8 in a coherent manner. (See Chapter 9 this volume and Ritchie et al, 2007 for a discussion of the First School model) In short, it is time to more fully, explicitly, and strategically embrace the full spectrum of children and families that are experiencing the transition to school, to deal more effectively with the settings that are responsible for that transition, and to move rapidly to create a far more effective system of developmental supports.

REFERENCES

Administration on Children, Youth and Families. (1999). *Head Start program performance measures: Second progress report.* Washington, DC: U.S. Department of Health and Human Services.

Administration on Children, Youth and Families. (2000). *Head Start program performance measures: Longitudinal findings from the FACES study.* Washington, DC: U.S. Department of Health and Human Services.

Administration on Children, Youth and Families. (2001). *Head Start program performance measures: Third progress report.* Washington, DC: U.S. Department of Health and Human Services.

Administration on Children, Youth and Families. (2002). *Head Start program information report* (National Level Summary, Report 5). Washington, DC: U.S. Department of Health and Human Services.

Barnett, W.S., Hustedt, J.T., Friedman, A.H., Boyd, J.S., & Ainsworth, P. (2007). *The state of preschool 2007: State preschool yearbook.* New Brunswick, NJ: National Institute for Early Education Research.

Barnett, W.S., & Yarosz, D. (2004). Who goes to preschool and why does it matter? *Preschool Policy Matters,* Issue 8. New Brunswick, NJ: National Institute for Early Education Research.

Bryant, D., Clifford, R., Early, D., Pianta, R., Howes, C., Barbarin, O., et al. (2002, November). *Findings from the NCEDL Multi-State Pre-Kindergarten Study.* Annual meeting of the National Association for the Education of Young Children. New York.

Bryant, D., Clifford, R., Saluga, G., Pianta, R., Early, D., Barbarin, O., et al. (2004). *Diversity and directions in state pre-kindergarten programs.* Chapel Hill, NC: Frank Porter Graham Child Development Institute.

Capps, R., Fix, M.E., Ost, J., Reardon-Anderson, L., & Passel, J.S. (2004). *The health and well-being of young children of immigrants.* Urban Institute. Retrieved from http://www.urban.org/UploadedPDF/311139_Childrenimmigrants.pdf

Citro, C.F., & Michael, R.T. (Eds.). (1995). *Measuring poverty: A new approach.* Washington, DC: National Academies Press.

Clifford, R., Barbarin, O., Chang, F., Early, D., Bryant, D., Howes, C., et al. (2005). What is pre-kindergarten? Characteristics of public pre-kindergarten programs. *Applied Developmental Science, 9,* 126–143.

Duncan, G.J., & Brooks-Gunn, J. (1997). *Consequences of growing up poor.* New York: Russell Sage Foundation.

Early, D.M., Maxwell, K.L., Burchinal, M., Alva, S., Bender, R.H., Bryant, D., et al. (2007). Teachers' education, classroom quality, and young children's academic skills: Results from seven studies of preschool programs. *Child Development, 78*(2), 558–580.

Education Commission of the States. (2003). *Eight questions on teacher preparation: What does the research say? A summary of the findings.* Denver, CO: Education Commission of the States.

Espinosa, L.M. (2007). English-language learners as they enter school. In R.C. Pianta, M.J. Cox, & K.L. Snow (Eds.), *School readiness and the transition to kindergarten in the era of accountability* (pp. 175–196). Baltimore: Paul H. Brookes Publishing Co.

Espinosa, L., Laffey, J., Whittaker, T., & Sheng, Y. (2006). Technology in the home and the achievement of young children: Findings from the early childhood longitudinal study. *Early Education & Development, 17*(3), 421–441.

Gruendel, J., & McQuillan, M. (2009). A Connecticut case study. *Linking ready kids to ready schools: A report on policy insights from the governors' forum series* (pp. 21–24). Denver, CO: Education Commission of the States, and Battle Creek, MI: W.K. Kellogg Foundation. Retrieved from http://www.ecs.org/docs/4208_COMC_report_forweb.pdf

Hamre, B., Bridges, M., & Fuller, B. (2003). *Early care and education staff preparation, quality, and child development.* Unpublished manuscript.

Heckman, J.J., & Masterov, D.V. (2007). The productivity argument for investing in young children. *Review of Agricultural Economics, 29*(3), 446–493.

Helburn, S.W. (1995). Center structure: Staff policies and characteristics. In S.W. Helburn (Ed.), *Cost, quality, and child outcomes in child care centers: Technical report* (pp. 91–124). Denver, University of Colorado at Denver, Economics Department.

Hernandez, D., & Charney, E. (1998). *From generation to generation: The health and well being of children in immigrant families.* Washington, DC: National Academies Press.

Hernandez, D.J., Denton, N.A., & Macartney, S.E. (2007). Demographic trends and the transition years. In R.C. Pianta, M.J. Cox, & K.L. Snow (Eds.), *School readiness and the transition to kindergarten in the era of accountability* (pp. 217–282). Baltimore: Paul H. Brookes Publishing Co.

Howes, C., Burchinal, M., Pianta, R., Bryant, D., Early, D., Clifford, R., et al. (2008). Ready to learn? Children's pre-academic achievement in pre-kindergarten programs. *Early Childhood Research Quarterly, 23,* 27–50.

Jacobson-Chernoff, J., Flanagan, K.D., McPhee, C., & Park, J. (2007). *Preschool: First findings from the preschool follow-up of the Early Childhood Longitudinal Study, Birth Cohort (ECLS-B).* NCES 2008-025. Washington, DC: U.S. Department of Education.

Kagan, S.L. (2009). Moving from "transitions" to policy change: Next steps for linking ready kids to ready schools. *Linking ready kids to ready schools: A report on policy insights from the governors' forum series* (pp. 7–10). Denver, CO: Education Commission of the States, and Battle Creek, MI: W.K. Kellogg Foundation. Retrieved from http://www.ecs.org/docs/4208_COMC_report_forweb.pdf

Kauerz, K., & Howard, M. (2009). Policy recommendations. *Linking ready kids to ready schools: A report on policy insights from the governors' forum series* (pp. 25–30). Denver, CO: Education Commission of the States, and Battle Creek, MI: W.K. Kellogg Foundation. Retrieved from http://www.ecs.org/docs/4208_COMC_report_forweb.pdf

Lopez, E., & de Cos, P. (2004). *Preschool and child care enrollment in California.* Sacramento, CA: California Research Bureau.

Magnuson, K.A., Ruhm, C.J., & Waldfogel, J. (2007). *Does prekindergarten improve school preparation and performance?* Working paper 10452. Cambridge, MA: National Bureau of Economic Research.

Mashburn, A., Pianta, R., Hamre, B., Downer, J., Barbarin, O., Bryant, D., et al. (2008). Measures of classroom quality in pre-kindergarten and children's development of academic, language, and social skills. *Child Development, 79*(3), 732–749.

Miller, S., & Close, J.T. (2009). An Ohio case study. *Linking ready kids to ready schools: A report on policy insights from the governors' forum series* (pp. 17–20). Denver, CO: Education Commission of the States / Battle Creek, MI: W.K. Kellogg Foundation. Retrieved from http://www.ecs.org/docs/4208_COMC_report_forweb.pdf

National Association for the Education of Young Children. (2009). *Early childhood inclusion.* A joint position statement of the Division for Early Childhood (DEC) and the National Association for the Education of Young Children (NAEYC). Washington, DC: Author.

National Association for Regulatory Administration. (2007). The 2007 Child Care Licensing Study. Lexington, KY: NARA and National Child Care Information and Technical Assistance Center.

National Center for Education Statistics. (1999). *America's kindergartners.* Washington, DC: U.S. Department of Education.

National Center for Education Statistics. (2000). *America's kindergartners.* Washington, DC: U.S. Department of Education.

National Center for Education Statistics. (2003). *Overview and inventory of state education reforms: 1990–2000.* Washington, DC: U.S. Department of Education, Institute of Education Sciences.

National Education Goals Panel. (1995). *National education goals report executive summary: Improving education through family-school-community partnerships.* Washington, DC: Author.

National Education Goals Panel. (1998). *Ready schools.* Washington, DC: Author.

National Governors Association Center for Best Practices. (2004). *NGA task force on school readiness: A discussion framework.* Washington, DC: National Governors Association.

National Institute for School Leadership. (2009). *Aligning and connecting birth through grade 3 development and learning experiences: A front-end analysis.* Washington, DC: Author.

National Institute of Child Health and Human Development Study of Early Child Care and Youth Development. (2002). Early child care and children's development prior to school entry: Results from the NICHD Study of Early Child Care. *American Educational Research Journal, 39,* 133–164.

National Institute of Child Health and Human Development Study of Early Child Care and Youth Development. (2004). Does class size in first grade relate to changes in child academic and social performance or observed classroom processes? *Developmental Psychology, 40*(5), 651–664.

National Institute of Child Health and Human Development Study of Early Child Care and Youth Development. (2005). A day in third grade: Observational descriptions of third grade classrooms and associations with teacher characteristics. *Elementary School Journal, 105*(3), 305–323.

Phillipsen, L.C., Cryer, D., & Howes, C. (1995). Classroom processes and classroom structure. In S.W. Helburn (Ed.), *Cost, quality and child outcomes in child care centers: Technical report* (pp. 125–158). Denver, CO: Economics Department, University of Colorado at Denver.

Pianta, R.C. (2005). Standardized observation and professional development: A focus on individualized implementation and practices. In M. Zaslow and I. Martinez-Beck (Eds.), *Critical issues in early childhood professional development* (pp. 231–254). Baltimore: Paul H. Brookes Publishing Co.

Pianta, R.C., Belsky, J., Houts, R., Morrison, F., & National Institute of Child Health and Human Development Early Child Care Research Network. (2007). Opportunities to learn in America's elementary classrooms. *Science, 315,* 1795–1796.

Pianta, R.C., & Kraft-Sayre, M. (2003). *Successful kindergarten transition: Your guide to connecting children, families, and schools.* Baltimore: Paul H. Brookes Publishing Co.

Pianta, R.C., La Paro, K.M., Payne, C., Cox, M.J., & Bradley, R. (2002). The relation of kindergarten classroom environment to teacher, family, and school characteristics and child outcomes. *Elementary School Journal, 102*(3), 225–238.

Pianta, R.C., & Rimm-Kaufman, S. (2006). The social ecology of the transition to school: Classrooms, families, and children. In K. McCartney & D. Phillips (Eds.), *Handbook of early childhood development* (pp. 490–507). Malden, MA: Blackwell Publishing.

Pianta, R.C., & Walsh, D.J. (1996). *High-risk children in schools: Constructing sustaining relationships.* New York: Routledge.

Rimm-Kaufman, S.E., & Pianta, R.C. (2000). An ecological perspective on the transition to kindergarten: A theoretical framework to guide empirical research. *Journal of Applied Developmental Psychology, 21*(5), 491–511.

Ripple, C.H., Gilliam, W.S., Chanana, N., & Zigler, E. (1999). Will fifty cooks spoil the broth? The debate over entrusting Head Start to the states. *American Psychologist, 54,* 327–343.

Ritchie, S., Maxwell, K., & Clifford, R.M. (2007). FirstSchool: A new vision for education. In R.C. Pianta, M.J. Cox, & K.L. Snow (Eds.), *School readiness and the transition to kindergarten in the era of accountability* (pp. 85–96). Baltimore: Paul H. Brookes Publishing Co.

Rumbaut, R.G. (1999). Assimilation and its discontents: Ironies and paradoxes. In H. Charles, J.D. Wind, and P. Kasinitz (Eds.), *The handbook of international migration: The American experience* (pp. 172–195). New York: Russell Sage Foundation.

Sewell, W., & Hauser, R. (1975). *Education, occupation and earnings.* New York: Academic Press.

Vecchiotti, S. (2003). Kindergarten: An overlooked educational policy priority. *Social Policy Report, 17*(2), 3–19.

Zaslow, M. (in press). *Measuring quality in early childhood settings.* Washington, DC: Child Trends.

4

Transitions

Perspectives from
the Majority World

Kathy Bartlett and Caroline Arnold with Sadaf Shallwani and Saima Gowani

INTRODUCTION

Throughout the world, young children make many transitions. Among the first ones are the transitions from the family to the wider community and from the community to primary school. They may or may not participate in an early childhood program as part of this transition process. This chapter addresses the experience of much of the world's children, to whom our conventional understandings of transition do not apply and for whom new meanings of transition need to be developed. We use the term *majority world* to refer to these children, rather than terms such as *developing world* or *Third World,* due to the disparaging or outdated connotations that are sometimes associated with the latter terms and the implication that wealthy countries have somehow finished developing. *Majority world* also highlights the fact that the majority of the world's population lives in these countries. Although a great deal has been written about transitions for children and families in the minority world, far less attention has been accorded to children in the majority world.

BACKGROUND

Why is it important to consider children's transitions in the majority world? The answer, quite simply, is that transition is the period most urgently in need of attention and is the time during which systems fail children the most. Early transitions in children's lives represent critical points that are key opportunities for children's growth and learning. They lay the foundation for life-long growth and development (Entwistle & Alexander, 1998). Yet they are also precarious times of risk and vulnerability, and the way that they are experienced by young children varies greatly across contexts.

Until very recently, limited attention was paid to transition[1] issues in the majority world. Attention to these issues has increased as a result of three factors:

1. Better analysis of data demonstrated that the major crisis in education occurs right at the beginning of primary school. Until now, donors and national governments have focused their attention on getting more children to complete primary school; graduation rates from primary school remain dismal in many countries. Completion of this level of schooling is a key goal within the United Nations Millennium Development Goals and the United Nations Educational, Scientific and Cultural Organization (UNESCO) Education for All (EFA) goals, yet little attention has been given to the specific point where education efforts break down. Now, analysis of grade-disaggregated data has found that there are high dropout and repetition rates in Grade 1 and that persistent patterns of underachievement are established early in children's educational experience (Arnold, Bartlett, Gowani, & Merali, 2006; UNESCO, 2005, 2006, 2008).

2. Powerful evidence from minority and majority world countries alike shows that early childhood development (ECD) programs improve enrollment, retention, and achievement and provide a host of much broader social and economic benefits. These benefits are particularly pronounced for disadvantaged and excluded children.

3. We now have a better understanding of the devastating consequences that occur when children lack good support for ECD (including, but not limited to, inability to access ECD programs) and specific attention is not given to the early years of primary school across most majority world countries.

Notions of readiness and transition are closely related in all parts of the world. In this chapter, we look at children's readiness for school in the majority world and the key factors underlying their readiness. We also examine an equally important issue: schools' readiness for children and what factors right at the beginning of primary school either assist or undermine children's transition into school. We draw out some of the similarities and differences between majority and minority world countries and across the immense diversity of the majority world, and we propose an overarching rights framework for early transition. This analysis prompts a number of questions that, while they are particularly applicable to the majority world, may also resonate for many minority world countries:

1. Why is it that, despite the internationally accepted definition of the early years as birth to 8, early childhood professionals and policy makers ignore 6- to 8-year-olds, limiting their focus to the preschool years?

2. Why isn't more happening in the course of large-scale education sector reform and within school improvement programs to ensure that children experience a welcoming environment and receive developmentally appropriate learning opportunities during those vital early years of formal school?

3. How can we improve the way we conceptualize and implement work to ensure that deliberately linked ECD and early primary components are part of a whole perspective and that there is continuity of good practices and learning?

The concepts of *ready children, ready families,* and *ready schools* that have been used by many experts (Boethel, 2004; Kids Count, 2005; Myers, 1997; Organisation for Economic Co-operation and

---

[1]The term *transition* in this chapter refers to the period before and after a child moves from either home or an early childhood program into primary school and to the passage from one environment to the other.

Development, 2006) are helpful in minority and majority contexts alike. However, much of the research and discussion in the majority world that is related to transition has not evenly addressed all three pieces (children, families, and schools). A good deal of attention has been placed on getting children ready for school by increasing the number of organized early childhood programs. This effort is understandable and is much needed, given the limited access that many children have to ECD programs. However, primary education has a broader reach than do ECD programs, and the lack of serious attention that has been given to make schools ready for children (beyond generalized attempts to make them "child friendly") has been a significant gap. It is equally important that we pay more attention to the contexts in which families are operating so that these contexts can better support families and enable them to provide vital support for their children's overall development, including assisting them with their transitions.

Starting around 2004, there has been an encouraging growth in awareness of, and action on, these issues. New research is underway, and the range of initiatives and discussions across many countries is expanding. There are promising efforts to increase access to early childhood services and improve supports for lower primary grades in a coordinated way. Some of these initiatives are highlighted by Arnold and colleagues (2006), who provide examples from a number of international agencies, including the Bernard van Leer Foundation, Save the Children, the Open Society Institute, the United Nations Children's Fund (UNICEF), and the Aga Khan Foundation, among others. Still, much remains to be done—and urgently needs to be done—for the millions of children who, from an early point in life, are not offered the range of supports that will facilitate their growth, development, and well-being.

MAJORITY WORLD CONTEXT FOR TRANSITION

What are some of the factors that make the context for transition so different in much of the majority world? This section examines the implications of pervasive and often extreme poverty in terms of not only income but also access to adequate health, education, and other services, including early childhood services.

Overall Trends

International economic and political trends—such as the increasing disparity between rich and poor people, more families migrating to find work, more people moving away from their extended families, increasingly heavy workloads for girls and women, globalization, the transition from planned to market economies, armed conflict, and HIV/AIDS—affect every aspect of young children's lives. Families struggle to survive and thrive, and many lack access to a range of needed services and supports for their young children.

Poverty   Around the world, poverty has a profound and negative impact on children. Children's lives, and thus their early transitions to the school environment, are negatively influenced by poverty—not just by inadequate income, but also by the marginalization, exclusion, and disempowerment that are so integral to poverty. Within families, communities, and countries, a lack of resources undermines people's capacity to provide sufficiently for children and to afford them opportunities to thrive. Children living in poverty may suffer from inadequate food and shelter, and they may lack access to education, health, and other social services and supports. Even when families are not effectively excluded from local services, these services are often woefully inadequate and may lack both competent staff and supplies of basic medicines or learning materials.

Even families' day-to-day interactions are constrained by lack of resources. The adults may have little time to simply enjoy talking and playing with their children in a comfortable and safe environment. In a life of grinding poverty, adults feel little sense of agency or control, and it is not surprising that the most disadvantaged families feel powerless to promote their children's best interests.

Poverty compounds other problems. Natural disasters are far more devastating for families that are already living in flimsy housing. Poor families are also the most vulnerable when armed conflict erupts (Consultative Group on Early Childhood Care and Development, 2009).

Poverty is a serious risk factor that impairs children's learning everywhere in the world (Grantham-McGregor et al., 2007). In the United States, Canada, Japan, and Western Europe, poverty, exclusion, and marginalization (due to lack of economic opportunities or to discrimination on the basis of ethnicity, religion, race, or gender) have a consistent negative impact on children's health, sense of self, access to and success in school, and overall well-being (Organisation for Economic Co-operation and Development, 2006). Poverty is widespread and disparities are increasing in wealthier countries, but the prevalence of absolute poverty is at another level entirely in the majority world.

In majority world countries, deep poverty is pervasive. Four out of ten children in sub-Saharan Africa live on less than one dollar a day (United Nations, 2007). In South Asia, the rate is 3 out of 10. Such widespread and extreme poverty has a profound impact on virtually all aspects of the experience of vast numbers of (and, in some places, most) children. The difficulties faced by these families are different in scale and nature from those faced by families in the minority world, and they are severely exacerbated by a serious lack of functioning infrastructure and services. Preschool programs usually do not even exist. Notions of ready children and ready families, and what these concepts mean for transitions, unfold in critically distinct ways in such a context.

Health and Nutrition   Poor health and malnutrition are facts of life for many children in low-income countries. In sub-Saharan Africa, for example, more than 40% of children under age 5 are physically stunted (Chabbott, 2006). A ground-breaking series on child development in developing countries (Lancet Global Health Network, 2007) highlights the fact that 200 million children under age 5 fail to reach their developmental potential due to poverty, poor health (including respiratory diseases, malaria, and parasites), malnutrition and inadequate levels of micronutrients, and inadequate care (Grantham-McGregor et al., 2007). Chronically malnourished children have more difficulty adjusting to, performing in, and progressing through school (Ames, Rojas, & Portugal, 2009; Grantham-McGregor et al.). The effects are both immediate and long-term (Bartlett, 2010). Children who are sick or malnourished lack the energy and interest to be active learners (Grantham-McGregor et al.). Studies have repeatedly found that children who are affected by health and nutrition problems at an earlier age demonstrate later cognitive deficits, lower school achievement, and higher dropout rates—the impacts of which extend throughout the school years and beyond (Lancet Global Health Network, 2007; Sakti et al., 1999; Walker et al., 2007). For families with children who are affected by HIV/AIDS, supports may be minimal or nonexistent, and the consequences may be catastrophic (O'Gara & Lusk, 2002). Furthermore, a growing body of literature demonstrates how poverty-related stress erodes the cognitive capacity of children and impacts the physiology of their brain development, especially when poverty is of long duration (Farah, Noble, & Hurt, 2005).

A large percentage of young children and their families thus face significant challenges in successfully managing transitions during the early childhood years. These challenges include

1) a lack of adequate resources within home and community contexts; 2) poor access to, and poor quality of, health and ECD programs; 3) inadequate access to, and inadequate quality of, primary school; and 4) ineffectiveness of linkages among home, school, and community. All of these factors directly affect children's developmental trajectories from their earliest years.

ECD Services in the Majority World

There is far more evidence regarding the benefits of a good start in life in the majority world than was available in the late 1990s. ECD enrollments are increasing, but far too slowly, and they often fail to reach those most in need. The failure on the part of both national governments and the international community to make adequate investments in ECD will have long-term consequences for development.

The Benefits   We now understand that ECD programs can be key in countering the challenges that are outlined in the previous section. Investments in ECD offer outstanding returns, both in human and financial terms. Numerous studies have demonstrated that ECD can provide improvements in education, health, social development, and economic growth indicators (Barnett, 1998; Engle et al., 2007; Kagitcibasi, Unar, & Beckman, 2001). The World Bank and leading economists such as Nobel laureate James Heckman have concluded that "well targeted ECD programs cost less and produce more dramatic and lasting results than education investments at any other level" (van der Gaag, 2002, pp. 74–75). ECD programs help reduce the social and economic disparities and gender inequalities that divide societies and perpetuate poverty, and they are preferable to costly remedial action.

An analysis of the relationship between preschool enrollment and primary school completion or repetition rates in 133 countries provides a strong case for placing a higher priority on ECD during education sector discussions (Mingat & Jaramillo, 2003). The authors found completion rates of 50% in communities that lacked preschool and around 80% in communities where about half the children had access to some sort of preschool or ECD center. They found the grade repetition rate was 25% where no children enrolled in preschool and just 12% where 45% of children enrolled in preschool. Controlling for GDP made little difference in the analysis.

Enrollment in ECD Programs   What does the enrollment picture in the majority world look like? Access to relevant, quality early childhood supports—whether they are formal or informal—remains problematic in most majority world countries. There are a few notable exceptions, such as Cuba. In this country, nearly all children participate in a range of ECD programs that begin before birth and target both children and parents. Cuban third graders significantly outperform their counterparts in much wealthier surrounding countries (Tinajero, 2009).

Most data focus on enrollment in preprimary classes rather than on a broader range of ECD services, especially ECD programs that serve children ages birth to 3 years. Data that do exist, paint a bleak picture. The 2009 EFA Global Monitoring Report states that the preprimary gross enrollment ratio (GER) is 36% for developing countries, 79% for developed countries, and 62% for countries that are in transition.

Breakdown by region is even more telling. In sub-Saharan Africa, although the number of children enrolled in an ECD program between 1999 and 2006 is up by 43%, the preprimary GER is just 14%. In practice, this means that 86% of children are entering primary school with no preschool experience. More than half the sub-Saharan Africa countries report a GER of less than 10%; in Mali, it is just 3%. In South Asia, the preprimary GER stands at 39% (up significantly from 21% in 1999). Yet in countries like Afghanistan it is less than 1%. In the Arab States, the GER is only 18%, and sub-Saharan Africa saw better growth in GER between 1999 and 2006 than the Arab States did during that period. In Latin America, the regional GER for preschool is 65%, but GERs differ substantially from country to country. In Cuba, virtually all children attend preschool, but in Guatemala only 29% do.

Failure to Reach Disadvantaged Children
Global disparities are mirrored in wide gaps within countries, especially between the richest and poorest children. In some countries, such as Syria, Mongolia, and Kyrgyzstan, children from the wealthiest 20% of households are at least 5 times as likely to attend preschool programs as children from the poorest 20% of households. Table 4.1 uses data from the EFA Global Monitoring Report (2009, p. 54) to highlight these stark disparities.

Preschool-age children who live in low-income households with low parental education levels in Ethiopia, Peru, Vietnam, and the Indian state of Andhra Pradesh are much less likely to be enrolled in preschool than their better-off counterparts (Ames et al., 2009; Woodhead et al., 2009). Fees and other "hidden costs" often make it difficult for low-income families to send their children to school. In Vietnam, 65% of urban children have access to ECD services, but only 36% of rural children do (Young Lives, 2007). In Ethiopia the situation is even worse: The corresponding figures are 58% (urban) and 4% (rural).

In the minority world, France and most Scandinavian countries have near-universal preschool enrollment and ECD services are often an entitlement. In contrast, in the United States ECD services are not universal, and only 45% of poor children are enrolled in preschool education, compared with 75% of children from high-income families (UNESCO, 2008).

Rates of participation in ECD programs also differ by gender. In some countries, girls face unique barriers to accessing preschool education, especially in rural areas (Woodhead et al., 2009). Gender discrimination may begin before birth, with high rates of abortion of female fetuses in some Asian countries. It may also lead to disparities in feeding practices (boys receive more and better quality food) and health-care–seeking behaviors. On a more positive note, statistics indicate that overall gender disparities in ECD enrollment tend to be minor in most countries (UNESCO, 2008). Furthermore, a program in Nepal showed that ECD can be an effective strategy for promoting greater gender equity in primary school (Save the Children, 2003; UNESCO, 2003, 2004).

UNICEF's Multiple Indicator Cluster Surveys, which were used in its 2006 State of the World's Children Report, and a report by the UNESCO Institute for Statistics (2005) point to

Table 4.1. Disparities in preschool enrollment (3- and 4-year-olds) in selected countries

Country	Richest 20%	Poorest 20%
Kyrgyzstan	47%	7%
Vietnam	80%	35%
Mongolia	73%	9%
Syria	18%	3%
Cote d'Ivoire	24%	1%

From UNESCO. (2008). *EFA global monitoring report 2009: Overcoming inequality: Why governance matters* (p. 54). Paris: Author; reprinted by permission.

the same conclusion regarding disparities in access: Children from the most marginalized backgrounds are considerably less likely to access ECD programs than are children from wealthier backgrounds, although they have been repeatedly shown to benefit the most (Arnold et al., 2006; UNESCO, 2006).

Across minority and majority world contexts, the failure to reach disadvantaged children is extremely worrisome. Despite the fact that EFA Goal 1 specifically prioritizes services for "the most vulnerable and disadvantaged children," in reality it is largely the wealthy who succeed in accessing the limited opportunities that are available, both when these opportunities are public and when they are free.

Reliability of Data   Data on access to ECD programs and supports are not always reliable. For example, governments may underreport the provision of ECD services by entities other than the state—especially when these organizations are informal and the government has no coordinating role. Nonstate provision (by Civil Society Organizations and private providers) accounts for an estimated half of ECD services in the majority world (49%). In sub-Saharan Africa, the figure is 53% (EFA Global Monitoring Report, 2009).

What makes the analysis of ECD services more complex is that nonstate providers are a diverse set of organizations, including very small local community development organizations, individually owned preschools, private for-profit preschools, faith-based preschools, and early childhood centers that are supported by local nongovernmental organizations (NGOs) (Aga Khan Foundation, 2007). In other words, private provision of services does not necessarily mean expensive and exclusive provision for wealthy families. Many of the NGO services, in fact, target excluded, poor families, though virtually all providers charge fees and seek in-kind and other supports from local communities. Botswana, Congo, Gambia, Lesotho, Togo, Uganda, Madagascar, Namibia, and Ethiopia all report that a very high percentage of their preprimary children are enrolled in private programs—90% or more (UNESCO, 2008).

Quality   In addition to generally having very poor access to early childhood programs, disadvantaged children lack access to quality services (Woodhead et al., 2009). This fact is particularly worrisome given that a small, but growing, body of research from the majority world is showing, not surprisingly, that higher quality ECD environments result in better outcomes for children—for example, children enrolled in high-quality programs often show both cognitive and psychosocial benefits (Aboud, 2006; Aboud, Hossain, & O'Gara, 2008; Moore, Akhter, & Aboud, 2008; Mwaura, 2008). What is critical here is that improving the quality of programs requires educators to have an array of learning materials available for children to use. The ECD teachers also need to receive in-depth professional training, as well as follow-up support, to help them apply new ideas and knowledge to support children's cognitive and psychosocial development in the classroom (Moore et al., 2008). Culturally appropriate training of local ECD staff who speak the children's language and are known (and often selected) by parents, along with provision of sufficient relevant teaching and learning materials, lies at the heart of quality programs operating in the majority world.

Unfortunately, these solutions are very different from the one that often is given priority in policy discussions: raising the formal education requirements for ECD teachers. This policy often means that only teachers coming in from the outside are qualified. As ECD policies become formalized and the field of ECD becomes professionalized, there are both intended and unintended consequences. Some of the unintended consequences can lead to poor and marginalized communities becoming further disadvantaged. There is much discussion of increasing standards for ECD staff qualifications—most often measured by formal (accredited) courses—across majority world countries. While this action frequently may improve the learning opportunities for children, the situation is complex.

These qualification requirements can be problematic, particularly when they do not acknowledge the value of teachers' practical work experience with young children and when their implications are not fully considered. Local people in remote rural villages or urban slums simply may not have the required qualifications. The result may be serious service gaps or the recruitment of outsiders who may not understand the local culture or speak the language. Local communities or NGOs that have been operating ECD activities may not be able to register as official providers because they do not meet new requirements or are unable to afford the cost of registration (including transport to a larger urban center and the time it takes to work through the process). While they may be closely attuned to local values and expressed needs and may be delivering valuable services, they are rarely validated within the emerging "professional" requirements.

Failure to Provide Adequate Resources for ECD   Low preschool enrollment rates signify a massive failure on the part of both national governments and international organizations to provide adequate financial resources for ECD. The Creditor Reporting System Aid Activity Database (International Development Statistics, 2009) indicates that

- Average annual aid to ECD programs (1999–2007) from bilateral and multilateral donor agencies (e.g., the United Nations, Western countries' development aid agencies) was $44 million.

- Average annual aid to primary education (1999–2007) was $2.266 billion.

Thus, donor support to ECD was just 1.9% of the total support to primary education. (Note that this support comes mostly from grants and does not include the significant World Bank loans[2] for ECD). There are, of course, problems in trying to estimate ECD investment. This type of investment may be hidden within basic education or broad social sector support as a subarea of work. Nevertheless, the fact remains that the resources allotted to ECD are wholly inadequate.

ADDRESSING TRANSITIONS IN THE MAJORITY WORLD

Given that ECD programs have enormous benefits for children's successful transition (and therefore are a valuable way to meet EFA and poverty reduction goals), a top priority must be to increase funds allocated to ECD—both funds in national budgets and funds from donors. Meanwhile, it is vital also to respond effectively to the reality, highlighted in the previous section, that only a small percentage of children and families have access to ECD programs of any kind. This means that the major transition for the vast majority of children in low-income countries is from their home to primary school. Therefore, it is even more critical to look at what happens as children enter Grade 1 and move through their early primary school years. As we will see in the next section, this transition period is highly precarious, and large numbers of children simply never make it through more than a few months or a year. We are faced with the urgent challenge of ensuring that primary schools are ready for children—*all* children—whether or not they are

---

[2]As of 2007, the World Bank has loaned $1.7 billion to 91 projects in 52 countries. These projects include stand-alone projects and projects that have subcomponents related to ECD.

"ready for school." It is critical that schools to play an active and positive role throughout this important transition period.

In order for a school to be "ready" for children, it must develop an environment in which all children feel a sense of belonging and are able to learn. This means that teachers must welcome and appreciate children's efforts, ensure their safety and sense of security, and provide learning opportunities that enable children to interact effectively with their world.

Although a school's ability to provide a positive learning environment has an important impact for all children. the importance is greatly magnified for younger children who are entering school for the first time. How young girls and boys fare, how they feel in the early days and weeks, and how they are viewed and treated as learners is critical. It can be a time of stress, anxiety, and insecurity, or it can be a time of anticipation, new friends and challenges, enjoyment of learning, and confidence.

Access to Primary Education: The First Gate

Access to primary education has increased dramatically in recent years in the majority world, with a primary GER of 106% and a net enrollment ratio (NER)—enrollment of the official age group for a given level of education expressed as a percentage of the corresponding population (UNESCO Institute of Statistics)—of 85% (UNESCO, 2008). The change is significant considering that, traditionally, enrollment has been low across much of the majority world and especially in sub-Saharan Africa and South Asia. Yet, while the vast majority of children now enroll in school, many of them do not complete the primary cycle. An estimated 75 million primary-school–age children do not complete primary school, either because they drop out or because they never have the chance to enroll in the first place (Save the Children, 2009). The same inequities that exclude so many children from ECD programs conspire against children enrolling and staying in school: low family income, low maternal education, challenges of geography (including distance to school), gender discrimination, and minority (e.g., ethnic, religious) status.

Various in-school factors, such as inadequate teaching, irrelevant curriculum, a poor or non-existent infrastructure, and a lack of learning materials can undermine young students' confidence and enthusiasm for learning from the start. These problems are analyzed further in the sections that follow. In addition, conflict and violence within schools and communities, entrenched cultural biases (e.g., attitudes toward girls and women), and factors such as distance to school affect parents' decisions about whether and when to allow their children to enroll and attend classes.

For numerous children, even those as young as 5 or 6 years, the possibility of starting school must compete with other possibilities, such as providing assistance in the household's livelihood and survival strategies. Assistance of this kind may mean helping to care for younger siblings, watching over the family livestock, collecting firewood and water, and chasing wild animals away from the family agricultural plots. However, across the majority world disadvantaged families are increasingly aware of the importance of education and the possibilities that it may offer children to break out of poverty. If children are learning, families often make great sacrifices to keep them in school.

This commitment on the part of many families makes it all the more disturbing that such vast numbers of children who do enter school drop out before completing the primary grades. In sub-Saharan Africa as a whole, one third of pupils leave school before they even reach Grade 5 (UNESCO, 2008). School completion rates have changed little in countries such as Uganda despite massive increases in initial enrollment. In order to address these challenges effectively, it is vital to know the point at which children are dropping out. When does the system fail them?

Dropouts, Repetition, and Underachievement: The Crisis in Early Primary School Undermining Successful Transition

In Uganda, one third (32%) of children who enroll in school drop out during their first year (UNESCO, 2006). Analysis of grade-disaggregated data demonstrates beyond doubt that the real crisis is in the early years. Dropout rates are highest in Grade 1, according to the data in recent Global Monitoring Reports (UNESCO, 2005, 2006, 2008). In many countries, high dropout levels often are combined with even worse repetition rates. In Guinea-Bissau, Rwanda, Equatorial Guinea, Madagascar, and Nepal, more than half the children who enroll either repeat first grade or drop out (Arnold et al., 2006). When dropout information is available by grade, Grade 1 dropout rates are usually at least double those of Grade 2. For example, in South Asia, children are 3 times as likely to drop out of Grade 1 as they are to drop out of Grade 4. Even in Latin America, where overall progress toward the EFA goals has been made, some areas show poor outcomes: In Colombia, 19% of children dropped out before completing Grade 1, and in Belize, 31% of children repeated Grade 1. Additional and often stark disparities exist within countries such as India, where Grade 1 dropout rates range from 2% in the state of Kerala to 21% in the state of Rajasthan (Arnold et al.).

Of those who stay in school, many children repeat classes and become established in persistent patterns of underachievement. Millions of children leave school without having attained basic literacy and numeracy skills. For example, a study of students' ability to read a simple sentence by Grade 5 found that in Peru the figure was just 18% for girls and boys alike, and in Ghana it was 19% for boys and only 12% for girls (Gilles & Quijada, 2008). National assessments in Uganda indicated that 46% of third graders are not reaching expected levels of competency in literacy (National Assessment of Progress in Primary Education, 2007). Along the same lines, a survey of learning achievement in 549 districts in India found that 47% of Grade 5 children could not read a story text at a Grade 2 level of difficulty (Pratham, 2007). The ability to read affects students' later progress across all subject areas and thus the likelihood of a successful transition through early primary school and into subsequent years of school.

In sum then, repetition and failure to learn stops or severely stymies children's successful transition. The next section focuses on and starts to unpack some of the in-school factors that contribute to this dire situation in which schools routinely fail the very children they have been established to serve. It highlights the need for us to focus attention on the neglected early primary classes.

What Happens in School

The most powerful determinant of children's successful transition in majority world countries is what actually goes on within the classroom—the way teachers teach and how much they teach. However, the physical environment can have a profound impact on transitions by directly affecting factors such as attention, concentration, behavior, and comfort, as well as by influencing social interaction. In this section, therefore, we will start with a brief look at one particular aspect of the physical environment, class size, before going on to examine several aspects of quality of teaching and instruction that children experience in school.

Class Size   In some of the poorest countries (particularly those in sub-Saharan Africa), the number of children who share a single classroom during the first year of primary school has mushroomed, reaching 100 or more (Abadzi, 2006). The learning environment in many Grade 1 classes is thus extremely challenging. Very large class sizes impede teachers' ability to teach and children's ability to learn (Gilles & Quijada, 2008; O'Sullivan, 2006), especially in the earliest years. Classes that may already have issues related to ventilation, light, warmth, noise, and sufficient quantities of the most basic furniture are now seriously overcrowded. In these classrooms, one teacher is faced with trying to provide meaningful learning opportunities for far too many children, often confronting an extreme range of ages and abilities, a lack of seating space, and a dire shortage of learning materials (Arnold et al., 2006; Gilles & Quijada, 2008).

Teacher Competence   Teacher competence is a multidimensional construct that includes 1) teacher capacity, 2) teacher motivation, and 3) teacher–child interactions, and that has major implications for instructional quality. First, many Grade 1 teachers lack the skills and competencies in classroom management and developmentally appropriate teaching and learning methods to build critical foundations in language, literacy, numeracy, and problem-solving skills. A number of factors contribute to this deficiency. Work with the upper primary grades is almost always accorded a higher status than work with the early grades. Therefore, the newest and least experienced teachers often are assigned to the early grades, usually through a centralized and hierarchical process (Abadzi, 2006). Research in India and Brazil has found that teachers' level of education is a significant predictor of their students' achievement, even in the early grades (Bartlett, 2010). Given that many early-grade teachers in low-income countries have minimal education themselves, they critically need good supplementary training and professional development. Too often, though, training reflects the same rote practices that take place in the classroom and makes little attempt to ensure that teachers understand the material presented or to provide clearly structured, hands-on experiences that teachers can then implement with their students.

Second, high absentee rates of primary teachers in majority world countries are a significant problem, along with a lack of engagement when they are in school. Many teachers spend significant amounts of school time outside the classroom, and it is not uncommon for teachers to hand over their duties (and a small fraction of their pay) to untrained substitutes while they tend to other obligations (Save the Children, 2007).

Third, the quality of interactions and teaching and learning approaches often falls short. Schools can be stressful places for young children. Physical punishment and humiliation are common even in lower grades and undermine learning and enjoyment. The way that teachers interact with students affects whether children want to stay in school and whether they learn anything at all (Research and Analysis Working Group, United Republic of Tanzania, 2008). Evidence from Brazil, Nepal, and Uganda demonstrates the benefits of warmer and more encouraging teacher responses, which, of course, are not independent of the mode of instruction (Bartlett, in press). In Tanzania, children defined a good teacher as someone who is not threatening, teaches until the children understand, and gives extra help and support when it is needed (Research and Analysis Working Group, United Republic of Tanzania).

Effective strategies for teaching in crowded early-grade classrooms are largely absent. Not enough attention is given to ensuring that teachers in the lower primary grades have sufficient knowledge and coherent and accessible teaching strategies to enable young children to gain the necessary basic skills, concepts, and interest in learning. Although there have been many efforts over the last 20 years promoting "active learning," these methods are often only partially understood by teachers and by those who supervise and support them. For example, many teachers have heard that lecture methods are old-fashioned and "not good," but they have not been helped to organize the alternative, group work. They may therefore place students' desks together to encourage mutual learning and support, but then continue to assign exercises that involve no cooperative work. The actual time that students spend on task is often hugely inadequate and may be less than 50% of the time officially allotted to the activity (Gilles & Quijada, 2008; Kaul,

Ramachandran, & Upadhayay, 1993). In the majority world, scheduled contact time for Grade 1 children averages only 700 hours a year (compared with 850 hours in high-income countries). Furthermore, many factors reduce actual class time, so there may be 200–300 fewer hours of instruction than are officially indicated (Bartlett, in press).

Reading   Remarkably little systematic attention has been given to ensuring that all children are able to become successful readers—including children whose homes have no reading materials and who speak a native language different from the language of instruction in school. Yet literacy is fundamental to ensuring students' progress through the formal education process. Research suggests that if children cannot read after about 3 years of education, they probably never will (Abadzi, 2006); they may be promoted regularly and may complete school, but will remain functionally illiterate. In short, failure during the first year or two of school to establish basic literacy skills "creates inefficiencies that reverberate all through the system" (2006, p. 136).

Many of the whole-language approaches that have been promoted through numerous projects over the last 2 decades have failed to deliver benefits for disadvantaged children because they depended on children having a literate context in the home and coming to school with preexisting literacy and numeracy-related knowledge. The current drive in certain places for phonics-based approaches has in part been a reaction to this. However, phonics has severe limitations because it fails to give adequate attention to making meaning, without which there is no reason to read (Snow, 2002; Tolhurst, 2008). Far more explicit and systematic instruction in reading is needed, especially for children who are struggling with a second language.

Language of Instruction   In the majority world, significant numbers of children enter primary school speaking a language different from the one that is used as the medium of instruction. It is estimated that 50% of the world's out-of-school children live in families and communities where the language of instruction in school is rarely used (MacKenzie, 2006). New policies in a number of countries now promote the use of a majority local language during the first years of primary school. However, because most teachers are assigned to schools by a centralized process, they often do not speak the home language of their students, and their first language may not even be the official language of instruction. There are often multiple languages in a classroom—students' home languages, the teacher's mother tongue, and the official language(s) of instruction.

The language of instruction is a key factor that can support or undermine children's successful transition (Abadzi, 2006; Benson, 2005). Children who come to school unfamiliar with the language of instruction are challenged cognitively and also challenged in terms of their confidence and sense of identity; they are more likely to end up repeating and dropping out of school (Bartlett, in press). Children's attendance levels are higher when instruction at school is in the same language as the one that is spoken at home, and this relationship varies according to other social factors (Smits, Huisman, & Kruijff, 2008). In Malawi, researchers have found that students whose home language is the same as their teacher's language (even if the language of instruction is different) perform significantly better in primary school (Chilora, 2000; Chilora & Harris, 2001).

Availability of Teaching and Learning Materials   The availability of basic learning materials and their appropriate use demonstrably improves children's school achievement, most strongly in places where material assets are low (Bartlett, in press). Of course, it is schools in the most impoverished communities that suffer the greatest dearth of teaching and learning materials. Considerable effort has been made across many countries to improve and update curricula and associated textbooks. The distribution of these materials in a timely manner, however, remains a challenge, particularly in more remote areas. Textbooks are often shared between several children or are written at levels that are too advanced for the learners. There are rarely sufficient resources beyond the key textbooks. When additional materials are provided, too often they are either at an inappropriate level or locked away in cupboards so that they do not get "spoiled." Yet an immersion in print and the opportunity to read for pleasure are recognized as crucial factors for the development of strong reading abilities. Concrete materials are equally important in aiding children's comprehension of basic mathematical and scientific concepts (Bartlett, in press).

Home–School–Community Linkages

In many parts of the majority world, the local school is not seen as part of the fabric of the community and is particularly not a structure that parents can influence. This attitude allows few effective avenues for engagement between home and school. In some cases, this situation results from the cultural and linguistic discontinuities between home and school in culturally diverse contexts; parents' ability to advocate for their children is clearly hampered when they do not speak the language that is used in the school.

Other times, the gap is related to educators' limited communication with parents and the lack of parents' involvement in school decision making. This situation may not be surprising given that schools' lines of control and reporting generally stretch upward through the system to Ministries of Education, not outward to the community. Yet parents' engagement with their children's education is one of the most robust predictors of successful transition and learning achievement (UNESCO, 1998).

This section outlined a number of serious problems and gaps in the provision of relevant quality education for young children as they make the key transition to primary school. These problems influence enrollment and retention. Equally important, they influence whether children learn anything and whether they think of themselves as capable learners. These problems amount to a crisis in education that occurs right at the beginning of schooling, yet school improvement programs and other sector reform efforts across the majority world traditionally have given little attention to the early years of primary education. In addition, educators working in ECD rarely forge effective links to primary schools. Likewise, primary schools do not reach out to ECD stakeholders in their surrounding area to ensure that there is good communication and to smooth the transition process. Families, ECD providers, and primary schools all must play an active role in this fragile transition period. We need a useful framework for conceptualizing efforts to address these challenges.

AN OVERARCHING FRAMEWORK FOR TRANSITIONS IN THE MAJORITY WORLD: CONTINUITY OR RIGHTS?

There is much discussion on the importance of continuity within the literature on transition (Lombardi, 1992; Myers, 1997). However, the degree of inequity and depth of poverty within most of the majority world are so extreme that we feel that it is important to pose the question of whether continuity is the appropriate organizing framework when many families in the majority world do not receive even the most basic level of support from government systems.

If a child enrolling in an ECD center comes from a home where she is left alone for long periods, where the parents are so exhausted from working to put food on the table that they have no time or energy to interact with her, and where there is no access to health care, is it continuity that is needed? If an ECD center runs in a tiny dark room and has no materials for children and the teacher receives no support, is it continuity that we want when the child transitions to primary school? The answer to such questions is probably "yes and no." Continuity is critical in many areas, such as using the mother tongue; being familiar with local teachers; protecting cultural identity; ensuring that all children, families, and teachers feel welcome; and recognizing, respecting, and building on what caregivers and teachers already know and do for their children. Yet the institutions and communities that are so lacking in basic resources must be transformed, in partnership with those same families and teachers. Continuity as a more general principle becomes a goal as the situation for families, and the services and supports that they access, improve.

A Rights Framework

The United Nations Convention on the Rights of the Child (CRC) establishes a set of legal norms for the protection and well-being of all children (United Nations General Assembly, 1989). Children's rights include fundamental needs (e.g., good health, learning opportunities, care, protection from harm), and adults have an obligation to meet these needs. The state is obliged both to protect the individual child and to help create the conditions in which all children can develop their potential. The younger the child, the more dependent that child is on adults to protect his or her rights. The CRC is legally binding on state parties and has more signatories than any other international convention. It provides a strong basis for initiating public dialogue and action on behalf of young children. It also provides the basis for demanding that governments be more accountable to young children and their families. A rights framework ensures that advocates for children's rights and education will increase their efforts to influence government policy as a key to achieving sustained change, whether through delivery of services or the protection of children through the legal system. However, while almost all governments have signed the CRC, there is often no functional system in place to ensure its implementation. This lack makes close partnership with civil society all the more critical. Civil society is a critical supporter and catalyst for ECD and in many places continues to be the main provider of ECD services.

The CRC states that ensuring children's rights includes the provision of support programs for children's physical, mental, spiritual, moral, and social development, enabling them to grow to their fullest potential. Families are the front line for ensuring their children's rights. A child's development is viewed primarily as the responsibility of the family, though the family may receive assistance from the government in the form of facilities and services for the care of children. (See Preamble and Articles 5, 6, and 18.) In essence, quality early childhood and transition programs aim to ensure the conditions under which children's rights are honored and met. Three fundamental features of a children's rights approach to transition are 1) attention to the whole child and the principle of "best interests of the child," 2) addressing discrimination and exclusion, and 3) working at multiple levels to meet obligations to children.

Attention to the Whole Child   A holistic view of children's well-being, while by no means new, has been validated and encouraged by the CRC. With the impetus of the CRC, many agencies and governments are adopting this comprehensive view of ECD. Majority world nations including the Philippines, Vietnam, Nepal, Jamaica, Kenya, and minority world countries such as the United Kingdom and France have policies that attend to the whole child. Holistic planning frameworks, which recognize sector and field realities, are key.

Addressing Discrimination and Exclusion   A fundamental characteristic of human rights is that they are universal and therefore, by definition, are concerned with addressing exclusion. Transition programs can be a highly effective way to work against deep-rooted patterns of disadvantage and marginalization. Working with parents empowers them not only to better support their children's development but also to demand services and supports from other duty-bearers. Inclusive center-based programs and schools are crucial bridges for many hard-pressed families and unlock opportunities for children.

Working at Multiple Levels for Children Before and After They Enter School
A rights approach emphasizes the necessity of working at multiple levels if we are to achieve the sort of fundamental shifts in values and social mores that we are seeking. ECD and transition initiatives are concerned with influencing the contexts in which children grow up so that 1) they are supportive of children's overall development and 2) they address issues that impede and damage that development. By *contexts,* we mean all of the different environments that affect young children—families, communities, health centers, ECD centers, schools, community organizations, district bodies, national policy bodies, and donors.

Thus, transition initiatives cover a wide range of activities, from working directly with families to changing systems that marginalize or exclude some children. They include work at the following six levels:

1. Interactions within the family—building family members' understanding, confidence, and skills to support their young children's development, aid their successful transitions, and hold government and other duty-bearers accountable to make quality services available

2. Community planning—working with communities to make the environment safer for young children, ensure inclusive ECD provision that reaches disadvantaged children, and provide health services for all

3. Provision of center-based ECD services that focus on providing safe, healthy, and stimulating environments for young children (e.g., child care centers, home-based child care, preschools, workplace child care)

4. Influencing the early years of primary education to provide consistent sustained support for children's overall development and learning in a welcoming environment that effectively supports the establishment of basic literacy, numeracy, and problem-solving skills as well as confidence and social skills

5. Strengthening national resources and building capacity to enable countries to provide good supports for young children's overall development and their successful transition into and achievement in school

6. Advocacy for legal, policy, and systemic change, or increased social and economic allocations for programs for young children

It may be useful to further consider these six areas of activity under the headings of pedagogy, program, and policy, as explicated elsewhere in this book.

Pedagogy, Program, and Policy:
The Rights Framework and the Way Forward

What are some of the key recommendations that emerge?

Pedagogy   The central concerns of center-based ECD services and the early years of primary school are quality pedagogy. In the majority world, access is also a key concern, particularly for ECD programs but also for primary education. At the center of pedagogy are the relationship between learners and teachers and the learning environment within which they interact. The quality of interactions that adults—including children's first and most influential teachers (their families), early childhood program staff, and primary school teachers—have with children are at the heart of this concern. As majority world governments take more interest in ECD, it is vital to

- Avoid a downward extension of Grade 1 and overformalized approaches in ECD programs. Instead, the focus should be on improving primary schools' readiness to support children's learning by encouraging the "pushing up" of good practices that are characteristic of ECD programs into the lower primary grades. These practices include the creation of a welcoming environment, particularly for families that did not have prior access to ECD service (the vast majority of families in many places) and hence that may be interacting with an educational institution for the first time. Also important are laying firm foundations in language, creating enthusiasm for learning, and fostering social development.

- Focus in early primary grades on improving the teaching of reading and math in enjoyable, systematic, and structured ways that ensure success for children who often may not come from literate contexts. This teaching should involve 1) intensive and interactive practice to improve language knowledge, 2) mother tongue teaching of reading and basic concepts, and 3) the availability of books that children can take home with them.

- Provide specific in-service training and mentoring for both ECD and lower primary school teachers (some of which can be conducted jointly). Build understanding, skills, and competencies regarding how young children learn, and generate practical ways to support diverse learners (e.g., those of different ages, children with and without ECD program experience).

- Ensure the availability and use of core teaching and learning materials for both ECD and early primary classes. Many of these materials can be made with locally available resources and should draw on local knowledge, culture, and traditions by involving parents or community members in classes. In addition, families can be encouraged to use local stories, songs, and games and to make learning materials to use at home.

Program and Policy   These two areas are so intertwined that, in order to avoid repetition, we must discuss them under one heading. While the emphasis on influencing government, which is central to a rights-based approach, is crucial, it is important to remember that the government's role is not always to provide for all rights, but to ensure that rights are realized. Moral obligations to children long precede any treaty and extend throughout society. Civil society has long played a central role in shaping ECD services.

ECD Programs   It is critical for governments to find ways to work with a broad range of civil society organizations and with communities in ways that reach out and genuinely engage families. Programs must strengthen community-level supports and work through local civil society as well as government. Analysis of what civil society organizations are doing, often through interventions that build bridges between government initiatives and local communities, can help to build strong ECD programs (Aga Khan Foundation, 2007).

ECD Policies

In many countries, ECD policies are being developed for the first time. Some of these policies follow a holistic framework and are multisectoral in nature; others are more sector specific and often sit within education. Whatever framework is used, communities need a broad and inclusive network of ECD services that effectively links with primary schools. The delivery of quality learning opportunities in ways that engage with the diversity of learners and communities at hand is a key policy and program issue.

Across many developing countries, policies are emerging that add 1 or more years of preschool to basic education. This expansion of access is for the most part a very positive step. However, there are two important points to recognize:

- Preprimary classes should not become a downward extension of uninspiring primary classes in a misguided attempt to give children an academic edge. (See the earlier pedagogy section.) Rather, policy should promote the uptake of good ECD practices by early primary grades.

- There should be concerted efforts to build on and create links with existing early childhood services in the community. Inclusive policies should link all types of ECD providers with local primary schools. This effort requires flexibility and responsiveness to local situations in the course of phasing in new policies (such as policies stipulating qualification requirements, as we discussed earlier). Interface and cooperation between state and nonstate providers is key in addressing both access and quality issues.

Early Primary School

The percentage of children enrolled in ECD programs is, as we have noted, small in most developing countries. Of this number, most of the children do *not* come from the disadvantaged groups that most need services. Therefore, it is all the more urgent to ensure that there is adequate policy and program attention to the quality of the first years of primary school. The important policy point here is that we need to reconceptualize the way that the massive school improvement efforts across the majority world are designed so that attention and resources for the early grades are prioritized. This work would include finding ways to influence and change the status of the lower primary grades, as well as recruiting and assigning experienced and capable teachers to the lower grades.

Evidence-Based Programs and Policy

Analysis of core enrollment, retention, and achievement data and examination of the effects of different interventions and programs are fundamental to planning effective programs for young children (Arnold et al., 2006). Emphasis is on the following points:

- Ensure regular and clear analysis of key data as an essential step in changing policies, programs, and practice.

- Develop an Early Transition Report that can provide information at local or national levels to look at the following statistics: poverty levels (the percentage of children under age 8 who live in poverty), rates of stunting (height lower than the average for the child's age), rates of participation in ECD programs, teacher–child ratio in Grade 1 (compared with the average ratio in the primary grades), dropout and repetition rates for Grades 1 and 2 compared with those rates at the end of primary school, teacher absenteeism, mother tongue policies and actual use of the mother tongue in ECD settings and early primary grades, student–textbook ratios in Grade 1 versus overall student–textbook ratios for the primary grades, specialized training for lower primary teachers (preservice, but especially in-service), and time spent on task and assessment of reading proficiency in Grade 2 or 3.

In minority world countries, there has been a rich and diverse range of research-related activities to inform policy and programs. A number of activities have been longitudinal and have provided the impetus for changing program funding—including the funding of programs focused on transition issues. This chapter has highlighted some of the growing evidence of the benefits of attention to the early years that is emerging from research in majority world countries. Evidence of benefits has been critical in influencing government policies in a number of countries. More efforts like the Young Lives study are needed. Young Lives is a long-term international research project investigating the changing nature of childhood poverty. Such longitudinal research in the majority world is essential to understanding and informing programs and policies. In addition, the promotion of ready children, families, and schools to improve transition is being undertaken by international and national agencies—and continues to create ongoing reports and research from program experiences across majority world countries. Yet, more longitudinal research evaluating the impact of programs is critical if more children are to enter school, stay there, and learn effectively.

SUMMARY AND CONCLUSIONS

In the majority world, attention to transition is central to addressing the acute crisis of high dropout and repetition rates during the early primary years and the establishment of persistent patterns of failure. Transition frameworks deliberately link ECD programs with early primary components, work to expand ECD initiatives, and also bring increased attention to the first years of primary schooling. In addition, they strengthen parents' own interactions with and support to their children.

This chapter recommends that action be taken on the following five fronts: 1) more and better ECD programs to reach all children, including the most disadvantaged ones; 2) improved links, coordination, cooperation, and understanding between ECD programs and primary school systems; 3) prioritization of attention to and resources for the early grades of primary school as a central component of education reform; 4) improved partnership between parents, civil society, and government; and 5) gathering of better information and data. The rights-based framework that we propose emphasizes a number of cross-cutting themes that apply to all of the preceding actions. First, we need to make deliberate efforts to reach and include marginalized children and families. Second, we need to do work at multiple levels to influence practice and governance. Third, we need to take a holistic approach that keeps the best interests of the child front and center.

Early childhood interventions ensure that children are ready for school and ready to make the most of many opportunities in life. But equally important, schools must be ready to educate all children—whether or not the children have had the opportunity to participate in an ECD program. This readiness would dramatically improve the chances of meeting the EFA and Millennium Development Goals and would make an important contribution to addressing entrenched cycles of poverty and exclusion. Work with the neglected early primary grades, concurrent with support for children's overall development before they enter school, is a powerful combination for successful transitions.

REFERENCES

Abadzi, H. (2006). *Efficient learning for the poor: Insights from the frontier of cognitive neuroscience.* Washington, DC: World Bank.

Aboud, F. (2006). Evaluation of an early childhood preschool program in rural Bangladesh. *Early Childhood Research Quarterly, 21*(1), 46–60.

Aboud, F., Hossain, K., & O'Gara, C. (2008). The Succeed Project: Challenging early school failure in Bangladesh. *Research in Comparative and International Education, 3*(3).

Aga Khan Foundation. (2007). Non-state providers and public–private–community partnerships in education. Contributions towards achieving EFA: A critical review of challenges, opportunities and issues. Background paper for the *EFA Global Monitoring Report 2008, Education for All by 2015: Will we make it?* Geneva.

Ames, P., Rojas, V., & Portugal, T. (2009). *Starting school: Who is prepared? Young Lives' research on children's transition to first grade in Peru* (Working Paper No. 47). Retrieved from http://www.younglives .org.uk/publications/working-papers/wp-summaries/summary-working-paper-47

Arnold, C., Bartlett, K., Gowani, S., & Merali, R. (2006). Is everybody ready? Readiness, transition and continuity: Reflections and moving forward. *EFA Global Monitoring Report 2007, Strong Foundations: Early Childhood Care and Education.*

Barnett, S. (1998). *Long-term cognitive and academic effects of early childhood education on children in poverty.* Ypsilanti, MI: HighScope Educational Research Foundation.

Bartlett, S. (2010). *Improving learning achievement in the early grades in low-income countries: A review of the research.* Geneva: Aga Khan Foundation.

Benson, C. (2005). *Girls, educational equity and mother tongue-based teaching.* Bangkok: United Nations Educational, Scientific and Cultural Organization.

Boethel, M. (2004). *Readiness: School, family, and community connections. Annual Synthesis 2004.* National Center for Family and Community Connections with Schools, Southwest Educational Development Laboratory. Retrieved from http://www.sedl.org/connections/resources/readiness-synthesis.pdf

Chabbott, C. (2006). *Accelerating early grades reading in high priority EFA countries: A desk review.* USAID EQUIP program. Retrieved from http://www.equip123.net/docs/E1-EGRinEFACountriesDeskStudy. pdf

Chilora, H. (2000, March). *Language policy research and practice in Malawi.* Paper presented at the Comparative and International Education Society Conference, San Antonio, TX.

Chilora, H., & Harris, A. (2001). *Investigating the role of teacher's home language in mother tongue policy implementation: Evidence from IEQ research findings in Malawi.* USAID Document No. PN-ACL-068. Improving Educational Quality Project. Retrieved from http://www.ieq.org/pdf/Investigating_Role_ Language.pdf

Consultative Group on Early Childhood Care and Development. (2009, March). *The path of most resilience: Early childhood care and development in emergencies, principles and practice.* Paper prepared for the INEE Global Consultation, Istanbul, Turkey.

Engle, P., Black, M., Behrman, J., Cabral de Mello, M., Gertler, P., Kapiriri, L., et al. (2007). Strategies to avoid the loss of developmental potential in more than 200 million children in the developing world. *The Lancet, 369*(9557), 229–242.

Entwistle, D.R., & Alexander, K.L. (1998). Early schooling as a "critical period" phenomenon. *Research in Sociology of Education and Socialization, 8,* 27–55.

Farah, M., Noble, K., & Hurt, H. (2005). Poverty, privilege and brain development: Empirical findings and ethical implications. In J. Illes (Ed.), *Neuroethics in the 21st century.* New York: Oxford University Press.

Gilles, J., & Quijada, J.J. (2008). *Opportunity to learn: A high impact strategy for improving educational outcomes in developing countries* (EQUIP2 Working Paper). Washington, DC: EQUIP2, AED, and USAID.

Grantham-McGregor, S., Cheung, Y., Cueto, S., Glewwe, P., Richter, L., Strupp, B., et al. (2007). Developmental potential in the first 5 years for children in developing countries. *The Lancet, 369*(9555), 60–70.

International Development Statistics. (2009). Online databases on aid and other resource flows. Retrieved from http://www.oecd.org/dac/stats/idsonline

Kagitcibasi, Ç., Unar, D., & Beckman, S. (2001). Long-term effects of early intervention: Turkish low-income mothers and children. *Applied Developmental Psychology, 22,* 333–361.

Kaul, V., Ramachandran, C., & Upadhayay, G.C. (1993). *Impact of ECE on retention in primary grades: A longitudinal study.* New Delhi: National Council of Education Research and Training.

Kids Count. (2005). *Getting ready: Findings from the National School Readiness Indicators Initiative.* Rhode Island: Author. Retrieved from http://www.gettingready.org/matriarch/d.asp?PageID=303&PageName2=pdfhold&p=&PageName=Getting+Ready+%2D+Full+Report%2E.pdf

Lancet Global Health Network. (2007). *Child development for developing countries.* Author. Retrieved from http://www.thelancetglobalhealthnetwork.com/archives/169

Lombardi, J. (1992). Beyond transition: Ensuring continuity in early childhood services. ERIC Digest. *Clearinghouse on Elementary and Early Childhood Education.* Urbana, IL: ERIC.

MacKenzie, P. (2006, November). *The use of mother tongue languages in education: Global pressure, local response.* Presentation at Society for International Development–Washington Education for Development, Washington, DC.

Mingat, A., & Jaramillo, A. (2003). *Early childhood care and education in sub-Saharan Africa: What would it take to meet the Millennium Development Goals?* Washington, DC: World Bank.

Moore, A., Akhter, S., & Aboud, F. (2008). Evaluating an improved quality preschool program in rural Bangladesh. *International Journal of Educational Development, 28*(2), 118–131.

Mwaura, P. (2008). *The quality of pedagogical ecology at Madrasa Resource Centre preschools in East Africa.* Unpublished manuscript.

Myers, R. (1997). Removing roadblocks to success: Transitions and linkages between home, preschool and primary school. *Coordinators' Notebook, 21,* 1–27. Retrieved from http://www.ecdgroup.com/download/cc121ari.pdf

National Assessment of Progress in Primary Education. (2007). Uganda Ministry of Education and Sports. Retrieved from http://www.education.go.ug/index.htm

O'Gara, C., & Lusk, D. (2002). The two who survive: The impact of HIV/AIDS on young children, their families and communities. *Coordinators' Notebook: HIV/AIDS and Early Childhood, 26,* 3–21. Retrieved from http://www.ecdgroup.com/pdfs/CN26withphotos.pdf

Organisation for Economic Co-operation and Development. (2006). *Starting strong II: Early childhood education and care.* Paris: Author.

O'Sullivan, M. (2006). Teaching large class sizes: The international evidence and a discussion of some good practice in Ugandan primary schools. *International Journal of Educational Development, 26,* 24–37.

Pratham. (2007). *ASER 2006: Annual status of education report.* New Delhi, India: Author.

Research and Analysis Working Group, United Republic of Tanzania. (2008). *Tanzanian children's perceptions of education and their role in society: Views of the children 2007.* Dar es Salaam, Tanzania. Retrieved from http://www.repoa.or.tz/documents_storage/Research%20and%20Analysis/Views_of_the_Children_2007.pdf

Sakti, H., Nokes, C., Hertanto, W., Hendratno, S., Hall, A., Bundy, D., et al. (1999). Evidence for an association between hookworm infection and cognitive function in Indonesian school children. *Tropical Medicine & International Health, 4*(5), 322.

Save the Children. (2003). *What's the difference? The impact of early childhood development programs: A study of the effects for children, their families and communities.* Kathmandu, Nepal: Save the Children & United Nations Children's Fund.

Save the Children. (2007). *Finding hope in troubled times: Education and protection for children in Nepal.* Kathmandu, Nepal: Save the Children Norway & Save the Children US.

Save the Children. (2009). *State of the world's mothers 2009: Investing in the early years.* Washington, DC: Author.

Smits, J., Huisman, J., & Kruijff, K. (2008). Home language and education in the developing world. Paper commissioned for the EFA Global Monitoring Report 2009, Overcoming inequality: Why governance matters.

Snow, C. (2002). *Reading for understanding: Toward an R&D program in reading comprehension.* Santa Monica, CA: Rand Corporation.

Tinajero, A.R. (2009, May). *A systemic view of Cuba's Educate Your Child Program: Strategies and lessons from the expansion process.* PowerPoint prepared for an ECD conference organized by the Wolfensohn Center at the Brookings Institute. Washington, DC.

Tolhurst, F. (2008). *Learning to read.* Unpublished note prepared for Aga Khan Foundation, Geneva, Switzerland.

UNESCO Institute of Statistics. Retrieved from http://www.uis.unesco.org/glossary/Term.aspx?name=NET%20ENROLMENT%20RATE%20%28NER%29&lang=en

United Nations. (2007). *The millennium development goals report 2007.* New York: Author.

United Nations Children's Fund. (2005). *State of the world's children 2006: Excluded and invisible.* New York: Author.

United Nations Children's Fund. (2008). *State of the world's children 2009: Maternal and newborn health*. New York: Author.

United Nations Educational, Scientific and Cultural Organization. (1998). *Wasted opportunities: When schools fail. Repetition and drop-out in primary schools*. Education for All status and trends 1998. Paris: Author.

United Nations Educational, Scientific and Cultural Organization. (2003, 2004). *EFA global monitoring report 2003/4: Gender and education for all: Leap to equality*. Paris: Author.

United Nations Educational, Scientific and Cultural Organization. (2005). *EFA global monitoring report 2006: Literacy for life*. Paris: Author.

United Nations Educational, Scientific and Cultural Organization. (2006). *EFA global monitoring report 2007: Education for all by 2015—Strong foundations: Early childhood care and development*. Paris: Author.

United Nations Educational, Scientific and Cultural Organization. (2008). *EFA global monitoring report 2009: Overcoming inequality: Why governance matters*. Paris: Author.

United Nations Educational, Scientific and Cultural Organization Institute for Statistics. (2005). *Children out of school: Measuring exclusion from primary education*. Montreal, Canada: Author.

United Nations General Assembly. (1989). Convention on the rights of the child. *Treaty series, 1577*, 3.

van der Gaag, J. (2002). From child development to human development. In M.E. Young (Ed.), *From early child development to human development: Investing in our children's future* (pp. 63–78). Washington, DC: World Bank.

Walker, S., Wachs, T., Meeks Gardner, J., Lozoff, B., Wasserman, G., Pollitt, E., et al. (2007). Child development: Risk factors for adverse outcomes in developing countries. *The Lancet, 369*, 145–157.

Woodhead, M., Ames, P., Vennam, U., Abebe, W., & Streuli, N. (2009). *Access, equity and quality in early education and transitions to primary school: Evidence from young lives research in Ethiopia, India and Peru* (Working Paper 55). The Hague, The Netherlands: Bernard van Leer Foundation.

Young Lives. (2007). *Education for All in Vietnam: High enrollment, but problems of quality remain* (Policy Brief 4). Department of International Development, University of Oxford, UK. Retrieved from http://www.younglives.org.uk/pdf/publication-section-pdfs/policy-briefs/Policy-brief4.pdf

5

Transitions for Children with Disabilities

Mary Beth Bruder

The Ira Allen Early Intervention Center was a regional public school program in a small city in the Northeast that served approximately 60 preschool children of varying types and levels of disability. The program provided home-based services for children beginning at birth, and many of these children had received services from Ira Allen ever since they had been diagnosed with a special need. The children moved to a new classroom each year from age 3 until they exited the program at age 5 or 6. Upon graduation from the program, the children enrolled in their local public primary schools.

The preschool program included four classrooms containing up to eight children each. The program ran two half-day sessions, and children attended for 5 days a week. The classrooms were led by a certified early childhood special education teacher, a teaching assistant, a graduate student, and an undergraduate student. The program also employed a full-time occupational therapist, a physical therapist, a speech-language pathologist, and an assistant for each of these specialists to increase the number of children who could receive these services. The program also had a nurse, a social worker, parent educators, and a follow-up consultant whose job was to work with school systems to facilitate children's transitions back to their local schools to enter either kindergarten or first grade. The state in which the program operated had adopted a policy to include all children with education plans in classrooms with their typically developing peers, and the follow-up consultant was hired to facilitate this inclusion.

After the first group of children transferred out of Ira Allen under the policy of inclusion, it became evident that there were problems. In October of that year, the follow-up consultant met with the preschool teachers and explained that the area special education directors felt that the children from Ira Allen weren't ready to transition. The directors had suggested that the state should fund a primary classroom for children ages 6–9 years, after which the children might be ready to transition back to their home schools. The state special education director denied this request and instead charged the Ira Allen staff with making the children ready to transition back to their home schools. In other words, the responsibility for transition in this state was given to the sending program.

As a sending program, Ira Allen was faced with the challenge of changing its policies, practices, and pedagogy. The director of the program began this shift by sending the Ira Allen preschool teachers to visit child care centers and public school kindergarten classrooms to observe the behaviors of children in these typical environments and become familiar with the curriculum that was being taught. Public school kindergarten teachers also met with the Ira Allen teachers to assist in curriculum design.

These steps fueled a culture shift for the special education teachers, helping them look beyond the developmental sequence and behavioral strategies that they had been using to guide their curriculum and instead focus on skills such as social competence and engagement in group activities. In addition, a series of trainings was offered to the staff and families about facilitating transition of children with disabilities into typical classroom environments. Last, the preschool piloted an immersion classroom for children during the second part of the school year. Children who were slated to move out at the end of the year were placed in typical early childhood environments in their hometowns 1 half day 3–5 days a week, in addition to continuing in the Ira Allen preschool program for 5 half days a week. The teacher of these outplaced preschoolers was also given time every week to observe the children at the typical early care and education programs and consult with the teachers there. All the preschool teachers received this time during this year in order to revamp their program to better prepare the children for their transition into the next environment.

The pilot program proved to be successful, and the transition for the children who participated in it was successful. The children had learned skills from their peers and adjusted to the demands of the new environments better than the special education teachers had expected. The parents of these children also embraced this new model and began to see their children's similarities with their peers. As a result, all the parents of children who had not participated in the pilot program requested to have the option of having their children attend programs with typical peers near their home schools rather than at Ira Allen.

Over the next few years, the local public schools began to open inclusive early childhood services for children with disabilities. At the same time, the Ira Allen teachers changed the way that they defined their curriculum and taught children. They also learned to consult with others in order to collaborate more effectively with their early care and education colleagues. They requested that the remaining classrooms at Ira Allen, which still served children from the town in which it was located, become inclusive and also enroll typically developing children. Transition became the vehicle that drove a systemic change.

The challenges embedded in the description of Ira Allen highlight the complexities that are encountered by preschool children with disabilities who receive special education services as they transition among multiple services. The Ira Allen story invokes all three prongs of the structural transitions framework guiding this volume. First, the issues were governed by a state policy, a 10-year plan with the goal of educating every school-age child in his or her neighborhood public school. Second, the Ira Allen preschool modified components of its program, including parent partnership and early childhood community support. Last, the Ira Allen teachers changed their curriculum content and instructional strategies and also fundamentally changed their role as classroom teachers. The most impressive feature of the process was that all three of these components—policy, program, and pedagogy—were interrelated. A second impressive feature of this process was that it occurred from 1976 to 1978 in Burlington, Vermont, where I began my teaching career leading the first pilot cohort of children who went on to attend community preschools. Transitions for children with disabilities then and now, over 30 years later, continue to challenge our schools, our community programs, our service providers, our children, and their families.

This vignette was not just about transition but about the learning environments of children with disabilities and the location, expectations, membership, and expected outcomes related to these environments. Indeed, the meaning of the word transition is aligned with context and environment. *The Merriam-Webster's Collegiate Dictionary*® defines *transition* as . . . 1) a passage

By permission. From *Merriam-Webster's Collegiate*® *Dictionary, 11th Edition* © 2010 by Merriam-Webster, Incorporated (www.Merriam-Webster.com).

from one state, stage, subject, or place to another; 2) movement, development, or evolution from one form, stage, or style to another. That is, the very meaning of transition requires movement between two different sets of circumstances. Using this definition, we see that transitions occur constantly in the lives of children, particularly children with disabilities.

Transition has been a topic of interest in both research and practice in early childhood intervention for over three decades (Branson & Bingham, 2009; Fowler, 1982; Malone & Gallagher, 2009; McCormick, 2006; Rice & O'Brien, 1990; Rosenkoetter, Hains, & Fowler, 1994; Rous, Hallam, Harbin, McCormick, & Jung, 2007). The purpose of this chapter is to provide an overview of the construct of transition in the lives of infants and young children with disabilities as they adapt to the demands of changing learning environments, service providers, and behavioral and educational expectations. These children represent a range of backgrounds, family structures, and disability types. What they have in common is that, for some reason (biological risk, environmental risk, established risk, or a combination), their development has been compromised and they are experiencing a delay between what is expected behavior for their age and what they are able to do across one or more developmental domains (cognition, motor, communication, or adaptive). Indeed, the most common label used to qualify a child under the age of 5 for early intervention or special education services is developmental delay.

The chapter examines transitions for this broad definition of children. Children with disabilities may be served by any and all varieties of early care and education programs (Wolery, 1999), but the chapter focuses on children who are served by programs funded by the Individuals with Disabilities Education Improvement Act (IDEA) of 2004 (PL 108-446). Although *early intervention* is the term that is used under IDEA for services provided to children under the age of 3 years and *preschool special education* is the term that is used for services provided to children ages 3–5 years, this chapter will use the broad term *early childhood intervention* to describe services under IDEA for children from birth to age 5.

The chapter will first provide an overview of the field of early childhood intervention, including its legislative mandates and service delivery components. Next will be a description of practical guidelines and the research base in transition efforts for infants and young children with disabilities and their families, followed by recommendations for future policy, programmatic application, and pedagogy.

AN OVERVIEW OF EARLY CHILDHOOD INTERVENTION

More than 50 years of research supports the effectiveness of intervention for infants and young children with disabilities (Guralnick, 2008; Trohanis, 2008). Though some studies have been criticized because of their methodological limitations (e.g., heterogeneity of the population, lack of control groups, narrowly defined outcome measures, inappropriateness of standardized measures of intelligence for the population), the data collected thus far demonstrate that early learning and development can be affected by intervention (Guralnick, 2005; Roberts, Innocenti, & Goetze, 1999). As society and families have become more aware of the importance of the years from birth to age 5, early childhood intervention models, programs, and services that are guided by federal laws have become increasingly available.

Conceptualized from an ecological model of human development (Bronfenbrenner, 1992), early childhood intervention views child, parent, and family functioning as complex. The processes that influence early learning and development are produced by the interaction of the environments that a child experiences and the characteristics of the people (including the developing child) within those environments (Bruder, 2001; Dunst, 2007; Guralnick, 2005). This framework suggests that early learning and early development vary as a function of both personal and environmental characteristics and the combined influences and interactions between these characteristics (Garbarino, 1992). Both the nature of early development and the heterogeneity of children who are eligible for early childhood intervention add a dimension of complexity that is unique to service delivery for this age group (Bailey, 1989).

Service Characteristics

Because early childhood intervention services have complex content, a number of service characteristics are salient to their design and implementation. Three characteristics in particular form the core values of professional practice for infants and young children and their families: family-centered practice, collaborative processes, and natural and inclusive learning environments (Hanson & Bruder, 2001; Harbin, McWilliam, & Gallagher, 2000).

Family-Centered Practice   Family involvement is critical to the success of any intervention with infants and young children (Bailey et al., 2006; Dunst, 2007; Turnbull et al., 2007). Infants and young children develop and learn in the context of their families, so services and supports must target families as well as their children. Early childhood intervention must be delivered in a way that recognizes that 1) families and children represent an interdependent unit (Bruder, 2000a), 2) intervention is more powerful when families are involved and supported (Dunst & Trivette, in press; Dunst, Trivette, & Hamby, 2006), and 3) family members should participate in all aspects of service provision (Powell, Batsche, Ferro, Fox, & Dunlap, 1997).

Research has demonstrated that family-centered practices have immediate benefits to both families and children (Dunst & Trivette, in press). These practices include treating families with dignity and respect, being sensitive to cultural and socioeconomic diversity, providing choices to families that relate to their priorities and concerns, fully disclosing information to families so that they can make informed decisions, focusing on a range of informal community resources as parenting and family supports, and offering help in ways that are empowering and competency enhancing for the families (Dunst, 1999). Considerable literature has been amassed on the individual and collective use of these practices (e.g., Bruder, 2000a; Dunst, 2007), and this philosophy is the cornerstone of early childhood intervention.

Collaborations Across Teams and Agencies   Early childhood intervention is provided by a variety of service providers who represent different agencies, professional disciplines, training sequences, pedagogies, and competencies. A collaborative approach in which these providers work together as a team facilitates the integration of developmental and behavioral domains in infants and young children (Bruder, 2005a; Bruder et al., 2005; Foley, 1990). Rather than having someone from each discipline address a separate developmental domain with a child, early childhood intervention consolidates interventions that cross developmental areas (Bruder, 2000b; Hanson & Bruder, 2001). The primary purpose of this approach is to pool the expertise of team members to provide children and families with more efficient, comprehensive, and functional assessment and intervention services. When this type of integration occurs, the team style is referred to as *transdisciplinary*.

There are at least three features of a transdisciplinary approach to early childhood intervention (King et al., 2009). The first feature is an assessment that is conducted in tandem by professionals from different disciplines, the second is collaborative interprofessional teamwork during the group's design and implementation of an intervention plan, and the third is role release, which refers to the sharing of expertise and knowledge of discipline-specific strategies. The model is challenging, but it is essential to meeting a child's comprehensive developmental needs (Foley, 1990).

In addition to collaborations across service providers, interagency collaborations are critical to meeting the needs of infants and young children with disabilities and their families. Both the nature of intervention services and the implementation of statewide systems under IDEA require service delivery structures to be collaborative (Bruder & Bologna, 1993; Bruder & Chandler, 1993) because the needs of children and their families can span health, social service, and education sectors. Collaborations require the agencies and staff in the agencies to agree on a common philosophy and service goal, which can only be achieved when joint agency and staff activities focus on building relationships. They must invest their time and resources and be committed to collaboration in order to achieve success (Bruder, 1994).

Natural Learning and Inclusive Environments   The term *natural and inclusive* describes ideal practices that are associated with the provision of early childhood interventions in settings such as the home or with children who do not have disabilities. More than 30 years of research have demonstrated that young children with disabilities benefit from participating in groups with children who do not have disabilities (Bruder, 2000b; Bruder & Staff, 1998; Bruder, Staff, & McMurrer-Kaminer, 1997; Clawson & Luze, 2008; Guralnick, 1978, 2001). This practice has been cited as a quality indicator of early intervention (Stremel & Campbell, 2007) and has been adopted by professional organizations (Division for Early Childhood, 1993; Division for Early Childhood & National Association for the Education of Young Children, 2009).

Service delivery in natural and inclusive environments includes young children with disabilities and their families in everyday activities (Dunst, Bruder, Trivette, Hamby, & Raab, 2001; McWilliam, Casey, & Sims, 2009; Woods & Kashinath, 2007). Services that are provided in this way support the ecological model of learning and development, which suggests that behavior exists and is best understood in context (Dunst, 2007). For young children, these contexts include family and community programs such as child care programs and other early childhood experiences. Learning and development occur within these contexts either through 1) preplanned activities with goals and purposes or 2) opportunities and experiences that happen in all of the settings in which a child and family participate (Bruder, 2001; Dunst, 2001; Dunst, Hamby, Trivette, Raab, & Bruder, 2000). This policy contrasts with an intervention model of episodic, time-limited interventions that do not necessarily provide enough learning opportunities to affect child and family outcomes (Bruder, 2005a; Dunst, 2007).

Legislative Mandates

Young children with disabilities are entitled to receive intervention services under federal law and subsequent policies that began in the 1960s and remain in effect today. Head Start, which began in 1965, was the frontrunner of an abundance of model programs that were aimed at alleviating the effects of environmental risk on child outcomes. In 1968, the Handicapped Children's Early Education Assistance Act (PL 90-538) provided funds for demonstration programs that included infants and young children with established risk.

In 1975, The Education for All Handicapped Children Act (EHC: PL 94-142) was enacted. This law mandated a free appropriate public education (including special education if needed) for children with disabilities ages 6–21 years, regardless of the nature or severity of the disability.

The law was the culmination of many years of court decisions and legislation that were focused on expanding access to education for children with disabilities. The law defined special education as "specially designed instruction, delivered at no cost to the parent, to address the unique needs of the child" (34 U.S.C. §300.17, 1991) in accordance with an individualized education program (IEP). This instruction could be conducted in the classroom, in the home, in hospitals and other institutions, or in other settings (such as community programs). Additional related services were also available to eligible children, including transportation and the developmental, corrective, and other supportive services that are required to assist a child with a disability to benefit from special education. Some of these services are speech pathology and audiology, psychological services, physical and occupational therapy, recreation (including therapeutic recreation), early identification and assessment of disabilities in children, counseling services (including rehabilitative counseling), school health, social work services in schools, parent counseling and training, and medical services for diagnostic or evaluation purposes.

In 1986, Congress amended the Education of the Handicapped Act (EHA) of 1970 (PL91-230) and added a number of significant components that specifically applied to children under age 5. First, preschool-age children (ages 3–5 years) who were eligible for special education were extended all the rights and protections of Part B of EHA, including free appropriate public education in the least restrictive environment (42 U.S.C. §671[b][3]). This program, which became known as Section 619 of Part B, was to be administered by the state education agencies.

Second, Congress added amendments that created incentives for states to develop an early intervention entitlement program for children birth to age 2. The rationale for this downward extension of services was described in the preamble of this section of EHA. Congress identified an "urgent and substantial need" to enhance the development of infants and toddlers with disabilities, to minimize the likelihood of institutionalization for this population, to increase these individuals' access to special education services, and to enhance the capacity of families to meet the special needs of their infants and toddlers with handicaps (Education of the Handicapped Act Amendments of 1986, 42 U.S.C. §671[a]). This component of the law (Part H, now Part C) described a statewide system of interagency, multidisciplinary services that were available to eligible children.

The law left a number of decisions to the discretion of states. These decisions included the choice of the lead agency that would administer the program and the eligibility criteria for children to qualify for early intervention. Other state-specific administrative decisions involved the formation of an interagency coordinating council, the establishment of interagency agreements, a data collection system for the statewide program, and the development of an individualized family service plan (IFSP) for each eligible child that would include a statement of the natural environments in which services would occur. In addition, the law required that IFSPs address the transition of children at age 3 into preschool special education. Table 5.1 contains the regulations that govern transition under Part H (now Part C).

Although there are differences in administration and policies in different states, the EHA early intervention regulations listed some services that applied to all eligible children and their families nationwide (42 U.S.C. §671[b][3]). These services are listed in Table 5.2 along with a list of professionals who may provide these services. States may also define new occupational categories of service providers as necessary. In addition, Part H (now Part C) of the EHA mandated service coordination to provide assistance to families as they navigate the statewide system of early intervention. The role of the service coordinator is defined by law and consists of seven activities, one of which is to facilitate the development of a transition plan to preschool services, if appropriate (C.F.R. §303.302[d]). Other than following general guidelines, states have the discretion to develop their own policies and procedures for the implementation of service coordination in their state.

Table 5.1. Regulations from Part H of Public Law 99-457 on transition—content of the individualized family service plan (IFSP)

Transition at age 3

When the child reaches age 3, the IFSP must include the steps that should be taken to support the child's transition

1. To preschool services under Part B of the Act, to the extent that those services are considered appropriate
2. To other services that may be available, if appropriate

These required steps include

1. Discussions with and training of parents regarding future placement and other matters related to the child's transition
2. Procedures to prepare the child for changes in service delivery, including steps to help the child adjust to and function in a new setting
3. With parental consent, the transmission of information about the child to the local educational agency to ensure continuity of services, including evaluation and assessment information required by another section of the Act, and copies of IFSPs that have been developed and implemented in accordance with other sections of the Act

Adapted from regulations for Public Law 99-457, Sec. 303.344.

Table 5.2. Services and professional disciplines under IDEA Part C

Services	Disciplines
Family training, counseling, and home visits	Family therapist
Special instruction	Special educator
Speech–language pathology and audiology services, and sign language and cued language services	Speech-language pathologist Audiologist
Occupational therapy	Occupational therapist
Physical therapy	Physical therapist
Psychological services	Psychologist
Service coordination services*	
Medical services only for diagnostic or evaluation purposes	Nurse Pediatrician and other physicians
Early identification, screening, and assessment services*	
Health services necessary to enable the infant or toddler to benefit from the other early intervention services	Dietician Nutritionist Nurse Pediatrician
Social work services	Social worker
Vision services	Orientation and mobility specialist
Assistive technology devices and assistive technology services*	
Transportation and related costs that are necessary to enable an infant or toddler and the family to receive another service described here*	

*These services do not have disciplines assigned to them.
Adapted from regulations for Public Law 99-457, Sec. 303.344.

In 1990, amendments renamed the EHA the Individuals with Disabilities Education Act (IDEA, PL101-476). These amendments emphasized the needs of traditionally underrepresented populations and included the provision of transition services for all IDEA-eligible students. Although the major focus was the transition of students from school to work, the transition from preschool special education to primary school was implicitly addressed. IDEA also expanded the definition of special education from a place to a service delivery structure that could be implemented in a variety of settings (e.g., early childhood community-based programs). Related services were also expanded beyond the original list in EHA to include other developmental, corrective, or supportive services, as required to assist a child with a disability.

Additional amendments to IDEA were made in 1997 and again in 2004, although there have been no major changes to service provisions in Part C (infants and toddlers) and Part B, Section 619 (children ages 3–5 years). These amendments have added specificity to the assurances that states must make regarding transitions from Part C to Part B (619). For example, a transition meeting must occur at least 90 days prior to a child's third birthday if the child seems to qualify for Part B services, and the early childhood agency should initiate the meeting. States must report their compliance with this provision in their Annual Performance Report to the U.S. Department of Education.

System Components

As a result of the federal mandate to serve eligible infants and young children who have disabilities in statewide systems of intervention, increasing numbers of children are being identified as eligible for services under IDEA (Gilliam, Meisels, & Mayes, 2005; Trohanis, 2008). Service systems and options for this population, as well as for the broader population of infants and young children who do not have disabilities, also are growing rapidly. Unfortunately, coordination among these growing systems of care is becoming increasingly complex, and this issue has increased the variability of early childhood intervention service structures across and within states (Dunst, 2007).

In an effort to address this variability and systematize what we know about early childhood intervention, Guralnick (2005) proposed a developmental systems model to describe the structural components (and the relationships among them) of an early childhood intervention service system. Each component represents a separate yet continuous phase of early childhood intervention. The components are illustrated on Figure 5.1 (Guralnick, 2001). These system components are contained in law and provide a framework for early childhood intervention service delivery (Bruder, 2005b; Dunst, 2007).

As Figure 5.1 shows, early childhood intervention begins with a referral for a screening to decide whether a child is eligible for further evaluation under IDEA. There are multiple models for developmental and medical screening programs (Gilliam et al., 2005; McLean, 2003), but all screenings are conducted on a large population in order to detect and refer children who need further evaluation. Unfortunately, there is usually no coordination of screening programs across populations of children and service sectors, and eligibility criteria for services can vary, so families and primary referral sources are sometimes confused about when and what to screen.

Despite its shortcomings, this system component creates the first opportunity for a state to collaboratively develop an efficient system in which all children receive regularly scheduled developmental and behavioral screens that can lead to further evaluation, and which includes a comprehensive assessment across domains of behavior (Wolraich, Gurwitch, Bruder, & Knight, 2005). This assessment can serve a diagnostic function and create an accurate portrayal of a

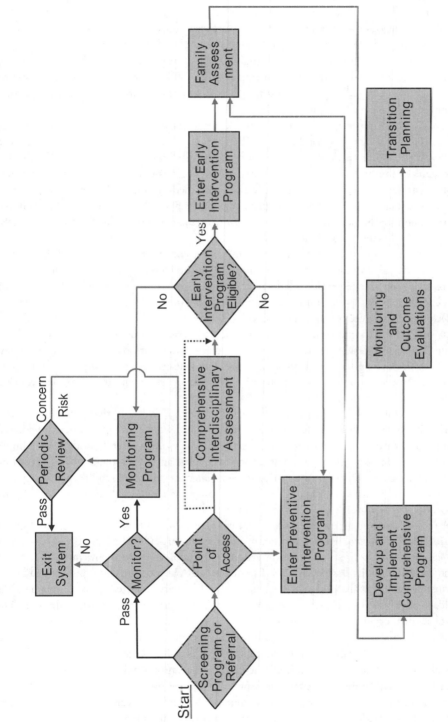

Figure 5.1. Developmental Systems Model. (From Guralnick, M.J. [2001]. A developmental/systems model for early intervention. *Infants and Young Children, 14*[2], p. 17; adapted by permission.)

child's needs across medical, educational, and social systems perspectives. It should be noted that it is not productive to assess a very young child using traditional procedures (e.g., professionals representing different disciplines who are unfamiliar to the child using contrived activities in an unfamiliar setting), and that in fact, such procedures may prove counterproductive (Meisels & Fenichel, 1996). Effective early childhood assessment protocols must be sensitive to the age of the child, the nature of his or her delay or disability, the family context, and the integration of a child's behaviors across developmental domains (McLean, Wolery, & Bailey, 2003). In order for the assessment to be valid, it must be culturally sensitive; family centered; and representative of the families' values, concerns, and priorities.

Once a child is enrolled in early childhood intervention, a program is developed using either an IFSP for infants and toddlers or an IEP for preschoolers. These plans must be comprehensive and collaborative and must focus on outcomes for both the child and the family. The components of the written plans include integrated objectives that cross discipline and agency boundaries as needed (including coordination of social, medical, and health needs). In addition, service providers who meet the state's highest personnel standards must be identified to implement the plan in either a child's natural environment (infants and toddlers) or least restrictive environments (preschool-age children).

A comprehensive program is then implemented according to the IFSP or IEP. The program must include instructional practices and therapeutic techniques to ensure that both the what and the how of intervention are detailed for monitoring purposes (Bruder, 1997a). These details can then be embedded into a developmentally appropriate curriculum through explicit instruction using evidence-based practices (Noonan & McCormick, 2006). For example, responsive teaching methods include a variety of instructional practices to enhance a child's learning. The key to utilizing these practices as responsive interventions is that the practices have to match the individualized objectives and learning opportunities for each child and use the least intrusive strategies to promote the learning of skills within developmentally appropriate routines and activities (Bruder, 1997b).

Once intervention begins, the IFSP and IEP outcomes and objectives must be continuously monitored to ensure the effectiveness of the plan and service providers. A comprehensive program can only be effective if data are collected regularly on child and family service implementation, learning opportunities, intervention strategies, and developmental and behavioral outcomes. Like other components of early intervention, data collection requires a philosophy of coordination and integration, because services and outcomes should only be measured within a collaborative framework (Bruder, 2005b; Roberts et al., 1999).

A recent requirement of state systems in early intervention (Part C) and preschool special education (619) is to report child and family outcomes as articulated by the U.S. Department of Education, Office of Special Education Programs. Data on these outcomes must be collected on each child and family that receives services under IDEA at program entry and exit, and these data must be submitted to Congress. The data for children are collected in the following areas: 1) children have positive social-emotional skills (including social relationships), 2) children demonstrate acquisition and use of knowledge and skills (including early language/communication and early literacy), and 3) children use appropriate behavior to meet their needs. The outcomes that are required for families include the following: 1) families know their rights, 2) families effectively communicate their children's needs, and 3) families help their children develop and learn. The last component of the developmental systems model is transition, though, as we can see in Figure 5.1, transition occurs throughout a child and family's engagement with the early childhood intervention system; both legislation and the subsequent evaluation of state and local service delivery systems have created multiple opportunities for change in service providers, services, and programs to occur.

TRANSITIONS IN EARLY CHILDHOOD INTERVENTION

Successful transitions have been a primary goal of early childhood intervention since the early 1980s (e.g., Fowler, 1982; Hains, Fowler, & Chandler, 1988; Hanline, 1988; Hutinger, 1981; Johnson, Chandler, Kerns, & Fowler, 1986; McCormick & Kawate, 1982; Murphy & Vincent, 1989; Vincent, Laten, Salisbury, Brown, & Baumgart, 1980; Walter & Vincent, 1982). For children with disabilities, transition has been defined as an outcome-oriented process (Will, 1985) and as a series of well-planned steps that results in the smooth placement and subsequent adjustment of the child and family into another setting (Hutinger, 1981). Within the field of early childhood intervention, transition is a dynamic process of moving from one program or service delivery mode to another (Chandler, 1992). Such transitions should address four objectives: 1) continuity of services, 2) minimal disruptions to the family system, 3) the ability of children to function in their new placement, and 4) compliance with legal requirements (Wolery, 1989). A last objective would be to facilitate both child and family competence along a continuum of skills that are both developmentally and individually appropriate.

Although formal vertical transitions for young children with disabilities typically occur at age 3 (into preschool) and age 5 (into kindergarten), horizontal transitions between services, providers, and programs also occur throughout these early years. Children with disabilities and their families move among different service providers, programs, and agencies as the child's needs change (Bruder & Chandler, 1996) and as required by law.

For example, transition can begin for some children at the moment of birth if their health status requires transfer to a special care nursery (Bruder & Walker, 1990). The families of these infants may then interact with at least two different hospital staff and two medical facilities (birthing hospital and special care hospital). Some of these children are then transferred back to a community hospital prior to being discharged home.

When hospital discharge does occur, the subsequent move to home and the community can present another set of transition-related service issues. These issues range from the costs of providing the quality care and services that the infant requires to the shortage of trained professionals who are available to provide those services. In addition, families must learn to negotiate a maze of community services that vary on the basis of philosophy, eligibility criteria, delivery options, staffing patterns, and service settings. Overriding these concerns is a family's need to reestablish its equilibrium through the use of individual coping mechanisms and support systems (Affleck, Tennen, Rowe, Walker, & Higgins, 1990; Bruder & Walker, 1990; Hadden, 2000).

Infants who are enrolled in early intervention programs and their families may experience many transition points during service delivery. The type, number, and intensity of intervention services and the professionals who are providing these services may change according to child need and/or family request (Hanson, 2005; McCormick, 2006). (See Table 5.2.) As children age into preschool services, the opportunities for transition points increase. For example, a child may be enrolled in a child care program or a community program such as Head Start or other preschool program, as well as a special-education–sponsored program. These programs may differ on a number of dimensions, not the least of which is the increase in the number of service providers, who may differ according to their own programs' philosophies and funding base. These complexities only add to the potential for confusion, miscommunication, and breaks in service. Needless to say, the type of planning and practices that are employed can influence the success of transition and the satisfaction of families with the transition process.

Transition in Practice

Transitions in early childhood intervention have been addressed in legislation for many years. The existence of legislative mandates has facilitated many service delivery models, guidebooks, and recommended practices to assist with the transition process for infants and young children with disabilities (Branson & Bingham, 2009; Fowler, 1988; Fox, Dunlap, & Cushing, 2002; Hadden, Fowler, Fink, & Wischnowski, 1995; Hanson, 2005; Malone & Gallagher, 2009; Noonan & Ratokalau, 1991; Rosenkoetter, Whaley, Hains, & Pierce, 2001; Rous et al., 2007; Rous, Hemmeter, & Schuster, 1999; Wischnowski, Fowler, & McCollum, 2000).

Two examples of special-education–sponsored programs are Project TEEM (Ross-Allen & Conn-Powers, 1991) and project STEPs (Rous, Hemmeter, & Schuster, 1994). These model demonstration projects were funded in Vermont and Kentucky, respectively. Both were subsequently funded to conduct outreach and implement their models throughout the country. Both included transition components and procedures such as the establishment of a transition planning team that was composed of a child's parents, service providers from both the sending and receiving programs (typically a preschool special education program and kindergarten, respectively), and relevant administrators. In both models, the roles and responsibilities of all people involved in the transition process were identified, transition timelines were established, and procedures for conducting referral and evaluation were set. The models provided family support activities, child preparation activities, a specific transition meeting, and follow-up support and evaluation procedures for the child after the transition.

Both project-specific guidebooks (Bruder, 1988; Conn-Powers, Ross-Allen, & Holburn, 1990; Fink, Borgia, & Fowler, 1993; Gallagher, Maddox, & Edgar, 1984) and published books (Lazzari, 1991; Rosenkoetter et al., 1994; Rous & Hallam, 2006) also provided specific models and general procedures to guide the transition process for children with disabilities. The procedures include 1) the identification of key players, 2) assessments of next and future environments, 3) the development of an interagency transition plan, 4) the establishment of transition planning teams, 5) surveys of future environments, 6) the establishment of transition goals, and 7) evaluation and follow-up. These guides also contain many practical suggestions, strategies, forms, and evaluation measures to ensure that there are both structural and child and family components in any transition. An additional feature of the Rous and Hallam (2006) transition guide is a theoretical model developed by the authors (Rous et al., 2007).

Another initiative to guide transition for infants and young children with disabilities has been the development of recommended transition practices for children under age 5. The first entity to do this was the Division for Early Childhood, Council for Exceptional Children. In 1993, this organization developed 11 areas of recommended practices to guide the field of early childhood intervention. The recommended practices were research or value based, family centered, multicultural, cross disciplinary, collaborative, and developmentally and chronologically age appropriate, and they followed the guidelines of the principles of normalization (Odom & McLean, 1996). The practices were initially developed by expert panels using focus group methodology. Then they were socially validated through a field sample of 500 professionals and families that were involved in early childhood intervention (Odom, McLean, Johnson, & LaMontagne, 1995). The final 22 recommended transition practices were organized into four categories on the basis of their relevance for agencies, programs, families and other caregivers, and children. The practices were further organized on the basis of the timing in which they occurred. Three phases of practice implementation were articulated for transitions: preparation, implementation, and follow-up and evaluation (Bruder & Chandler, 1993, 1996).

Another set of transition practices was identified by the National Early Childhood Technical Assistance System in 1996. The Center convened a Transition Policy Work Group that generated a list of supports related to early childhood transition policy development and practices. This list included recommendations for written policies, transition timelines, compliance monitoring of timelines and activities, stakeholder input, and interagency councils to ensure the timelines and success of transition (Rosenkoetter et al., 2001).

The National Early Childhood Transition Center also recently developed a set of recommended practices for early childhood transition for children with disabilities (Rous, 2008). This center has examined a number of issues and practices through research and policy reviews, which are available on its web site (http://www.hdi.uky.edu/NECTC). After generating a set of transition outcomes and practices from the literature, the center assessed educators' agreement with a set of recommended practices, gathering responses from 417 experts from the Division for Early Childhood of the Council for Exceptional Children and the National Association for the Education of Young Children. Seventy-five percent of the respondents agreed or strongly agreed with the practices listed in Table 5.3. It should be noted that these practices are similar in scope to the original practices put forth by the Division of Early Childhood of the Council for Exceptional Children.

Table 5.3.   Practices validated by the National Early Childhood Transition Center

Interagency service system
A primary contact person for transition is identified within each program or agency.
Community- and program-wide transition activities and timelines are identified.
Referral processes and timelines are clearly specified.
Enrollment processes and timelines are clearly specified.
Program eligibility processes and timelines are clearly delineated.
Agencies develop formal mechanisms to minimize disruptions in services before, during, and after the transition of the child and family.
Staff and family members are actively involved in design of transition processes and systems.
Staff roles and responsibilities for transition activities are clearly delineated.
Conscious and transparent connections are made between the curriculum and expectations for the child across programs and environments.
Methods are in place to support staff-to-staff communication within and across programs.
Families meaningfully participate as partners with staff in program- and community-wide transition efforts.

Child and family preparation and adjustment
Individual child and family transition meetings are conducted.
Staff follow up on children after the transition to support their adjustment.
Transition team members share appropriate information about each child who is making a transition.
Transition plans are developed that include individual activities for each child and family.
Staff know key information about a broad array of agencies and services available within the community.
Children have opportunities to develop and practice skills that they need to be successful in the next environment.
Families are aware of the importance of transition planning and have the information they need to actively participate in transition planning.
Families' needs related to transition are assessed and addressed.
Families have information about and are linked with resources and services to help them meet their specific child and family needs.
Families actively participate in gathering information about their child's growth and development.

From Rous, B. (2008). *Recommended transition practices for young children and families: Results from a validation survey.* (Technical Report #3). Lexington: University of Kentucky, Human Development Institute, National Early Childhood Transition Center. Available at http://www.ihdi.uky.edu/nectc/; reprinted by permission. The National Early Childhood Transition Center was funded through the U.S. Department of Education, Office of Special Education Programs, Cooperative Agreement #H324 V020031.

The Evidence Base in Transition

An active research agenda in early childhood intervention transition has paralleled advances in policy and practice. Most efforts have focused on identifying effective instructional practices to enhance a child's competence in the next educational environment. These practices attempt to align the pedagogy or curriculum between preschool special education and either early education or kindergarten. One of the first such studies was done by Walter and Vincent (1982), who surveyed kindergarten teachers regarding their requirements for kindergarten and generated a list of 84 behaviors that the teachers identified as critical to success in kindergarten. These behaviors were then grouped into curriculum targets such as working independently, participating with a group, following routines, communicating functionally, following directions, playing appropriately, and taking care of oneself. Although there is consensus on the pedagogy that enhances successful transitions for young children moving into kindergarten, it should be noted that this research has not been translated into accepted practice (Kemp & Carter, 2005).

Another line of transition research has focused on the program component of family involvement and satisfaction (Hains et al., 1988; Hanline & Halvorsen, 1989; Hanline & Knowlton, 1988; Janus, Lefort, Cameron, & Kopechanski, 2007; Johnson et al., 1986; Kemp, 2003; Lovett & Haring, 2003; Roberts, Rule, & Innocenti, 1998). Most studies assess parental perception of the transition process (Hamblin-Wilson & Thurman, 1990) or parent-identified supports to ease the stress of a transition (Hanson et al., 2000). Collectively, studies of families have found that the provision of supports such as giving parents information, providing them with placement choices, having them visit placement options before the transition meeting, having them participate in decision making, having opportunities to plan, and offering follow-up support facilitates a positive perspective on the transition. Positive relationships between families and providers have been identified as a mediator that eases the stress of transition for families (Rous & Hallam, 2006).

The process and structure that are used to facilitate the actual event of transition have also been studied as program components. They include transition time lines, transition teams, the transfer of records (e.g. IFSPs), transition plans, and interagency agreements (Dogaru, Rosenkoetter, & Rous, 2009; Fowler & McCollum, 2000; Hadden & Fowler, 2000; Repetto & Correa, 1996). One study revealed that early childhood leaders' concerns around the transition process were mediated by the level of state policy development and the use of local agreements. That is, early childhood leaders who had such structures in place had fewer concerns about the transition process (Shotts, Rosenkoetter, Streufert, & Rosenkoetter, 1994). Guidelines to writing interagency agreements exist, as do recommendations for enhancing their usefulness (Fowler, Donegan, Lueke, Hadden, & Phillips, 2000; Fowler & McCollum, 2000; LaCour, 1982; Rous & Hallam, 2006; Wischnowski et al., 2000).

Policy development and implementation is a final area of inquiry with respect to transitions for infants and young children with disabilities (Rosenkoetter et al., 2001). The National Early Childhood Transition Center has documented differences in Part C and Part B (619) policy applications, including stakeholder involvement in the selection of transition indicators and compliance review of transition benchmarks. Part C and Part B (619) state coordinators reported that coordination for transition occurred most frequently in preschool programs that provided educational interventions and least frequently in child care programs. Both sets of program coordinators noted the rare use of evidence-based transition strategies in interagency agreements. One important divergence between the Part C programs and Part B (619) programs was with respect to the values underlying the transition guidelines that are used within a state. Whereas 97% of Part C coordinators identified family-centered care as a core value, only 58% of Part B program coordinators did so. Legislation was identified as a guiding value by most coordinators (81% of Part C, 92% of Part B). It was no surprise that all respondents identified the inherent differences between the programs in terms of philosophy, the array of service options, and different eligibility criteria as a major barrier to smooth transitions between Part C and Part B (619) programs.

Additional policy evidence on transition can be identified through the State Performance Plans that are required by IDEA. The transition indicator for Part C is the percentage of children exiting Part C who receive timely transition planning by their third birthday to support their transition to preschool and other appropriate community services. Transition planning includes IFSPs with transition steps and services, notification to the Local Education Agency (LEA) if the child is potentially eligible for Part B, and a transition conference if the child is potentially eligible for Part B. In 2007–2008, 58 state Part C programs and territories reported on all three indicators. Thirty-nine percent reported substantial compliance on having transition steps in the IFSP, forty-five percent reported substantial compliance in notification to the LEA, and thirty-one percent reported substantial compliance with a transition conference. Full compliance on these indicators was found for only 19, 32, and 13 states on the three indicators, respectively. Just 29 states reported substantial compliance in the 619 indicator on the percentage of children eligible for Part B who had an IEP developed and implemented by their third birthday (National Early Childhood Technical Assistance Center, 2009a, 2009b).

Recent Research-Focused Literature Reviews

Three recent reviews of the literature have summarized research that has been conducted on early childhood transitions for infants and children with disabilities. Janus and colleagues (2007) reviewed the literature on transitions for children with special needs as they went to kindergarten. The authors found a relatively small number of research articles that included transitions of children with special needs. These articles identified the following barriers as most problematic to transitions: duplicate paperwork and child assessments, communication issues, intervention philosophy and training differences between two programs, family issues such as establishing new relationships and support networks, and the consistency and timing of practices used.

Malone and Gallagher (2009) focused on literature concerning the transition from infant–toddler programs (Part C) to preschools (Part B). The factors they identified that contribute to the existing transition process included the availability of technical assistance and collaboration, program quality, the availability of assistance for children and parents, and policy. The authors concluded that after 20 years of research and practice in this area, barriers to smooth transitions still remain, such as child identification and eligibility criteria and the timing of transition activities. Malone and Gallagher made a set of recommendations, emphasizing the need for investigations of child and family characteristics (culture, location, density of services) on the transition process, as well as an accounting of the resources expended on this process in relation to child and family outcome.

A thorough review of transition practices and child and family outcomes was conducted by the National Early Childhood Transition Center (Rosenkoetter et al., 2009). Of the 50 articles included in the review, 15 focused on young children with disabilities and their families, 33 focused just on children, and the rest focused only on families. The majority of studies were descriptive rather than experimental, and all focused on vertical transitions, particularly the transition into kindergarten. Methodology and outcomes were both analyzed, even though more than half of the studies did not include data in their publication. The authors concluded with recommendations for both practice and research: more rigor in research design, increased attention to children transitioning at age 3, and the inclusion of outcomes measures for children and families. Rosenkoetter and colleagues (2009) suggested that there was "no demonstrated linkage between specific transition practices/strategies and outcomes for young children with disabilities and their families" (p. 33) and that there was limited validation of specific family support strategies on child outcomes.

RECOMMENDATIONS

The current status of transitions for infants and young children receiving services under IDEA reflects the challenges facing the field of early childhood intervention. Scholars continue to search for evidence-based practices to support child and family outcomes, and it remains difficult to implement effective practices that result in positive child and family outcomes (Dunst, 2007; Odom, 2009). From the time that a child is suspected of being eligible for intervention services (and for many children, even before a formal referral occurs), families and children interface with a variety of service providers, programs, and service agencies, all of which may have differing philosophies, intervention priorities and strategies, and collaborative skills (Bruder & Bologna, 1993; Rous, 2004). Although many practices have been used to support transition in early childhood intervention, few have been validated through rigorous research designs. In addition, both families and professionals report that transitions are stressful and problematic (Hanson, 2005; Malone & Gallagher, 2009; Rosenkoetter et al., 2009). It is within this context that transitions continue to happen, albeit not always in a coordinated, timely, or effective manner.

It should be noted also that the practices, research, and legislative requirements presented in this chapter have addressed only formal vertical transitions, not the many horizontal transitions or the informal vertical transitions (e.g., into a higher age grouping at a child care facility, into a story group for older children at the library) that affect a family and a child with disabilities. IDEA mandates that transition occurs with a timeline and under the direction of the service coordinator for children leaving Part C programs into preschool special education or other early childhood programs. IDEA also implicitly requires that transition activities be included in the IEP for preschoolers who are moving into school-age programs. These programs also have challenging horizontal transitions, because the IFSP/IEP process allows providers, services, and locations to change as needed or requested. The overlapping components of the developmental systems model in early childhood intervention also illuminate the multiple transition events that occur throughout a child's enrollment in services under IDEA. The model illustrates transitions as only one component that contributes to the effectiveness and efficiency of the intervention process for each child and family.

Although it is tempting to list and describe recommendations to improve transitions for infants and young children with disabilities, this task has been done for more than 25 years, and readers are referred to the exemplary work that already embodies pedagogical, programmatic, and policy recommendations. Rather, the main recommendation of this chapter is that the field of early childhood intervention embrace the paradigm of continuity that forms the foundation of this book and examine transition outcomes for young children with disabilities in the broader service delivery system for early childhood. This recommendation does not ignore the challenges that are inherent in the transition process, nor the expanding intervention systems, service requirements, funding streams, and other variables related to the complexity of early childhood intervention. Rather, it acknowledges the fact that change and movement among service systems, structures, and providers occurs continuously for children with disabilities. It may be time for our field to embrace transition as an ongoing process that exists in the context of early childhood rather than as an artificial (and somehow stressful) event which is created by requirements that are inherent in service administration, provision, and allocation of resources by the service systems. A major paradigm shift is required to embrace transition within a continuous model of interventions, services, and supports available to all children and families.

The first step toward making this shift is to recognize and respect a number of highly evolved principles of early development that should be embedded within early childhood pedagogy, programs, and policy. For example, in 2000, the National Research Council summarized what was known about the science of early childhood development in its report *From Neurons to Neighborhoods* (Shonkoff & Phillips, 2000). This publication contains information that is critical to the development of systems to enhance children's competence and long-term developmental and behavioral outcomes. The report's recommendations are founded on 10 core concepts that include the importance of self-regulation and human relationships (including the construct of attachment) to subsequent healthy development and the need to minimize risk and enhance resiliency and protective factors to facilitate healthy development. These principles should be the foundation of early childhood systems, service delivery, and transitions for all children, especially children who have vulnerabilities such as disabilities.

Second to respecting the importance of developmental constructs in the design of early childhood systems and the inevitability of transition is to recognize the growth and change that has occurred in the field of early childhood intervention. Thirty years ago, transition processes were limited to young children with disabilities moving vertically into the one available option. Back in 1976, when the story presented at the beginning of the chapter occurred, the early childhood intervention teachers in Vermont numbered fewer than 15, as did the programs. In contrast, today countless early childhood initiatives are being implemented in every state. According to the 28th Annual Report to Congress, 282,733 children are served by 63,437 early interventionists in Part C and 701,949 children are served by 31,163 preschool teachers and over 100,000 related service personnel in Part B (619) programs. These numbers, which increase every year, further complicate and challenge the fidelity with which recommended transition practices occur, in part because our growing workforce may not be skilled at implementing practices as they were intended. As we move forward it is clear that our research agenda and training models must increasingly address the growth and heterogeneity in our field regarding children, families, providers, and systems.

Moe than 10 years ago, Guralnick (1997) proposed that the field of early childhood intervention adopt a new paradigm for research on effectiveness. His model of second-generation research requires specificity in both the design and outcome measurements of research. In particular, he suggested examining the impact of various contextual factors on program effectiveness—identifying program features that are associated with optimal child and family outcomes for certain subgroups of the population. This model seems promising for future research on transitions: As transitions become increasingly complex, we could use empirical findings to guide practice for specific groups of children with disabilities and their families.

Likewise, effective training models must be used to ensure that we are building the capacity of our workforce to implement evidence-based transition practices. Any training provided in early childhood should be based on the National Research Council's *How People Learn* (2000). Reduced from a list of principles laid forth by Knowles, Holton, and Swanson (1998), these recommendations emanate from the research base on adult learning and include 1) acknowledging learners' preexisting understandings, 2) using multiple examples to provide depth when teaching, and 3) integrating metacognitive learning opportunities. These principles are central to a methodology which ensures that learners retain and apply information to problems and gain confidence in their abilities to solve future problems (Dunst & Trivette, 2009). This type of training requires educators to commit to changing children's behavior in the context where the change is needed using strategies and technologies that are effective, and goes well beyond exposure to new methods as presented in workshops and conferences.

The third aspect of improving transitions is the adoption of evaluation strategies that focus on all of the variables that are shown to be important to successful outcomes. It was noted earlier that the field of early intervention is based on Bronfenbrenner's (1993) ecological framework. This orientation requires that attention be given to the multiple characteristics of a service system, suggesting that child and family outcomes are influenced by the individuals, organizations, agencies, cultures, communities, and states that are involved in the service delivery and system administration. Other variables that relate to the specific child and family include their history, values, culture, ethnicity, family structure, home routines and community activities, child disability, child age, economic status, and geographic location. There are also variables associated with service providers, including their attitudes, values, knowledge of resources and recommended practices, previous experiences, training, and skills that they bring to the service implementation endeavor. These characteristics of the child, the family, and the service provider also influence the multiple elements of service provision.

Finally, service delivery is influenced by the existing system infrastructure. The infrastructure is made up of multiple organizations, agencies, and programs that can facilitate or hinder effective service delivery. Families, service providers, and service system infrastructure are embedded within community contexts, all of which combine to influence not only the nature of early childhood intervention transition but also the outcomes. To analyze the interrelationships among these variables, a logic model can be used to examine the way in which each variable contributes to a program feature (e.g., transition). Variables can be grouped according to characteristics such as resources, process, outputs, and outcomes (Gilliam & Mayes, 2000; W.K. Kellogg Foundation, 2001).

One such model was designed to measure outcomes of systems, children, and families under Part C service coordination because transition is one activity that is required under this component (Bruder, 2005b; Bruder et al., 2005). The logic model was created as a result of a series of national surveys, focus groups, and interviews that identified the outcomes and practices of effective service coordination. A logic model, adapted from this original service coordination model and depicted in Figure 5.2, articulates the relationships among policy, programmatic, and pedagogical components of transition. It offers a vehicle in which to embed inputs, processes, and outputs as they relate to the measurement of child and family outcomes for children receiving services under IDEA. First, the input column includes the state level that is related to policy, the community level that is related to program practices, and the personnel level that forms the foundation of pedagogy. Second, process variables represent state policy development and implementation; programmatic options; and pedagogy that are recommended for service providers, notably teachers. Third, the output column is the attempt to consolidate recommendations for transition from this chapter: It encompasses policy, program practice, and pedagogy.

At the policy level, effective transitions require each family to have a designated transition coordinator to assist in the process and to determine the type, level, intensity, and scope of activities needed by each child and family as they experience transition. Under Part C this person is the service coordinator, but under Part B there is no such designation, though it is highly recommended such a point person exist.

A second, very important policy output is the delivery of seamless, continuous, and timely services for all children and families (Rosenkoetter et al., 2001). The programmatic output results in a community approach that embraces all children and their families. Collaborations and different intensity levels of support should be available to all community members as children experience both vertical and horizontal transitions (Kagan & Neuman, 1998).

The last output results from the pedagogy that is used by service providers. The first element is a climate in which positive relationships characterize all activities in early childhood intervention. Relationships are built by open and ongoing communication and individuals' willingness to

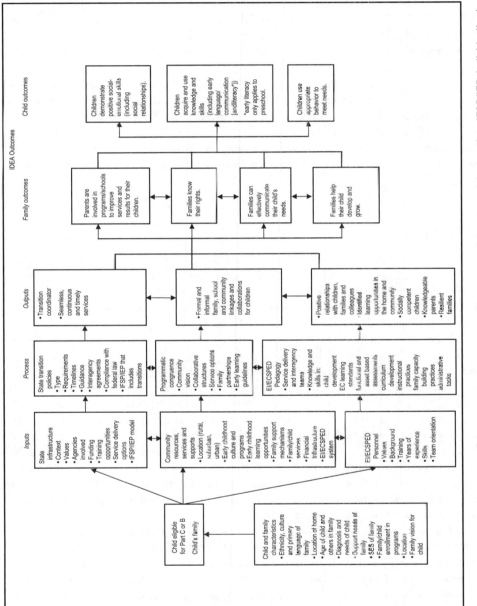

Figure 5.2. Transition logic model. *Key:* EI/ECSPED, early intervention/early childhood special education; IFSP/IEP, individualized family service plan/individualized education.

engage each other in common efforts (Hanson, 2005). Another element is the broadening applications in early childhood intervention of a model in which children are active learners in a variety of home and community routines and activities (Dunst & Bruder, 2002). Social competence is another output of pedagogy. This construct has been integral to school readiness (Ladd, 2005, 2008); a model in which developmental domains, including emotional regulation, is measured as an indicator of a child's social competence has been proposed by Guralnick (1992) and applied to toddlers with disabilities by Bruder and Chen (2007). Other components of effective pedagogy include knowledgeable parents (Bailey et al., 2006) and resilient families (Connelly, 2007). This last element may prove to be one of the most protective factors for both parents and children who encounter multiple transitions.

Whereas these outputs as displayed on a logic model are designed to articulate the interactions among variables that contribute to a successful transition, the ultimate outcome of transitions should be enhanced development for children and improved knowledge and skills for families. Combined, these outputs should contribute to a realization of improved child and family outcomes as a result of receiving early childhood intervention within a broader early childhood framework. This model is but one way to both unify and isolate variables that ultimately enhance transitions for children with disabilities and their families.

CONCLUSION

I would like to end this chapter the way I started it: with a story that is personal. I am sending my youngest daughter, age 3, to a public preschool program this fall. Annie has spent half her life in an orphanage or hospital in China, has had open-heart surgery, and developed complications as a result. She demonstrates both environmental and biological risk and has an IEP to document her needs and objectives for this upcoming school year. She will be going from an inclusive toddler child care class with 4 children into an inclusive magnet public school class with 18 children, the majority of whom will not have documented disabilities. Half the class comes from extreme poverty, and some do have IEPs. Like many children in the early childhood intervention system, Annie has had a number of vertical transitions, including six informal transitions into the next chronological age group in child care and three formal transitions into new programs, all of which occurred after she came home to the United States. These transitions have occurred over a relatively short time frame since she has been home. She also had 4 vertical transitions that I know of in China and more than 10 horizontal transitions across providers and within programs. On the spectrum of children with disabilities, Annie has mild to moderate developmental delays. She has received a typical array of services available to young children with disabilities; in fact, she has received less than what was recommended because I have limited her exposure to the early interventions that she has been eligible to receive.

What do I want for Annie's next transition? I want her to feel safe and secure in her new classroom and with her new teacher. I also want her to receive the interventions that are on her IEP the week school starts. My assumption is that she will be in a classroom that uses our state preschool benchmarks and the IDEA early childhood outcomes to guide her progress through a developmentally and individually appropriate curriculum. That's the big picture and the basic elements of an effective transition from my perspective as a mother. How I want this to occur relies less on formality and more on respect, communication, and collaboration as school practices are conceived and implemented.

Of course, there are other recommended practices that I would like to see in place for our transition. For example, before school starts I would like it if her current teacher and I could help choose a classroom that would meet Annie's individual needs. She has a slow-to-warm temperament and is extremely shy in new groups. Once she has been placed, I would like to have the opportunity to meet the new teacher and the staff. I would like the opportunity to share with the teacher who Annie is, what her history is, and what her favorite activities in her early care program were. I would like Annie's child care teacher to communicate in writing to the new preschool teacher about Annie's learning style and skills. I know that the child care teacher cannot go to meet the teacher in person, nor can the preschool teacher go to meet with the child care teacher and observe Annie in her current environment because of constraints on time, coverage of the current classrooms, and funds to cover extra hours of duty.

I would like all of Annie's records to be transferred to the new school before school starts, including assessments and the IEP. I would like Annie to spend time with the teaching staff to get to know them so that she may understand who her caregiver will be over the next year. I would like to be able to meet some of the other children in the class and their families so that we have some connections before the first day of school. I would like to know the curriculum they will be using, as well as the daily schedule, so that I can prepare Annie and know myself what her days will be like. Last, I would like her teacher and the special education staff to meet before school starts (or the first week before seeing Annie), so that they can go over Annie's plan, discuss how interventions will be incorporated into the daily routine, and decide who will be the one to communicate Annie's progress to all on a weekly basis.

At the transition point during the first day and weeks of school, I would like Annie to be met by the classroom teacher, to receive a name tag, and to be able to bring in a favorite toy and blanket from home. I would like the teacher to ask for a book to accompany Annie that contains pictures about her family, home life, and favorite things to do. I would like to be able to stay in the classroom as long as Annie needs to feel safe and secure. If I am not able to stay (because of my work demands), I would like to be able to plan with the teacher how to handle Annie's daily transition from me to her. Finally, I would like to see Annie's special services be implemented according to her IEP in collaboration with her teacher.

After transition, I would like to have daily updates on Annie's behavior in school and weekly updates on her progress in the curriculum and her IEP. I would like a communication system that will function for everyone on Annie's team (special education and classroom staff) so that joint planning can occur. I would like to know that Annie is doing well across all domains of behavior, especially social competence, which is one of her main areas of need.

Will that happen? We know it should, not just for Annie but for all young children making a transition.

REFERENCES

Affleck, G., Tennen, H., Rowe, J., Walker, L., & Higgins, P. (1990). Mothers' interpersonal relationships and adaptation to hospital and home care of high risk infants. In R. Antonak & J. Mulick (Eds.), *Transitions in Mental Retardation (Vol. V)*. Norwood, NJ: Ablex Publishing.

Bailey, D.B., Jr. (1989). Issues and directions in preparing professionals to work with young handicapped children and their families. In J. Gallagher, P. Trohanis, & R. Clifford (Eds.), *Policy implementation and P.L. 99-457: Planning for young children with special needs* (pp. 97–132). Baltimore: Paul H. Brookes Publishing Co.

Bailey, D.B., Bruder, M.B., Hebbeler, K., Carta, J., DeFosset, M., Greenwood, C.R., et al. (2006). Recommended outcomes for families of young children with disabilities. *Journal of Early Intervention, 28*(4), 227–251.

Branson, D.M., & Bingham, A. (2009). Using interagency collaboration to support family-centered transition practices. *Young Exceptional Children, 12*(3), 15–31.

Bronfenbrenner, U. (1992). Ecological systems theory. In R. Vasta (Ed.), *Six theories of child development: Revised formulations and current issues* (pp. 187–249). Philadelphia: Kingsley.

Bronfenbrenner, U. (1993). The ecology of cognitive development: Research models and fugitive findings. In R.H. Wozniak & K.W. Fischer (Eds.), *Development in context: Acting and thinking in specific environments* (pp. 3–44). Mahwah, NJ: Erlbaum.

Bruder, M.B. (Ed.). (1988). *Transition practices in early childhood for Connecticut*. Farmington, CT: Author.

Bruder, M.B. (1994). Working with members of other disciplines: Collaboration for success. In M. Wolery & J.S. Wilbers (Eds.), *Including children with special needs in early childhood programs* (pp. 45–70). Washington, DC: National Association for the Education of Young Children.

Bruder, M.B. (1997a). Early childhood intervention. In J.W. Wood & A.M. Lazzari (Eds.), *Exceeding the boundaries: Understanding exceptional lives* (pp. 534–569). Fort Worth, TX: Harcourt Brace & Co.

Bruder, M.B. (1997b). The effectiveness of specific educational/developmental curricula for children with established disabilities. In M.J. Guralnick (Ed.), *The effectiveness of early intervention: Directions for second generation research* (pp. 523–548). Baltimore: Paul H. Brookes Publishing Co.

Bruder, M.B. (2000a). Family centered early intervention: Clarifying our values for the new millennium. *Topics in Early Childhood Special Education, 20*(2), 105–115.

Bruder, M.B. (2000b). Renewing the inclusion agenda: Attending to the right variables. *Journal of Early Intervention, 23*(4), 223–230.

Bruder, M.B. (2001). Infants and toddlers: Outcomes and ecology. In M.J. Guralnick (Ed.), *Early childhood inclusion: Focus on change* (pp. 203–228). Baltimore: Paul H. Brookes Publishing Co.

Bruder, M.B. (2005a). Early intervention services for infants and their families. In W.M. Nehring (Ed.), *Core curriculum for specializing in intellectual and developmental disability: A resource for nurses and other health care professionals* (pp. 109–122). Boston: Jones & Bartlett Publishers.

Bruder, M.B. (2005b). Service coordination and integration in a developmental systems approach to early intervention. In M.J. Guralnick (Ed.), *The developmental systems approach to early intervention* (pp. 29–58). Baltimore: Paul H. Brookes Publishing Co.

Bruder, M.B., & Bologna, T.M. (1993). Collaboration and service coordination for effective early intervention. In W. Brown, S.K. Thurman, & L. Pearl (Eds.), *Family-centered early intervention with infants and toddlers: Innovative cross-disciplinary approaches* (pp. 103–127). Baltimore: Paul H. Brookes Publishing Co.

Bruder, M.B., & Chandler, L.K. (1993). Transition. In Division for Early Childhood (Ed.), *DEC recommended practices: Indicators of quality in programs for infants and young children with special needs and their families*. Reston, VA: Council for Exceptional Children.

Bruder, M.B., & Chandler, L.K. (1996). Transition. In S. Odom & M. McLean (Eds.), *Early intervention/ early childhood special education: Recommended practices* (pp. 287–307). Austin, TX: PRO-ED.

Bruder, M.B., & Chen, L. (2007). Measuring social competence in toddlers: Play tools for learning. *Early Childhood Services, 1*(1), 49–70.

Bruder, M.B., Harbin, G.L., Whitbread, K., Conn-Powers, M., Roberts, R., et al. (2005). Establishing outcomes for service coordination: A step toward evidence-based practice. *Topics in Early Childhood Special Education, 25*(3), 177–188.

Bruder, M.B., & Staff, I. (1998). A comparison of the effects of type of classroom and service characteristics on toddlers with disabilities. *Topics in Early Childhood Special Education, 18*(1), 26–37.

Bruder, M.B., Staff, I., & McMurrer-Kaminer, E. (1997). Toddlers receiving early intervention in childcare centers: A description of a service delivery system. *Topics in Early Childhood Special Education, 17*(2), 185–208.

Bruder, M.B., & Walker, L. (1990). Discharge planning: Hospital to home transitions for infants. *Topics in Early Childhood Special Education, 9*(4), 26–42.

Chandler, L.K. (1992). Promoting children's social/survival skills as a strategy for transition to mainstreamed kindergarten programs. In S.L. Odom, S.R. McConnell, & M.A. McEvoy (Eds.), *Social competence of young children with disabilities* (pp. 245–276). Baltimore: Paul H. Brookes Publishing Co.

Clawson, C., & Luze, G. (2008). Individual experiences of children with and without disabilities in early childhood settings. *Topics in Early Childhood Special Education, 28*(3), 132–147.

Conn-Powers, M.C., Ross-Allen, J., & Holburn, S. (1990). Transition of young children into the elementary education mainstream. *Topics in Early Childhood Special Education, 9*(4), 91–105.

Connelly, A.M. (2007). Transitions of families from early intervention to preschool intervention for children with disabilities. *Young Exceptional Children, 10*(3), 10–16.

Division for Early Childhood. (1993). Position statement on inclusion. *DEC Communicator, 19*(4), 4.

Division for Early Childhood & National Association for the Education of Young Children. (2009). *Early childhood inclusion: A joint position statement of the Division for Early Childhood (DEC) and the National Association for the Education of Young Children (NAEYC)*. Chapel Hill: The University of North Carolina, FPG Child Development Institute.

Dogaru, C., Rosenkoetter, S., & Rous, B. (2009). *A critical incident study of the transition experience for young children with disabilities: Recounts by parents and professionals. Technical Report #6.* Lexington University of Kentucky, Human Development Institute, National Early Childhood Transition Center. Retrieved from http://www.hdi.uky.edu/nectc.home

Dunst, C.J. (1999). Placing parent education in conceptual and empirical context. *Topics in Early Childhood Special Education, 19*(3), 141–146.

Dunst, C.J. (2001). Participation of young children with disabilities in community learning activities. In M.J. Guralnick (Ed.), *Early childhood inclusion: Focus on change* (pp. 307–333). Baltimore: Paul H. Brookes Publishing Co.

Dunst, C.J. (2007). Early intervention for infants and toddlers with developmental disabilities. In S.L. Odom, R.H. Horner, M. Snell, & J. Blacher (Eds.), *Handbook of developmental disabilities* (pp. 161–180). New York: Guilford Press.

Dunst, C.J., & Bruder, M.B. (2002). Families and their role in their children's learning. *Children's Learning Opportunities Annual Report.*

Dunst, C.J., Bruder, M.B., Trivette, C., Hamby, D., & Raab, M. (2001). Characteristics and consequences of everyday natural learning opportunities. *Topics in Early Childhood Special Education, 21*(2), 68–92.

Dunst, C.J., Hamby, D., Trivette, C.M., Raab, M., & Bruder, M.D. (2000). Everyday family and community life and children's naturally occurring learning opportunities. *Journal of Early Intervention, 23*(3), 151–164.

Dunst, C.J., & Trivette, C.M. (2009a). Capacity-building family-systems intervention practices. *Journal of Family Social Work, 12* 119–143.

Dunst, C.J., & Trivette, C.M. (2009b). Using research evidence to inform and evaluate early childhood intervention practices. *Topics in Early Childhood Special Education, 29*(1), 40–52.

Dunst, C.J., Trivette, C.M., & Hamby, D.W. (2006). *Family support program quality and parent, family and child benefits.* Asheville, NC: Winterberry Press.

Education for All Handicapped Children Act of 1975, (EHC), PL94-142, 20 U.S.C. §§ 1400 *et seq.*

Fink, D.B., Borgia, E., & Fowler, S.A. (1993). *Interagency agreements: Improving the transition process for young children with special needs and their families.* Retrieved September 15, 2009, from http://facts.crc.uiuc.edu/facts1/facts1.html

Foley, G.M. (1990). Portrait of an arena evaluation: Assessment in the transdisciplinary approach. In E.D. Gibbs & D.M. Teti (Eds.), *Interdisciplinary assessment of infants: A guide for early intervention professionals* (pp. 271–286). Baltimore: Paul H. Brookes Publishing Co.

Fowler, S.A. (1982). Transition from preschool to kindergarten for children with special needs. In K.E. Allen & E.M. Goetz (Eds.), *Early childhood education: Special problems, special solutions* (pp. 229–242). Rockville, MD: Aspen.

Fowler, S.A. (1988). Promising programs: Transition planning. *Teaching Exceptional Children, 20,* 62–63.

Fowler, S.A., Donegan, M., Lueke, B., Hadden, D.S., & Phillips, B. (2000). Evaluating community collaboration in writing interagency agreements on the age 3 transition. *Exceptional Children, 67,* 35–50.

Fowler, S.A., & McCollum, J.A. (2000). Supports and barriers to writing an interagency agreement on the preschool transition. *Journal of Early Intervention, 23,* 294–307.

Fox, L., Dunlap, G., & Cushing, L. (2002). Early intervention, positive behavior support, and transition to school. *Journal of Emotional and Behavioral Disorders, 10*(3), 149–157.

Gallagher, J., Maddox, M., & Edgar, E. (1984). *Early childhood interagency transition model.* Seattle: Edmark.

Garbarino, J. (1992). *Children and families in the social environment* (2nd ed.). New York: de Gruyer.

Gilliam, W.S., & Mayes, L.C. (2000). Development assessment of infants and toddlers. In C.H. Zeanah (Ed.), *Handbook of infant mental health* (2nd ed., pp. 236–248). New York: Guilford Press.

Gilliam, W.S., Meisels, S., & Mayes, L. (2005). Screening and surveillance in early intervention systems. In M.J. Guralnick (Ed.), *The developmental systems approach to early intervention* (pp. 73–98). Baltimore: Paul H. Brookes Publishing Co.

Guralnick, M.J. (Ed.) (1978). *Early intervention and the integration of handicapped and nonhandicapped preschool children.* Baltimore: University Park Press.

Guralnick, M.J. (Ed.). (1997). *The effectiveness of early intervention.* Baltimore: Paul H. Brookes Publishing Co.

Guralnick, M.J. (1992). A hierarchical model for understanding children's peer related social competence. In S.L. Odom, S.R. McConnell, & M.A. McEvoy (Eds.), *Social competence of young children with disabilities* (pp. 37–64). Baltimore: Paul H. Brookes Publishing Co.

Guralnick, M.J. (2001). A developmental systems model for early intervention. *Infants and Young Children, 14*(2), 1–18.

Guralnick, M.J. (2005). An overview of the developmental systems model for early intervention In M.J. Guralnick (Ed.), *The developmental systems approach to early intervention* (pp. 3–28). Baltimore: Paul H. Brookes Publishing Co.

Guralnick, M.J. (2008). International perspectives on early intervention: A search for common ground. *Journal of Early Intervention, 30*(2), 90–101.

Hadden, D.S. (2000). The long anticipated day: Strategies for success when a premature infant comes home from the neonatal intensive care unit. *Young Exceptional Children, 3*(2), 21–27.

Hadden, D.S., & Fowler, S.A. (2000). Interagency agreements: A proactive tool for improving the transition from early intervention to preschool special education services. *Young Exceptional Children, 3*(4), 2–8.

Hadden, S., Fowler, S.A., Fink, D.B., & Wischnowski, M.W. (1995). *Writing an interagency agreement on transition: A practical guide. Family and child transitions into least restrictive education (FACTS/LRE).* Champaign: University of Illinois at Urbana-Champaign.

Hains, A.H., Fowler, S.A., & Chandler, L.K. (1988). Planning school transitions: Family and professional collaboration. *Journal of the Division for Early Childhood, 12*(2), 108–115.

Hamblin-Wilson, C., & Thurman, S.K. (1990). The transition from early intervention to kindergarten: Parental satisfaction and involvement. *Journal of Early Intervention, 14*(1), 55–61.

Handicapped Children's Early Education Assistance Act (PL90-538).

Hanline, M. (1988). Making the transition to preschool: Identification of parent needs. *Journal of the Division for Early Childhood, 12*(2), 98–107.

Hanline, M., & Halvorsen, A. (1989). Parent perceptions of the integration transition process: Overcoming artificial barriers. *Exceptional Children, 55*(6), 487–492.

Hanline, M., & Knowlton, A. (1988). A collaborative model for providing support to parents during their child's transition from infant intervention to preschool special education in public school program. *Journal of the Division for Early Childhood, 12*(2), 116–125.

Hanson, M.J. (2005). Ensuring effective transitions in early intervention. In M.J. Guralnick (Ed.), *A developmental systems approach to early intervention: National and international perspectives* (pp. 373–398). Baltimore: Paul H. Brookes Publishing Company.

Hanson, M.J., Beckman, P.J., Horn, E., Marquart, J., Sandall, S.R., Greig, D., et al. (2000). Entering preschool: Family and professional experiences in this transition process. *Journal of Early Intervention, 23*(4), 279–293.

Hanson, M.J., & Bruder, M.B. (2001). Early intervention: Promises to keep. *Infants and Young Children, 13*(3), 47–58.

Harbin, G.L., McWilliam, R.A., & Gallagher, J.J. (2000). Services for young children with disabilities and their families. In J.P. Shonkoff & S.J. Meisels (Eds.), *Handbook of early childhood intervention* (pp. 387–415). New York: Cambridge University Press.

Hutinger, P.L. (1981). Transition practices for handicapped young children: What the experts say. *Journal of the Division for Early Childhood, 2*, 8–14.

Individuals with Disabilities Education Improvement Act (IDEA) of 2004, PL 108-446, 20 U.S.C., §§ 1400 *et seq.*

Janus, M., Lefort, J., Cameron, R., & Kopechanski, L. (2007). Starting kindergarten: Transition issues for children with special needs. *Canadian Journal of Education, 30*, 628–648.

Johnson, R.J., Chandler, L.K., Kerns, G., & Fowler, S.A. (1986). What are parents saying about family involvement in school transitions? A retrospective transition interview. *Journal of the Division for Early Childhood, 11*, 10–17.

Kagan, S.L., & Neuman, M.J. (1998). Lessons from three decades of transition research. *The Elementary School Journal, 98*(4), 365–381.

Kemp, C. (2003). Investigating the transition of young children with intellectual disabilities to mainstream classes: An Australian perspective. *International Journal of Disability, Development, and Education, 50*, 403–433.

Kemp, C., & Carter, M. (2005). Demonstration of classroom survival skills in kindergarten: A five-year transition study of children with intellectual disabilities. *Educational Psychology, 20*, 393–411.

King, G., Strachan, D., Tucker, M., Duwyn, B., Desserud, S., & Shillington, M. (2009). The application of a transdisciplinary model for early intervention services. *Infants and Young Children, 22*(3), 211–223.

Knowles, M.S., Holton, E.F., III, & Swanson, R.A. (1998). *The adult learner: The definitive classic in adult education and human resources development* (5th ed.). Houston, TX: Butterworth-Heinemann.

LaCour, J.A. (1982). Interagency agreement: A rational response to an irrational system. *Exceptional Children, 49*(3), 265–267.

Ladd, G.W. (2005). *Children's peer relations and social competence: A century of progress.* New Haven, CT: Yale University Press.

Ladd, G.W. (2008). Social competence and peer relationships for young children and their service-providers. *Early Childhood Services, 2*(3), 129–148.

Lazzari, A.M. (1991). *The transition sourcebook: A practical guide for early intervention programs.* Tucson, AZ: Communication Skill Builders.

Lovett, D.L., & Haring, K.A. (2003). Family perceptions of transitions in early intervention. *Education and Training in Developmental Disabilities, 38*(4), 370–377.

Malone, D.G., & Gallagher, P. (2009). Transition to preschool special education: A review of the literature. *Early Education and Development, 20*(4), 584–602.

McCormick, L. (2006). Transitions. In M.J. Noonan & L. McCormick (Eds.), *Young children with disabilities in natural environments: Methods and procedures* (pp. 317–329). Baltimore: Paul H. Brookes Publishing Co.

McCormick, L., & Kawate, J. (1982). Kindergarten survival skills: New directions for preschool special education. *Educating and Training of the Mentally Retarded, 17,* 247–252.

McLean, M. (2003). Assessment and its importance in early intervention/early childhood special education. In M. McLean, M. Wolery, & D. Bailey (Eds.), *Assessing infants and preschoolers with special needs* (3rd ed., pp. 1–21). Upper Saddle River, NJ: Prentice Hall.

McLean, M., Wolery, M., & Bailey, D. (2003). *Assessing infants and preschoolers with special needs* (3rd ed.). Upper Saddle River, NJ: Prentice Hall.

McWilliam, R.A., Casey, A.M., & Sims, J. (2009). The routines-based interview: A method for gathering information and assessing needs. *Infants and Young Children, 22*(3), 224–233.

Meisels, S.J., & Fenichel, E. (1996). *New visions for the developmental assessment of infants and young children.* Washington, DC: Zero to Three.

Murphy, M., & Vincent, L.J. (1989). Identification of critical skills for success in day care. *Journal of Early Intervention, 13*(3), 221–229.

National Research Council. (2000). *How people learn: Brain, mind, experience and school.* Washington, DC: National Academies Press.

Noonan, M.J., & McCormick, L. (2006). *Young children with disabilities in natural environments: Methods and procedures.* Baltimore: Paul H. Brookes Publishing Co.

Noonan, M.J., & Ratokalau, N.B. (1991). PPT: The preschool preparation and transition project. *Journal of Early Intervention 15,* 390–398.

Odom, S.L. (2009). The tie that binds: Evidence-based practice, implementation science, and outcomes for children. *Topics in Early Childhood Special Education, 29*(1), 53–61.

Odom, S.L., & McLean, M.E. (Eds.). (1996). *Early intervention/early childhood special education: Recommended practices.* Austin, TX: PRO-ED.

Odom, S.L., McLean, M.E., Johnson, L.J., & LaMontagne, M.J. (1995). Recommended practices in early childhood special education: Validation and current use. *Journal of Early Intervention, 19*(1), 1–17.

Powell, D.S., Batsche, C.J., Ferro, J., Fox, L., & Dunlap, G. (1997). A strength-based approach in support of multi-risk families: Principles and issues. *Topics in Early Childhood Special Education, 17*(1), 1–26.

Repetto, J.B., & Correa, V.I. (1996). Expanding views on transition. *Exceptional Children, 62*(6), 551–563.

Rice, M.L., & O'Brien, M. (1990). Transition: Times of change and accommodation. *Topics in Early Childhood Special Education, 9*(4), 1–14.

Roberts, R.N., Innocenti, M.S., & Goetze, L.D. (1999). Emerging issues from state level evaluations of early intervention programs. *Journal of Early Intervention, 22*(2), 152–163.

Roberts, R.N., Rule, S., & Innocenti, M.S. (1998). *Strengthening the family-professional partnership in services for young children.* Baltimore: Paul H. Brookes Publishing Co.

Rosenkoetter, S.E., Hains, A.H., & Fowler, S.A. (1994). *Bridging early services for children with special needs and their families: A practical guide for transition planning.* Baltimore: Paul H. Brookes Publishing Co.

Rosenkoetter, S.E., Schroeder, C., Rous, B., Hains, A., Shaw, J., & McCormick, K. (2009). *A review of research in early childhood transition: Child and family studies* (Technical Report #5). Lexington: University of Kentucky, Human Development Institute, National Early Childhood Transition Center. Retrieved September 15, 2009, from http://www.hdi.uky.edu/Libraries/NECTC_Papers_and_Reports/Technical_Report_5.sflb.ashx

Rosenkoetter, S.E., Whaley, K.T., Hains, A.H., & Pierce, L. (2001). The evolution of transition policy for young children with special needs and their families: Past, present, and future. *Topics in Early Childhood Special Education, 21*(1), 3–14.

Ross-Allen, J., & Conn-Powers, M.C. (1991). *TEEM: A manual to support the transition of young children with special needs and their families from preschool into kindergarten and other regular education environments.* Burlington, VT: University of Vermont, University Affiliated Program, Center for Developmental Disabilities.

Ross-Allen, J., & Conn-Powers, M.C. (1991). Transition of young children into the elementary education mainstream. *Topics in Early Childhood Special Education, 9*(4), 91–105.

Rous, B. (2004). Perspectives of teachers about instructional supervision and behaviors that influence pre-school instruction. *Journal of Early Intervention, 26*(4), 266–283.

Rous, B. (2008). *Recommended transition practices for young children and families* (Technical Report #3). Lexington, KY: University of Kentucky, Human Development Institute, National Early Childhood Transition Center. Retrieved September 15, 2009, from http://www.hdi.uky.edu/Libraries/NECTC_Papers_and_Reports/Technical_Report_3.sflb.ashx

Rous, B.S., & Hallam, R.A. (2006). *Tools for transition in early childhood: A step-by-step guide for agencies, teachers and families*. Baltimore: Paul H. Brookes Publishing Co.

Rous, B., Hallam, R., Harbin, G., McCormick, K., & Jung, L. (2007). The transition process for young children with disabilities: A conceptual framework. *Infants and Young Children, 20*(2), 135–148.

Rous, B., Hemmeter, M.L., & Schuster, J. (1994). Sequenced transition to education in the public schools: A systems approach to transition planning. *Topics in Early Childhood Special Education, 14*(3), 374–393.

Rous, B., Hemmeter, M.L., & Schuster, J. (1999). Evaluating the impact of the STEPS model on development of community-wide transition systems. *Journal of Early Intervention, 22*(1), 38–50.

Shonkoff, J.P., & Phillips, D.A. (Eds.). (2000). *From neurons to neighborhoods: The science of early childhood development*. Washington, DC: National Academies Press.

Shotts, C.K., Rosenkoetter, S.E., Streufert, C.A., & Rosenkoetter, L.I. (1994). Transition policy and issues: A view from the states. *Topics in Early Childhood Special Education, 14*, 395–411.

Stremel, K., & Campbell, P.H. (2007). Implementation of early intervention within natural environments. *Early Childhood Services, 1*(2), 83–105.

Trohanis, P.L. (2008). Progress in providing services to young children with special needs and their families: An overview to and update on the implementation of the Individuals with Disabilities Education Act (IDEA). *Journal of Early Intervention, 30*(2), 140–151.

Turnbull, A.P., Summers, J.A., Turnbull, R., Brotherson, M.J., Winton, P., Roberts, R., et al. (2007). Family supports and services in early intervention: A bold vision. *Journal of Early Intervention, 29, 3*.

Vincent, L., Laten, S., Salisbury, C., Brown, P., & Baumgart, D. (1980). Family involvement in the educational processes of severely handicapped students: State of the art and directions for the future. In B. Wilcox & R. York (Eds.), *Quality educational services for the severely handicapped: The federal perspective* (pp. 164–179): U.S. Department of Education, Division of Innovation and Development.

Walter, G., & Vincent, L.J. (1982). The handicapped child in the regular kindergarten program. *Journal of the Division for Early Childhood, 6*, 82–95.

Will, M. (1985). Transitioning: Linking disabled youth to a productive future. *OSERS News in Print, 51*, 11–16.

Wischnowski, M.W., Fowler, S.A., & McCollum, J.A. (2000). Supports and barriers to writing an interagency agreement on the preschool transition. *Journal of Early Intervention, 23*(4), 294–307.

W.K. Kellogg Foundation. (2001). *Using logic models to bring together planning, evaluation, and action: Logic model development guide*. Battle Creek, MI: Author.

Wolery, M. (1989). Transition in early childhood special education: Issues and procedures. *Focus on Exceptional Children, 22*, 1–16.

Wolery, M. (1999). Children with disabilities in early elementary school. In R.C. Pianta & M.J. Cox (Eds.), *The transition to kindergarten* (pp. 253–280). Baltimore: Paul H. Brookes Publishing Co.

Wolraich, M.L., Gurwitch, R.H., Bruder, M.B., & Knight, L.A. (2005). The role of comprehensive interdisciplinary assessments in the early intervention system. In M.J. Guralnick (Ed.), *The developmental systems approach to early intervention*. Baltimore: Paul H. Brookes Publishing Co.

Woods, J.J., & Kashinath, S. (2007). Expanding opportunities for social communication into daily routines. *Early Childhood Services, 1*(2), 137–154.

6

Developing and Learning in More than One Language

The Challenges and Opportunities for Transitions in Early Education Settings

Eugene E. García

About 5 million students in the United States are learning English as a second language (García & Jensen, 2009). After they leave the home environment, these children are immediately thrust into a series of significant transitions as they enter U.S. educational venues that most likely do not reflect their everyday language and culture. Addressing these transitions has become a key aspect of the early learning activities developed for these children. If they are successfully addressed, these transitions allow the children to lay a solid educational foundation for later educational success and achievement.

Several terms are used in the literature to describe U.S. school children whose native language is not English. These terms include *English language learner, English learner,* and *limited English proficient.* The terms are used interchangeably to refer to students whose native language is not English and who have not developed academic English proficiency. In this chapter, we will use *dual-language learner* (DLL), to emphasize students' learning and progress in two languages at early stages of language development. An analysis of young children who spoke a language other than English in the United States indicated that most children who live in predominantly non-English environments also are exposed substantially to English (Hernández, Denton, & Macartney, 2008). Therefore, the term DLL recognizes and more appropriately emphasizes that these children's knowledge, skills, and abilities are a product of dual-language environments in both home and school settings and facilitates a better understanding of the types of transitions they face.

A DEMOGRAPHIC AND SERVICE IMPERATIVE FOR ENHANCED EARLY CARE AND EDUCATION FOR DUAL-LANGUAGE CHILDREN

The demography of DLL students are thoroughly examined in two reports. *The New Demography of America's Schools* by Randy Capps and colleagues (2005) at the Urban Institute and *Children in Immigrant Families* by Donald Hernández and colleagues (2008) at the University at Albany, State University of New York. These reports use U.S. census data to describe the ethnic, linguistic, economic, domestic, educational, and geographic (including their origins and destinations) characteristics of immigrant children and families. The data in the reports were drawn from the 2000 census, but the information provided remains useful to project the future demographic characteristics of U.S. students. Certainly, the 2010 census was expected to shed further light on the characteristics of students and in some cases to correct misguided projections that were based on 2000 data. Until those data were analyzed, these reports continued to be helpful tools that can orient our understanding of the future challenges and opportunities for educators serving children of immigrant origins who learn English as a second language.

At least one in five children ages 5–17 years in the United States has a foreign-born parent (Capps et al., 2005), and many, though not all, of these children learn English as their second language. It is important to note that DLL students and children from immigrant families (i.e., children with at least one foreign-born parent) are not identical populations, though they are closely related. Most children from immigrant households are English learners at some point in their lives.

The overall population of children speaking a non-English native language in the United States rose from 6% in 1979 to 14% in 1999 (García & Jensen, 2009). The number of students speaking a minority language in K–12 schools has been estimated to be more than 14 million (August, 2006). The representation of DLLs in U.S. schools is highest in early education facilities (preschools and primary schools), because DLL children in preschool or kindergarten tend to develop oral and academic English proficiency by third grade. The percentage of DLL students from prekindergarten to Grade 5 rose from 4.7% to 7.4% between 1980 and 2000, while the percentage of DLL students in Grades 6–12 rose from 3.1% to 5.5% during the same period (Capps et al., 2005). Young DLLs (up to 8 years old) have been the fastest growing student population in the country over the past few decades. This population has grown primarily because of increased rates of legal and illegal immigration and also because of high birthrates among immigrant families (Hernández et al., 2008).

A majority of DLLs come from Spanish-speaking immigrant families. During the 2000–2001 school year, Spanish was the native language of 77% of English learners nationally (Hopstock & Stephenson, 2003). But the group represents many national origins and more than 350 languages. In 2000, more than half of DLLs came from Latin American immigrant families (Capps et al., 2005). Nearly 40% of children came from Mexican immigrant families (Hernández et al., 2008). The Caribbean, East Asia, and Europe, in combination with Canada and Australia, each account for 10%–11% of the overall population of children from immigrant families; Central America, South America, Indochina, and West Asia each account for 5%–7% of the total; and the former Soviet Union and Africa account for 2%–3% each. At least 3 out of 4 children from immigrant families are born in the United States (Capps, 2001), though U.S. nativity is higher among elementary-school–age children of immigrant families than among students of immigrant families attending secondary school (Capps et al., 2005).

Therefore, as immigrant families settle into new destinations due to labor demands (Zúñiga & Hernández-León, 2005), DLL students increasingly attend school in districts and states that served few or no DLL children prior to the 1980s. Although the rise in DLL students is a national phenomenon, affecting all sectors in the United States, immigrant families continue to be concentrated in California, Texas, New York, Florida, Illinois, and New Jersey (Capps et al., 2005). Several other states have witnessed rapid increases in their immigrant populations. Between 1990 and 2000, seven states experienced over 100% increases in the numbers of children from immigrant families attending pre-K–fifth grade: Nevada, North Carolina, Georgia, Nebraska, Arkansas, Arizona, and South Dakota (in order from greatest to smallest percentage increase) (Capps et al.). During the 1990s, Nevada, Nebraska, and South Dakota saw increases of 354%, 350%, and 264% in their DLL populations, respectively. These increases led several school districts and states to frantically seek out and provide educational resources for children who were English language learners. In such circumstances, families, children, and communities engage in a series of transitions: Parents relocate their families and take on new working and living conditions, children attend new educational institutions, and schools and local communities adapt to new populations of families and students.

EARLY CARE AND EDUCATIONAL CIRCUMSTANCES

We cannot adequately understand the academic performance patterns of DLL students as a whole without comparing these students' social and economic characteristics with those of native English speakers and considering the institutional history of U.S. schools (Jensen, 2008b). Although a great deal of socioeconomic variation exists among DLLs, they are more likely than native English-speaking children, on average, to live in poverty and to have parents whose formal education is limited (García & Cuellar, 2006). In addition, DLL students are more likely to have ethnic or racial minority status (Capps et al., 2005). Each of these factors—low income, low parental education, and ethnic or racial minority status—decreases group achievement averages across academic areas, resulting in the relatively low overall performance of DLL students.

In their analyses of a national data set of academic performance in early elementary school, Reardon and Galindo (2006) found that reading and mathematics achievement patterns from kindergarten–third grade varied according to home language environments among Hispanic students. Hispanic students who were living in homes that were categorized as primarily Spanish speaking or only Spanish speaking lagged further behind white children than did Hispanics who lived in homes that were categorized as primarily English speaking or only English speaking.

Given that educational risk factors for DLL students are associated with one another (Collier, 1987; Jensen, 2007), it is valuable to consider the impact of language background on achievement outcomes. Variables such as parental education, segregated living conditions, and family poverty are also associated with achievement gaps for DLL students.

Thus, rather than pointing to one or two student background factors as explanations for the low achievement of DLL students, we understand that educational risk, in general, is attributable to a myriad of interrelated child background factors, including parental education levels, family income, parental proficiency in English, mother's marital status at the time of the child's birth, and status of the home as a single-parent or dual-parent home (National Center for Education Statistics, 1995). The more risk factors that affect a child, the less likely it is that the child will do well in school. Because DLL children, on average, exhibit three of the five risk factors at higher rates than do native English speakers, they are generally at greater risk for academic underachievement (Hernández et al., 2008). Using data from the 2000 census, Capps and colleagues (2005) found that 68% of DLL students in pre-K–fifth grade lived in low-income families, compared with 36% of English-proficient children. The percentages changed to 60% and 32% respectively, for 6th- to 12th-grade students. Moreover, 48% of DLL children in pre-K–5th grade and 35% of DLLs in the higher grades had a parent with less than a high school education, compared with 11% and 9% of English-proficient children in the same grades (Capps et al.). Teachers of DLL children must be able to address these challenging educational circumstances.

CONCEPTUAL FRAMEWORK FOR UNDERSTANDING TRANSITIONS

The data presented in the preceding section suggest directly that DLLs are in a double-jeopardy situation, at a minimum. All children must transition from home to school, but when these children make the transition, there are fewer transcending similarities between home and school than is the case for most children. Any understanding of transitions for this population must address the linguistic and cultural diversity of DLL children and their families in order to properly assess and improve the early learning environments that are designed for them (García, 2005; García & Frede, in press; Portes, 2005.)

This view is supported by research that suggests that the educational failure of diverse student populations is related to a culture clash between home and school. In essence, researchers have suggested that educational endeavors for DLL students are likely to fail if they do not attend to culture. We steer away from the notion that understanding general principles of development alone can help us understand the diversity of children and families and respond to them in ways that support their own positive efforts to enhance development and learning. Rather, we suggest that a variety of approaches to address cultural and linguistic diversity fall along a continuum of responsive practice, as depicted in Figure 6.1.

These approaches, supported by the literature, recommend alternatives for integrating cultural diversity into the development of practices that improve the early learning conditions of diverse students (particularly DLLs). Theoretically, such students do not succeed academically because the difference between school culture and their home culture leads to a harmful dissonance. The challenge is to identify critical differences between and within DLL populations and to incorporate this information into practices at school. This effort focuses attention on the individual and the cultural milieu in which that individual resides.

Advances in research design (particularly in developmental science), analysis, and theory have produced principles concerning how children from diverse linguistic and cultural roots develop in environments that are designed for care, teaching, and learning (García, 2005; Gardner, 2006; Gutierrez & Rogoff, 2003). From this work, some consensus has emerged. At the conclusion of their efforts to synthesize the scientific knowledge base of development, Bransford and colleagues (2000) argue that understanding of learning and development involves understanding about developmental processes, developmental environments, instruction, and sociocultural processes.

In order to build a research base, we require a strong theoretical framework that describes the social and cultural context of learning (Nasir & Hand, 2006). Curriculum, instruction, program design, and policy researchers need a thorough, shared understanding of the cultural

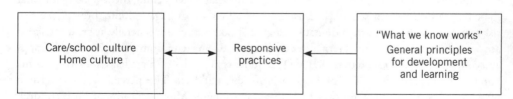

Figure 6.1. Addressing cultural and linguistic diversity: a continuum of theoretical perspectives.

processes that shape learning inside the home and classroom—the ways in which environments within and outside school interact to shape student engagement and learning (García, 2005). This more articulated notion that language, culture, and learning are interconnected in the social environments of the child helps us to better understand issues related to transitions for dual-language children.

NEED FOR A SOCIOCULTURAL MODEL OF STUDENT LEARNING WITH AN EYE ON TRANSITIONS

To date, a comprehensive, uniting model of the sociocultural processes that shape student learning has not been proposed (Jensen, 2008a). Various models emphasize different elements of what could be a unifying framework. For example, the work of Cole and Engeström (1993) emphasize ways in which knowledge is accumulated through the lens of history and organized from a cultural perspective. This work is relevant to student learning because information that is shared in classrooms and schools is filtered by students through their personal histories and family cultures. Another example is the work of Rogoff (2003), a psychologist who is interested in the collaboration between children and adults across different cultures. Her work introduced important concepts to psychology, including the idea of "guided participation" in cultural activity, in which adults who have little formal schooling parent (and teach) their young children very differently from adults who have extensive school experience (Rogoff, Mistry, Göncü, & Mosier, 1993).

Additional pieces of a model of sociocultural student learning have been suggested, including the notions of *situated cognition* (Brown, Collins, & Duguid, 1989), *cognitive apprenticeship* (Brown & Campione, 1996), *intersubjectivity* (Vygotsky, 1978), *engagement* (Skinner, Pappas, & Davis, 2005), "learning as shifts in social relations" (Nasir & Hand, 2006), *power in social structure* (Freire, 1970; McDermott & Varenne, 1995), *meaning in cultural tools and artifacts* (Cole, 1996), and *responsive pedagogy* (Garcia, 2005). Each of these pieces is important to the whole. García relies heavily on these conceptual and theoretical underpinnings and places a heavy emphasis on issues of culture and the antecedents of culture as mediating variables in addressing the formal education of linguistically and culturally diverse students. These same issues are a critical part of understanding transitions for DLLs.

Cultural Mediation

No concept is as elusive, yet significant, in the social realm as *culture* (Geertz, 1973). Definitions of the term abound, though none is exhaustive. The complexity of culture often repels social scientists (depending on their discipline and training), which may prevent policy makers from considering important cultural processes and, therefore, the public good, particularly in education. Compounding the insufficient attention to culture in policy circles and in the professional training of school personnel (García, 2005) is the fact that the term tends to be misunderstood and even used erroneously. For example, *culture* is often used as a substitute for *nationality* or *ethnicity,* suggesting that cultural homogeneity exists across thousands or even millions of people (Rogoff, 2003).

Perhaps the most useful perspective from which to understand culture is to think of it as a process (Cole, 1996, p. 129) rather than as an outcome, independent variable, or "collection of things whether tangible or abstract" (Hutchins, 1996, p. 354). It is not simply what people do, but the values, customs, practices, symbols, and beliefs that mediate their knowledge, skills, and relationships (Miller, 2002; Rogoff, 2003). It guides the ways in which groups respond to their environments and think over time. Thus, a human mind and the culture of that mind are inseparable.

As we have mentioned, conflict may occur when different cultural communities share time and space to engage in a common activity (Rogoff, 2003). *Different* does not equate to *deficient,* although the two concepts are often confused by persons who are projecting their own cultural values on others. Typically, these persons are detached from the metacognitive exercise of *cultural understanding* (García, 2005). To avoid cultural conflict in school, communities frequently segregate themselves by race, ethnicity, and/or socioeconomic class (Boulton, 1995; Ellis, 1997).

As different communities interact within schools, however, cultural practice evolves over time, whether the change is recognized or not (Valdés, 1996). Change in cultural practice that is attributable to conflict and differentiation is, and will continue to be, typical of the human experience. Understanding, predicting, and even shaping that change between home and school and within schools with an eye toward building engaging learning environments is necessary—and must be undertaken deliberately—in order to provide equitable educational opportunities to all students (Lesgold, 2004). This imperative is consistent with John Dewey's (1938) writing on education and experience. This grand educator of America's past was very cognizant of intersecting cultures and transitions between cultures.

In terms of developmental science, building *cultural bridges* is a means of connecting situated experience in care and learning environments with students' prior knowledge (Bransford, Brown, & Cocking, 2000; Bransford, Derry, Berliner, Hammerness, & Beckett, 2005; Driscoll, 2000; Lesgold, 2004). Thus, promoting successful transitions entails constructing these bridges. An assessment of prior knowledge must consider children's developmental histories in the context of their family histories (Cole & Engeström, 1993). Cultural fit, in other words, entails a three-pronged effort: 1) assessing child and family history, 2) evaluating the child's formal care and early schooling history, and 3) negotiating cultural practices. The third aspect is perhaps the most challenging one (Greenwood, Horton, & Utley, 2002; Guthrie, Rueda, Gambrell, & Morrison, 2008).

This work, combined with other studies of cultural practice in education (Gonzalez, Moll, & Amanti, 2005; Guthrie et al., 2008; Well & Mejía Arauz, 2005), clarifies theoretical constructs that are related to learning and associated cultural practices in the home and formal developmental or learning environments. These constructs demonstrate that development and learning must be understood in terms of institutional and family histories. We cannot ignore the role of families as they engage with the formal activities that are constructed by society to care for their children and foster their development.

This process of assessing family and school histories, and also noting associated cultural factors that influence student learning, is, however, insufficient to actually bridge cultural differences—that is, to engage students and enhance their learning opportunities through meaningful classroom activity. As we have mentioned, a cultural psychology that is developed in order to improve student learning must not only assess student, family, and school histories separately and comparatively but also thoughtfully connect these histories by developing meaningful and empirically based educational practice. Many cultural studies in education describe cultural and historical differences in family and school practices, yet very few, unfortunately, provide empirically supported ways to negotiate differences while enhancing student engagement and learning (Banks et al., 2007). Conventional research tends to examine how children are socialized to accept participation rules, authority, and linguistic norms while leaving the inferential work of determining what school and classroom inputs actually raise student achievement to policy analysts and others. These others, in turn, tend to underestimate cultural mediation (Fuller & Clark, 1994).

In order to improve school effectiveness and student learning by implementing responsive policies, programs, and practice, there must be a merger of cultural and inferential research. Bruner reflected

> Given all the work, given the surge of effort since the cognitive revolution, are we any better able to improve the education of children suffering the blight of poverty, discrimination, alienation? Have we developed any promising leads about how to organize the culture of school in ways to help children toward a fresh start? What does it take to create a nurturing school culture that empowers the young effectively to use the resources and opportunities of the broader culture? (1996, p. xiv)

In his book on culturally oriented and empirically supported solutions to the learning gap between students at risk (particularly children who have racial and ethnic minority backgrounds) and their peers, Portes asserted that "[t]he three most important predictors of school success remain parent involvement, adult–child ratios, and academic learning time" (p. 98). Referring to these predictors, he continued:

> These are no accident since they are quite interrelated. All three maximize learning activity related to what schools expect, teach, and value and are directly related to social class and tests. The adult present or level of assistance in the home and school available for tasks and experiences valued at school seems, in fact, to account for how parental involvement is defined. . . . What is needed then is a brainy, reliable way to ensure that combinations of factors are maximized and integrated in the lives of [students placed at risk] from underrepresented groups at multiple levels. We need to understand the reasons why some variables such as teaching characteristics (content and instructional expertise), leadership, collaboration, and similar school factors differ from others structured socially from a multifaceted view. It cannot be expected that interventions focusing on individual level factors such as self-esteem or character can close the gap any more than vouchers or high expectations at other levels. A comprehensive plan must direct strategies toward a common purpose and anticipate the social impact and costs of altering learning or economic outcomes. (2005, pp. 98–99)

Embedded in this quote are understandings that language, culture, and their accompanying values are acquired in the home and community environment; that children come to early care and learning environments with some knowledge about what language is, how it works, and what it is used for; that children learn higher level cognitive and communicative skills as they engage in socially meaningful activities; and that children's development and learning are best understood as the interaction of linguistic, sociocultural, and cognitive knowledge and experiences in consistent and positive socioemotional contexts. A more appropriate perspective of development and learning, then, is one that recognizes that development and learning are enhanced in contexts that are both socioculturally and linguistically meaningful for the child and the family. García (2005) and Fuller et al. (2007) further emphasize that children learn best and parents and teachers feel most satisfied when they are encouraged to become allies in the care and learning process. Therefore, a more appropriate approach to early childhood practice is one that recognizes that development and learning are enhanced when they occur in contexts that emotionally, socioculturally, linguistically, and cognitively reflect the child's and family's history and culture.

Such meaningful contexts have been notoriously inaccessible to linguistically and culturally diverse children, particularly young DLLs. In fact, schooling practices and teachers, who are the architects and engineers of instruction, often contribute to educational vulnerability (Valenzuela, 1999). The monolithic culture transmitted by common forms of care, pedagogy, curricula, instruction, classroom configuration, and language dramatizes the lack of fit between the DLL child and his or her experience. The prevailing culture is reflected in practices such as

- The systematic exclusion of the histories, languages, experiences, and values of these children

- *Tracking,* which limits some students' access to academic courses and which justifies retaining these students in learning environments that do not foster academic development, socialization, or self-perception as competent learners and language users

- A lack of opportunities to engage in developmentally and culturally appropriate learning in ways other than teacher-led instruction

- Absence of linguistic and cultural bridges in construction of important transitions

Construction of Responsive Communities of Practice

The adoption of a responsive approach would have profound implications for DLL populations (García, 2005). The new interest in developing responsive practices redefines our efforts to better serve diverse children and families. It might be described as practices of empowerment, cultural learning, or a cultural view of providing developmental assistance or guidance. In any case, it argues for practices that respect and integrate students' values, beliefs, histories, and experiences and that recognize the active role played by families and children in the processes of development and learning. It therefore implies a *responsive community of practice,* one that encompasses practical, contextual, and empirical knowledge and a worldview of education that evolves through meaningful interactions among parents, family members, children, caregivers or teachers, and other community members. This responsive set of strategies expands children's knowledge and well-being beyond their own immediate experiences and uses those experiences as a sound foundation for cultivating well-being.

To further clarify this approach, Table 6.1 summarizes the conceptual dimensions for high-performing responsive communities as formal interventions in early care and early learning circumstances.

In sum, a *responsive community* recognizes that care and learning have their roots in processes that build transitions across various contexts and circumstances. Such a conceptual framework rejects the Americanization/assimilation strategy, extends beyond the policy and practice frameworks of equal opportunity, and concludes that a focus on broader issues of culture is useful but insufficient to serve culturally diverse students effectively in today's early care and learning environments. Instead, a focus on responsive engagement with families and children encourages participants in the approach to engage in the positive construction and reconstruction of meaning and to reinterpret and augment past knowledge within a nurturing context. Diversity is perceived and used as a resource for enhancing development and learning instead of being seen as a problem. A focus on what children and families bring generates an asset- and resource-oriented approach rather than a deficit- or needs-assessment approach. Within this knowledge-driven, responsive, and engaging environment, skills are tools for acquiring knowledge, not a fundamental target of interventions.

This mission requires an understanding of how individuals with diverse sets of experiences seen through the lens of their own cultures "make meaning," communicate that meaning, and

Table 6.1. Conceptual dimensions of addressing cultural and linguistic diversity in responsive development and learning communities supporting transitions

Agencywide practices	Caregiver and teacher practices
• Define the vision by accepting and valuing diversity. • Treat classroom practitioners as professionals and colleagues in school development decisions. • Foster collaboration, flexibility, and enhanced professional development. • Eliminate (gradually or immediately) policies that seek to categorize diverse children, thereby rendering their experiences inferior or limiting. • Reflect and connect to the surrounding community—particularly to the families of the children served—through the formal construction of cultural and linguistic bridges.	• Employ bilingual/bicultural skills and awareness. • Maintain high expectations of diverse children and families. • Treat diversity as an asset—with specific articulation of program bridges to language and culture. • Engage in ongoing professional development to learn about issues of cultural and linguistic diversity and to learn which practices are most effective. • Provide basic services to address cultural and linguistic diversity: 1) Pay attention to and integrate home language/cultural practices. 2) Focus on maximizing children's and families' interactions across categories (e.g., language proficiency, academic performance, immigration status, etc.). 3) Make regular and consistent attempts to access and build on family and community resources. 4) Take a thematic approach to early learning activities, and integrate various skills, events, and learning opportunities. 5) Focus on language development through meaningful interactions and communications combined with direct skill-building in content-appropriate contexts.

extend that meaning, particularly in social contexts that are designed for early care and learning. Such a mission requires an in-depth treatment of the processes that are associated with producing diversity, namely, issues of socialization in and out of formal care and early learning experiences. It also requires educators to examine how such understanding is actually transformed into care, pedagogy, and curriculum that results in enhanced social, emotional, cognitive, and linguistic development for DLL children.

WHAT CONTRIBUTES TO SUCCESSFUL TRANSITIONS FOR DLLS?

The breadth and depth of language and literacy development is particularly important during the first 5 years of life, and literacy development in the schooling context is especially significant through the third grade, when complex literacy practices are introduced. This development includes, of course, the expressive and receptive vocabulary development of non-English languages spoken by DLL children. Early language learning has important relevance for the social, emotional, and cognitive development of children throughout their lives. Thus, cultural notions of language learning can inform the building of bridges between home environments and caregiving environments outside the home, including preschools.

The effectiveness of programs targeting young DLLs is a widely contested issue. Debates over which types of programs best develop the academic skills of these children continue to cause tumult among practitioners, academics, and policy makers. The fundamental issue underlying this argument is whether bilingual or English-only approaches are more effective in boosting and sustaining the learning and care of young DLL children. Early research surrounding this issue was inconclusive. Some scholars, such as Baker and de Kanter (1981) and Baker and Pelavin (1984), asserted that the research evidence did not support the effectiveness of bilingual instruction—in other words, that bilingual education simply does not work. Other scholars, such as Willig (1985), refuted this argument with evidence to support the efficacy of bilingual programs.

Most research related to the efficacy of program efforts has not included early learning venues, but it is still relevant. Greene (1998) was one of the first researchers to conduct a systematic meta-analysis of the effectiveness of bilingual education in early grades. Out of 75 previous studies, he included 11 in his analysis that met minimal standards for the quality of their research design (e.g., randomization). Greene found overall that bilingual programs produced 0.21 of standard deviation improvement on reading tests and 0.12 of a standard deviation improvement on math tests measured in English.

More recently, Slavin and Cheung (2005) published a "best evidence synthesis" which reviewed experimental studies that compared bilingual and English-only reading programs for DLLs. In this review, the authors employed a systematic literature search, quantified outcomes as effect sizes, and extensively discussed individual studies ($N = 17$) that met inclusion criteria. Thirteen of the seventeen studies focused on elementary school reading abilities in students for whom Spanish was their dominant language. Slavin and Cheung weighted the results by sample size to calculate an effect size of 0.33 in favor of programs that used bilingual approaches.

Rolstad, Mahoney, and Glass (2005) presented another meta-analysis. In this piece, the authors included 17 studies that have been conducted since 1985 on the effectiveness of bilingual approaches compared with English-only approaches. The authors found that bilingual approaches were consistently better than English-only approaches. Controlling for DLL status, analysis yielded a positive effect for bilingual programs at 0.23 of a standard deviation.

Finally, Borman, Hewes, Reilly, and Alvarado (2006) did not assess program differences directly, but conducted a meta-analysis on the achievement effects of certain nationally disseminated and externally developed school improvement programs. These programs, which are known as *whole-school* or *comprehensive* reforms, have been implemented in schools that serve Hispanic DLL students predominantly. The authors also compared the specific achievement effects of the 12 most widely implemented models of comprehensive school reform (CSR) for these students and found that the effects of CSR for schools serving these students were somewhat limited. The current body of evidence does suggest, however, that CSR programs that show particular promise for Hispanic DLL students "are built around valuing and teaching relevant culture and traditions, and address language directly" (Borman et al., p. 38). The research results that we have cited echo the need for building bridges of transition that are linguistically and culturally responsive. Not to do so ignores the empirical connection between these types of programmatic bridges and DLL student success.

DUAL-LANGUAGE PROGRAMS

Dual-language (DL) programs—also known as *two-way immersion*—are relatively new in the United States. Unique among program alternatives, DL programs aim to provide high-quality instruction simultaneously to students whose first language is not English and to English-speaking students who are learning a second language. Care centers and schools offering DL programs thus teach children language through content, with teachers adapting their instruction to ensure children's comprehension and using content lessons to convey vocabulary and language structure (García, 2005).

The Center for Applied Linguistics (2005) has compiled a report on research-based strategies and practices that are associated with DL program development and implementation. Titled *Guiding Principles for Dual-Language Education,* the report discusses seven dimensions of planning and ongoing implementation of DL programs: 1) assessment and accountability, 2) curriculum, 3) instruction, 4) staff quality and professional development, 5) program structure, 6) family and community, and 7) support and resources.

The installation of DL programs is based on a strong theoretical rationale and is supported by empirical research findings concerning both first and second language acquisition (Genesee, 1999). This rationale grows out of the aforementioned sociocultural model, which maintains that learning occurs through naturalistic social interaction (Vygotsky, 1978). That is, the integration of native English speakers and speakers of other languages facilitates second language acquisition because it promotes natural, substantive interaction among speakers of different languages.

Currently in the United States there are more than 400 DL programs, and the number is growing rapidly (Center for Applied Linguistics, 2004). While the vast majority of programs offer instruction in Spanish and English, there are also DL programs conducted in Korean, Cantonese, Arabic, French, Japanese, Navajo, Portuguese, and Russian (García, 2005; Howard, Sugarman, & Christian, 2003).

Research suggests that dual-language immersion is an excellent model for academic achievement for both language-minority and majority children (Cobb, Vega, & Kronauge, 2005; García, 2005; Howard et al., 2003; Sugarman & Howard, 2001). Positive effects of DL programs have also been found for young Hispanics during the early years of schooling (ages 3–8 years). Figueroa (2005) conducted a study with 24 Spanish-speaking kindergartners (10 girls, 14 boys) in a DL program that looked at associations between the development of prereading knowledge in Spanish and the development of English skills. She examined scores on tests of phonological reasoning and oral fluency during the fall, winter, and spring of the children's kindergarten year. She found that participants made significant gains both in Spanish and English for every subtest of phonological awareness and at each of the three waves of data collection. Moreover, all participants were meeting or exceeding district requirements.

In an experimental study, Barnett, Yarosz, Thomas, and Blanco (2006) compared the effects on children's learning of a DL and a monolingual English immersion (EI) preschool program. Children in the study ($N = 150$) were from both English and Spanish home-language backgrounds. Eighty-five children were randomly assigned to the DL program and sixty-five were randomly assigned to the EI program in the same school district. The two programs were compared on measures of children's growth in language, emergent literacy, and mathematics. Compared with those in the EI group, children in the DL program produced larger and more significant gains in Spanish vocabulary. In addition, all the children in the DL program (including native Spanish and native English speakers) made greater phonological awareness gains in English, yet no group differences were found on measures of English language and literacy development.

Thus, the present evidence suggests that programs that use both English and the native language of children whose home language is not English may lead to positive achievement outcomes for both language minority and language majority students, especially for young children who are developing fundamental language and literacy skills. Research supports the notion that higher order cognitive and literacy skills transfer between languages, that developing native language skills can improve second-language skills, and that the DL program model corresponds well with these findings (Christian, Genesee, Lindholm-Leary, & Howard, 2004). DL programs are one very direct way to bridge the language and culture of DLL students, they facilitate transitions by allowing children to build on their natural linguistic talents in ways that are culturally conducive in learning settings outside the home.

CONCLUSION

This chapter began by introducing a new term, *dual-language learner*—(DLL) to describe children in the United States who do not speak English as their primary language when they come to school. It made the case that DLL students can best be served by understanding and acting on the bridges that link their dual languages and dual cultures. Therefore, the best *transition* for DLLs depends on minimizing the cultural and linguistic discontinuities that they experience and on building bridges between home and school. To that end, a dual-language program might very well be the best programmatic transition strategy available. DLL children face many challenges that relate to their languages, social and economic circumstances, and, most important, the English-only schooling situations that await too many of them. Instead, a dual-language learning environment that mirrors their ongoing nonschool experience and bridges the linguistic and cultural divide between home and school settings provides a grand opportunity for these students.

REFERENCES

August, D. (2006). Demographic overview. In D. August & T. Shanahan (Eds.), *Report of the national literacy panel on language minority youth and children*. Mahwah, NJ: Lawrence Erlbaum Associates.

Baker, K.A., & de Kanter, A.A. (1981). *Effectiveness of bilingual education: A review of the literature*. Washington, DC: U.S. Department of Education.

Baker, K.A., & Pelavin, S. (1984). *Problems in bilingual education*. Paper presented at the annual meeting of the American Education Research Association, New Orleans.

Banks, J., Au, K.H., Ball, A.F., Bell, P., Gordon, E.W., Gutiérrez, K.D., et al. (2007). *Learning in and out of school in diverse environments: Life-long, life-wide, life-deep*. Seattle: The LIFE Center.

Barnett, W.S., Yarosz, D.J., Thomas, J., & Blanco, D. (2006). *Two-way and monolingual English immersion in preschool education: An experimental comparison*. New Brunswick, NJ: National Institute for Early Education Research.

Borman, G.D., Hewes, G.H., Reilly, M., & Alvarado, S. (2006). *Comprehensive school reform for Latino elementary-school students: A meta-analysis*. Commissioned by the National Task Force on Early Childhood Education for Hispanics. University of Wisconsin-Madison.

Boulton, M.J. (1995). Patterns of bully/victim problems in mixed race groups of children. *Social Development, 3*, 277–293.

Bransford, J., Derry, S., Berliner, D., Hammerness, K., & Beckett, K.L. (2005). Theories of learning and their roles in teaching. In L. Darling-Hammond & J. Bransford (Eds.), *Preparing teachers for a changing world: What teachers should learn and be able to do*. San Francisco: Jossey-Bass.

Bransford, J.D., Brown, A.L., & Cocking, R.R. (2000). *How people learn: Brain, mind experience, and school*. Washington, DC: National Academies Press.

Brown, A.L., & Campione, J.C. (1996). Psychological theory and the design of innovative learning environments: On procedures, principles, and systems. In L. Schauble & R. Glaser (Eds.), *Innovations in learning: New environments for education*. Mahwah, NJ: Lawrence Erlbaum Associates.

Brown, J.S., Collins, A., & Duguid, P. (1989). Situated cognition and the culture of learning. *Educational Researcher, 18*(1), 32–42.

Bruner, J. (1996). *The culture of education*. Cambridge, MA: Harvard University Press.

Capps, R. (2001). Hardship among children of immigrants: Findings from the 1999 national survey of American families (Policy Brief). Washington, DC: The Urban Institute. Retrieved March 17, 2002, from http://www.urban.org/publications/310096.html

Capps, R., Fix, M.E., Murray, J., Ost, J., Passel, J.S., & Hernández, S.H. (2005). The new demography of America's schools: Immigration and the No Child Left Behind Act. Washington, DC: The Urban Institute. Retrieved July 16, 2005, from http://www.urban.org/url.cfm?ID=311230

Center for Applied Linguistics. (2004). *Directory of two-way bilingual immersion programs in the United States*. Washington, DC: Author. Retrieved December 14, 2004, from http://www.cal.org/twi/directory/

Center for Applied Linguistics. (2005, March). *Guiding principles for dual language education*. Washington, DC: Author.

Christian, D., Genesee, F., Lindholm-Leary, K., & Howard, L. (2004). *Project 1.2 two-way immersion: Final progress report.* Berkeley: University of California, Center for Research on Education, Diversity & Excellence.

Cobb, B., Vega, D., & Kronauge, C. (2005). *Effects of an elementary dual language immersion school program on junior high school achievement of native Spanish speaking and native English speaking students.* Paper presented at the American Education Research Association annual conference, Montreal, Canada.

Cole, M. (1996). *Cultural psychology: A once and future discipline.* Cambridge, MA: Belkap Press.

Cole, M., & Engeström, Y. (1993). A cultural–historical approach to distributed cognition. In G. Salomon (Ed.), *Distributed cognitions: Psychological and educational considerations.* New York: Cambridge University Press.

Collier, V.P. (1987). Age and rate of acquisition of second language for academic purposes. *TESOL Quarterly, 21*(4), 617–641.

Dewey, J. (1938). *Experience and education.* New York: Collier Books.

Driscoll, M.P. (2000). *Psychology of learning and instruction* (2nd ed.). Needham Heights, MA: Allyn & Bacon.

Ellis, S. (1997). Strategy choice in sociocultural context. *Developmental Review, 17,* 490–524.

Figueroa, L. (2005). *The development of pre-reading knowledge in English and Spanish: Latino English language learners in a dual-language education context.* Paper presented at the American Education Research Association annual conference, Montreal, Canada.

Freire, P. (1970). *Pedagogy of the oppressed.* New York: Herder & Herder.

Fuller, B., Bein, E., Bridges, M., Halfon, N., Jang, H., Kuo, A., et al. (2007, May). *Latino children's early development: Roots of the immigrant paradox?* Paper presented at the National Institutes of Health Conference on ECLS-B Analyses, Bethesda, MD.

Fuller, B., & Clark, P. (1994). Raising school effects while ignoring culture? Local conditions and the influence of classroom tools, rules, and pedagogy. *Review of Educational Research, 64*(1), 119–157.

García, E.E. (2005). *Teaching and learning in two languages: Bilingualism and schooling in the United States.* New York: Teachers College Press.

García, E.E., & Cuellar, D. (2006). Who are these linguistically and culturally diverse students? *Teachers College Record, 108*(11), 2220–2246.

García, E., & Frede, E. (in press). Enhancing the knowledge base for serving young English language learners: A research and policy agenda. In E. García & E. Frede (Eds.), *Developing the research agenda for young English language learners.* New York: Teachers College Press.

García, E.E., & Jensen, B.T. (2009). Language development and early education of young Hispanic children in the United States.

Gardner, H. (2006). *The development of education of the mind.* New York: Routledge.

Geertz, C. (1973). *The interpretation of cultures.* New York: Basic Books.

Genesee, F. (Ed.). (1999). *Program alternatives for linguistically diverse students.* Berkeley: University of California, Center for Research on Education, Diversity & Excellence.

Gonzalez, N., Moll, L., & Amanti, C. (2005). *Funds of knowledge: Theorizing practices, households, communities, and classrooms.* Mahwah, NJ: Lawrence Erlbaum Associates.

Greene, J.P. (1998). *A meta-analysis of the effectiveness of bilingual education.* Claremont, CA: Thomas Rivera Policy Institute.

Greenwood, C.R., Horton, B.T., & Utley, C.A. (2002). Academic engagement: Current perspectives on research and practice. *School Psychology Review, 31*(3), 328–349.

Guthrie, J.T., Rueda, R., Gambrell, L., & Morrison, D. (2008). Roles of engagement, valuing, and identification in reading development of students from diverse backgrounds. In L. Morrow, R. Rueda, & D. Lapp (Eds.), *Handbook of research on literacy instruction: Issues of diversity, policy, and equity.* New York: Guilford.

Gutierrez, K., & Rogoff, B. (2003). Cultural ways of learning: Individual traits and repertoires of practice. *Educational Researcher, 32*(5), 19–25.

Hernández, D.J., Denton, N.A., & Macartney, S.E. (2008). Children in immigrant families: Looking to America's future. *Social Policy Report: A Publication of the Society for Research in Child Development, 22*(3), 1–24.

Hopstock, P.J., & Stephenson, T.G. (2003). *Native languages of LEP students: Descriptive study of services to LEP students and LEP students with disabilities* (special topic report no. 1) Arlington, VA: Development Associates, Inc., and U.S. Department of Education, Office of English Language Acquisition.

Howard, E.R., Sugarman, J., & Christian, D. (2003). *Trends in two-way immersion education: A review of the research.* Washington, DC: Center for Applied Linguistics.

Hutchins, E. (1996). *Cognition in the wild*. Cambridge, MA: MIT Press.

Jensen, B.T. (2007). Understanding immigration and psychological development: A multi-level ecological approach. *Journal of Immigrant and Refugee Studies, 5*(4), 27–48.

Jensen, B.T. (2008a). Raising questions for binational research in education: An exploration of Mexican primary school structure. In E. Szecsy (Ed.), *Resource book: Second binational symposium*. Tempe, AZ: Arizona State University. Retrieved April 3, 2007, from http://simposio.asu.edu/docs/2007/cdrom/book/jensen_PDF.pdf

Jensen, B. (2008b). *Understanding differences in binational reading development: Comparing Mexican and U.S. Hispanic students*. Paper presented at the annual meeting for the American Educational Research Association, New York.

Lesgold, A. (2004). Discussion: Contextual requirements for constructivist learning. *International Journal of Educational Research, 41*, 495–502.

McDermott, R., & Varenne, H. (1995). Culture as disability. *Anthropology & Education* Quarterly, 26*(3)*, 324–348.

Miller, P.H. (2002). *Theories of developmental psychology* (4th ed.). New York: Worth Publishers.

Nasir, N.S., & Hand, V.M. (2006). Exploring sociocultural perspectives on races, culture, and learning. *Review of Educational Research, 76*(4), 449–475.

National Center for Education Statistics. (1995). *Approaching kindergarten: A look at preschoolers in the United States* (National household survey). Washington, DC: U.S. Department of Education, Office of Educational Research and Improvement.

Portes, P. (2005). Dismantling educational inequality: A cultural–historical approach to closing the achievement gap. New York: Peter Lang Publishing.

Reardon, S.F., & Galindo, C. (2006). Patterns of Hispanic students' math and English literacy test scores. Report to the National Task Force on Early Childhood Education for Hispanics. Tempe, AZ: Arizona State University.

Rogoff, B. (2003). *The cultural nature of human development*. New York: Oxford University Press.

Rogoff, B., Mistry, J., Göncü, A., & Mosier, C. (1993). Guided participation in cultural activity by toddlers and caregivers. *Monographs of the Society for Research in Child Development, 58*(8), 1–179.

Rolstad, K., Mahoney, K., & Glass, G.V. (2005). The big picture: A meta-analysis of program effectiveness research on English language learners. *Educational Policy, 19*(4), 572–594.

Skinner, C.H., Pappas, D.N., & Davis, K.A. (2005). Enhancing academic engagement: Providing opportunities for responding and influencing students to choose to respond. *Psychology in the Schools, 42*(4), 389–403.

Slavin, R.E., & Cheung, A. (2005). A synthesis of research on language of reading instruction for English language learners. *Review of Education Research, 75*(2), 247–284.

Sugarman, J., & Howard, L. (2001). Two-way immersion shows promising results: Findings from a new study. *Language Links*. Washington, DC: Center for Applied Linguistics.

Valdés, G. (1996). *Con respeto: Bridging the distances between culturally diverse families and schools*. New York: Teachers College Press.

Valenzuela, A. (1999). *Subtractive schooling: U.S. Mexican youth and the politics of caring*. Albany, NY: State University of New York Press.

Vygotsky, L.S. (1978). *Mind in society: The development of higher order psychological processes*. Cambridge, MA: Harvard University Press.

Well, G., & Mejía Arauz, R. (2005). Toward dialogue in the classroom: Learning and teaching through inquiry. *Working Papers on Culture, Education and Human Development, 1*(4). Retrieved November 12, 2005, from http://www.uam.es/otros/ptcedh/2005v1_pdf/v1n4eng.pdf

Willig, A.C. (1985). A meta-analysis of selected studies on the effectiveness of bilingual education. *Review of Educational Research, 55*(3), 269–317.

Zúñiga, V., & Hernández-León, R. (Eds.). (2005). *New destinations: Mexican immigration in the United States*. New York: Russell Sage.

II

Pedagogical Perspective

7

Aligning the Content of Early Childhood Care and Education

Catherine Scott-Little and Jeanne L. Reid

In the past decade, efforts have accelerated to create a coordinated system of early care and education. As part of the prekindergarten (pre-K)[1]–third grade movement, also termed the *PK* movement, education policy makers have begun to reconceptualize preschool through third grade as a seamless, high-quality experience for children (Bogard & Takanishi, 2005). Standards, curriculum, and assessments offer the critical architecture for cohesive instructional content and smooth transitions during these formative years of learning and development.

The desire to build a systematic approach to children's early learning has been motivated by concerns about children's progress that have been quantified by research findings. First, children's learning and development from age 3 to 8 years is the foundation for their subsequent academic success. Children need to finish third grade with core literacy skills or they may have trouble "catching up" later (Bogard & Takanishi, 2005; Hamre & Pianta, 2005). Moreover, research has found that children gain substantially from high quality pre-K programs, but these gains often fade out in the early elementary grades (Magnuson, Ruhm, & Waldfogel, 2007). This finding has prompted some policy makers who have made substantial investments in pre-K to expand their focus to sustaining early education gains in the elementary school years (Dinkes, 2008) and to focus on strategies that help children make effective transitions into formal schooling.

Parents, teachers, and policy makers alike are increasingly concerned about whether their children are receiving high-quality early education. This concern has prompted educators to seek a more intentional and coordinated approach to educating children, and to focus on children's progress over time, with increasing attention to transitions that support children's learning rather than disrupt children's progress. Three components of instruction provide a foundation for an intentional and coordinated approach to education and effective transitions: *standards* articulate goals for children's learning, *curriculum* is the framework for how to teach, and *assessments* help answer the questions "How did we do?" "What could we do differently for these children or this child?" and "Where do we go from here?" This type of intentional and reflective

---

[1] *PK* refers to pre-K programs that are state-funded and often have the goal of school readiness.

109

pedagogy that recognizes the multiple transitions that characterize children's learning is perhaps the core of quality early childhood education (Burchinal et al., 2008; Pianta & Hadden, 2008).

The importance of familiarizing children with the environment to which they are transitioning and other activities to promote coordination between programs have long been recognized as a component of transition planning. But smooth transitions for young children require much more than creating memoranda of understanding, transferring children's records to their new schools, and having them visit their new classrooms ahead of time. Far more important is maintaining consistency between the content that they learn and the pedagogy that is used to teach the content.

Aligned standards, curricula, and assessments provide both a road map for what we want children to learn across the years and feedback on what children are learning. These tools support a planned, intentional, and sustained approach to pedagogy over time, in contrast to the uncoordinated, unintentional, and episodic approach that has characterized much of early education. Rather than focusing on structural components of quality such as class size, teacher education, and curriculum, the new approach focuses more on the nature and quality of learning opportunities over the critical years of early development in order to promote quality educational experiences at each age and continuity across age and grade levels (Pianta & Hadden, 2008).

In this chapter we provide a brief history of early learning standards, their relationship to curriculum and assessment, and working definitions of the types of alignment. We then analyze the complexities of alignment, describing what alignment is, what it is not, and what challenges it poses. Acknowledging that this conceptualization of alignment may be daunting, we present two examples of how it has been applied in the field. While the technologies for alignment are evolving and incomplete, we offer an approach to support transitions in early education that are characterized by continuity of instruction for a diverse population of children.

EARLY LEARNING STANDARDS AND THE NOTION OF ALIGNMENT

Although the field of early education has long had program standards to guide its efforts to promote quality, early learning guidelines or standards that articulate expectations for children's knowledge and abilities represent a more recent and somewhat controversial development. Some scholars see standards as the necessary starting point of a systematic approach to effective pedagogy and transitions for children who participate in early childhood programs. Others view standards with caution. Standards in early childhood can represent a fundamental shift in the pedagogical starting point, moving from the child's own interests to a prescribed content. A central tension in any effort to articulate standards, therefore, is the challenge of defining uniform goals for children's growth.

Several factors have combined to increase the attention and energy that are focused on early learning standards for very young children. The early childhood field has a long history of defining outcomes that are important for children before they enter school. During the early 1990s, the National Education Goals Panel Technical Work Group on Goal 1 defined school readiness and described five domains of children's development that are important for success in school (Kagan, Moore, & Bredekamp, 1995). In the late 1990s, the Head Start Child Outcome Framework outlined indicators of learning and development that Head Start programs should assess (Head Start Bureau, 2001). In addition, the Early Child Outcomes requirements of the Office of Special Education Programs established three broad outcomes for children with disabilities. Early intervention and early childhood special education programs must report the percentage of children being served who make progress on the three outcomes (Hebbeler & Barton, 2007). These initiatives sparked considerable debate at the national level about what outcomes are appropriate for young children.

The No Child Left Behind Act of 2001 (PL 107-110) created intense pressures on early education programs to raise quality, bolster children's academic skills, and establish accountability (Stipek, 2006). In 2002, the federal Good Start, Grow Smart initiative required states to develop voluntary early learning guidelines in the areas of early literacy and mathematics. Although states were required to develop the early learning guidelines, early education programs were not required to use them (Good Start, Grow Smart Interagency Workgroup, 2006).

At the state level, policy makers and leaders have embraced standards and accountability measures to protect their substantial investments in pre-K programs. In 2008, 38 states spent $4.6 billion—a 23% increase from the previous year—to enroll 1.1 million children in preschool with the goal of preparing them to succeed in school (Barnett, Epstein, Friedman, Boyd, & Hustedt, 2008).

Taken together, these policy initiatives at the federal and state levels served as an impetus for states to develop early learning standards. Today every state in the country has early learning standards for preschool programs (Scott-Little, Cassidy, Lower, & Ellen, 2010). In addition, 22 states have established standards for their infant and toddler programs (Scott-Little et al., 2010). Standards can create a binding thread in the often fragmented array of early childhood programs that pulls them together with a consistent agenda for the content of children's learning and development.

Types of Alignment

The creation of standards is not a stand-alone achievement. They are meaningful only when they are used to guide program development and pedagogy. Standards should reflect a seamless progression in children's development across the years of their early care and education to support their learning and development as they transition from one age level to the next. Indeed, standards, curriculum, and assessments that are *aligned* both within and across the preschool–to–third-grade years are the structural underpinnings of a cohesive approach to effective pedagogy in early childhood.

Alignment has been conceptualized in two ways. *Horizontal alignment* refers to the degree to which standards, curriculum, and assessments are consistent within a given age cohort. *Vertical alignment* refers to the degree to which standards, curriculum, or assessments are synchronized between age cohorts. Figure 7.1 illustrates the links among standards, curricula, and assessments that constitute alignment.

At the simplest level, horizontal alignment requires the curriculum to reflect the content that is expressed in the standards and requires assessments to assess what teachers are trying to teach. Horizontal alignment can promote consistency in the goals and expectations across programs that serve children of the same age. Given that significant variations in resources, philosophy, and pedagogy are common across early care and education programs, horizontal alignment with a common set of standards can promote more effective transitions by requiring the different programs to align their curricula and assessments to common goals for children. We recognize that variation across early care and education programs can be an asset to the field because it offers parents choices about the type of program that their child experiences. But we are suggesting that horizontal alignment to a common set of standards could decrease the wide variation (and inequities) in children's skills and knowledge at kindergarten entry because the programs would be working toward common goals. Horizontal alignment would therefore promote effective transitions by increasing the likelihood that children attending different early care and education programs all would experience a learning environment that stimulates their knowledge and development in the areas that are addressed in their state's early learning standards.

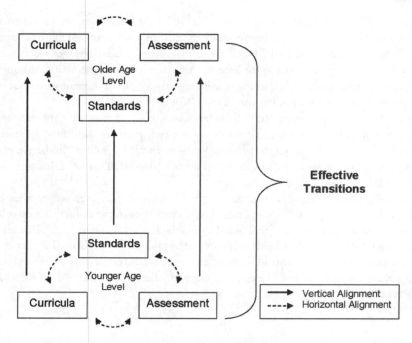

Figure 7.1.   Content alignment among standards, curricula, and assessments.

Vertical alignment ensures that schooling is organized so that children "have learning experiences that build on those in the previous years and connect closely with those to come" (Bogard & Takanishi, 2005, p. 3). Horizontal and vertical alignment work together to create continuity in pedagogy, resulting in more effective transitions for children. While the logic of this interdependency is clear, the disparate genesis of standards, curriculum, and assessment, both within and across age levels, has often meant that alignment is an afterthought rather than a guiding premise in their development. The early learning standards, curriculum, and assessments in each state generally have been developed by separate groups at different times (Scott-Little, Kagan, & Frelow, 2005). For example, standards are often written by a variety of stakeholders at the state level, whereas new curricula generally have been designed and tested by private companies, model programs, and teachers, and assessment tools have been developed independently by psychometricians. The result of this lack of cohesion is an urgent need to align these important structural components of children's educational experience.

THE COMPLEXITIES OF ALIGNMENT ANALYSES

Alignment methodologies have developed rapidly since No Child Left Behind mandated the creation of reading and mathematics standards and the periodic assessment of children's progress toward meeting those standards beginning in third grade. Although many people see assessment as the most prominent component of this mandate, it is important to evaluate alignment across all three aspects of education—standards, curricula, and assessments—in the K–12 years. Such efforts take us closer to valid measurement of student progress by asking the questions "What do we want to learn?" "Are we teaching the specified content?" and "Are we measuring it?" (Bhola, Impara, & Buckendahl, 2003; Flowers, Browder, & Ahlgrim-Delzell, 2006).

With this goal in mind, several states have begun the task of aligning multiple documents. In many cases, their purpose has been to ensure that the content of standards, curricula, and assessments matches to an acceptable degree within a given age group. Often, states use crosswalk matrices to determine whether enough similarity exists across documents to qualify them as "matching." The conceptualization of alignment described in this chapter expands our understanding of a systematic approach to pedagogy from a consideration of how well two or three documents "match" to a deeper analysis of the quality of alignment between content addressed in the different documents and how the content fits together both within and across the early years of learning. Relatively simple assessments of "match" are often termed *low-complexity analyses,* while multidimensional analyses that consider questions of quality are often termed *high-complexity analyses*. In the sections that follow, we offer a conceptualization of high-complexity alignment that evaluates the coherence of standards, curricula, and assessments along multiple dimensions both within and across age levels.

Horizontal Alignment Analyses

Horizontal alignment is a logical starting point for analysis because establishing the coherence of standards, curricula, and assessments within an age or grade level is a prerequisite for assessing their congruence over time. Determining whether the content across the three documents that are used within a given age level matches in both content and quality is thus a necessary step, and yet it is only the beginning for analyses that strive to support continuity, effective pedagogy, and smooth transitions.

Several methodologies have been proposed to evaluate alignment for K–12 standards, curriculum, and assessments (Blank, 2002; Porter, Smithson, Blank, & Zeidner, 2007; Webb, 2007). For example, Webb offered four criteria for alignment studies: categorical concurrence, depth of knowledge consistency, range of knowledge correspondence, and balance of representation. Categorical concurrence is essentially an assessment of how well items or indicators match across documents. The remaining three criteria address questions of quality. Depth of knowledge examines the relative difficulty or cognitive challenge posed by different objectives. Range of knowledge and balance of representation are analyses of individual objectives and also a more transcendent evaluation of the developmental goals served by a particular document. The Webb analysis is conducted in two stages: 1) reviewers code the depth of knowledge that the standards articulate as the appropriate content for pedagogy, and 2) reviewers code the depth of knowledge levels for corresponding assessment items and curriculum objectives. Findings are then reported for each of the four criteria. Importantly, reviewers or their sponsors must make the qualitative judgment regarding what level of alignment or concurrence across the documents is acceptable.

This analysis and other K–12 methodologies are not immediately transferable to early childhood education, however, because the early years of learning and development pose unique challenges to alignment efforts. Five challenges must be addressed when horizontal alignment analyses are conducted and interpreted in early childhood.

The first challenge is to determine the level at which to conduct the analysis. In early childhood, standards fall under multiple developmental domains, usually socioemotional skills, physical or motor development, cognitive skills and general knowledge, language and literacy, and approaches to learning. Within these domains, authors usually articulate multiple standards, which are then broken down into multiple indicators that reflect the operational components of the broader goals expressed in each standard. Assessments of alignment can thus occur on several different levels: domains, standards, indicators or items, and/or transcendent constructs of development and learning. Consequently, alignment reviewers must consider the appropriate level or levels of analysis across documents.

A second challenge is that early childhood standards, curricula, and assessments have rarely been developed by the same people, posing further problems for horizontal alignment analyses and hindering the interpretation or use of results from the analyses. Standards, the logical cornerstone of this pedagogical infrastructure, have often been the last of the three documents to emerge. Consequently, standards and curriculum may reflect different approaches to or philosophies of child development and learning. For example, while the standards may be holistic in their approach to development, curriculum and/or assessments may focus more on discrete skills in areas such as mathematics or literacy. While neither approach is right or wrong, the disjuncture poses challenges to conducting alignment analyses and is likely to result in analyses which indicate that the standards and curriculum are misaligned.

When standards and the curriculum have disparate authors, there may be different levels of emphasis on particular skills, knowledge, or learning dispositions. Alignment analyses will identify areas of misalignment in these cases, but it may not be immediately clear whether these different levels of emphasis reflect misalignment that should be corrected or whether the difference appropriately reflects the different functions of the documents, one to specify pedagogical goals (i.e., "what" teachers should address) and the other to guide the pedagogical process in the classroom (i.e., "how" teachers should teach).

Another challenge to conducting and interpreting horizontal alignment analyses is the disjuncture in the genesis of standards and assessments. We know intuitively that the content of standards should determine the content of assessments, and that the assessments should measure how well teachers have taught and children have learned the expected content. Yet in the real world, assessments often come first, prompting the unfortunate but understandable situation in which persons writing standards may think, "This is what will be assessed, so we should make sure that we articulate it in our standards." Though standards and assessments may be considered "aligned" within this framework, they are not the product of a comprehensive approach to the articulation of learning goals and do not use this approach to choose curricula and assessments that support the fulfillment of those goals.

A fourth challenge to alignment efforts is that there are differences in the nature of standards and assessments. By necessity, assessments are typically more parsimonious than standards. Indeed, few people would advocate assessing every standard, a mandate that might require educators to spend more time performing assessment than facilitating learning in the classroom. Given this premise, however, the harder question is, "What standards should we assess?" Alignment reviewers must exercise considerable judgment about this qualitative question in order to conclude whether there is appropriate alignment between standards and assessments. Quantitative alignment analyses may reveal patterns of alignment and misalignment, but considerable thought must be given to the conclusions that are drawn from the analyses to determine whether the assessment has addressed a sufficient number of standards and whether the standards that are being addressed in the assessment reflect content that is developmentally significant.

Finally, horizontal alignment analyses are challenging because the number and type of assessments that are available differ across the areas of children's learning and development that are addressed in early learning standards. We have yet to develop a comprehensive set of assessments to evaluate all of the components of early development and learning. Although tools to assess reading and mathematics skills are plentiful, assessments for social-emotional skills and approaches to learning are evolving (Snow & Van Hemel, 2008). Furthermore, the types of assessments that are used to collect data often vary according to the area of learning and development that is being addressed. Children's social-emotional growth and approaches to learning may more often be assessed with naturalistic, observational measures, whereas areas such as emergent literacy or mathematical knowledge may be assessed with standardized, on-demand tasks. Therefore, alignment analyses are complicated by the fact that the content addressed in different areas within the standards may be assessed differently and by the unevenness in the availability of assessments to address different areas of children's learning and development.

Vertical Alignment Analyses

The content of standards, curricula, and assessments should progress over time, with the broad goal of constructing the foundation of skills, knowledge, and a love of learning that will support a child's achievement in school and beyond. Teachers should be responsive to individual children's successes and pitfalls in ways that nurture their progress both within grades and across the continuum of preschool and elementary education. Vertically aligned standards, curriculum, and assessments could support this type of coherent instruction that facilitates children's ability to experience transitions with natural ease, rather than disjuncture. Indeed, vertical alignment is more commonly thought of as an important element of effective transitions than is horizontal alignment.

Although vertical alignment is intuitively appealing, it is conceptually and technically challenging in practice due to the complexities and unanswered questions about early learning and development. As with horizontal alignment, "match" among the content of standards, assessment, and/or curricula is a necessary, but not sufficient, component of vertical alignment, because "match" among standards, curricula, and assessments for different ages does not guarantee that the documents will promote high-quality educational experiences.

The quality of the alignment among standards, curricula, and assessments across age and grade levels must also be evaluated. Two major considerations related to the quality of vertical alignment must be addressed.

First, vertical analyses need to consider the process of development over time. Content that is appropriate for one age cohort simply may be inappropriate for another. It may also be critical for students to master certain content in order to learn other content in a later year, yet the precursor skills "drop out" of the standards as children age. For example, nurturing young children's attachment to caring and consistent adults is a natural component of infant–toddler programs, but it is unlikely to be an explicit element of pedagogy in subsequent years. Instead, standards, curricula, and assessments are more likely to address children's relationships with adults and peers in preschool and early elementary school, a component of development that is affected by early attachment relationships but is nevertheless a different construct. Clearly, the idea of alignment as a simple match of content over time is inadequate for vertical alignment.

In this context, a challenge for current vertical alignment analyses is the general lack of established learning trajectories for specific areas of learning and development in early childhood. Sufficient research has not been done to document the explicit paths of children's learning across the ages in order to document how specific areas of development and learning unfold over time. Thus, we do not have data to substantiate how particular areas of learning progress across ages. While scholars are making progress in articulating these common patterns, the lack of a consensus regarding the progression of early learning in many areas leaves alignment analyses without an important source of knowledge.

We do have research in some areas of development (such as children's language and literacy development) that indicates general patterns or learning trajectories, but within these areas there are individual differences in learning that may not conform to the patterns. For example, while we do have research that indicates a developmental sequence of language development that is similar for all children, the rate of learning across and within languages can vary greatly (Bowman, Donovan, & Burns, 2001). So even if we have documented learning trajectories within a specific area of learning, individual differences in children's development within this area mean that the documented learning trajectories are not applicable for all children, which presents further challenges for vertical alignment analyses.

A second element that relates to the quality of vertical alignment is the fact that early learning differs from later learning in ways that pose unique challenges to efforts to align early childhood education. Because early learning is episodic and integrated in nature, it is often more difficult to specify the discrete skills and knowledge that young children should possess by a certain age than it is to specify them in older learners. Skills learned at one age may combine with knowledge learned at another age to nurture a new and more advanced skill that may emerge gradually. For example, fine motor skills that emerge in the first years of life combine with print awareness later to foster early writing skills.

Indeed, early learning differs fundamentally from later learning in its orientation around domains of development that are interdependent. Whereas early learning is often understood as a complex orchestration of skills across developmental domains, later learning is usually divided among academic subject areas such as mathematics, reading, science, social studies, and the arts. The shift from a developmental orientation to an academic orientation is gradual and inexact in its timing. How to configure this progression in alignment analyses is an unavoidable tension in efforts to create congruence of instructional content over time.

Common Concerns for Horizontal and Vertical Alignment Analyses

Layered on top of the fundamental complexities of early learning is the dramatic individual, cultural, and linguistic diversity that characterizes children in the United States. Articulating aligned standards, curricula, and assessments is challenging enough, and developing ideas about what learning should look like for children with different abilities and disabilities, cultures, and languages over time further complicates the task. The particularly uneven nature of development and learning among children with disabilities increases the difficulty of alignment efforts. Children with disabilities may advance remarkably in several areas but struggle to integrate their advances among domains. Alignment analyses to date have given minimal attention to the learning patterns and needs of these children.

The incomplete research base on the educational implications of cultural differences for learning is also a serious weakness. The meaning of a child's silence, for instance, can differ across cultures. Likewise, we have limited knowledge of how English language learners gain knowledge related to concepts and simultaneously acquire language skills in two languages.

The conceptualization of both horizontal and vertical alignment is thus quite complex in practice and lacks the foundation of a complete knowledge base. In spite of these challenges, the need to establish both types of alignment across the early years of learning cannot wait. An aligned, coherent pedagogy is necessary in order to support effective transitions for children among the notoriously fragmented array of early childhood programs.

RECONCEPTUALIZING ALIGNMENT TO PROMOTE EFFECTIVE TRANSITIONS

To capture the complexity of progress within and across age cohorts and to serve the diverse children who attend early education programs, alignment analyses must move beyond the consideration of matching content across documents. Using crosswalks to compare content across programs for children of a particular age or over time for a cohort of children is a good start, but this work will not collect the data that we need in order to analyze the continuous instructional quality that standards, curriculum, and assessment should support. Similarly, efforts to back-map content from one age to another—that is, simplifying the content from an older age group and including it in a young age group—in order to create the appearance of alignment are ill advised. These efforts include taking standards from an older age group and reconfiguring them in a similar form for a younger age group. Such an approach could lead to the push-down of academic pedagogy that inappropriately presents advanced academic content during the early years of care and schooling—all in an effort to create seamless transitions.

Instead, we recommend a more labor-intensive and thoughtful process that begins by considering where children are in their development and where we want them to go. This approach to alignment involves some collective discussions among stakeholders about developmental philosophies and our hopes for our children. Stakeholders might ask themselves questions such as "What areas of learning do we consider uniformly important for our children and why? How will we nurture diverse learning styles across cultures? How do we think instruction should change as children move through the age or grade levels of our educational system?" These are not easy questions, but their answers can inform any alignment effort.

Alignment analyses in early childhood need to be highly complex, technical endeavors that consider both match and quality of instructional content within and across age cohorts. Whereas the technical process of an alignment effort may be conducted by a small group of individuals, the philosophical process that defines its purpose and the use of its results must occur on a broader, more inclusive level. Indeed, this challenge requires a collaboration of stakeholders to articulate thoughtfully values and goals to inform the process from the start and to guide the interpretation of the results, with the goal of nurturing meaningful and coherent transitions for children. In our own work, we have tried to apply some of these considerations to varying degrees in two examples that follow.

Promoting the Use of Aligned Curricula and Assessments: Minnesota's Experience

In 2006, Minnesota began to plan a pilot Quality Rating and Improvement System (QRIS). Plans called for the QRIS to be tested in four local communities and then eventually to be implemented on a statewide basis. QRIS planners recognized the importance of curricula and assessments in shaping the experiences of children in infant–toddler and preschool classrooms, and they felt that the QRIS must incorporate some requirements for the curricula and assessments that would be used in participating programs in order to promote high quality. As a result, the planners decided to develop a process to approve curricula and instructional assessments, the use of which would then be required of programs participating in the QRIS program. The Department of Human Services convened a committee to develop criteria and an approval process. Programs from the QRIS pilot areas were asked to submit curricula and assessments for review and approval.

The review committees that were charged with developing criteria for approving curricula and assessments decided that alignment with Minnesota's early learning standards, the Minnesota Early Childhood Indicators of Progress, was a fundamental requirement in order for curricula and assessments to be approved (Minnesota Parent Aware, n.d.). The committees operationalized alignment at three levels.

First, the curriculum or assessment had to address each of the six domains that were included in the early learning standards: social and emotional development, approaches to learning, language and literacy development, creativity and the arts, cognitive development, and physical and motor development.

Second, the goals and objectives of a curriculum and the specific areas that were addressed within an assessment had to be "reasonably aligned" with the Early Childhood Indicators of Progress in order to be approved. The committee expected to see at least a modest degree of consistency with the early learning standards within each domain.

Finally, the committee considered the approach of the curricula and assessments when deciding which ones should be approved. They felt that it was important for curricula and assessments to be generally consistent with the holistic and child-centered approach to early education that was articulated in the Early Childhood Indicators of Progress. Curricula were required to address all domains, include a balance of teacher-initiated and child-initiated instructional strategies, and provide a variety of types of learning experiences in order to be approved. Assessments had to address all domains of development and be observation based in order to be approved. While this alignment requirement was somewhat less concrete than the others, it addressed the notion that alignment is more than a simple "match" between the areas of children's learning and development that are addressed. In addition to simply looking at whether the content of the curricula and the assessments matched the standards, the committee sought to promote curricula and assessments that were also aligned or consistent with the values, goals, and philosophy of their early learning standards.

This example has relevance to effective transitions. By requiring the programs that participate in the QRIS to use recommended curricula and assessments, Minnesota is hoping to increase the likelihood that children's experiences will help them develop specified skills and knowledge, no matter what program they attend. The goal is to decrease the disparities in what children know and are able to do when they enter kindergarten, thereby promoting effective transitions.

Analyzing Horizontal and Vertical Alignment: Pennsylvania's Experience

Pennsylvania is developing an accountability system to provide data on the nature of the state's early childhood programs and on the learning and development of children who are enrolled in these programs. As part of this effort, Pennsylvania has recognized alignment as a fundamental requirement of the accountability system. Standards and assessments must be aligned horizontally and vertically in order to promote continuity for children and to infuse consistent accountability requirements across the early care and education system.

The state commissioned an in-depth study of alignment among the standards for birth through third grade and alignment among the standards and assessments for birth through pre-K (the Ounce Scale and the Work Sampling System). The study also included a more cursory analysis of consistency between the pre-K assessment and the third grade assessments. The Office of Child Development and Early Learning (OCDEL) asked Drs. Sharon Lynn Kagan of Teachers College, Columbia University; and Catherine Scott-Little of the University of North Carolina at Greensboro to conduct alignment analyses to guide OCDEL's future decisions about the standards and assessments used in their early childhood programs and early elementary grades.

The research team knew that these alignment analyses would differ from commonly used alignment analyses in early childhood education because the study would examine both horizontal and vertical alignment across a far greater age span than is typical—birth through third grade. Results from a thorough review of the K–12 alignment literature indicated the need to implement a series of high-complexity alignment analyses in order to gain a complete picture of the degree to which the various documents were aligned. A unidimensional approach that simply looked at the "match" between standards of different ages and between standards and assessments would not be sufficient to support meaningful coherence in the content of multiple programs.

Recognizing that there were multiple levels of domains, standards, and indicators in both the standards and assessments, and that a wide age span was under analysis, the team decided to develop a common metric of learning and developmental constructs that could be used to compare and analyze data from multiple documents addressing the first 8 years of life. The first step was to develop a template that described the constructs of learning and development that are important from birth through third grade. The team began with a template developed from previous analyses of infant–toddler and prekindergarten (pre-K) standards and modified it to incorporate content that is appropriate for kindergarten through third grade. The resulting template included 100 constructs, each of which operationally defines a skill or knowledge area. The 100 constructs are organized into five domains—physical, social-emotional, approaches toward learning, language and communication, and cognitive development. The content of both standards and assessments can be assigned, or "coded," to constructs within the template. For example, an infant–toddler standard that states "begin to link the sound or words with their meaning" would be coded as the construct "vocabulary, meaning, and linguistic concepts." A kindergarten standard that states, "Name and describe new concepts" would be coded the same way. Because the template is applicable across age levels and across both standards and assessments, the results of the coding process yielded data that could be compared or analyzed to determine the degree to which alignment is evident.

The second step in the alignment analyses was to determine the dimensions or elements of alignment that should be examined. As we have described, it is possible for the content of standards and/or assessments to match but to be of poor quality, perhaps leaving out important content or covering the same content but in different degrees of thoroughness. Therefore, informed by Webb's (2007) framework, the group determined that the quality of alignment would be assessed on the basis of the consistency of the content across four parameters:

- *Balance:* Are the domains of development and learning emphasized equally across the documents?

- *Coverage:* Do the documents address the same constructs?

- *Depth:* Are the specific constructs within the domains addressed or emphasized to the same degree?

- *Difficulty:* Is the cognitive "complexity" or difficulty of standards roughly equivalent to the complexity or difficulty indicated by the assessments for the same age level, and do the standards for different age levels reflect a reasonable progression in difficulty?

Once the methodology was established, the team conducted a number of alignment analyses:

- Horizontal analyses to examine the alignment between the infant–toddler standards and the Ounce Scale assessment and to examine alignment between the pre-K standards and the Work Sampling System

- Vertical analyses to examine the alignment between the infant–toddler, pre-K, kindergarten, first, and second-grade standards

- Vertical analyses to examine the alignment between the pre-K assessment (Work Sampling System) and the standardized assessment used in third grade (the Pennsylvania System of School Assessment or PSSA)

Although a detailed description of the findings from these analyses is beyond the scope of this chapter, we present some of the significant findings to illustrate the implications of this type of high-complexity analysis for improving alignment and, ultimately, the coherence of transitions for children. Further information is reported by Kagan, Scott-Little, and Reid (2009).

The horizontal alignment analyses indicated that, overall, there was generally acceptable alignment between the standards and assessments that were used in programs serving children from birth through pre-K. The balance analyses indicated that there was a high degree of alignment between the domains covered by the pre-K standards and the Work Sampling System. However, the horizontal analyses of alignment between the infant–toddler standards and the Ounce Scale suggested a lower degree of alignment. The two documents were organized by different age levels, and the degree to which they addressed each of the five domains was inconsistent. Furthermore, the pattern of alignment between the standards and the assessment differed for each of the five age levels within the infant–toddler period. Results suggested that the standards and the Ounce Scale may have somewhat different philosophical orientations regarding which areas of infant–toddler development should be emphasized. In addition, the coverage and depth analyses to examine horizontal alignment between the standards and the Ounce Scale or Work Sampling System indicated some misalignment between the standards and assessments. The standards often addressed a broader array of constructs than did the assessments. As with the balance analyses, these findings were particularly true for the infant–toddler documents. Finally, the difficulty analyses indicated that there was some misalignment between the cognitive complexity or age level of the expectations articulated by the standards and the assessments.

Vertical analyses of the standards from birth through third grade also yielded examples of both alignment and misalignment. The balance analyses showed that the standards for infants and toddlers emphasized developmental domains to a greater extent than did the standards for pre-K and kindergarten, while the pre-K, kindergarten, and first- through third-grade standards placed a greater emphasis on academic areas. Findings from the coverage and depth analyses indicated that some constructs were addressed in one age level and not in another, sometimes with "starts and stops" across the age levels. In these cases, the construct was addressed in the standards for one age level, was not addressed at the next age level, and then was addressed again for the following age level. The analyses also indicated differences in the degree to which constructs within the same domain were addressed across the age levels. Difficulty analyses indicated that there was an appropriate progression of difficulty. Generally, the pre-K standards were more difficult than the infant–toddler standards, and the kindergarten standards were more difficult than the pre-K standards. There were, however, examples in which the difficulty level was deemed to be equal across the two age levels that were being compared, and examples in which the standards written for younger children were deemed to be more difficult than those for older children.

Finally, the vertical analyses comparing the pre-K assessment with the third-grade assessment provided evidence of both alignment and misalignment. For example, the types of assessments used at the two age levels were quite different, which created misalignment in the basic nature of the assessments. Whereas the Work Sampling System is a naturalistic, observation-based assessment, the third grade PSSA is a standardized, paper-and-pencil assessment administered in a testing situation. Beyond this obvious source of misalignment, the team sought to examine the constructs addressed by the two assessments to determine whether they provided data on relatively consistent areas of children's learning. Again, an obvious source of misalignment was noted—the Work Sampling System collects data on all five domains of development and learning, while the PSSA only addresses reading and mathematics.

To examine alignment more thoroughly, the team analyzed the reading and mathematics constructs that were addressed by the two assessments. The results indicated that there was a relatively high degree of alignment between the early literacy constructs addressed by the Work Sampling System and the reading constructs addressed by the PSSA. The mathematics constructs addressed by the two assessments also were similar; the PSSA addressed only one construct (data analysis and probability) that was not addressed on the Work Sampling System. For both literacy and mathematics, the Work Sampling System addressed precursor skills that were either directly or indirectly related to the literacy and mathematics skills addressed by the third-grade PSSA. Results suggest that there was a reasonable degree of alignment within the two specific content areas, reading and mathematics, that were assessed by the PSSA.

Results from these analyses provided in-depth data on alignment that Pennsylvania used to revise its early childhood standards. Because the analysis used a multidimensional approach, the data rendered a robust set of implications for policy and practice. At the domain level in both the horizontal and vertical analyses, the evidence of misalignment in some areas of development suggested opportunities to reexamine the philosophy of child development and pedagogy that the standards should reflect. Differences in the types of assessments and the areas of learning and development that are assessed also suggested that the state should consider adopting a comprehensive assessment strategy that is coherent both within and across age levels. At the indicator level, revisions to the standards to eliminate areas of misalignment across the first 8 years of life could prevent the disjuncture in pedagogical practice that too often characterizes early education programs across the country.

The goal in any such analysis is to improve alignment across multiple parameters to provide a more coherent basis for teaching, learning, and assessments within and across age and grade levels and, ultimately, to provide more continuity for children. The systemic approach to aligning standards and assessments across multiple age levels will promote smoother transitions for children.

ALIGNMENT, PEDAGOGY, AND TRANSITIONS FOR CHILDREN

Alignment should be viewed as a core element of transitions. Alignment analyses that simply create crosswalks to determine the extent to which standards for different age levels or standards, assessment, and curricula within a particular age level "match" are insufficient and do not do justice to the complex nature of alignment across and within age or grade levels. The analyses also must look across multiple parameters of alignment to determine the degree to which the documents are in sync and the degree to which the collective group of documents are high quality (i.e., address all the areas of children's development and learning that are important, and do so in a coherent manner).

This process requires us to do some deep thinking about children's development. Instead of simply asking, "Are our children getting proper exposure to emergent mathematics skills in preschool?" we might also ask, "How does the progression of social-emotional growth support mathematics learning, and what should this learning look like in our diverse population of children?" Instead of simply asking, "Are we assessing the proper literacy skills in preschool?" we might also ask, "How are we nurturing approaches to learning that will foster progress in literacy and other domains, and do we want to try to capture this progress in an assessment?" As children age, analyses should address fundamental questions regarding how development in the various domains is interrelated, how development at one stage supports development at the next stage, and when and how academic content should be introduced to children. Alignment analyses can thus yield data on the extent to which the content that is addressed at earlier ages is foundational to the content that is addressed later and whether the developmental progression of content is evident across the age and grade levels.

Alignment analyses also must take into account the extent to which the standards, curricula, and assessments reflect common values about how children should be educated and which areas of development and learning should be emphasized. Alignment in the philosophy that underlies standards, curricula, and assessments is perhaps just as important as alignment of the content in these documents. Although this type of alignment is somewhat less precise than alignment analyses that focus solely on content, the degree to which the standards, curricula, and assessments emanate from a shared understanding of early childhood development is equally important. Alignment in the philosophical underpinning of early care and education is a key element of effective transitions, minimizing the disjunctures or inconsistencies that children experience as they transition from one setting to another.

Although the idea of using results from the alignment analyses to produce greater continuity for children is logical and seems to hold great promise for improving children's transitions, the movement toward greater alignment across grade levels will not be easy. Results of the analyses suggest that some fundamental questions must be addressed, questions that reveal philosophic differences at the very heart of education. For instance, one source of misalignment relates to differences between a developmental approach and an academic approach to content. The standards for older children tend to exhibit more academic content, whereas standards for younger children reflect a more developmental approach. The challenge now is to look more systematically at how the domains and academic subject areas are introduced and to what extent they are emphasized within the content of the standards across the age and grade levels.

A second fundamental challenge to alignment analyses relates to differences in beliefs about how children should be educated. Across the country, the standards and assessments that are used by programs serving children before they enter kindergarten typically reflect a more child-centered and holistic approach, whereas the standards and assessments for kindergarten through third grade reflect a more traditional K–12 education approach where content is back mapped, instruction is less integrated, and assessments are less holistic. This shift in orientation is apparent in both the standards and the assessments and is likely to be evident in the nature of the classrooms and instruction that children experience when they enter elementary school. In order to promote smooth transitions, educators need to address this disjuncture in the fundamental approaches that undergird teaching and learning in different settings across the age span of birth through third grade. It is possible that a forward-mapping approach to developing standards and alignment (an approach that starts with the standards and/or assessments for the younger age and uses them to determine the content that should be addressed at older ages) holds promise as a means for ensuring that the content at each age level is appropriate, developmentally significant, and aligned across age and grade levels.

We recognize that this is no easy task, but to promote continuity in children's experiences as they move from early care and learning settings to elementary school, the shift from a child-centered approach to a more direct instruction approach must be articulated and implemented intentionally. This shift should be undertaken with an eye toward what can best support young children's learning and development at each age and grade level. The state must address questions such as "What is the most appropriate balance between teacher-initiated and child-initiated instruction and how should that balance change across the age levels?" and "When and how can integrated, developmentally oriented teaching and subject-area teaching complement each other across the age levels?" Examining alignment of standards and assessments is a good first step, but in order for the alignment analyses to promote continuity and effective transitions, states will need to build on results from the alignment analyses to answer these complex questions.

CONCLUSION

We have suggested that alignment of standards, curricula, and assessments is a key element of efforts to promote effective transitions for children. We also have advocated for alignment analyses to address multiple parameters in order to evaluate the degree to which the standards, curricula, and assessments that are used in preschool and primary settings promote continuity for children. Efforts to promote effective transitions must do more than prepare children to move from one physical setting to another: The settings and all that children experience within them must be realigned to promote continuity. Because standards, curricula, and assessments are the heart of the pedagogy that guides the instruction children receive, it is important to look at how well they are aligned as part of transition efforts. Indeed, high-complexity alignment analyses must be used to determine the quality of the alignment between standards, curricula, and assessments in order to promote quality programming and smooth transitions for children.

Case Study—The Wisconsin Model Early Learning Standards

An Aligned Approach to the Content of Early Learning Programs

Jeanne L. Reid

In April 2002, the federal government announced the Good Start, Grow Smart initiative, which required states to create voluntary early learning standards for young children who were enrolled in state-funded child care. In return, programs were given greater flexibility to spend their federal child care funds as they wished. Wisconsin responded with an ambitious effort to create standards that would reflect the complex nature of learning and development during the first 6 years of a child's life, up to the beginning of first grade. These standards would be useful to a variety of early childhood educators who are independently making curricular and assessment choices. The result is an approach that is aligned both horizontally and vertically to standards that provide the basis for high-quality early care and education.

General Description   Katherine McGurk is a leader in the effort and a child care planner in the Department of Workforce Development[2] at the Wisconsin Bureau of Early Childhood Education. According to her, the state began developing its standards by looking inward and creating an inventory of the benchmarks that existed for early learning within local school districts, then looking outward and assessing how other states had tackled the challenge of early standards and the lessons they could offer. "We learned from them, 'Do not create the standards in a silo,'" said McGurk (personal communication, July 1, 2009). The result was a collaborative approach to developing standards that would establish a platform for cohesive content across a diverse array of early care and education programs.

McGurk and colleagues at the Department of Workforce Development reached out to their counterparts in the Department of Public Instruction and the Department of Health and Family Services, as well as leaders in early childhood special education, the Head Start Collaboration Project, the state's Cooperative Educational Service Agencies (12 regional agencies that provide support services to school districts across the state),

---

[2]The Bureau of Early Childhood Education is now in a newly formed Department of Children and Families.

the Wisconsin affiliate of the National Association for the Education of Young Children, and professional organizations representing the multifaceted early childhood workforce. Their efforts to forge a diverse coalition of people representing state and local governmental and nongovernmental agencies were richly rewarded with a collaboration that has endured despite leadership and staff changes along the way.

The participants were organized into an 11-person steering committee and a larger advisory committee that was composed of the many stakeholders whose participation was critical to the implementation of the standards. The steering committee's job was to do background work, put ideas on paper, and ultimately write the standards, while the advisory committee conducted a review process to provide feedback on the steering committee's work. "We learned that we really had to have a collaborative workgroup from the beginning and then we would take it out through the advisory committee to the workforce and focus groups to share materials and to establish relationships to have their buy-in from the start," said McGurk (personal communication, July 1, 2009).

The steering committee was faced with the challenge of creating standards that would be appropriate for multiple programs serving a diverse population of children of different ages, and it had to overcome a substantial obstacle: how to depict a common trajectory of learning and development over time that would be inclusive of all young children. As McGurk explained,

> We had a very strong voice on the steering committee who did not want any type of [age-specific] checklist to be created. The concern was that a school district might use the list to disadvantage some children. Our belief was that schools should be ready for children, not that the children should be ready for schools. After very long discussions, that became a premise of the committee's work. (Personal communication, July 1, 2009)

The committee proceeded with caution, mindful that articulating age-specific norms of child development could be construed as a tool to label children in negative ways.

The first step was to agree on guiding principles:

- A child's early learning and development is multidimensional.

- Expectations for children must be guided by knowledge of child growth and development.

- Early relationships matter.

- Children are individuals who develop at various rates.

- Children are members of cultural groups that share developmental patterns.

- Children exhibit a range of skills and competencies within any domain of development (Wisconsin Department of Public Instruction, 2008, p. 1).

Guided by these premises, the committee took a careful look at the research on child development. "It was not a process of looking at the academic standards and backing them up. We started by looking at the research on how children grow. We wanted a document for both typically and nontypically developing children, a document that could be used with all parents," McGurk said (personal communication, July 1, 2009).

After much discussion, the committee decided to abandon the idea of using age bands to indicate the typical timing of children's growth. The bands, which are common in other state standards, would have given users an idea of when to expect a child to demonstrate a particular skill or knowledge. Instead, the committee decided to offer developmental continuums, which present the progression of learning and development that most children follow in mastering a particular skill, but that do not indicate the ages at which this progression should occur. Wisconsin has a single set of standards for children from birth to the beginning of first grade with no age markers for the sequence of learning and development that the standards depict.

The developmental continuums offered a way for the steering committee to create continuity in the content of early childhood programs over time that would reflect the complexity of children's development, without being subject to the disadvantages associated with specific age markers. The committee wrote, 'While children generally develop in similar stages and sequences, greatly diverse patterns of behavior and learning emerge as a result of the interaction of several factors, including genetic predisposition and physical characteristics 'socioeconomic status' and the values, beliefs, and cultural and political practices of their families and communities" (Wisconsin Department of Public Instruction, 2008, p. 4). The state's approach to vertical alignment thus emphasizes the typical progression of learning and development across the early years, not the typical age at which any step in this progression should occur.

The goal is for any teacher, caregiver, or parent to be able to locate a child on the continuum, regardless of the child's age, and to consider strategies for supporting the child's development. This common resource on early learning and development, in turn, would nurture continuity in the content of programs that serve children up to the beginning of first grade. The steering committee explained, "These standards support the development of optimal learning experiences that can be adapted in response to the individual developmental patterns of children" (Wisconsin Department of Public Instruction, 2008, p. 4). In this way, the standards depart from offering a specific road map for pedagogy and instead foster a deeper understanding of child development, which caregivers and teachers may then use to inform their own practice (Brown, 2007). Rather than reading the standards to learn what they should be doing and when, teachers and caregivers can read them as a primer in the complex and uneven patterns of child development.

To this end, the standards are organized into five domains: health and physical development, social and emotional development, language development and communication, approaches to learning, and cognition and general knowledge. Within each domain, the standards appear as performance standards, which specify the demonstrable skills and knowledge that each standard involves. Developmental continuums suggest where the particular skills or knowledge fit into children's growth over time, program standards outline what program elements would support the standard, and sample strategies offer ideas for how adults may interact with children to support the learning and development articulated in the standard.

After an intensive research, writing, and review process, in 2003 the steering committee produced an initial set of early learning standards for children from age 3 through the completion of kindergarten. Despite the committee's concerted efforts to build a broad coalition, the response from professionals in the infant and toddler field was a loud, "Why didn't you include us?" (K. McGurk, personal communication, July 1, 2009). As a result, the steering committee went back to work and produced a set of early learning standards for children from birth to the beginning of first grade, which were completed in 2008.

Implementation   To ensure that the standards are used as intended—to create continuity in the content of instruction—across programs in the early years of children's development, the three Wisconsin departments that led the initiative (Workforce Development, Public Instruction, and Health and Family Services) have jointly sponsored training programs at the local level. The state has approved 70 early learning standard trainers who provided some 55 training sessions to 968 people in 2008 (*Wisconsin Model Early Learning Standards Training Report,* 2008). (Not all trainers conduct training every year.) The goal of the training is to make the standards a common language that all programs and families can use to enhance their work with children (K. McGurk, personal communication, July 1, 2009).

The training is very much communitywide and includes birth-to-three early intervention programs, child care providers, Head Start programs, preschools for 3-year-olds and 4-year-olds, teachers of 4-year-old and 5-year-old public school kindergarten children, special education programs for ages 3 through 5, and families. "You get them all into the same room, and they're all hearing the same things about the standards, and you get a lot of 'Ahas!' They learn as much from each other as from the trainer," said Arlene Wright, a state-sponsored early learning standards coach who helps to organize the training (personal communication, July 6, 2009). The goal is to create cross-system dialogue and collaboration that mirrors the cross-system work at the state level. Jill Haglund, a steering committee member in the Department of Public Instruction, says, "The learning at the local level is equally as important as what we are doing at the state level" (personal communication, July 13, 2009).

How programs and parents use the standards to alter their practice may nevertheless diverge. For example, Wright explains, "Child care providers are learning to emphasize each one of the domains, to think about what they are teaching and how they are teaching it, to develop lesson plans to reflect the standards, to use more of a child-centered project approach instead of 'my favorite teaching units' approach, and how to focus on small groups of children who are at different levels, including children with disabilities" (personal communication, July 6, 2009). In contrast, the teachers of 4-year-old and 5-year-old kindergartners use the standards "as a guide to develop their local benchmarks or learning targets and as a guide to develop or review curricula and assessment" (Ibid.). In each case, the common language of the standards brings the various programs into better content alignment.

An important obstacle to the content alignment of Wisconsin's early learning programs is the lack of consistency in the curriculum and assessment tools that early care and education providers use. Wisconsin harbors a deeply rooted respect for local control of its school systems, which makes it anathema for the state to tell school districts or early care and education providers what curriculum and assessments to use. Instead, the state has integrated information and facilitation regarding the use of various curricula and assessment tools into the training. The aim is to ensure that the standards align with the curriculum and assessments that localities choose. Wright explained that she hopes to prompt thinking such as "What do our curriculum and assessments look like now that I understand the standards? Maybe they do not align. Maybe they do not align. Maybe we need to consider using the standards as a guide to review our current curriculum and assessment and think about using something else" (personal communication, July 6, 2009).

In the training and on the state's web site, participants can find resources to help them learn more about various curricula and assessment tools. The state also informs web-site users and training participants about alignment studies that are conducted by outside parties—sometimes the curriculum-developing companies themselves—regarding the congruence of these materials with Wisconsin's standards. By offering this information, the state hopes to foster the alignment of curriculum and assessment tools with the standards, without mandating it. Wright noted, 'We are not going to give them something in stone that they have to use, but we suggest that they use the standards to develop their benchmarks and choose a curriculum. And we want them to know where their children are on the continuum, which involves ongoing assessment" (personal communication, July 6, 2009).

The intended result of the standards will be higher quality programs that offer continuity in their content even as children transition from home to a program, from one program to another, and from preschool to kindergarten. With this goal in mind, the committee has reached out to higher education leaders in the state to ensure that the standards become part of the curriculum in early childhood education courses. Though the job of embedding the standards in the daily practice of multiple providers across departments is ongoing, McGurk believes that already "the standards have provided a common language for us to use and a layout of the continuum of development. When I am out and about at various initiatives, people ask me, 'How does this connect back to the early learning standards?' Certainly they are known and a variety of folks are thinking about how other things fit in with them" (personal communication, July 1, 2009).

Lessons Learned   As the hard work of integrating the standards into practice continues, the steering committee has continued to nurture the coalition that led the development and implementation of the standards. McGurk says that its members are bound by "an ongoing relationship and a common desire to do what is right for children," and sustaining such effective collaboration is critical to maintain the momentum of the standards effort. "What we are doing also has to be right for each department. We have shared ownership" (personal communication, July 1, 2009). Awareness of the standards initiative among the three departmental leaders and their ongoing support has also been critical to keeping the collaboration together over time. Perhaps most important, McGurk recommends keeping "a laser focus on your common purpose. It is a framework for shared expectations for school readiness—you keep saying those words, over and over and over" (personal communication, July 1, 2009).

Future Directions   To increase the impact of the standards, Wisconsin is translating them into Spanish and Hmong. The three lead departments also continue to focus on two issues: 1) developing their training and 2) aligning with elementary school standards.

First, in terms of training, steering committee members recognize that the training represents an integral piece of their effort to create horizontal and vertical content alignment across programs and ages of children. Without training, the standards might gather dust on shelves or be used in idiosyncratic ways that would foster program quality, but not continuity across programs. But the committee also believes that one-shot training is not enough. "We are looking for ongoing professional development for implementation of the materials, additional mentoring, and training," says McGurk (personal communication, July 1, 2009).

The second issue is how best to align the early learning standards with the academic standards that guide the K–12 system. The Department of Public Instruction is revising the Wisconsin Model Academic Standards for Mathematics and English Language Arts. The revisions will include Grade Band Focus Areas. Wright believes that the new pre-K–2 Grade Band Focus Areas will complement, rather than compete with, the early learning standards for birth through the entrance to first grade. "I crosswalked the early learning standards with the Mathematics PK–2 Focus Areas and Learning Continuum and they work beautifully. The idea of a learning continuum for PK–2 is similar to the developmental continuum of the early learning standards. We are encouraging people to use both because we are developing a system, not separate pieces" (K. McGurk, personal communication, July 6, 2009).

The thinking regarding how to integrate the two approaches in the classroom continues. One step that the state has taken to foster the combined use of both sets of standards was to use the same numbering system in both of them, as well as using some of the same nomenclature, such as *performance standards*, which articulate how a child might be expected to demonstrate a particular skill or knowledge. McGurk says, "We are not done with that yet. We are thinking about how our standards fit into what school districts are doing because the language for the domains is not the same. But the content—things like developing curiosity and creativity—is the same" (personal communication, July 1, 2009). The need to extend continuity in the content of early education into the elementary grades is a critical challenge of this and any effort to foster effective transitions for young children.

Conclusion   Despite the challenges it has faced, Wisconsin has made concrete steps toward creating continuity in the instructional content of its early education programs. By writing standards that are applicable to a highly diverse population of children and that focus on children's development from birth to the beginning of first grade, the state has created a valuable model of how to nurture substantive connections across programs in the content of these programs' work with young children. Within each age group, Wisconsin has also addressed variations in curricular and assessment choices by offering intensive training on how to align standards, curriculum, and assessments. Together, these efforts are redrawing transitions for young children from a fragmented array of programs to a collage of programs that are far more unified in content and purpose.

Case Study—Early Care and Education in France
A Model of Content Alignment
Kate Tarrant

France has long held a deep commitment to the education of its young children, one that has often been the envy of other nations (Organization for Economic Co-operation and Development, 2004). In 1989, the passage of the Education Guidance Act[3], which made preschool an entitlement and established the primary school cycle system as the national curriculum, sealed the country's commitment to early childhood education (Neuman, 2007). This system sets expectations for children's learning from age 3, the time that they begin public preschool, and continues through their primary school years. Specifically, the law created a structure for the national curriculum: three multi-year cycles with one cycle that transcends the preschool and primary school grades (Organization for Economic Co-operation and Development, 2004). By delineating key learning objectives based on developmental principles for children from age 3 to the

---

[3]Translated from the French *loi d'orientation sur l'éducation.*

end of primary school, the cycles ensure that early childhood education content is vertically aligned. The cycles also provide the foundation for assessment and pedagogy, facilitating horizontal alignment. Thus, the primary school cycle system provides the structural underpinnings for smooth transitions for young children as they move from preschool to primary school.

General Description   Curricular reform in France grew out of mounting criticism of the French educational system that surfaced in the 1980s. Cross-national research revealed that young children were underperforming, and studies cited early care and education as an important mechanism to promote student achievement (Organization for Economic Co-operation and Development, 2004; Pepper, 2008). In response to these results, authorities sought a way to link early childhood education with formal education to develop a primary school cycle system that was based on aligned educational expectations throughout the early years. All public schools in France are expected to implement this curriculum. This effort has several goals: to give children the literacy and numeracy skills they need to succeed in elementary education, to establish continuity between the different school levels, and to provide children with smooth transitions to elementary education. To achieve these objectives, the Ministry of Education's curriculum defines the skills that students should acquire in the course of each cycle. At the same time, the policy maintains teacher autonomy regarding specific teaching methods and curriculum design to allow for individualized instruction.

Since the curriculum was first introduced in 1989, it has undergone several revisions. In February 2002, the Ministry of Education modified the curriculum to promote a more play-based approach to early education (Neuman, 2007). At that time, the curriculum was reoriented around domains of activities rather than around subject areas. With its focus on "life and future learning," literacy and language development was at the center of the reform and was designed to transcend learning areas.

In July 2006, the Ministry of Education further refined the primary school cycle system by introducing the *socle commun: de connaissances et de competences*—common foundation: knowledge and competencies (International Review of Curriculum and Assessment Frameworks, 2008). The *socle commun* defines the skills and core content that students are expected to acquire by the end of compulsory education. It extends beyond students' knowledge and skills to outline ideal attitudes associated with academic achievement. For example, "In mastering a foreign language, a student is expected to become more open-minded and to develop a desire to communicate with his/her European neighbors and other foreigners" (International Review of Curriculum and Assessment Frameworks, 2008, section 5.2.2). The *socle commun* is the starting point for the development of curriculum, assessment, and pedagogy.

Implementation   Instantiated in policy, the primary school cycle system provides a structure for pedagogical alignment in early childhood education. As its implementation reveals, the primary school cycle system exemplifies both vertical and horizontal alignment of preschool and primary school education. The alignment ensures consistency within a given grade level and continuity as children transition from one grade level to the next.

Vertically Aligned Learning Objectives   In France, the Ministry of Education sets national education policies, operations, and curricula from preschool entry all the way through higher education (Organization for Economic Co-operation and Development, 2004). During the development of curricula, the national curriculum council (the *Conseil*

National des Programmes) advises the Ministry on the content that should be included at each level of education. One of the council's main goals is to ensure continuity in the curriculum across the entire education spectrum. The council sets the content of every discipline for each cycle.

The curriculum is divided into three cycles. The first cycle outlines expectations for children in the first 2 years of the *école maternelle,* France's universal voluntary preschool system for children ages 3–5. Cycle two, the basic learning cycle, delineates key learning objectives, including basic language and mathematical thinking skills, for children in the last year of *école maternelle* through the second year of primary school. It bridges the preschool and primary school years. The third cycle is the consolidation cycle and it provides learning objectives for children in their third, fourth, and fifth year of elementary education. It focuses on the further development of the basic learning skills.

To carry out instruction in school, teachers within a given cycle (regardless of grade levels) collaborate around the specific needs of their students. For example, teachers engaged in one cycle meet to examine student achievement. When children struggle to learn the content, teachers meet with family members and they develop an individualized learning plan called a Projects of Educational Success (PRE) to support the child's learning difficulties. Teachers collaborate around curriculum design as well. Every 4 years, each school proposes a school project that guides the curriculum. The project transcends grades, thereby providing an opportunity for teachers and children to work on similar content.

Horizontally Aligned Learning Objectives, Assessment, and Teaching   In addition to guiding vertical alignment of curricular content, the primary school cycle system facilitates horizontal alignment of content, assessment, and teaching. There are two types of assessment, and each draws on the learning objectives that are outlined in the primary school cycle system: child assessment and program assessment. "The Ministry of Education has developed evaluation tools (CD-ROM) for teachers to use at the end of *maternelle* and the first year of elementary school" (Organization for Economic Co-operation and Development, 2004, p. 25). These tools are used to assess school readiness and to inform instruction. A record of achievement is kept and passed on to a child's primary school teachers.

Alignment is also encouraged through program assessment. One set of assessors monitors teachers in both early childhood settings and elementary schools every 3 years. Their task is to evaluate schools' progress toward meeting pedagogical objectives, including objectives that are related to transitions and alignment, addressed in meetings between teachers to "discuss children's learning, identify areas of difficulty, and plan strategies to smooth transitions from one stage of education to the next" (Organization for Economic Co-operation and Development, 2004, p. 25).

Instruction is also horizontally aligned in the primary school cycle system. The primary school cycle system informs the unified teacher preparation system that is provided by University of Teachers Training Institutes. Moreover, elements of the curriculum, such as schoolwide projects, encourage collaboration among preschool and primary school teachers and directors. Therefore, both teacher preparation and school practices align with the curricular content and assessment procedures to establish horizontal alignment. These instructional practices also transcend grades to ensure pedagogical continuity as children transition from preschool to primary school.

Lessons Learned   The primary school cycle system has raised tension between the need to balance teacher-directed and child-centered approaches to instruction. Lessons should be culturally relevant and engaging and should provide children with necessary skills for school success. The 2006 revision to the learning cycles introduced greater flexibility in time allocation to achieve a more child-centered environment. The new timetable provides a weekly time allocation for language and mathematics, around which the remainder of the curriculum is built. Flexibility built into the timetable enables teachers to provide holistic instruction that is based on projects and blocks of time that vary according to the nature of the content. Teachers are encouraged to integrate language and, since 2008, history-of-arts instruction throughout the curriculum (INCA, 2008).

Another lesson stems from the Ministry's efforts to support the most vulnerable students: children of immigrant families, children with learning difficulties, and children with disabilities. The school week duration shifted in September 2008 to add 2 hours a week of small-group remedial instruction for children with learning difficulties.

Future Directions   Guided by the primary school cycle system, the Ministry of Education has developed an aligned system for children from the time they begin preschool until they graduate. However, a chasm between preschool and services for children under 3 years old remains a major challenge to achieving a fully integrated system and aligned pedagogy (Neuman, 2007). Governance contributes to this divide, with the Ministry of Education responsible for preschool while infant–toddler child care is a joint responsibility of the Ministry of Health and Solidarity and the Ministry of Employment, Social Cohesion, and Housing. Moreover, preschool is a universal entitlement in France, while child care resembles a market characterized by a diversity of providers with demand exceeding supply (Neuman, 2007). In spite of these cleavages, efforts are taking hold across the country to bridge the gap between the two sectors. Many municipalities, for instance, have early childhood coordinators who are responsible for linking services, providing training, supporting teachers, and helping children navigate early childhood services. In addition, preschools in some municipalities have established transition programs (*classes passerelles*) that are focused on 2- to 3-year-old children who have not attended early childhood programs (Passarelles, EJE, 2006). These "bridging activities" familiarize families with the education system and provide children with opportunities to socialize with others and experience separation from their families (Neuman, 2007). Despite these local efforts, much work remains to be done at the national level to bridge child care services for children under 3 years of age with preschool services.

Another major objective for the Ministry of Education is to improve services for the youngest children (2 to 3 years old) for whom *école maternelle* is the first contact with a group environment. These children often struggle to adapt to the pace and rhythms of the preschool day. Many of these efforts support children with special needs and others at risk of underachievement.

Conclusion   Since the Ministry of Education in France established aligned expectations for young children, school achievement has increased: In 1975 approximately 50% of students repeated a grade, but in 2007 the percentage was only 20%. To be sure, several efforts—such as reduced class size and greater attention to early education—contribute to these results. Nevertheless, the primary school cycle system is one element of a reform effort that has improved achievement.

As outlined in this case study, the primary school cycle system incorporates the knowledge, skills, and attitudes for young children in France. The content is based on a developmental continuum that transcends grade levels to create vertical alignment. The primary school cycle system also provides the basis for assessment, curriculum design, and teaching to ensure horizontal alignment. Simply stated, France's primary school cycle system provides the structural under-pinnings that are necessary to provide content alignment and smooth transitions for young children.

REFERENCES

Barnett, W.S., Epstein, D.J., Friedman, A.H., Boyd, J.S., & Hustedt, J.T. (2008). *The state of preschool 2008*. New Brunswick, NJ: National Institute of Early Education Research.

Bhola, D.S., Impara, J.C., & Buckendahl, C.W. (2003). Aligning tests with states' content standards: Methods and issues. *Educational Measurement: Issues and Practice, 22*(3), 21–29.

Blank, R. (2002). *Models for alignment analyses and assistance to states: Council of Chief State School Officers summary document*. Washington, DC: Council of Chief State School Officers.

Bogard, K., & Takanishi, R. (2005). PK–3: An aligned and coordinated approach to education for children 3 to 8 years old. *Social Policy Report, 19*(3), 3–24.

Bowman, B.T. (2006, September). Standards at the heart of educational equity. *Beyond the Journal*. Retrieved from http://journal.naeyc.org/btj/200609/BowmanBTJ.pdf

Bowman, B.T., Donovan, M.S., & Burns, M.S. (Eds.). (2001). *Eager to learn: Educating our preschoolers*. Washington, DC: National Academies Press.

Brown, C.P. (2007). It's more than content: Expanding the conception of early learning standards. *Early Childhood Research and Practice, 9*(1). Retrieved from http://ecrp.uiuc.edu/v9n1/brown.html

Burchinal, M., Howes, C., Pianta, R., Bryant, D., Early, D., Clifford, R., et al. (2008). Predicting child out-comes at the end of kindergarten from the quality of pre-kindergarten teacher–child interactions and instruction. *Applied Developmental Science, 12*(3), 140–153.

Dinkes, M. (2008, June). Aligning Georgia's PK–3 system. *The State Education Standard*, 52–54. Retrieved from http://nasbe.org/index.php/file-repository/func-startdown/760/

Flowers, C., Browder, D., & Ahlgrim-Delzell, L. (2006). An analysis of three states' alignment between language arts and mathematics. *Exceptional Children, 72*(2), 201–215.

Francis, V. (2009). French primary schools: History and identity. In R.M. Clifford and G.M. Crawford (Eds.), *Beginning school: U.S. policies in international perspective* (pp. 32–52). New York: Teachers College Press.

Good Start, Grow Smart Interagency Workgroup. (2006). *Good Start, Grow Smart: A guide to Good Start, Grow Smart and other federal early learning initiatives*. Retrieved from http://www.acf.hhs.gov/programs/ccb/initiatives/gsgs/fedpubs/GSGSBooklet.pdf

Hamre, B.K., & Pianta, R.C. (2005). Can instructional and emotional support in the first grade classroom make a difference for children at risk of school failure? *Child Development, 72*(2), 949–967.

Head Start Bureau. (2001, April). Head Start Child Outcomes Framework. *Head Start Bulletin, 70*, 44–50.

Hebbeler, K., & Barton, L. (2007). The need for data on child and family outcomes at the federal and state levels. *Young Exceptional Children Monograph Series, 9*, 1–15.

International Review of Curriculum and Assessment Frameworks. (2008). *France: Curricula (age 3–19)*. Retrieved from http://inca.org.uk/1380.html

Kagan, S.L., Moore, E., & Bredekamp, S. (1995). *Reconsidering children's early development and learning: Toward shared beliefs and vocabulary*. Washington, DC: National Education Goals Panel.

Kagan, S.L., Scott-Little, C., & Reid, J. (2009). *Pennsylvania early learning standards alignment study. Executive summary*. Harrisburg: Pennsylvania Office of Child Development and Early Learning.

Magnuson, K., Ruhm, C., & Waldfogel, J. (2007). The persistence of preschool effects: Do subsequent classroom experiences matter? *Early Childhood Research Quarterly, 22*(1), 18–38.

Minnesota Parent Aware. (n.d.). Child assessment review process summary. St. Paul, MN: Author. Retrieved from http://www.parentawareratings.org/providers-educators/preparation.html

Neuman, M.J. (2007). *Governance of early care and education: Politics and policy in France and Sweden.* Unpublished doctoral dissertation, Columbia University, New York.

No Child Left Behind Act of 2001, PL 107-110, 115 Stat. 1425, 20 U.S.C., §§6301 *et seq.*

Organization for Economic Co-operation and Development. (2004). *Early childhood education and care policy in France* (OECD Country Note). Directorate of Education, OECD. Retrieved from http://www.oecd.org/dataoecd/60/36/34400146.pdf

Passerelles, EJE.(2006). Jardins d'enfants: classes passarelles. Retrieved from http://www. passerelles-eje. info/dossiers/dossier_245_jardins+enfants+classes+passerelles.html

Pepper, D. (2008). *Primary curriculum change: directions of travel in 10 countries.* Qualifications and Curriculum Authority. Retrieved from http://inca.org.uk/Primary_curriculum_change_INCA_probe.pdf

Pianta, R.C., & Hadden, D.S. (2008, June). What we know about the quality of early education settings: Implications for research on teacher preparation and professional development. *The State Education Standard,* 20–27. Retrieved from http://nasbe.org/index.php/file-repository?func=fileinfo&id=762

Porter, A.C., Smithson, J., Blank, R., & Zeidner, T. (2007). Alignment as a teacher variable. *Applied Measurement in Education, 20*(1), 27–51.

Scott-Little, C., Cassidy, D.J., Lower, J., & Ellen, S. (2010). Early learning standards and quality improvement initiatives: A systemic approach to supporting children's learning and development. In P. Wesley & V. Buysse (Eds.), *The quest for quality: Promising innovations for early childhood programs.* Baltimore: Paul H. Brookes Publishing Co.

Scott-Little, C., Kagan, S.L., & Frelow, V.S. (2005). *Inside the content: The depth and breadth of early learning standards.* Greensboro, NC: University of North Carolina, SERVE Center for Continuous Improvement.

Scott-Little, C., Kagan, S.L., Frelow, V.S., & Reid, J. (2008). *Inside the content of infant–toddler early learning guidelines: Results from analyses, issues to consider, and recommendations.* Greensboro, NC: University of North Carolina.

Snow, C.E., & Van Hemel, S.D. (Eds.). (2008). *Early childhood assessment: What, why, and how?* Washington, DC: National Academies Press.

Stipek, D. (2006). No Child Left Behind comes to preschool. *The Elementary School Journal, 106*(5), 455–465.

Webb, N.L. (2007). Issues related to judging the alignment of curriculum standards and assessments. *Applied Measurement in Education, 20*(1), 7–25.

Wisconsin Department of Public Instruction. (2008). *Wisconsin Model Early Learning Standards* (2nd ed.). Madison, WI: Wisconsin Child Care Information Center. Retrieved from http://www.collaborating-partners.com/EarlyLS_docs.htm

Wisconsin Model Early Learning Standards Training Report, 2005–2009. (2009). Madison, WI: Department of Children and Families. Retrieved from http://dcf.wisconsin.gov/childcare/quality/wmels_summary05_09.pdf

8

Aligning Curriculum and Teaching

A Child-Focused Approach

Sue Bredekamp

No other period of life is marked by as much growth and change as the years from birth through age 8. Children undergo almost incomprehensible transformations as they progress from being totally reliant on others to becoming relatively independent actors who strive for mastery of skills. In the midst of all of these changes, children's development during those years is marked by certain continuities, including continuity in relationships with their family members and connections to their cultural and linguistic group. Children also show relative consistency as they develop in individual traits such as personality and temperament (Shonkoff & Phillips, 2000).

The title of this volume indicates its premise: that the settings in which children are served must be responsive to their needs for both continuity *and* change in educational experiences if early schooling is to be successful. *Continuity* refers to the continuous nature of child development and the need for coherence and connectedness among children's experiences at home and school and from preschool through the elementary grades. By contrast, the primary definition of *transition* is change; efforts directed at transition tend to focus on easing children into and preparing them for the inevitable changes that occur as they move through the educational system.

Head Start, federal and state departments of education, foundations that focus on education, and education advocacy groups are calling for greater *alignment* of prekindergarten (pre-K) Grade 3 as a strategy to improve outcomes for children and address the transition challenges they face during the early years of school. Advocates for increased alignment emphasize the need to ensure that what comes before a transition is "in line with" what comes after it and that the experiences that follow clearly build on the ones that came before (Barbour & Seefeldt, 1993; Foundation for Child Development, 2008; Shore, 2009; Takanishi & Kauerz, 2008).

Despite these worthy goals, recent efforts to promote pre-K–3 alignment have been met with suspicion by many preschool educators, who assume that the burden of change will fall on programs for younger children rather than on elementary schools. For example, one of the more controversial aspects of the recently revised position statement of the National Association for the Education of Young Children (NAEYC) on developmentally appropriate practice was the association's call for "improved, better connected education for preschool and elementary children" (2009a, p. 3). Many readers assumed that this would inevitably lead to pushing elementary school practices that are neither developmentally appropriate nor effective even for older children down to the preschool level.

In fact, educational *alignment* activities tend to focus less on changes in actual classroom practices and more on written documents such as state standards and curricula. Attempts to align teaching strategies usually involve updating standards for teacher certification or guidelines for teacher preparation to reflect current knowledge about child development and effective practices (NAEYC, 2009b). Such efforts to align written standards and policies are an important first step in improving young children's transitions. However, high-quality, coherent educational experiences will occur only if the overarching goal is to help each child make ongoing learning and developmental progress. To accomplish this goal, we must make the needs of individual children central in any effort to align curriculum and teaching.

The purpose of this chapter is to discuss strategies for achieving such pedagogical continuity—designing a more coherent, connected framework of curriculum and teaching practices across the pre-K–3 continuum. The fact is that the quality of educational experience needs to be improved across the full continuum of preschool through primary grades (Bogard & Takanishi, 2005; Ritchie, Maxwell, & Bredekamp, 2009). Rather than focusing on the weaknesses of either preschool or elementary education, educators and policy makers need to take a "best of both worlds" approach and draw on the science of child development and learning to transform early schooling for all children (Barbarin & Wasik, 2009; NAEYC, 2009a; Ritchie, Maxwell, & Clifford, 2007). Although programs for infants and toddlers should also be part of this framework, we will focus in this chapter on programs for preschoolers and elementary school children. We begin with a brief discussion of definitional issues.

TOWARD ALIGNMENT OF DEFINITIONS

Of all educational constructs, *curriculum* is perhaps the most difficult to define. Because there is no agreed-upon definition, it is not surprising that attempts to align curricula between educational levels can be difficult. A fundamental barrier to the conversation is a difference in the way that educators think of curricula in preschool and in elementary school.

Curriculum at the Preschool Level

The preschool curriculum has traditionally focused on the process of teaching and learning rather than on the content that children are learning. The emphasis has been on child-initiated, constructivist approaches to teaching and learning in response to children's interests and needs as exemplified in the *HighScope Preschool Curriculum* and *The Creative Curriculum*. These curricular approaches provide guidance on structuring learning environments, information about how teaching and learning should occur, goals for children's learning and development, and assessment tools. Effective implementation depends on teachers' ability to promote individual children's development and learning within the framework; therefore, these models include professional development for teachers. Within the past few years, both *HighScope* and *Creative Curriculum* have added more content in the areas of literacy and mathematics.

In addition to the development of these broad-based curriculum models, there has been an explosion in domain-specific preschool curricula that focus more on the content to be learned than on the process. The focus is most often on early literacy but may also be on mathematics and social-emotional skills. Despite the increased attention to learning goals, particularly in the area of early literacy, there is still enormous resistance in the field to such preplanned curricula (Frede & Ackerman, 2007; Ginsburg, Lee, & Boyd, 2008). The strong tradition of emergent curricula in the field leads many preschool educators to use pejorative terms such as *curriculum in a box* or *canned curriculum* to describe any published curriculum resource, regardless of its source or content.

Little information is available on the extent to which preschool programs utilize specific curricula. An 11-state study of pre-K programs conducted by the National Center for Early Development and Learning provides some evidence about curriculum use in state-funded preschool programs (Early et al., 2005). Only 4% of teachers reported having no curriculum, while 14% used a locally developed curriculum and 9% used a state curriculum. The most widely used curricula are *HighScope,* found in 38% of classrooms, and *Creative Curriculum,* found in 19% of classrooms. *HighScope* and *Creative Curriculum* are also the two mostly frequently used curricula in Head Start (Zill, Sorongon, Kim, Clark, & Woolverton, 2006).

Curriculum at the Primary Level

By contrast, the main focus of the curriculum in the primary grades is content. The opposite of the emergent child-centered curriculum, an elementary school curriculum is likely to be a commercially published program that is based on a predetermined scope and sequence. The scope and sequence in a subject area such as mathematics or reading determines what knowledge and skills are taught and when. It is estimated that more than 80% of primary-grade teachers use some form of published curriculum, particularly to teach reading (Shanahan, 2006).

Preschool educators tend to be wary of content-driven scope-and-sequence approaches to curriculum planning because they believe that these approaches will be too rigid and will not be sufficiently responsive to children's interests, individual differences, and cultural and linguistic diversity. At times, the primary-grade curriculum seems to assume that all children can be taught the same thing, at the same time, with the same results. In fact, given the great diversity in prior experience and knowledge that children bring to school, the only way for every child to achieve at high levels is for the curriculum and instruction to be responsive to their individual and cultural variation.

Toward Consistent Definitions

The NAEYC and the National Association of Early Childhood Specialists in State Departments of Education (NAECS/SDE) developed a joint position statement on curriculum, assessment, and program evaluation for birth through age 8 that broadly defines curriculum:

> Curriculum is more than a collection of enjoyable activities. *Curriculum* is a complex idea containing multiple components, such as goals, content, pedagogy, or instructional practices. Curriculum is influenced by many factors, including society's values, content standards, accountability systems, research findings, community expectations, culture and language, and individual children's characteristics. (2003, p. 6)

The NAEYC and the NAECS/SDE also addressed the question of whether programs should use published curricula or whether it is better for teachers to develop their own curricula:

> The quality of the curriculum should be the important question. If a published, commercially available curriculum—either a curriculum for one area such as literacy or mathematics or a comprehensive curriculum—is consistent with the position statement's goals and values, appears well suited to the children and families served by the program, and can be implemented effectively, then it may be worth considering, *especially as a support for inexperienced teachers* [emphasis added]. (p. 6)

As for teacher-developed curriculum, the position statement cautions that

> If staff have the interest, expertise, and resources to develop a curriculum that includes clearly defined goals, a system for ensuring that those goals are shared by stakeholders, a system for determining the beneficial effects of the curriculum, and other indicators of effectiveness—then the program may conclude that it should take that route. (p. 6)

Developing an effective curriculum "from scratch," so to speak, is a daunting task, especially for most preschool teachers who are likely to have little knowledge of or experience in curriculum development. Alignment of a pre-K–3 curriculum has the potential to provide preschool teachers with thoughtfully planned, research-based curriculum resources, allowing them to spend more time on adapting the curriculum and their teaching for individual children's abilities, needs, and interests. At the same time, such alignment needs to support primary-grade teachers as they adapt their instruction to individual and cultural variation among children.

CURRICULUM ALIGNMENT

Several major initiatives are working toward the goal of pre-K–3 alignment to ease children's transitions from preschool to elementary school. One example is the Early Childhood Education Network of the National Association of State Boards of Education (NASBE), funded by the W.K. Kellogg Foundation. This project reports having made impressive progress on aligning sets of learning standards, curriculum, assessment, teaching practices, professional development, evaluation, and accountability systems in six states (National Association of State Boards of Education, 2009). Another example is FirstSchool at the University of North Carolina, a particularly comprehensive project. FirstSchool is a well-conceptualized, visionary approach to providing the best possible education for 3- to 8-year-olds that gathers together all of the stakeholders who play a role in bringing about change (Ritchie et al., 2007; see also Chapter 9, this volume).

Despite such impressive model projects, however, barriers continue to persist. The sections that follow describe some strategies and considerations that have potential for moving the country toward the goal of aligning curriculum and teaching with a focus on children. These strategies include basing curricula on research, establishing state standards, using developmental and learning continua, and supporting the development of foundational processes.

Using a Research-Based Curriculum

Since the No Child Left Behind Act was passed in 2001, great emphasis has been placed on the use of scientifically based curriculum in primary grades. This trend found its way into preschool through Early Reading First grants that required programs to use structured literacy curricula. The 2008 reauthorization of Head Start calls for K–3 alignment and the use of scientifically based curricula, although confusion remains about what this requirement actually means. If Head Start takes a clearer stand and provides more guidance on what constitutes an acceptable curriculum, these mandates could have a major impact on the quality of teaching and learning in programs and achieve alignment of the curriculum from preschool to third grade.

In general, the scientific basis of a curriculum is judged in one of two ways. The first strategy is to design the curriculum by drawing on research findings. For example, alphabet knowledge and phonological awareness predict later success in learning to read, according to the National Early Literacy Panel (2008). Therefore, a research-based early literacy curriculum is likely to include the goals of acquiring these skills and the strategies for teaching them. A second, far more rigorous approach to developing a research-based curriculum begins with a strong foundation in research and then systematically evaluates whether the particular curriculum effectively produces positive learning outcomes for children. This method of evaluating curricula is the most valid one, but it is also extremely difficult to control for extraneous variables such as teacher behaviors and learning contexts in order to attribute outcomes to the curriculum itself. For example, a large-scale study of the effectiveness of various preschool curricula found that there were very few significant differences between the literacy curricula being evaluated and the curricula in control classrooms (Preschool Curriculum Evaluation Research Consortium, 2008). One explanation for this result is that most preschool classrooms, including the control groups, now teach literacy to a greater extent than in the past.

Evidence suggests that a well-planned curriculum is an essential component of an effective early childhood education program (Bowman, Donovan, & Burns, 2001; Klein & Knitzer, 2007; Landry, 2005a, 2005b; National Association for the Education of Young Children, 2005). Using a research-based curriculum, as opposed to taking a more open-ended approach, has greater potential for alignment across the pre-K–3 continuum. A research-based curriculum is more likely to have consistent, clearly defined goals and proven effective learning experiences than a curriculum that is developed by an individual teacher or school. Yet little research has been done on the effectiveness of specific curricula, and data on effective curricula for children whose home language is not English and for children with disabilities are sparse (NAEYC Specialists in State Departments of Education, 2003). Evaluation of a focused mathematics curriculum in the Preschool Curriculum Evaluation Research Consortium study is one exception. Children from low-income families made startling gains in mathematics knowledge when they followed a preschool curriculum that included preplanned, sequenced math experiences in small groups and computer activities (Preschool Curriculum Evaluation Research Consortium, 2008). The mathematics curriculum was developed on the basis of a rigorous research design such as the one described previously. The control groups in the study, like most early childhood classrooms, provided very little mathematics teaching.

Basing a curriculum on research and evaluating its effectiveness are important steps in the right direction. These practices would minimize the number of situations in which curriculum is ill defined at best or irrelevant and ineffective at worst. However, much more work needs to be done in order for this strategy to be effective in pre-K–3 curriculum alignment.

Using State Learning Standards and Benchmarks

As was discussed in Chapter 7, state learning standards are an important vehicle for improving quality and consistency of curriculum and therefore, content alignment. Written standards guide and often mandate the development of curriculum and assessment tools. Standards have the potential to create a bridge between what research says that children should be learning and the kinds of teaching and learning that actually occur (Cross, Woods, & Schweingruder, 2009).

In the context of curriculum alignment, a few points about standards are relevant. The first is that state standards vary considerably in terms of quality, quantity, and other variables (Scott-Little, Kagan, & Frelow, 2005). Therefore, they are not uniformly useful in guiding curriculum development within or across states, much less aligning the curriculum and teaching for individual children. The common core standards in English language arts and mathematics developed by the Council of Chief State School Officers and the National Governor's Association in 2010 is a step in the right direction, potentially alleviating the problem of having 30 different sets of state standards.

Concerns also arise over the quality of the standards. To begin with, the process used to develop standards does not always yield the best results. The outcome is often a compromise among diverse stakeholders and political perspectives.

A still graver issue is that the standards themselves may not be developmentally appropriate because they have not been validated by research (Neuman & Roskos, 2005). That is, some standards or benchmarks are not achievable by most children in the age range for which they are intended, even if the children have good teaching and learning experiences. For example, a developmentally *inappropriate* preschool standard is for children to blend and segment individual phonemes, a skill that is more achievable in late kindergarten and first grade. Similarly, expecting all children to read at a certain level by the end of kindergarten, a benchmark that is becoming more common, is setting up many children for failure. This expectation is especially problematic for children from low-income families and children whose home language is not English and who have not had sufficient opportunity to learn precursor skills prior to kindergarten.

Another concern about using standards as the basis of curriculum alignment is that although standards describe content knowledge and skills fairly well, they give scant attention to domain-specific process standards. For example, the National Council of Teachers of Mathematics standards for school mathematics include processes such as problem-solving, reasoning, communicating, and connecting that cut across all mathematics content areas and relate to other curriculum areas as well. These processes are essential for understanding and applying mathematics knowledge, yet they are seldom given the attention they deserve in standards and thus in the curriculum (Cross et al., 2009).

State standards can be effective in aligning the curriculum at the broad planning level, but they are less reliable tools for aligning the curriculum with the needs of individual children. By their very nature, benchmarks are most often tied to specific grade or age levels. This connection can have the unintended consequence of causing curricula to be planned narrowly according to specific age or grade-level expectations. It also can contribute to teachers assuming that children should have fully mastered the benchmarks of the previous level by the time they move on to the next one (Wasik & Newman, 2009).

Standards have an important role to play in achieving consistency of curriculum content, but standards are not curricula. Alignment that serves children's interests is best accomplished by conceptualizing curriculum goals on a continuum, as we will discuss next.

Using Developmental and Learning Continua to Guide Curriculum and Teaching

Early childhood education has moved away from thinking about milestones of development, or ages and stages, to viewing development and learning as a continuum. A continuum is a predictable, but not rigid, sequence of typical developmental accomplishments within age ranges (McAfee & Leong, 2007). A learning continuum, also known as a *learning trajectory* or *path,* is a predictable sequence of knowledge or skills in a content area such as mathematics, with each level more sophisticated than the last and building on the previous level (Clements & Sarama, 2009; Cross et al., 2009; Sarama & Clements, 2009).

In 2009, the National Research Council (NRC) released a report on early childhood mathematics education that identified detailed learning paths for children from age 3 through 6 in the areas of numbers and operations, geometry and spatial relations, and measurement. The report concluded that children's mathematics learning, especially that of children from low-income families, can be improved if children experience a planned, sequenced curriculum that is based on these teaching–learning paths.

Research-based developmental and learning continua can serve as the basis for planning the scope and sequence of a curriculum beginning in preschool and continuing through the primary grades. While it is true that a sequenced discipline such as mathematics lends itself particularly well to this approach, using developmental and learning continua has great potential for improving curriculum alignment in other subjects, too. A growing body of research identifies content knowledge and skills that form the foundation for later learning and serve as important sequences of learning (Cross et al., 2009; National Council of Teachers of Mathematics, 2006; National Early Literacy Panel, 2008; Snow, Burns, & Griffin, 1998). Research also identifies continua in the social-emotional and physical domains of development (Gallahue & Ozmun, 2006; Thompson & Goodman, 2009), as well as in other curriculum areas.

State learning standards do not provide the same level of detail in articulating research-based learning paths as the level of detail in the learning paths identified by the NRC Committee on Early Childhood Mathematics, nor should they. Such work is better left to scholars and independent review groups. Nevertheless, by whatever name they are called—continua, learning paths, or learning trajectories—these constructs can be valuable for informing standards development and for planning and aligning curricula across age spans. In addition, teachers can use continua of development and learning to assess children and determine when, where, and how to provide individual instruction and scaffolding, discussed later in this chapter.

Supporting Foundational Competencies

Thus far, we have discussed curricula in terms of relatively traditional subject matter areas or developmental domains. However, recent findings from brain research, as well as cognitive and social-emotional developmental psychology, reveal that this approach takes far too narrow a view of curricula and of what really matters in early childhood education (Barbarin & Wasik, 2009).

Research indicates that there are several domain-general developmental processes that undergird and facilitate learning across all areas. These include, but are not limited to, self-regulation, executive function, symbolic representation, and memory (Barbarin & Wasik, 2009; Ritchie et al., 2009). Some states include a few early learning standards that are related to children's approaches to learning, such as curiosity, persistence, and focused attention (Scott-Little et al., 2005). On the whole, however, these general, albeit essential, processes do not fit neatly into a category and are not part of the curriculum and standards conversation. Including these domain-general processes as well as the domain-specific processes that we discussed earlier could have a profound effect on future curriculum development and teaching practices, reducing fragmentation of curriculum by subject area.

Self-regulation is the ability to adapt or control emotions, behavior, and thinking according to the demands of a situation (Bodrova & Leong, 2006). Vygotsky considered the development of self-regulation to be the primary goal of education for 4- and 5-year-old children. We now know that self-regulation in preschool and kindergarten predicts children's academic success in the primary grades, beyond variations in their intelligence or family backgrounds (Blair & Razza, 2007; McClelland, Acock, & Morrison, 2006). As most elementary school teachers would attest, when children enter school lacking the ability to self-regulate, trying to teach them academic skills is almost always a losing endeavor.

Depending on their area of expertise, researchers study self-regulation from varying perspectives—cognitive, social, or emotional. Therefore, the term is applied to various aspects of children's functioning. From a social-emotional perspective, self-regulation includes the ability to monitor and express emotions appropriately, the ability to control physical impulses, compliance with rules and the demands of social situations, and the ability to delay gratification (Calkins & Williford, 2009). From a cognitive perspective, self-regulation involves the overall cognitive construct called *executive function*. This construct includes the ability to focus attention on a required task (even when you'd rather be thinking about or doing something else), the ability to plan (thinking before acting), and a capacity for working memory (retaining new information long enough for it to be consolidated into long-term memory) (Bodrova & Leong, 2006). All of these processes are essential for success in school and life (Bodrova & Leong; Diamond, Barnett, Thomas, & Munroe, 2007).

Symbolic representation, the use and understanding of symbols, forms the foundation of all language and written communication. It is also an essential component of mathematics and science, both of which involve complex symbol systems that rely heavily on models or representations of highly abstract phenomenon.

Memory is essential for new learning, retrieval of prior knowledge, and conceptual development (Ornstein, Coffman, & Grammer, 2009). (Yet early childhood educators usually associate memory negatively with rote memorization.)

Each of these domain-general processes, and others such as attachment and language, should be fundamental goals of the early childhood curriculum from pre-K to grade 3 (Ritchie et al., 2009). There is substantial evidence that particular curriculum approaches and teaching strategies can help build these abilities. For example, the Vygotskian *Tools of the Mind* curriculum is designed for preschool through second grade (Bodrova & Leong, 2007). A major feature of the curriculum is helping children develop the ability to engage in mature sociodramatic play and planning. Such play involves roles, rules, props, a situation, and language interaction, and lasts 10 minutes or more. Mature sociodramatic play promotes self-regulation because it requires children to regulate their own behavior, regulate that of others, and in turn be regulated by others, all within the same context (Bodrova & Leong, 2006; Boyd, Barnett, Bodrova, Leong, & Gomby, 2005). For example, if several children are playing "airport," only one child can be the pilot. Others may be the ticket takers, flight attendants, passengers, and so forth. If a flight attendant decides to be the pilot, the play breaks down. In short, the flight attendant must regulate him- or herself by staying in the role, regulate others by keeping the passengers happy, and be regulated by others (no storming the cockpit).

Such mature play does not happen automatically, and teachers have a critical role in helping children gain play skills. For example, one of the features of *Tools of the Mind* is engaging children in play planning (i.e., drawing, dictating, and/or writing their plans), a practice that further contributes to children's representational abilities and planning skills. *Tools of the Mind* has been found to improve self-regulation and executive function among children from low-income families compared with other children in closely matched pairs. Children's levels of self-regulation also correlated with their literacy and mathematics achievement (Barnett et al., 2008; Diamond et al., 2007).

Similarly, the fundamental component of the well-researched *HighScope* curriculum is the plan–do–review process, in which children plan what they are going to do during choice time, engage in the learning experiences, and then reflect on what they learned and on what they will do next. These processes—planning with analysis—are all components of executive function, which most likely accounts for much of the effectiveness of the *HighScope* curriculum model. For decades, there have been heated debates in the field about the positive lasting effects of the child-centered *HighScope* curriculum, compared with a direct instruction model, on crime prevention and other prosocial behaviors (Schweinhart, Weikart & Larner, 1986; Schweinhart & Weikart, 1997). In retrospect, it is likely that exposure to the direct instruction model at preschool did not "cause" later crime and other negative social consequences, but that lack of exposure to decision making, planning, and other experiences that promote executive function and self-regulation did not prevent these consequences.

Curriculum approaches that actively promote these fundamental domain-general processes, in addition to domain-specific knowledge and skills, emphasize both content and process (what and how children learn). Such an approach could help align curriculum with teaching, as we discuss in the next section. As we saw in our discussion of definitions, separating curriculum and teaching is particularly difficult in early childhood education. We turn now to the related issue of aligning instructional practices.

ALIGNING TEACHING

Regardless of the curriculum that is used, the key factor in its effectiveness is the teacher. Teachers must make hundreds of decisions every day about how to respond and adapt instruction for children who inevitably do not fit neatly into the curriculum plan or meet the predetermined learning standard. What teachers do at each level of the pre-K–3 continuum has the greatest potential to ensure pedagogical continuity for children. First, we discuss effective teaching in general; then we turn to some specific elements of instruction that warrant attention.

Teacher–Child Interactions

A large body of research demonstrates that the interactions between children and teachers are the most important determinants of the quality of children's experiences, their academic achievement, and their social-emotional competence. These interactions determine both the emotional and the instructional climate of the classroom, each of which predicts outcomes for children across the pre-K–3 spectrum (Hamre & Pianta, 2001, 2005; Pianta, La Paro, & Hamre, 2008; Pianta & Stuhlman, 2003). Positive, responsive relationships between teachers and children are as important for primary-grade children as they are for preschoolers. At the same time, intentional scaffolding of children's learning is as much a part of the preschool teacher's role as it is the primary school teacher's.

Research using the Classroom Assessment Scoring System (CLASS) finds that the instructional climate of the classroom is the strongest and most consistent predictor of children's learning over time (Burchinal et al., 2008; Hamre & Pianta, 2005). Children benefit when teachers use strategies that build concept development (seeing how facts are organized and interconnected) and when they provide useful feedback and language modeling. In classrooms that have a positive instructional climate, teachers manage time so that children are actively engaged in learning opportunities and promote higher order thinking and creativity.

Results of large-scale studies, however, paint a disturbing picture. While the emotional climates of early childhood classrooms are generally acceptable, the quality of instruction is very poor in most preschool classrooms (Early et al., 2005; Hamre & Pianta, 2007). On the whole, teachers do not use a variety of methods to engage children, nor do they have extended discussions with children encouraging them to reason and solve problems. Most teacher talk consists of giving directions or assigning routine tasks. Preschools, especially those which serve children from low-income families, are marked by many missed opportunities for learning (Early et al.) and certainly don't promote the important domain-specific and domain-general processes that we discussed earlier.

Similarly, research reveals that students are exposed to low-quality instruction in primary-grade classrooms. In fact, the available evidence suggests that instructional quality is generally poor from preschool to third grade (Early et al., 2005; National Institute of Child Health and Human Development, 2002, 2003, 2005). Thus, across the early grades of schooling, children are rarely exposed to teaching strategies that are intended to stimulate higher order thinking and rarely get feedback beyond being told that they are correct or incorrect.

The urgency of improving teacher–child interactions in pre-K–3 classrooms is evident from a study by Hamre and Pianta (2005) that investigated whether high levels of instructional and emotional support from first-grade teachers could influence the trajectory of schooling for children who had been identified as at risk for school failure. By the end of first grade, students who had experienced strong instructional and emotional support had achievement scores and relationships with their teachers that were comparable to those of low-risk peers. On the other hand, children who were at risk for school failure and whose first-grade teachers provided less instructional and emotional support displayed lower achievement and more conflict with peers than did their low-risk peers.

Across the pre-K–third-grade continuum, the importance of the teacher's role is clear. It is equally clear that teacher–child interaction, especially the quality of instruction, needs considerable improvement. In addition, teaching strategies such as promoting conceptual development, engaging in instructional conversation, giving useful verbal feedback, and modeling language are effective from age 3 to Grade 3.

Building teachers' capacity to provide high-quality emotional and instructional climates—aligning pre-K–3 teaching—would be a major step toward achieving pedagogical continuity and smooth transitions for children. One professional development effort that was designed to achieve this goal is MyTeachingPartner (MTP). Developed by the same research team as the CLASS, MTP uses consultants who analyze videotapes of teachers working in their classrooms. Then the consultants target intensive, individualized professional development to improve specific teaching practices. Teachers review and reflect on the feedback that was given on the basis of videotapes of their own performance. Then, teachers and consultants interact via videoconference. MTP has significantly improved teachers' language interactions and the quality of their instruction, features that are related to positive outcomes for children, especially children living in poverty. (See http://www.myteachingpartner.net.)

Teaching–Learning Contexts from Pre-K–3

One difficult aspect of children's experience during the transition from preschool to the primary grades is the abrupt shift in instructional practices. A particular challenge for children is the way that they are grouped for instruction. In preschool, for example, children spend approximately 33%

of their time in learning centers or having choice time, but only 6% of the kindergarten day is devoted to such activity (Hamre & Pianta, 2007). By contrast, kindergarten and the early grades are dominated by whole-group instruction and independent seatwork. In the past, kindergarten teachers tended to lament the fact that their students hit a brick wall when they transitioned to first grade. Today, children encounter that brick wall even earlier as the expectations that they will pay attention to teachers and be regulated by them increase exponentially from preschool to kindergarten.

The issue of grouping as an instructional strategy needs more research and discussion across the pre-K–3 period. On the whole, preschool teachers tend to reject whole-group, teacher-directed instruction in favor of play and child-chosen activities, and they rarely use small groups. Ironically, preschool teachers usually read books to the whole class, rather than to small groups of four to six children, which would permit conversation about the book and promote vocabulary and literacy skills (Dickinson, 2001a; Lonigan & Whitehurst, 1998). The most effective mathematics curricula utilize a variety of teaching formats, including small-group instruction, whole-group instruction, play, routines, and computers (Cross et al., 2009).

As with every other aspect of education, teachers' behavior in the various learning contexts is what really matters. During optimum child-initiated experiences, teachers are not passive, nor are children entirely in control—although this ideal is not always realized in practice. During playtime in preschool, children's frequent one-to-one conversations with teachers and talk with peers correlate with high language and literacy scores in kindergarten and first grade (Dickinson, 2001b). Teachers' use of math talk during play is similarly effective (Cross et al., 2009). However, observational research finds that teachers tend to spend little time with children during free play (Dickinson; Seo & Ginsburg, 2004).

Whole-group instruction is not inevitably bad either. Correlational research demonstrates that, during large-group times, preschool teachers' explanatory talk and use of cognitively challenging vocabulary improves learning outcomes (Dickinson, 2001b). The key is that children should not be passive during teacher-guided instruction at any grade level. The most effective whole-group instruction includes elements such as brief teacher demonstrations, discussions, problem-solving in pairs, and physical activities (Cross et al., 2009). Children can be enthralled by an effective whole-group lesson, just as they can wander aimlessly during choice time. In either context, the outcome depends on the teachers' scaffolding of children's engagement and learning.

Using Formative Assessment to Scaffold Learning

Earlier in this chapter, we introduced the concept of using a learning continuum to achieve better curriculum alignment and therefore smooth transitions for young children. The success of this strategy depends on several factors. Teachers must be knowledgeable about the steps in the continuum; they must be skilled at formative assessment in order to determine where individual children are on the continuum; and they must have a large repertoire of teaching strategies to scaffold children's continued progress to the next levels.

There is widespread agreement that learning is most effective when it is meaningful and builds on prior knowledge (Bowman et al., 2001; Bransford, Brown, & Cocking, 2000). Putting this principle into practice is key to scaffolding children's learning. To apply it, teachers must be skilled in using formative assessment methods, including observing children, interviewing them, and evaluating their work products to find out what children already know and can do. Then they need to activate children's prior knowledge, using effective strategies such as open-ended questioning to reveal children's thinking and understanding—currently a rare occurrence in classrooms.

Building on prior learning becomes even more challenging when children's knowledge is obtained in a cultural or linguistic context that differs from their teacher's. English-speaking teachers may not recognize the competence of children who speak Spanish at home (Espinosa, 2007). Often teachers assume that children have no knowledge, when really the teachers are unable to access it.

Building on prior learning is essential for school success. Teaching children to read in a language that they do not speak is a failing proposition (Slavin & Cheung, 2005). Immersing Spanish-speaking preschoolers in English-only classrooms can damage teacher–child relationships, hinder child achievement, and lead to behavior problems (Barnett, Yarosz, Thomas, Jung, & Blanco, 2007). At the same time, there is a gap in background knowledge among children living in poverty and their more affluent peers that is already present in preschool (Neuman, 2006). Addressing this gap early on requires early childhood programs, especially Head Start and state-funded pre-K programs, to provide a consistent, coherent, intellectually engaging, and challenging curriculum and intentional teaching.

ACHIEVING CURRICULUM AND TEACHING ALIGNMENT

Aligning the curriculum and teaching from pre-K to Grade 3 is a daunting task. In this chapter, we suggested strategies for moving toward this goal. Some of these activities require major effort. Identifying agreed-upon developmental and learning continua across all curriculum areas would be highly worthwhile, but a challenging task. Designing an effective curriculum to develop domain-general processes such as executive function and self-regulation is difficult enough, but taking it to scale is another hurdle entirely. Preparing teachers to accurately use formative assessment and scaffold individual children's progress will require retooling teacher education and professional development.

On the other hand, some of the strategies that we propose are deceptively simple. Teaching strategies such as using What or Why questions to call children's attention to details, making connections to what children already know, and responding to children's interests are effective techniques whether the subject is mathematics or reading comprehension, and they also enhance memory ability. Focusing on deliberate memory strategies during first grade (at the outset of a child's school career) is especially important in order for the child to achieve later success (Ornstein et al., 2009). Such strategies are as basic as asking children what they remember about an event or to reflect on their memory ("How did you remember that?"). However, most teachers do not intentionally engage in these deliberate memory-enhancing strategies (Ornstein et al.). Adding these skills to teachers' repertoires could go a long way toward improving children's school success, especially for children who do not receive this kind of assistance at home.

Finally, aligning curriculum and teaching does not mean making them the same. By definition, what is developmentally appropriate will be different for different age groups. However, consistency and continuity are fundamental to healthy development and successful learning from birth through age 8. Establishing a positive relationship with each child requires effort and at times, specific skills, especially for children with challenging behaviors. Nevertheless, it takes as much effort to speak kindly to a child as to speak harshly. Given that the former is so much more effective, all teachers have a responsibility, if not an ethical obligation, to strive toward it. The ultimate goal is to align curriculum and teaching to promote the learning and meet the needs of every child.

Case Study—Aligning Curriculum and Teaching in Red Bank, New Jersey

Aleksandra Holod and Jocelyn Friedlander

In New Jersey's Red Bank Borough Public Schools, a commitment to developmentally appropriate practice has led naturally to the alignment of curriculum and teaching across the early grades. In addition to choosing and designing curricula for preschool through third grade that reflect common understandings about how young children learn, the district provides ongoing opportunities for teachers to adapt their instructional methods to meet children's needs. Joint planning meetings and peer-to-peer classroom observations provide opportunities for teachers to share effective strategies. Moreover, formal and informal student assessment data are used to drive ongoing professional development. Together, these strategies have resulted in common threads across grades and smoother transitions for children.

Red Bank's effort to improve classroom practice has occurred within the context of a larger state-level initiative to foster consistency from preschool through third grade. The Division of Early Childhood Education within the State Department of Education oversees administration of New Jersey's state-funded preschool program and implements the states' vision of pedagogical alignment for young children. Three key aspects of the state's policy framework support its pre-K–3 agenda (E. Wolock, personal communication, August 27, 2009). First, state learning standards are fully aligned from preschool to 12th grade. Second, the Division of Early Childhood Education has developed implementation guidelines for state-funded pre-K programs that emphasize transition planning and alignment of curriculum and instruction between preschool and later grades. Third, the Division offers professional development for district administrators that promotes the use of child-centered instructional strategies.

While the Department of Education continues to develop state-level infrastructure to support its pre-K–3 agenda, Red Bank has begun to establish the type of alignment that policy makers hope to see throughout New Jersey: It has translated transition policy into practice. Red Bank's efforts to improve transition began with the arrival of Superintendent Laura Morana in 2006. Superintendent Morana realized that teachers at different grade levels must coordinate their efforts in order to best meet the needs of all of the district's students, including the district's many low-income students and English language learners.

Implementation   At Red Bank, three strategies ensure pedagogical continuity: curricular alignment, shared instructional practices, and data-driven professional development. We describe each in turn.

Curricular Alignment   Pre-K and kindergarten classrooms in Red Bank use the Tools of the Mind (Metropolitan State College of Denver, n.d.) curriculum to teach literacy, mathematics, science, and other subjects. The Early Childhood Division of the New Jersey Department of Education recommends *Tools of the Mind* as one of five curricula that align with state standards and incorporate developmentally appropriate practice (New Jersey Department of Education, 2008). The curriculum, which is based on Lev Vygotsky's sociocultural theory of development, uses a combination of instructional techniques—individual work, cooperative paired learning, teacher scaffolding, and explicit instruction—to cultivate cognitive and socioemotional self-regulation. Opportunities for self-regulation are embedded in content work, and teachers regularly assess children's progress in order to individualize instruction. Guided by *Tools of the Mind,* the district has created consistency between pre-K and kindergarten classrooms, on features ranging from curriculum to physical classroom space and materials. Initially, only Red Bank's pre-K teachers received training on *Tools of the Mind.* The district later recognized the potential of the program to improve instruction and invested in *Tools of the Mind* training for kindergarten teachers and full-time paraprofessionals at both grade levels to improve transition and promote more developmentally appropriate practice. Kindergarten classrooms were also organized into activity centers with materials that mirrored those found in pre-K classrooms (L. Morana, personal communication, September 16, 2009). These changes created continuity and eased transitions for children as they moved from prekindergarten to kindergarten.

First- through third-grade teachers maintain pedagogical continuity as they teach reading and language arts. All three grades use *Treasures*, a MacMillan/McGraw-Hill teaching guide, within a balanced literacy framework. Like *Tools of the Mind,* the balanced literacy framework includes a combination of direct instruction, differentiated instruction in small groups, and independent practice at centers. The balanced literacy framework is well aligned with the child-centered instructional practices that are used in Red Bank's preschool and kindergarten classrooms. It builds nicely, for example, on incoming first graders' prior experience conducting independent inquiry at centers with a study partner and a variety of literacy materials (L. Morana, personal communication, September 16, 2009). Through their shared view of children as capable learners and their use of differentiated instruction, teachers of preschool through third grade in Red Bank maintain pedagogical alignment across the early grades.

Instructional Alignment   Red Bank also has improved transitions by providing multiple opportunities for teachers at different grade levels to meet with one another and discuss instructional strategies. Common planning periods allow teachers to develop consistent lesson plans, and transition meetings at the end of every school year provide a forum for teachers of different grade levels to discuss particularly successful instructional approaches. During one transition meeting, for example, kindergarten teachers informed first-grade teachers that they found the group discussion method recommended in *Tools of the Mind* to be especially effective. Using this approach, a teacher poses a question to the class and asks children to discuss the answer with partners while she walks around and listens. The teacher then summarizes what she heard and shares the most correct answer with the class. With kindergarten teachers' endorsements, first-grade teachers decided to adopt this "turn and talk" strategy in place of the more teacher-directed approach that they had been using of asking students to raise their hands and respond to the teacher at the front of the classroom.

Peer-to-peer classroom observations also allow teachers to strengthen instructional alignment. During these periods, observing teachers learn about the techniques and materials that are used in other grades and often come away with new ideas for their own classrooms. For example, first-grade teachers were interested in the short weekly student–teacher conferences that they observed kindergarten teachers conducting with all of their children during the morning literacy block. During the conferences, teachers and students review work from a child's portfolio, discuss progress as well as challenges encountered, and set learning goals for the following week. The conferences provide kindergarten teachers with an opportunity to guide classroom instruction and encourage children to take an active role in their learning. As a result of cross-grade classroom observations and follow-up discussions, first-grade teachers decided to replicate this practice in their own classrooms (J. Bombardier, personal communication September 16, 2009). By exposing teachers to effective instructional practices, this collaborative process has brought meaningful continuity to children's experiences.

Data-Driven Professional Development   To support alignment of curriculum and instruction, Red Bank employs instructional coaches who provide ongoing on-site professional development. This professional development contrasts with off-site workshops or brief, consultant-led trainings, which do not allow teachers opportunities to practice new skills and receive regular feedback. It also allows for greater continuity from grade to grade as coaches work with teachers at different grade levels to promote age-appropriate, child-centered practices. Coaches provide one-to-one support to teachers and workshops that are tailored to address specific needs identified through lesson plan review, classroom observation, and analysis of child assessment data (L. Morana, personal communication September 10, 2009).

Instructional coaches, administrators, and the superintendent also review all teachers' lesson plans weekly or biweekly to ensure that lesson plans reflect the curriculum with fidelity and utilize appropriate instructional approaches. Coaches give teachers feedback after reviewing their lesson plans and observing their classrooms. For example, they may encourage teachers to use more differentiated instruction or more varied learning activities. Coaches suggest strategies such as child-led investigation or compare-and-contrast examples, and they even model lessons for teachers who request more guidance. Teachers are also asked to reflect on the strengths and weaknesses of their teaching and lesson plans as the week goes on. Coaches, administrators, and the superintendent meet weekly to look for patterns in the feedback that is given to teachers or in teachers' reflections to find areas where professional development should be targeted. For example, the coach may develop a training session to help teachers strengthen a specific skill with which children appear to be struggling.

Child assessment data play an important role in informing professional development and classroom instruction in Red Bank. School improvement teams review state testing data over the summer to identify the specific underlying skills and concepts that children need to strengthen in order to make progress along the learning continuum in content areas such as literacy and mathematics. During the school year, teachers, instructional coaches, principals, and administrators analyze data from formative assessments of children's portfolios and quarterly benchmark assessments in weekly planning meetings. Participants develop action plans to address areas that need improvement (J. Bombardier, personal communication, September 16, 2009). For example, if children are scoring 3 out of 5 on writing assessments and grammar seems to be the primary challenge, teachers can design a mini-lesson on sentence-writing to scaffold children's learning. Through this type of data-driven professional development, teachers are able to employ instructional strategies that respond closely to children's position on the learning continuum.

Maximizing Time for Collaboration and Professional Development   Red Bank's ongoing process of assessment and adaptation assumes that teachers and school administrators will invest significant time in this effort. To accommodate busy schedules and union guidelines, the district has found creative ways to maximize opportunities for collaboration and professional development. Teachers using *Tools of the Mind* attend 5 days of professional development throughout the year. Additional professional development sessions are held for all teachers by converting unused snow days into professional development days at the end of the school year. Faculty meetings are also a time for teachers to consult with instructional coaches. Per union regulations, these meetings were traditionally held bimonthly for 50 minutes each. Recognizing the need for longer meetings, Superintendent Morana successfully negotiated for monthly meetings of double the length, which have allowed for more productive reflection. These are some of the strategies that Red Bank has used to ensure that staff's limited working hours outside the classroom are spent meaningfully (L. Morana, personal communication, September 10, 2009).

Lessons Learned   Smoothing transitions between grade levels required open-mindedness and flexibility from teachers. This requirement was particularly true for kindergarten teachers in Red Bank, who were asked to abandon the teacher-directed instructional approaches that they were accustomed to using and to adopt instead less familiar approaches that were characteristic of pre-K classrooms. Because the *Tools of the Mind* trainings took place quarterly, kindergarten teachers were not able to see the "big picture" of the curriculum until the end of the first school year that they used it, when the final training session occurred. In addition to adjusting their assumptions about teaching and learning, kindergarten teachers also had to confront the practical implications of changing curricula, such as rearranging their classrooms to accommodate learning centers. "We were asking teachers to change their whole method of delivering instruction. It was unknown to them; we had to get past that fear," explained John Bombardier, Red Bank Borough's Supervisor of Curriculum and Instruction (personal communication, September 16, 2009).

To support these shifts in kindergarten classrooms, administrators had to acknowledge teachers' previous efforts while they simultaneously asked them to adopt a different approach to instruction. The district learned two key lessons as they faced the challenge of providing instructional, motivational, and material support to teachers.

First, data played an important role in garnering support for change. According to Laura Morana, superintendent, "You have to use data to introduce an issue that needs attention" (personal communication, September 10, 2009). It was largely the review and discussion of student performance data that convinced skeptical teachers of the need for a new approach to classroom instruction. Later, they were won over by the effectiveness of the child-centered curriculum and instruction. Ms. Morana noted, "Teachers eventually became the spokespeople because they could see the curriculum was effective in improving performance. When you have the data to support you, it is easier."

Second, district and school administrators noted the importance of adequately budgeting for classroom materials and supplies. The district incurred substantial costs in the process of reorganizing kindergarten classrooms into activity centers and stocking them with new materials. By providing the funding that was needed to fully implement the new curricular initiative, the district ensured its success.

Above all, the crucial message from Red Bank's effort to improve instruction is that alignment must be grounded in an understanding of developmentally appropriate practice. When teachers understand where their children are developmentally and where they have been, they are equipped to scaffold children's learning. Looking beyond the similarities built into *Tools of the Mind* and the *Balanced Literacy Approach,* teachers in Red Bank have found ways to translate particularly effective classroom activities (e.g., turn and talk) for use at various grade levels. Opportunities for discussion and cross-grade classroom observation, as well as ongoing assessment and professional development, have allowed teachers to continually share and emphasize instructional practices that work and to drop the ones that do not. To foster alignment, Red Bank has gone beyond simply selecting curricula or textbooks—instead, the district has attempted to base instruction around strategies that are responsive to the needs of young children.

Future Directions   Having identified successful methods for improving classroom practice, Red Bank is working to establish stronger school improvement teams. Superintendent Morana's goal is to foster increased leadership capacity at the building level so that teachers develop their own creative and proactive approaches to enhancing student achievement with less involvement from district administrators. Driving this approach is the understanding that improvement at the classroom level cannot be a top-down process; rather, it depends on the active engagement of the staff who are working directly with children. When the district decided to update its math curriculum, for example, teachers were asked to participate in the review and selection of the new textbook, McGraw-Hill's *Everyday Mathematics*. Teachers will continue to play a primary role in planning as the district works to increase alignment of math instruction, thereby further supporting children's transition across the early grades (L. Morana, personal communication, September 10, 2009).

Conclusion   Red Bank Borough public school system has served as a trailblazer in New Jersey, where the State Department of Education has made transitions across the pre-K–3 continuum a priority. Red Bank Borough laid the groundwork for effective transition by selecting pedagogically aligned curricula and emphasizing developmentally appropriate instructional approaches. The district ensured the realization of its vision by providing teachers with professional development time to share effective teaching strategies and to develop plans on the basis of student assessment data. More and more districts are expected to adopt these practices as New Jersey's State Department of Education continues to support transition through regulatory guidance and professional development for administrators.

Case Study—Step by Step Moldova

Promoting Transitions Through Child-Centered Pedagogy
Alejandra Cortazar

Step by Step Moldova (SBSM) is a comprehensive educational reform program that aims to provide quality education for children in the Republic of Moldova from birth to age 10. SBSM uses two overarching strategies. First, it promotes a child-centered educational model that is suitable both for preschool and primary schools. SBSM's child-centered approach embraces ideas of individualized learning and active pedagogy and is based on the work of theorists and practitioners such as Jean Piaget, Erik Erickson, Karl Rogers, Lev Vygotsky, Maria Montessori, and Howard Gardner (Step by Step Moldova, n.d.). Second, SBSM works to improve the professional development system for preschool and primary school teachers in line with this child-centered approach. Both strategies promote pedagogical continuity between preschool and primary school, thereby facilitating children's transition between educational levels.

Participants   SBSM has successfully supported more than 383 preschool and 1156 primary school classrooms across the country. SBSM strives to serve disadvantaged children and families and works with many minority populations including Moldova's Russian, Ukrainian, Bulgarian, Jewish, Gagauz, and Roma communities (International Step by Step Association, n.d.).

Origins   SBSM began in 1994 as a joint effort between Children's Resources International and the Open Society Institute. Its child-centered methodology was initially introduced in 12 classrooms in five kindergartens. Well received, the program grew substantially in its second year, reaching 60 new classrooms. To meet the demands of parents and teachers for continuity, the program expanded in 1996 to primary schools where it was implemented in 20 experimental classrooms. The following year, the program added a component for children from birth to age 3. It also developed a new training module, to be offered through institutions of higher education, that was designed to help teacher education colleges and universities train preschool and primary school teachers to implement child-centered curricula. Nine institutions of higher education are working with SBSM to train new teachers in the child-centered approach (Step by Step Moldova, n.d.).

The program became a member of the International Step by Step Association (ISSA) in 1998, joining a network of countries in Central and Eastern Europe and Central Asia that were developing similar programs. Between 1998 and 2006, SBSM partnered with the Social Investment Fund in Moldova, a World Bank project, to improve early education by renovating school facilities. During this period, SBSM also increased its investments in teacher training, reaching teachers in more than 350 schools (C. Cincilei, personal communication, July 21, 2009).

Since 2007, SBSM has worked with the Ministry of Education in the Education for All Fast Track Initiative. Using a "train-the-trainer" model, the program provided training for 1,350 teachers from 2007 to 2008, with another 1,320 teachers slated to receive training in 2009 and 2010. In addition, after focusing on the classroom for many years, SBSM decided to expand its work to the larger school and community, creating programs not only for teachers but also for school administrators, staff, and the community (Step by Step Moldova, 2008).

SBSM also works to influence policy at the national level. In 2007, the program released national teacher standards and began formulating national early learning and development standards (C. Cincilei, personal communication, July 23, 2009).

Program Structure   SBSM is a nongovernmental, nonprofit, and nonpolitical organization. As a member of the ISSA, it is linked with early childhood development professionals and nongovernmental organizations in 29 countries that implement the Step by Step program (International Step by Step Association, n.d.). ISSA provides its members with the Step by Step pedagogical standards and helps them advocate for change at the national level (C. Cincilei, personal communication, July 21, 2009). SBSM's strategy is guided by this international effort that is affecting change for early childhood education in other nations as well.

The program is run by a core team of five individuals with a staff of approximately 50 trainers across the country (C. Cincilei, personal communication, November 11, 2008). A central office staff oversees the work of trainers who are distributed among six training centers throughout the country. SBSM also has a board of directors with representatives from partner and funding organizations, including the Soros Foundation Moldova, the Mott Foundation, the Moldovan Social Investment Fund, and the World Bank. The board also includes experts in the fields of community development and education (Step by Step Moldova, 2008).

Implementation   Working toward its mission of fostering child-centered practices at the preschool and primary school levels, SBSM provides support, training, and monitoring to preschool and primary school teachers and administrators in child-centered pedagogy. In addition to providing training for in-service teachers and administrators, SBSM offers support for preservice training.

The SBSM in-service training model is composed of 18 days of training spanning a 2-year period. Over the course of the training program, both preschool and primary school teachers are expected to complete home assignments and build a portfolio. At the end of the training, teachers are assessed and awarded a certificate in the SBS method. Training covers child-centered curriculum and philosophy, active learning, meaningful learning, partnership with families, classroom management, teachers' role in child-centered methodology, individualized learning, and integrated curriculum. The training program uses active pedagogy to encourage teachers' participation and learning and to model good practices (Step by Step Moldova, n.d.).

Over the past few years, decreases in funding have necessitated some changes to the training program. Although the 18-session training is considered ideal, SBSM has adjusted the number of sessions in some instances. For example, while teachers trained under the Social Investment Fund receive the full 18 days of instruction, teachers trained under the Education For All Fast Track Initiative receive between 5 and 7 days (C. Cincilei, personal communication, July 23, 2009).

SBSM trains at least two teachers per school, helping them integrate child-centered learning centers into their classrooms. The philosophy of the SBSM model is that these teachers will transmit their knowledge and skills to fellow teachers and administrators, promoting further change within their schools (C. Cincilei, personal communication, July 21, 2009). Classrooms that have received support from SBSM, considered "model classrooms," are used as demonstration classrooms for training other teachers in the school. Teachers throughout the school are encouraged to modify classroom routines and adult–child interactions to adopt SBSM's child-centered philosophy. They are also expected to encourage children's active participation. For example, both preschool and primary school teachers are expected to lead circle times during which children can ask and answer questions and teachers can integrate content areas such as language, mathematics, and science. Teachers are also encouraged to individualize activities according to each child's interests and needs (C. Cincilei, personal communication, July 23, 2009).

In addition to emphasizing classroom techniques, trainers help teachers extend the child-centered philosophy to family engagement. Specifically, teachers encourage parents to be more active in their children's education by inviting the parents to participate in classroom activities, by hosting sessions on topics of parent interest, and by asking parents to join in field trips outside the school.

Although some aspects of the teacher training are conducted separately for preschool and primary teachers, SBSM encourages collaborative work between these two groups. For example, in order to foster smooth transitions for children, preschool children are invited to visit primary school classrooms. In addition, primary school teachers visit preschool classrooms in order to become familiar with the preschool environment and to meet the children who will be enrolling in primary school. The fact that preschool and primary school teachers share a common pedagogical approach fosters meaningful continuity between these two education levels. SBSM trainers also advise university faculty in child-centered pedagogy and support them in designing preservice teaching programs for preschool and primary school teachers.

Highlights and Accomplishments   One of SBSM's greatest accomplishments is its reach. The organization has been able to work with multiple community-based organizations to create a vast network of five institutions implementing the SBS model in 1,539 classrooms. This reach has allowed SBSM to influence educational practices and policies on a national level (Step by Step Moldova, 2008). An example of SBSM's policy impact is its collaboration with the Ministry of Education through the Education for All Fast Track Initiative. Program Director Cornelia Cincilei believes that "being selected to train preschool teachers across the whole country on to implement child-centered education is an indicator of the trust the government has in the SBS model" (personal communication, July 21, 2009). SBSM continues to expand within and beyond Moldova; it has offered support and mentoring programs in child-centered methodology in Armenia and Tajikistan (Step by Step Moldova, n.d.).

Another highlight of SBSM's work has been the high regard in which its staff are held. These educators work with preservice teachers and with faculty members who conduct in-service training. The Step by Step model has gained recognition from the Ministry of Education as a valid institution for teachers' professional development and accreditation (C. Cincilei, personal communication, July 21, 2009).

Perhaps most important, evaluation results suggest that SBSM has had positive impacts on child outcomes. The Ministry of Education evaluated SBSM several times during the program's first years of implementation and concluded that SBSM was a good model of child-centred pedagogy, had positively influenced children's development, and had provided children with strong foundations for future learning. Specifically, the study revealed that children who attended child-centered classrooms were more inquisitive, creative, and able to think critically than children who did not participate in these types of classrooms (International Step by Step Association, n.d.).

Challenges   A main challenge for SBSM has been helping communities overcome the long-held belief that traditional teaching methods are more effective than child-centered methodologies at facilitating children's learning and development. Teachers were accustomed to a prescribed curriculum and they had to adapt their mindset and actions to accommodate a more open curriculum that encouraged children's active participation. Many teachers had the preconceived notion that children would learn at a slower pace with a child-centered approach than they would in a teacher-centered classroom. These initial concerns dissipated, however, once the first cohort of children finished primary school. Teachers found that the children in the child-centered SBSM program did not lag behind their peers, and in fact exhibited more advanced skills in some areas, including communication and problem-solving skills.

In addition to these attitudinal obstacles, structural obstacles impeded SBSM's implementation. When SBSM was first launched, primary school teachers were conforming to pressure from educational inspectors who assessed their performance according to standards that required a more directive role for teachers. This problem was mitigated in 2007 when Moldova's government, with the participation of SBSM, developed new standards for teachers that were consistent with a child-centered teaching philosophy (C. Cincilei, personal communication, July 21, 2009). The adoption of these standards as national policy is important evidence of SBSM's impact on what had been deeply entrenched understandings of how children learn and how teachers should teach.

Lessons Learned   To generate change inside a school, it is necessary to engage a team of staff; a strategy focused only on individual teachers is insufficient to change the pedagogical practices of a school. For this reason, SBSM opened its training to include administrators and community members so that the collective team could be agents of change inside the school community (C. Cincilei, personal communication, July 21, 2009).

It is necessary to present teachers with multiple ways of implementing the child-centered approach in order to increase the program's effectiveness. Specifically, providing teachers with multiple examples from training and model classrooms demonstrates that there is more than one way of enacting a child-centered approach. Teachers must be flexible and use self-reflection skills when they are implementing the SBS approach.

Using teachers from the best performing classrooms as trainers is more effective than using academics as trainers. Early childhood and primary school teachers are more practice oriented, a factor that is greatly appreciated by the teachers who participate in the SBSM professional development program.

In order to facilitate children's transitions, preschool and primary school teachers need to respect one another's work. SBSM has found that mutual respect between preschool and primary school teachers comes from a shared understanding of children's development, needs, learning processes, and pedagogical approaches. When they respect one another, teachers at each level forge successful collaborative relationships (C. Cincilei, personal communication, July 21, 2009).

Future Directions   Moving forward, SBSM's most ambitious goal is to implement large-scale change by helping schools become ready to receive preschool children. This goal is founded on SBSM's experience that it is more effective to change classroom practices when the entire school shares a common understanding of children's needs and appropriate practices (C. Cincilei, personal communication, July 21, 2009). SBSM will continue to promote and implement pedagogical alignment between preschools and primary schools. To accomplish this work, program personnel must advocate for revisions to align primary school content-based standards with the early learning standards that are currently being created for children from birth to 7 years. In addition, SBSM seeks to expand its professional development activities by working with community schools and alternative preschool programs that have not yet been involved in SBSM.

Conclusion   SBSM advocates for quality child-centered education for children in Moldova. By introducing a child-centered approach at both the preschool and primary school levels, SBSM has created pedagogical alignment in participating settings between these two educational levels. This pedagogical continuity has helped to bridge disparities that are commonly present between the preschool and primary school curricula, therefore easing children's transition from one level to the next.

REFERENCES

Barbarin, O.A., & Wasik, B.H. (Eds.). (2009). *Handbook of child development and early education: Research to practice.* New York: Guilford Press.

Barbour, N.H., & Seefeldt. C. (1993). *Developmental continuity across preschool and primary grades.* Wheaton, MD: Association for Childhood Education International.

Barnett, W.S., Jung, K., Yarosz, D.J., Thomas, J., Hornbeck, A., Stechuk, R., et al. (2008). Educational effects of the Tools of the Mind Curriculum: A randomized trial. *Early Childhood Research Quarterly, 23*(3), 299–313.

Barnett, W.S., Yarosz, D.J., Thomas, J., Jung, K., & Blanco, D. (2007). Two-way and monolingual English immersion in preschool education: An experimental comparison. *Early Childhood Research Quarterly, 22*(3), 277–293.

Blair, C., & Razza, R.C. (2007). Relating effortful control, executive functional and false belief understanding to emerging math and literacy ability in kindergarten. *Child Development, 78*(2), 647–663.

Bodrova, E., & Leong, D.J. (2006). Self-regulation as a key to school readiness: How early childhood teachers can promote this critical competency. In M. Zaslow & I. Martinez-Beck (Eds.), *Critical issues in early childhood professional development* (pp. 203–224). Baltimore: Paul H. Brookes Publishing Co.

Bodrova, E., & Leong, D.J. (2007). *Tools of the Mind: The Vygotskian approach to early childhood education.* New York: Merrill/Prentice Hall.

Bogard, K., & Takanishi, R. (2005). PK–3: An aligned and coordinated approach to education for children 3 to 8 years old. *Social Policy Report,* vol. 19(3).

Bowman, B., Donovan, M.S., & Burns, S. (Eds.). (2001). *Eager to learn: Educating our preschoolers.* National Research Council, Committee on Early Childhood Pedagogy. Washington, DC: National Academies Press.

Boyd, J., Barnett, W.S., Bodrova, E., Leong, D.J., & Gomby, D. (2005, March). *Promoting children's social emotional development through preschool* (Preschool Policy Report). New Brunswick, NJ: National Institute for Early Education Research.

Bransford, J.D., Brown, A.L., & Cocking, R.R. (Eds.). (2000). *How people learn: Brain, mind, experience and school.* Expanded edition. Washington, DC: National Academies Press.

Burchinal, M., Howes, C., Pianta, R., Bryant, D., Early, D., Clifford, R., et al. (2008). Predicting child outcomes at the end of kindergarten from the quality of pre-kindergarten teacher–child interactions and instruction. *Applied Developmental Science, 12*(3), 140–153.

Calkins, S.D., & Williford, A.P. (2009). Taming the terrible twos: Self-regulation and school readiness. In O.A. Barbarin & B.H. Wasik (Eds.), *Handbook of child development and early education: Research to practice* (pp. 172–198). New York: Guilford Press.

Clements, D.H., & Sarama, J. (2009). *Learning and teaching early math: The learning trajectories approach.* New York: Routledge.

Cross, C.T., Woods, T.A., & Schweingruder, H. (Eds.). (2009). *Mathematics learning in early childhood: Paths toward excellence and equity.* Committee on Early Childhood Mathematics, Center for Education, Division of Behavioral and Social Sciences and Education. Washington, DC: National Academies Press.

Diamond, A., Barnett, S., Thomas, J., & Munroe, S. (2007). Preschool program improves cognitive control. *Science, 318*(5855).1387–1388.

Dickinson, D.K. (2001a). Book reading in preschool classrooms: Is recommended practice common? In D.K. Dickinson & P.O. Tabors (Eds.), *Beginning literacy with language: Young children learning at home and school* (pp. 175–203). Baltimore: Paul H. Brookes Publishing Co.

Dickinson, D.K. (2001b). Large-group and free-play times: Conversational settings supporting language and literacy development. In Dickinson, D.K., & P.O. Tabors (Eds.), *Beginning literacy with language: Young children learning at home and school* (pp. 223–256). Baltimore: Paul H. Brookes Publishing Co.

Early, D.M., Barbarin, O., Bryant, D., Burchinal, M., Chang, F., Clifford, R., et al. (2005). *Prekindergarten in eleven states: NCEDL's multi-state study of pre-kindergarten and study of state-wide early education programs (SWEEP).* Chapel Hill, NC: FPG Child Development Institute.

Espinosa, L. (2007). English-language learners as they enter school. In R.C. Pianta, M.J. Cox, & K.L. Snow (Eds.), *School readiness and the transition to kindergarten in the era of accountability* (pp. 175–196). Baltimore: Paul H. Brookes Publishing Co.

Foundation for Child Development. (2008). America's vanishing potential: The case for pre-K–3rd education. New York: Author. Retrieved June 1, 2009, from http://www.fcd-us.org/resources/resources_show.htm?doc_id=711495.

Frede, E., & Ackerman, D.J. (2007). Preschool curriculum decision-making: Dimensions to consider. Retrieved June 5, 2009, from http://nieer.org/resources/policybriefs/12.pdf

Gallahue, D.L., & Ozmun, J.C. (2006). Motor development in young children. In B. Spodek & O.N. Saracho (Eds.), *Handbook of research on the education of young children* (2nd ed.) (pp. 105–120). Mahweh, NJ: Lawrence Erlbaum Associates.

Ginsburg, H.P., Lee, J.S., & Boyd, J.S. (2008). Mathematics education for young children: What it is and how to promote it. *Social Policy Report, XXII*(I), 3–23.

Hamre, B.K., & Pianta, R.C. (2001). Early teacher–child relationships and the trajectory of children's school outcomes through eighth grade. *Child Development, 72,* 625–638.

Hamre, B.K., & Pianta, R.C. (2005). Can instructional and emotional support in the first-grade classroom make a difference for children at risk of school failure? *Child Development, 76*(5), 949–967.

Hamre, B.K., & Pianta, R.C. (2007). Learning opportunities in preschool and early elementary classrooms. In R.C. Pianta, M.J. Cox, & K.L. Snow (Eds.), *School readiness and the transition to kindergarten in the era of accountability* (pp. 49–83). Baltimore: Paul H. Brookes Publishing Co.

International Step by Step Association. (n.d.). Retrieved from http://www.issa.nl/network/moldova/moldova.html

Klein, L.G., & J. Knitzer. (2007). Promoting effective early learning: What every policy maker and educator should know. New York: National Center for Children in Poverty. Retrieved June 1, 2009, from http://nccp.org/publications/pub_695.html

Landry, S.H. (2005a). *Effective early childhood programs: Turning knowledge into action.* Houston, TX: University of Texas-Houston, Health Science Center.

Landry, S.H. (2005b). *Texas Early Education Model (TEEM): Improving school readiness and increasing access to child care for Texas: Year 2 Findings.* Houston, TX: University of Texas-Houston, Health Science Center.

Lonigan, C.J., & Whitehurst, G.J. (1998). Relative efficacy of parent and teacher involvement in a shared-reading intervention for preschool children from low-income backgrounds. *Early Childhood Research Quarterly, 13*(2), 263–290.

McAfee, O., & Leong, D. (2007). *Assessing and guiding young children's development and learning* (4th ed.). Boston: Allyn & Bacon.

McClelland, M.M., Acock, A.C., & Morrison, F.J. (2006). The impact of kindergarten learning-related skills on academic trajectories at the end of elementary school. *Early Childhood Research Quarterly, 21*(4), 471–490.

Metropolitan State College of Denver. (n.d.). *Tools of the Mind.* Retrieved May 15, 2009, from http://www.mscd.edu/extendedcampus/toolsofthemind/curriculum/index.shtml

National Association for the Education of Young Children. (2005). *Curriculum: A guide to the NAEYC early childhood program standard and related accreditation criteria.* Washington, DC: Author.

National Association for the Education of Young Children. (2009a). *Developmentally appropriate practice in early childhood programs serving children from birth through age 8. Position statement.* Washington, DC: Author. Retrieved June 1, 2009, from http://www.naeyc.org/files/naeyc/file/positions/PSDAP.pdf

National Association for the Education of Young Children. (2009b). *NAEYC standards for early childhood professional preparation programs.* Washington, DC: Author.

National Association for the Education of Young Children & National Association of Early Childhood Specialists in State Departments of Education. (2003). *Early childhood curriculum, assessment, and program evaluation: Building an effective, accountable system in programs for children birth through age 8* (Position statement). Retrieved June 1, 2009, from http://www.naeyc.org/files/naeyc/file/positions/pscape.pdf.

National Association of State Boards of Education. (2009). Promoting quality in pre-K–grade 3 classrooms: Findings and results of NASBE's Early Childhood Education Network. *Issues in Brief.* Arlington, VA: Author.

National Council of Teachers of Mathematics. (2006). *Curriculum focal points.* Reston, VA: Author.

National Early Literacy Panel. (2008). *Developing early literacy: Report of the National Early Literacy Panel.* A scientific synthesis of early literacy development and implications for intervention. Washington, DC: National Institute for Literacy.

National Institute of Child Health and Human Development. (2002). The relation of first grade classroom environment to structural classroom features, teacher, and student behaviors. *The Elementary School Journal, 102,* 367–387.

National Institute of Child Health and Human Development. (2003). Social functioning in first grade: Predictions from home, child care and concurrent school experience. *Child Development, 74,* 1639–1662.

National Institute of Child Health and Human Development. (2005). A day in third grade: A large-scale study of classroom quality and teacher and student behavior. *The Elementary School Journal, 105,* 305–323.

Neuman, S.B. (2006). The knowledge gap: Implications for early education. In D.K. Dickinson & S.B. Neuman (Eds.), *Handbook of early literacy research* (Vol. 2). New York: Guilford Press.

Neuman, S.B., & Roskos, K. (2005). The state of state pre-kindergarten standards. *Early Childhood Research Quarterly, 20*(2), 125–145.

New Jersey Department of Education. (2008). *Preschool program implementation guidelines.* Retrieved June 30, 2009, from http://www.state.nj.us/education/ece/dap/impguidelines.pdf

Ornstein, P.A., Coffman, J.L., & Grammer, J.K. (2009). Learning to remember. In O.A Barbarin & B.H. Wasik (Eds.), *Handbook of child development and early education: Research to practice* (pp. 103–122). New York: Guilford Press.

Preschool Curriculum Evaluation Research Consortium. (2008). *Effects of preschool curriculum programs on school readiness (NCER 2008–2009).* Washington, DC: National Center for Education Research, Institute of Education Sciences, U.S. Department of Education. Washington, DC: U.S. Government Printing Office.

Pianta, R.C., La Paro, K.M., & Hamre, B.K. (2008). *Classroom Assessment Scoring System (CLASS).* Baltimore: Paul H. Brookes Publishing Co.

Pianta, R.C., & Stuhlman, M.W. (2003). Teacher–child relationships and children's success in the first years of school. *School Psychology Review, 33*(3), 444–458.

Ritchie, S., Maxwell, K., & Bredekamp, S. (2009). Rethinking early schooling: Using developmental science to transform children's early school experiences. In O.A. Barbarin & B.H. Wasik (Eds.), *Handbook of child development and early education: Research to practice* (pp. 14–37). New York: Guilford Press.

Ritchie, S., Maxwell, K., & Clifford, R.M. (2007). FirstSchool: A new vision for education. In R.C. Pianta, M.J. Cox, & K.L. Snow (Eds.), *School readiness and the transition to kindergarten in the era of accountability* (pp. 85–96). Baltimore: Paul H. Brookes Publishing Co.

Sarama, J., & Clements, D.H. (2009). *Early childhood mathematics education research: Learning trajectories for young children.* New York: Routledge.

Step by Step Moldova (n.d.). *PASCUPAS* Retrieved from http://www.pascupas.md/about/about_us/en.html

Step by Step Moldova (2008). *Annual report.* Retrieved from http://www.pascupas.md/docs/132-rapor-tanual.doc.doc

Schweinhart, L.J., & Weikart, D.P. (1997). *Lasting differences: The HighScope Preschool Curriculum Comparison Study through Age 16.* Ypsilanti, MI: HighScope Educational Research Foundation.

Schweinhart, L.J., Weikart, D.P., & Larner, M.B. (1986). Consequences of three preschool curriculum models through age 15. *Early Childhood Research Quarterly, 1*, 15–45.

Scott-Little, C., Kagan, S.L., & Frelow, V.S. (2005). Inside the content: The breadth and depth of early learning standards. Retrieved February 28, 2009, from http://www.serve.org/_downloads/publications/insidecontentfr.pdf

Seo, K.-H., & Ginsburg, H.P. (2004). What is developmentally appropriate in early childhood mathematics education? Lessons from new research. In D.H. Clements, J. Sarama, & A.M. DiBiase (Eds.), *Engaging young children in mathematics: Standards for early childhood mathematics education* (pp. 91–104). Mahwah, NJ: Lawrence Erlbaum Associates.

Shanahan, T. (2006). The worst confession: Using a scripted program. President's message. *Reading Today*, August/September, 14.

Shonkoff, J., & Phillips, D.A. (2000). *From neurons to neighborhoods: The science of early childhood development.* Washington, DC: National Academies Press.

Shore, R. (2009). The case for investing in pre-K–3rd education: Challenging myths about school reform. Retrieved June 1, 2009, from http://www.fcd-us.org/resources/resources_show.htm?doc_id=801522

Slavin, R.E., & Cheung, A. (2005). A synthesis of research on language of reading instruction for English language learners. *Review of Educational Research, 75*(2), 247–281.

Snow, C.E., Burns, M.S., & Griffin, P. (Eds.) (1998). *Preventing reading difficulties in young children.* Washington, DC: National Academies Press.

Takanishi, R., & Kauerz, K. (2008). PK inclusion: Getting serious about a P–16 education system. *Phi Delta Kappan, 89*(7), 480–87.

Thompson, R.A., & Goodman, M. (2009). Development of self, relationships, and socioemotional competence: Foundations for early school success. In O.A. Barbarin & B.H. Wasik (Eds.), *Handbook of child development and early education: Research to practice* (pp. 147–171). New York: Guilford Press.

Wasik, B.H., & Newman, B.A. (2009). *Teaching and learning to read.* In O.A. Barbarin & B.H. Wasik (Eds.), *Handbook of child development and early education: Research to practice* (pp.147–171). New York: Guilford Press.

Zill, N., Sorongon, A., Kim, K., Clark, C., & Woolverton, M. (2006). Children's outcomes and program quality in Head Start. *FACES 2003 Research Brief.* Washington, DC: Head Start B.

III

Programmatic Perspective

9

Ready or Not? Schools' Readiness for Young Children

Sharon Ritchie, Richard M. Clifford, William W. Malloy,
Carolyn T. Cobb, and Gisele M. Crawford

INTRODUCTION

Public education in the United States has been characterized by periods of expansion to make public school available and accessible to virtually all children between the ages of 5 and 18 years (Crawford, Clifford, Early, & Reszka, 2009). We are continuing this expansion by including increasing numbers of even younger children. By the beginning of the 21st century, nearly 1 in 4 children had their prekindergarten (pre-K) experience in an elementary school setting. (Clifford, Early, & Hills, 1999). This recent expansion has led to much discussion and debate about the role and nature of school for these young children. We know that children can benefit from early education experiences. But are schools ready and willing to make changes to accommodate the full range of needs of younger children and their families? While schools and policy makers invest in getting children ready for kindergarten, many families appear to be questioning the readiness of schools for their children.

Two trends have a bearing on the question of school readiness. First, while most 3- and 4-year-olds are still served in nonpublic school settings, many children are coming to elementary school at an earlier age. A substantial literature demonstrates the positive benefits for children of exposure to educational experiences earlier in life, so some 38 states now have established state-funded public pre-K programs (Barnett, Epstein, Friedman, Boyd, & Hustedt, 2008). Most of these programs serve children who are considered to be at risk of school failure in the elementary and secondary system. However, a few states now accept all children into their state pre-K programs 1 year before the children are eligible for kindergarten. By 2008, more than 1 million children were enrolled in these state programs in the United States (Barnett et al.). Many other children were in school-based Head Start programs, programs for children with special needs, or locally sponsored pre-K programs.

Second, in a seemingly contradictory trend, relatively large numbers of families are deciding to delay kindergarten entry for their children to allow them to have a year of additional development prior to entering the formal school setting. In a fascinating examination of the changing pattern of school entry, Deming and Dynarski (2008) show a strong pattern of children entering kindergarten at an older age. Between 1968 and 2005, the proportion of 6-year-old children in first grade declined from 96% to 84%. About three quarters of the decline is attributable to parents or school staff deciding to keep children out of kindergarten or first grade when the children are legally eligible to enter that level of schooling. In many cases, the families enroll their children instead in private preschool or its equivalent, but the fact is that they are choosing to delay entry into elementary school. This process, referred to as *red-shirting*, has increased at the same time that we have witnessed the downward extension of schools to serve children before they are eligible for kindergarten.

Another illustration of parents' hesitance to send their children to elementary school at a very young age is the increasing number of families who choose to home school their children for at least the first few years of school. By 2003, nearly 100,000 children (2.7% of the children in kindergarten) were home schooled for the kindergarten year (National Center for Education Statistics, 2006). The rate of home schooling at this age is much higher than the rate at other ages. For example, 1.8% of children in Grades 1–3 and 1.9% of children in Grades 4 and 5 were home schooled. So, while there is a push to start children's schooling at younger and younger ages through pre-K programs, a substantial number of parents feel that the highly structured nature of most schools is not what is best for their own young children.

These two trends illustrate critical issues that schools face as we move into the 21st century. Schools must be ready to receive very young children and to serve them appropriately through the early elementary years. In this chapter we will examine the concept of ready schools and describe the evidence in favor of implementing the concept. We will then detail school-level factors that facilitate transitions for young learners. Finally, we will describe school engagement policies that ensure continuity and effective practices for children as they start school.

What Are Ready Schools?

The National Education Goals Panel first addressed school readiness at the national level in the 1990s. This panel of policy makers and educators set 10 national education goals to be achieved by the year 2000, including ensuring that all children "enter school ready to learn," increasing the high school graduation rate to 90%, increasing student mastery in challenging subject areas, and producing a generation of world leaders in mathematics and science. In 1998, the Goals Panel recognized that expecting all children to be ready to learn was not sufficient; we also needed all *schools* to be ready for all children (Shore, 1998). The Panel identified key characteristics and practices of ready schools, including

- Ensuring a smooth transition for children between home and school
- Achieving continuity between early care and education and elementary schools
- Helping every child to achieve success
- Introducing practices that have been shown to raise achievement
- Taking responsibility for results
- Having strong leadership.

North Carolina was one of the first states to formally address school readiness with a task force of early childhood educators and K–12 educators. The task force was convened by then Governor

James Hunt and Superintendent Michael Ward and produced a report titled *School Readiness in North Carolina: Strategies for Defining, Measuring, and Promoting Success for All Children* (Ahearn, Nalley, & Marsh, 2000). The report noted that school readiness has a multipart definition, encompassing "ready kids" and "ready schools" supported by "ready families and communities." The National Governors Association (2005) built on this multipart definition in its 2005 report on school readiness to include "ready states," which would provide a policy and program context for local school systems and communities.

The work of creating a national Ready Schools movement has been furthered by the support of private foundations, especially the W.K. Kellogg Foundation and the Foundation for Child Development, and by national education associations such as the Council of Chief State School Officers, the National Association of Elementary School Principals, the Education Commission of the States, and the National School Boards Association.

As the definition of ready schools has been further refined by national and state work, the term has come to include the understanding that accountability for the education of young children must extend from birth to age 8 and certainly must span ages 3–8. Thus, the term pre-K–3 (or "age 3 to Grade 3") describes an approach to school reform that shares similar goals and approaches with ready schools, both of which, at their core, focus on smoothing transitions among the settings and services for young children and their families.

State and local efforts are beginning to study how to create effective linkages between and across early education (preschool) and early elementary grades, as well as how to identify the characteristics of an elementary school that have the capacity to sustain and increase children's learning in the early grades. Some of the pre-K–3 policy work focuses on structural and policy components of schooling, promoting universal pre-K, full-day kindergarten, smaller class sizes, reduced retention rates, and the alignment of teacher preparation and professional development with children's development and learning (Bogard & Takanishi, 2005). A critical aspect of this work is using instructional and human resources to better ensure coordination, alignment, and quality across the grades (through appropriate school environments, curriculum and instruction alignment, increased collaboration and shared leadership among teachers, and family and community involvement) (Reynolds, Magnuson, & Ou, 2006). The focus of all efforts to improve pre-K–3 education is sustained coherence and alignment in the education of children across ages 3–8.

Why Are Ready Schools and Pre-K–3 Important?

In the 21st century, educators must meet the multiple demands of national, state, and local entities. These expectations are based on the federal regulations in the No Child Left Behind Act of 2001 (PL 107-110), guidelines from state and local boards of education, and district mandates and standards. Teachers at all grade levels feel the pressure of this increased accountability and need to make their students meet increasingly stringent requirements. The stakes are high for all students and schools. Yet, in spite of decades of educational reform, we still face persistent achievement gaps between minority and nonminority students, children who are poor and those who are not, and English language learners and native English speakers. A study of achievement and economic consequences in this country by McKinsey & Company (2009) found that there is an education achievement gap between the United States and other countries, as well as a persistent achievement gap by race and income within our own country. Achievement as early as fourth grade can be linked to life outcomes. In short, McKinsey & Company assert that the loss of human capital represented by the achievement gap amounts to a "permanent recession."

At the same time, research over the last two decades has shown that learning begins early, that brains develop most rapidly in the earliest years, and that early learning experiences are critical for the long-term success of children. The National Research Council Report *From Neurons to Neighborhoods* (Shonkoff & Phillips, 2000) makes the compelling case that the earliest years—birth through the primary grades—are critical to the long-term educational and life success of all children. In addition, evidence suggests that gains in cognitive and social-emotional skills may be greatest for children who are furthest behind when quality interventions are provided (Peisner-Feinberg et al., 2000; Shonkoff & Phillips).

Although the early years of schooling may be the key to long-term success for students, as well as to positive and cost-effective social and economic outcomes for both students and society, research reveals that the quality of schooling at these ages is poor—or at best, variable. The National Center for Early Development and Learning, for example, conducted a multistate study of pre-Ks and found wide variation in the quality of environments and instruction. Almost two thirds of the time, observers saw no teacher–child interaction, and most of the interactions that were observed focused on routine, maintenance activities (FPG Child Development Institute, 2005).

Stuhlman and Pianta (2009) analyzed profiles of more than 800 first-grade classrooms across the United States in terms of the emotional climate and instructional dimensions of quality. Classrooms were classified as *high quality, mediocre quality,* or *low quality,* and were rated on the basis of emotional climate and academic demand. The types of classrooms varied widely both within and across schools. "Children whose preschool achievement scores were lowest, whose ethnicity was non-white, and who were from poor or working-poor families were about twice as likely to be in the low overall quality classrooms than they were to be in the high overall quality classrooms" (pp. 334–335).

These findings make it clear that the foundations for success are not in place. The quality of the early grades must be consistently high in order to yield ongoing positive results—both academic and social and both short-term and over time. Schools must actively engage with early care and education and with families, and they must continue to work to establish high-quality learning environments at all grade levels.

Although numerous research studies have found that high-quality preschool experiences lead to better academic and other outcomes for children, pre-K programs or similar interventions alone cannot eliminate the achievement gap or maximize learning for our most vulnerable students. While the benefits of pre-K do not disappear, they may begin to fade by third or fourth grade if quality instruction is not sustained through the primary years (Shore, 2009). Coherent, high-quality educational and instructional approaches across the pre-K–3 span will yield the best results for success and the highest likelihood that children will exit Grade 3 prepared to master an increasingly difficult academic curriculum (Bogard & Takanishi, 2005).

In *The Case for Investing in PreK–3rd Education: Challenging Myths About School Reform,* Shore (2009) argues for "a more reasoned approach to school reform—one that builds a solid foundation for learning by providing coordinated, enhanced learning opportunities every year from Pre-Kindergarten (for three- and four-year-olds) through Third Grade" (p. 2). But how do we know that this approach works? Several studies provide evidence that multiyear, high-quality programs yield long-term benefits and positive outcomes both for the child and society. Four programs, in particular, are frequently cited as having long-term educational, social, and economic benefits for their participants:

- *HighScope Perry Preschool Curriculum* (Schweinhart et al., 2005) provided 2 years of high-quality preschool, regular home visits with families, and focused transition to kindergarten. Long-term results show increased academic achievement, lower dropout rates, lower crime rates, and higher employment.

- *Carolina Abecedarian Project* (Campbell & Ramey, 1995) provided full-time, high-quality educational intervention in a child care setting for children from low-income families from infancy to kindergarten entry. An additional school-age component used a family-support model for a subsample of the children in the study. Evaluations showed that the preschool intervention produced greater intellectual and academic outcomes than the school-age intervention. In addition, there was some evidence that academic gains increased as a function of the number of years (0–8years) that children were involved in the program (Ramey & Campbell, 1991).

- The Chicago Child–Parent Center program (Reynolds, 2003) was developed to promote academic success among low-income children. The program included a half-day preschool, half- or whole-day kindergarten, parent centers in schools, and 2 or 3 years of school-age intervention (i.e., reduced class sizes, family support, and instructional support in classrooms) in colocated elementary schools. Studies over the course of several years showed that prekindergarten programs combined with high-quality elementary services significantly increased long-term academic achievement and resulted in lower grade retention rates, lower rates of special education placement, higher rates of high school graduation and full-time employment, and lower rates of Medicaid receipt and arrests for violence (Reynolds & Temple, 2008).

- Dimensions of pre-K–3 education that were available in the Early Childhood Longitudinal Study–Kindergarten (ECLS–K) database were analyzed for their impact on children's academic success (Reynolds et al., 2006). Pre-K–3 variables used in the regression analyses included whether children had attended preschool or full-day kindergarten, whether they had experienced a stable K–2 school environment, whether they had been taught by certified teachers in K–3, how involved their parents were in their schooling, and the amount of time they spent on reading and language arts instruction in kindergarten. The authors found that children who had more of these *combined* dimensions of pre-K–3, compared with children who had fewer or none of the dimensions, had higher achievement levels in reading and math, lower retention rates, and slightly lower special education placement rates. Of critical importance, the effects were most notable for disadvantaged children.

Together, this evidence strongly suggests that a coherent approach to educating children from preschool through the primary grades that includes multiple, high-quality components of ready schools is most likely to lead to successful children by the end of third grade. And children who are successful in third grade are more likely to be successful throughout their school careers, to reach higher level outcomes, and to experience lifelong success. In order to realize these benefits, schools must unite the best aspects of early childhood, elementary, and special education.

SCHOOL-LEVEL FACTORS THAT FACILITATE TRANSITIONS

We define transition as a life-change process that occurs when children move from one environment to another. Physical and academic environments need to change along a seamless continuum to meet the developmental and learning needs of children as they grow, social environments need to help children gain the skills to negotiate prosocial relationships across and between their learning environments, and emotional environments need to support children's strong sense of themselves no matter where they are. The goals of coordinating children's transition are to make the experiences of children, family members, and educators seamless and to recognize and correct the problem when the gulf between experiences is too great for children to navigate successfully.

We define transition coordination as work that motivates and guides the collaborative efforts of families, the school, and the community to positively influence transitions by facilitating the integration of a child's current experience with new and unfamiliar situations.

Schools need to place a far higher value on the importance of transitions and develop a far more complex understanding of what they entail. The many factors that contribute to effective, coherent pre-K–3 experiences include time allocation, support services, collaborative structures, grouping, and curriculum alignment.

Time Allocation

"We don't have time!" This is perhaps the most universal complaint from educators. Specifically, they don't have time for planning, meeting with colleagues, spending meaningful time with individual students, or engaging with families (Ritchie & Crawford, 2009). Because the cognitive and social development that promotes learning occurs in an interactive context for both children and adults (Pianta & Walsh, 1996; Vygotsky, 1986), it is essential that schools focus on reprioritizing the use of staff time to promote communication among interdisciplinary education professionals, children, families, and community service providers (Darling-Hammond & Bransford, 2005).

In order to optimize relationship building, communication, and coordination, the allocation of time must value meaningful participation opportunities at all levels. To promote student involvement, teachers might redesign the classroom to provide more time and opportunities for peer involvement. To help educators participate, more time might be scheduled for horizontal and vertical planning. At the administrative level, increased time might be allotted to collaborative program development that requires representation from all members of the school community. Families and teachers might prioritize opportunities to discuss the child's progress and needs and develop meaningful partnerships that increase parents' roles in decision making. Allowing educators the time that they need to be effective may demand a complete restructuring of the traditional school day and year.

Support Services

We have known for many years that children do not reach their full academic potential if they are hungry, abused, neglected, or homeless. Studies published in the early 1990s (Children's Defense Fund, 1991; National Commission on Children, 1991) proved to be very effective in encouraging educators and policy makers to support families' efforts to raise children. Furthermore, the Carnegie Task Force on Meeting the Needs of Young Children (1994) suggested that a "quiet crisis" was emerging. The study implied that poverty, inadequate child care, and an increasing lack of parental care were damaging the health and welfare of young children. It became evident to educators and policy makers that this "quiet crisis" was having a deleterious effect on public education, yet education's one-dimensional approach was not equal to the task of resolving the complex challenges presented by this changing environment for young children.

As a result, Franklin and Allen-Meares (1997) suggested that increased attention be given to the need to provide a supportive service system within schools and between schools and human service agencies. Cunningham and Cardiero (2000) assert that it is the role of student support services to assist students as they transition from one developmental stage to another. They suggest that the people best able to do this are counselors, psychologists, social workers, therapists (e.g., speech, occupational, and physical therapists), health care professionals, special educators, remedial educators, and visiting teachers. Support service providers should have the knowledge, skills, and cultural competence to work with preschool and school-age children within a culturally sensitive environment and to include the perspectives and values of family members. As we struggle to improve the school experiences of our most vulnerable children, it is essential to ensure that their basic physical and emotional needs are met.

Collaborative Structures

According to Lambert (1998), collaboration involves the development of reciprocal processes within a trusting environment that evoke the potential of members to challenge assumptions, construct new meanings, and promote new actions. In order to develop and sustain collaborative work, it is essential for us to reexamine school structures with the joint aims of prioritizing time for communication and developing and maintaining relationships among teachers and children, family members, and other professional staff members. Henderson and Milstein (2003) suggest that collaboration works best when schools communicate about how organizational processes and relationships work and when they involve all members of the school community in policy development. Examples of collaborative structures that support communication and generate multiple perspectives include vertical and horizontal teams, professional learning communities, mental health teams, study groups, child study teams, and team teaching.

Vygotsky's (1936) ideas on the contribution of social interaction to learning have powerful implications for collaboration. A collaborative process enables the people who are working together to coconstruct ideas and strategies using the best available scientific research as well as the wisdom and values of the varied partners. This is an inquiry model—a way to learn what other people believe and to struggle for common understandings to broaden the collective intellect. A particular challenge of this work is in establishing trust among people who have different perspectives and who are in situations where, traditionally, the power of status, race, and gender dictate outcomes. Breaking this pattern requires them to commit to moving slowly, reflecting on various practices, listening carefully, and integrating the ideas of all partners in a significant and discernible manner.

Curriculum Alignment

Work with the curriculum must focus on aligning children's experiences to support the developmental sequence of growth and learning (New, Palsha, & Ritchie, 2009). This means working both within and across grade levels. The more cohesive the alignment of children's physical, cognitive, social, and emotional experiences along a developmental continuum, the greater the school's capacity for achieving successful transitions for children and families. The collaborative structure of professional learning communities provides ongoing opportunities for educators to examine their curriculum and instructional approaches by using a variety of assessment data that include both formal and informal and formative and summative assessments across and within grade levels. Within these learning communities, educators focus on understanding the children in their classrooms and designing intentional and balanced learning opportunities for them.

Grouping

A variety of terms are used in discussions of theoretical and practical issues related to age-grouping practices. The terms *ungraded, nongraded, continuous progress, mixed-age grouping,* and *multiage grouping* are often used interchangeably. All these terms generally refer to grouping children into classes whose age range is greater than 1 year. Classes that are structured around grouping employ a teaching philosophy and curriculum practices that maximize the benefits of interaction and cooperation among children of various ages; provide for more than 1 year of contact between a given group of children and their teacher; and allow children with different experiences who are at different stages of development to get help from one another with all aspects of classroom activity, including mastery and application of basic literacy and numeracy skills.

According to Ubben, Hughes, and Norris (2001), decisions about effective instruction are based on the grouping of children according to the size, composition, and flexibility of the group. Grouping according to size requires educators to identify the ideal group size. Pate-Bain, Achilles, and Boyd-Zaharias (1992) suggested that smaller classes allow children to receive more personal attention from the teacher. Grouping according to composition involves providing instruction that is related to individual students' capabilities. Grouping by composition has the potential to be the most volatile strategy because of the controversy surrounding heterogeneous versus homogenous grouping. Grouping by flexibility focuses on the extent to which certain groups should remain intact. Educators have voiced concern about the disproportionate numbers of minority and poor white children who remain locked into stigmatized, low-track classes. Using research to inform the composition of classrooms can make a difference for children's adjustment as they move through school and can improve their eventual outcomes, particularly for the most vulnerable children. When and how children develop varies by individual and by early childhood program, and schools need to focus more on developmental processes than on test scores and age when they make decisions about grouping.

FACING THE COMPLEXITY OF TRANSITIONS IN PRACTICE

These chapters and the conceptual frame offered in this volume show that people who are thinking intently about transitions have moved far beyond shallow definitions and simplistic approaches. The task remains to support individual educators and school communities as they develop their understanding of a much larger and more complex view of transitions. Achieving the ready schools mind-set that schools are responsible for meeting the needs of every child requires educators to be willing to ask questions about what factors contribute to patterns of success and failure in schools. Such self-reflection and honest critique are not easy. Engaging in an inquiry process means examining school policies and practices; addressing difficult issues; developing and sustaining collaborative structures; working effectively with multiple stakeholders; using evidence and data as a source for dialogue and professional development; and taking every opportunity to ask hard questions about what works, what does not, for whom it works, and who is left out. This change process requires commitment to a long-term effort and buy-in at the district and school levels. It requires a secure and supportive administrative environment that encourages teachers to identify their most serious classroom problems and to work with other school and community personnel and with families to address these problems.

The bottom line is that there are no shortcuts to improving experiences and outcomes for young children and their families. If we are to make a real difference in the lives of children and families, it is essential that we determine pathways to create the durable continuity of pedagogy, programs, and policies that is espoused in this volume. Offering children the opportunity for optimal transitions into and throughout school involves altering the institution of school.

In this section, we will draw on our experience with three initiatives—projects that are helping schools develop a more complex view of transitions. First, in 2005, the FPG Child Development Institute at the University of North Carolina at Chapel Hill launched an initiative called FirstSchool. Its goal is to help schools across the United States that are serving children ages 3 to 8 years unite the best of early childhood, elementary, and special education in the process of rethinking how schools should serve young children and their families. Second, the Ready Schools Initiative supported by the North Carolina Partnership for Children provides grants to communities to support their development of ready schools, provides technical assistance and coaching to ready-schools communities, and is creating a ready-schools toolkit to assist communities in their development efforts. Third, the North Carolina Department of Public Instruction launched the Power of K Initiative in 2007 to identify successful kindergarten teachers and offer them opportunities to further improve their capacity as teachers. The end result of the initiative is to develop a team of highly successful kindergarten leaders who can launch a movement to improve kindergarten programs statewide. Power of K focuses on returning kindergarten to its developmentally appropriate roots and empowering kindergarten teachers to make the case for how those more appropriate practices benefit children and improve their outcomes later in school.

FirstSchool encourages schools to grapple with philosophical and practical change around fundamental questions: 1) What do we believe about the educational and social needs of young children? 2) How do we improve the school experiences of our most vulnerable children? 3) How do we use data to reveal the successes and challenges we face? 4) What are the implications of data for professional development? 5) What if research drove practice?

What Do We Believe About the Educational and Social Needs of Young Children?

The divisions between early childhood, elementary school, and special education separate teacher knowledge and values into different and often conflicting camps. The FirstSchool challenge is to create an educational system that unites the best practices of all three into a coordinated continuum of learning and care. In order to design and implement effective practices across the pre-K–3 spectrum, we must 1) develop a process for understanding and aligning curriculum content across the age span; 2) use knowledge of child development as a lens for designing instruction and learning environments; 3) link curriculum with children's families, culture, and language; and 4) focus on balanced and intentional instructional approaches.

All early education programs need to develop shared beliefs about the educational and social needs of young children and gather data to determine how best to meet those needs. In a rural district in North Carolina, one elementary school, using data from a variety of assessments, concluded that its teachers needed professional development that focused on differentiated instruction, integrated curricula, and transitions. FirstSchool designed 3 days of professional development aimed at helping the teachers understand the underlying school issues that had been making their focus areas difficult for them; providing a structure and process that they could use to examine their instructional practices for effectiveness; helping them use the Standard Course of Study to develop a schoolwide project that addressed both transitions and the social studies competencies across pre-K–3; and helping them align their literacy goals to the school project. At the conclusion of the 3 days, the participants discussed strategies for working collaboratively with the rest of the faculty and staff to continue development and implementation of their ideas, and they identified ways that FirstSchool could offer ongoing support as they institutionalize new structures and practices.

How Do We Improve the School Experiences of Our Most Vulnerable Children?

Within a FirstSchool framework, schools take responsibility for identifying and implementing strategies that help the most vulnerable children. Specifically, data on dropout rates, retention, and discipline, as well as annual testing results, repeatedly point to the failure of schools to meet the needs of minority boys. Boys seem to have problems with early adjustment to school due to the requirements of the typical public school classroom (Nieto, 1999). The structure and processes of most classrooms reward skills in which boys tend to be deficient, and they devalue and discourage the abilities that are often boys' preferred ways of engaging the world. Minority boys tend to be even more at odds with standard school expectations than are white boys in our society.

In order to improve the school experiences of minority boys, FirstSchool provided a year of professional development to aligned teams composed of pre-K–3 teachers from three schools. The goal of the effort was to make meaningful changes in the teachers' practices and their environment. For example, the teachers noted that children encounter a large number of arbitrary rules in the course of the day: sitting with legs "criss-cross applesauce," standing in line with their hands behind their backs, and sitting for long periods in their chairs. Children who broke these rules often were chastised, which made them shut down and not pay attention, miss recess, or use everyone's time while the teacher waited for compliance. Instead of rigidly enforcing these rules, teachers came up with ways to provide individual water bottles for thirsty children, ways to give children flexibility and choice about where to sit, stand, and lie down while working, and ways to engage children in interesting observations as they moved through the hallways. These changes pleased both the teachers and the children and resulted in increased harmony. Other changes that had positive effects for minority boys were offering different types of books and using small-group instruction. In general, teachers found that their new strategies increased the boys' attentiveness and improved their own relationships with them. As we move toward the ready schools mind-set, it is essential that we remove the burden of the achievement gap from the shoulders of small children and place it squarely in the laps of schools.

How Do We Use Data to Reveal the Successes and Challenges We Face?

Schools use a variety of data sources to get information about children's progress in school. One of the goals of using multiple sources of data is to look beyond state tests in gauging school success and improvement. The Professional Learning Community movement is helping schools maximize ways to use data to make instructional and curricular changes that support the needs of every child.

One source of data is the HighScope Ready Schools Assessment (HighScope Educational Research Foundation, 2006), which helps schools critically examine general policies and practices of a school, emphasizing areas that are most relevant to pre-K–3 classrooms, teachers, children, communities, and parents. The school uses the measure to collect evidence on the successes and challenges of detailed criteria in each of eight dimensions: Leadership; Engaging Environments; Transitions; Teacher Supports; Family, School, and Community Partnerships; Effective Curriculum, Instruction, and Assessment; Diversity; and Assessing Progress and Assuring Quality. On the basis of this evidence, the school team then develops a consensus on the scores that the school has earned for each criterion. Data are entered into the HighScope web site and reports are provided to schools. Figure 9.1 is an example of a report focused on transitions. The team uses the scores to make decisions about how to move forward in areas where the data indicate that the school is encountering challenges.

In order to address alignment across the pre-K–3 span, the Emergent Academic Snapshot (Ritchie, Howes, Kraft-Sayre, & Weiser, 2001) assesses the amount of time that teachers spend in different activity settings throughout the day. These data provoke dialogue around issues such as the change in children's experiences as they move from pre-K to kindergarten (moving from 136 minutes of free choice to 16 minutes and from 76 minutes of whole-group time to 128 minutes) and the amount of time that children spend in "basics," which include using the bathroom,

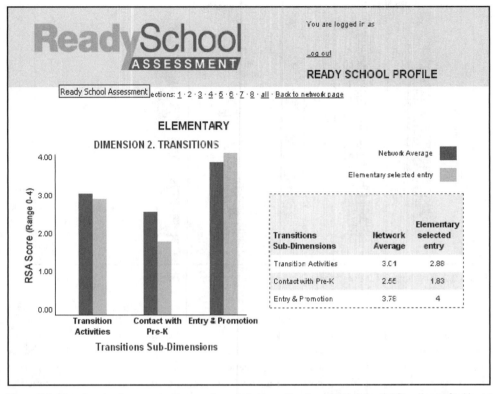

Figure 9.1. Ready school assessment: sample report. From *Ready or Not? Schools' Readiness for Young Children.* (p. 118) Ypsilanti, MI: HighScope Press. © 2010 HighScope Educational Research Foundation. Used with permission.

washing their hands, waiting, and moving between learning environments both within the classroom and the school (see Figure 9.2). Additional data from this same measure help teachers see the amount of time that children spend on oral language development, other literacy activities, social studies, math, and so forth, and how much time teachers spend in direct and scaffolded instruction. Teachers use these data to stimulate conversations that focus on their own philosophy of instruction; the federal, state, and local mandates that constrain or support their philosophy; and the professional development that they need in order to make progress in areas that prove difficult.

What Are the Implications for Professional Development?

Educators who are committed to change are looking for answers to many questions: "How do I get my principal to understand that children need a variety of ways to engage with materials and information?" "How do I get my teachers to understand the pressure I am under to improve the end-of-year test scores?" "How can we more effectively engage with our children's parents and families?" "How do I effectively teach children who do not speak English?" "How do we find more time in the day to plan and communicate with one another?" "How do I include more science and social studies for the children?" and "What does it mean to be intentional?"

The Power of K is one of North Carolina's responses to some of these professional development needs. The initiative is a 3-year effort that involves the development of a statewide learning community of kindergarten teachers. The teachers have regular meetings, receive individual coaching and mentoring, have access to national experts, and are encouraged to use data to guide and monitor change. The initiative is intended to help teachers design appropriate learning environments for kindergarten children, integrate literacy and math into both teacher- and child-initiated

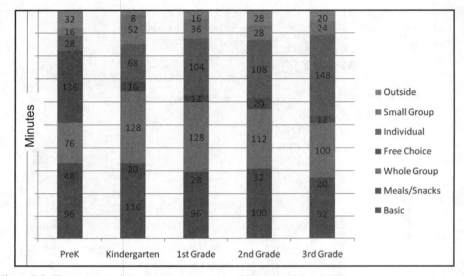

Figure 9.2. The amount of time teachers spend in different activity settings.

experiences, and articulate their practices to others. Teaching educators how to talk about what they do and why they do it is an important component of the Power of K. Even teachers who are very good at what they do may rarely have the chance to talk about it. Teachers become better at their work when they are able to share their ideas with others, provide rationales for their practices to principals and parents, and explain how their work supports the goals of the standard course of study and the curriculum. This project focuses on kindergarten classrooms as the entry point to elementary school for most students and, thus, as the key opportunity to promote a successful transition from a variety of preschool environments to the primary grades.

What if Research Drove Our Practice?

A teacher who participated in a pre-K–3 quality improvement project explained the remarkable improvement in her classroom by saying, "You gave me permission to do what I learned from my college classes." Fear that students would earn low test results has been a major impetus for implementing practices that often run counter to what we know is good for young children. In the search for the silver bullet that would ensure high test scores, many school districts have turned to highly prescribed curricula and have required more and more rote learning from children at younger and younger ages. Yet over the past several decades, research has provided us with validation for the kind of developmentally appropriate practices that we are seeing less and less often in the early grades. FirstSchool is helping schools reexamine their ideas about what is basic to learning for young children by using research findings to support teachers' choices regarding curricula, instructional practices, and professional development needs.

We know, for example, that vocabulary development is an essential predictor of reading and that our most vulnerable children have serious deficits in this area (Snow, Burns, & Griffin, 1998). We also know that the amount of time students spend on out-of-context phonics and letter identification is far greater than the time they spend on oral language development (meaningful and reciprocal conversation between teachers and students and among peers). Recommendations for improving specific early academic skills emphasize using a variety of modalities and incorporating rich, hands-on experiences. The National Research Council's book

Preventing Reading Difficulties in Young Children (Snow et al., 1998) reviews the early literacy research and argues that young children's conversations with adults, exposure to books, and experiences with activities that are designed to promote phonological awareness, such as rhyming games, are all linked to later reading ability.

Developmental scientists tell us that the approach to instruction is as important as the content (Ritchie, Maxwell, & Bredekamp, 2009). Most early childhood professionals agree that scaffolded instruction is generally preferential to didactic instruction in terms of helping children understand new information and skills more deeply and maintaining children's interest and motivation. *Scaffolding* refers to interactions in which the teacher works within the child's "zone of proximal development." Children's knowledge and skills advance when the needed supports are provided (Berk & Winsler, 1995; Bodrova & Leong, 1996; Vygotsky, 1978).

However, didactic instruction clearly has a place in the early childhood classroom. Repetition and recitation help children to consolidate new knowledge (Cornell, Senechal, & Broda, 1988), and different children respond to different types of instruction (Doyle & Rutherford, 1984; Hopkins, McGillicuddy-De Lisi, & De Lisi, 1997). Didactic instruction is more rote in nature and involves the provision of information from teachers to children. Teachers using a didactic approach provide information to the children through modeling, practice, explanation, recitation, and closed-ended questioning (Smerdon, Burkam, & Lee, 1999). Highly skilled teachers have a variety of teaching approaches in their repertoire guided by research; good instruction involves balancing and blending the different approaches and choosing them to suit the individual needs of children.

CONCLUSION

Altering the institution of school to become a place that ensures smooth transition in its largest sense requires an alignment between beliefs and actions, between data and professional development, and between research and practice. Decisions about time allocation, support services, collaborative structures, the curriculum, and grouping must be informed by developmental science as much as by administrative pressures. Schools and educational policies must support educators to be reflective; to value inquiry; to use data to monitor and guide change; to master the best of early childhood, elementary, and special education; to work effectively with families; and to collaborate with one another. It is essential that we design and implement support for teachers who currently feel stymied in their ability to converse with children, feel buried by a demanding curriculum, are unable to effectively reach all of the children in their classroom, and lack the time or skill to do the kind of teaching that research suggests is best. State, district, and local policies, professional development, and the current testing and accountability climate will have to change dramatically to align with the ideas presented in this chapter and throughout this volume.

This discussion points to the need to rethink what schools should look like as they move to serving younger children. The fundamental question is "Are the facilities, personnel, and programs geared to meet the full range of needs of each child served by the school?" This question encompasses both what happens to children within their classes and what transitions children face as they enter and move through the graded system of schools in the United States. The evidence regarding the movement to add pre-K to schools indicates that we have a long way to go to ensure that environments are welcoming to young children and their families. It is time for us to listen to the families who have voted with their actions by postponing their children's entry into the formal school setting. We must work carefully to make children's first school experience one that will meet their present needs and launch them on a successful trajectory.

Case Study—FirstSchool at South Lexington Elementary School

Aleksandra Holod

FirstSchool is a new preK–3 education initiative developed by the FPG Child Development Institute at the University of North Carolina, Chapel Hill, that embodies the concept of ready schools. Using data-driven professional development and technical assistance, FPG works with partner schools to make pre-K–3 an integrated experience and to change the culture of schools so that they are more responsive to young children's needs. FirstSchool also draws on best practices from the fields of early childhood, elementary, and special education to create school environments that foster success for all children, especially those who are vulnerable due to poverty and minority status.

FirstSchool aims to improve the quality of young children's transitions in three ways. FirstSchool consultants help teachers increase parent participation and develop closer relationships with families, thereby easing children's transitions between home and school across the pre-K through Grade 3 spectrum. Second, consultants improve transition between pre-K and the primary grades by facilitating dialogue and collaboration between early childhood and elementary educators. Third, FirstSchool staff support schools as they collaborate with other community partners to develop a more coordinated and systematic approach to transition for young children and their families. Through these approaches to transition, FirstSchool endeavors to improve classroom quality and close the achievement gap between children of different racial and socioeconomic backgrounds. Easing the transitions from home to school and from pre-K–3 are FirstSchool's central goals.

Origins   The FirstSchool initiative was born out of studies of state-funded pre-K which revealed that pre-K classrooms tended to have minimal overall quality as measured by environmental rating scales (Early et al., 2005). These studies, which were conducted in 11 states by the National Center for Early Learning and Development at FPG, also found that children were not engaged in any learning activities—including art, math, or looking at books—for 44% of the day in the average pre-K program (Early et al., in press). In six of the states, researchers followed pre-K students to kindergarten, where scores on quality measures were also lower than expected, and where children were not engaged in any learning activities for 40% of the day (Burchinal et al., 2008).

FirstSchool was designed to address these weaknesses. To develop a model of teaching and transition strategies, FPG engaged in a collaborative, 3-year planning process with principals, teachers, families, and other community members. Planning committee members examined school management issues, classroom teaching practices, and family needs, all of which affect children's early school experiences. They also identified policies and governance issues that influence children's transitions to school. This inclusive planning process led to the development of the FirstSchool framework, which is in the early stages of implementation at three pilot schools (S. Ritchie, personal communication, June 3, 2009).

Implementation at South Lexington Elementary

About South Lexington Elementary School   South Lexington Elementary School is one of FPG's three pilot schools. It is located in Lexington, North Carolina, an economically depressed community where unemployment and poverty are high due to the closure of local textile and furniture mills, which were once major employers in the area. South Lexington is a Title I school; 90% percent of its 450 students are eligible for the federal free-and-reduced-price lunch program (J. Miller, personal communication, June 8, 2009). The school's catchment area includes the town's public housing developments, as well as the local homeless shelter and domestic violence shelter. Because South Lexington Elementary is located in a community in great need of support and the school offers four pre-K classrooms, it was a perfect setting in which to pilot the FirstSchool model.

The school principal has led various reform efforts in recent years. South Lexington utilized a comprehensive school reform grant to implement the Comer School Development Program, a reform effort that encourages schools to address all of the needs of children, including their physical, psychological, linguistic, social, ethical, and cognitive needs. The school has also participated in the North Carolina Ready Schools Initiative, a state-wide intervention effort to engage in collaborative assessment and planning to improve classroom quality and family partnerships. In addition, South Lexington participated in a state-funded dropout prevention program led by members of the FirstSchool team (J. Miller, personal communication, June 8, 2009). Because African American and Latino boys tend to drop out at the highest rates when they get to high school, the initial stage of the FirstSchool work focused on improving these children's early school experiences (S. Ritchie, personal communication, September 15, 2009).

Data-Driven Reform   The work at South Lexington began with intensive data collection. The FirstSchool team collected Emerging Academic Snapshot data, an instrument developed by the director of FirstSchool, Dr. Sharon Ritchie, and her colleagues (Ritchie et al., 2001). Four boys of color were selected in each participating classroom, including the two boys of color who had the closest relationship to the teacher and the two boys of color who had the most conflicted relationship with the teacher. This choice was determined by having teachers complete the Student–Teacher Relationship Scale (Pianta, 2001) on each boy of color in the classroom. The snapshot data indicated how much time the focal children spent in small groups, in large groups, or doing individual work. It also showed how much time children spent engaged in teacher-led versus child-directed learning activities; how much time children spent engaged in literacy, math, science, and other subjects; and what teaching approaches were utilized. The data were analyzed and presented at professional development sessions to help teachers understand how their classrooms facilitated or challenged the learning and engagement of the boys.

The Learning Community Responds to the Data   Learning community meetings, in which teachers, principals, and other building staff come together to look at and discuss the data, are an important part of the FirstSchool process. At South Lexington, the teachers were surprised to see that the data indicated that children were spending a substantial portion of the day on routine activities, such as getting in line and waiting in the hallway. As South Lexington's principal Jackie Miller says, "Working with FirstSchool gave us insight into things we weren't aware of. Looking at the data helped us realize we could be faster, that we could improve transitions throughout the day." Teachers discussed this issue and devised a solution to take better advantage of this portion of the day. Teachers decided that they would engage children in learning activities during routine activity times, such as having children count the number of steps they take when they walk in the hallway, making systematic observations as the class moves through the building, or encouraging the children to engage in quiet exchanges with peers.

The FirstSchool learning community at South Lexington also examined classroom practices and expectations across grades to see whether steps could be taken to ease children's vertical transitions as the children progress from pre-K through third grade. For example, FirstSchool snapshot data indicated that children experienced a drastic reduction in choice time as they entered kindergarten. Pre-K–3 teachers discussed this lack of alignment between pre-K and kindergarten. What could the role of choice be as the children get older? Teachers also discussed their expectations regarding children's social, emotional, and learning skills. Through extensive dialogue, teachers became aware that children encountered varying expectations as they moved from grade to grade. As a result, pre-K teachers began to focus more on teaching children the learning behaviors that they would need when they entered kindergarten, while K–3 teachers focused more on the developmental needs of the children who were entering their classrooms. Teachers' efforts to align classroom management practices increased the continuity of children's school experiences.

The type of collaboration seen between early childhood and elementary grade teachers at South Lexington demonstrates the importance of relationships within schools. The FirstSchool learning community allowed teachers to build relationships across the early grades by including pre-K teachers in the professional development sessions that were offered to K–3 teachers—a rare practice in public elementary schools. Giving pre-K and primary grade teachers time to dialogue together fostered a stronger sense of community and collaboration (S. Ritchie, personal communication, July 7, 2009).

Lessons Learned   Everyone involved in South Lexington's FirstSchool process learned about the challenges involved in implementing changes to the schools' teaching and administrative practices. As discussed next, the process requires involvement from all staff at the school, not just the teachers. Furthermore, reform requires that school personnel reflect on the educational culture that drives their practice.

All Staff Members Matter   Lead teachers and principals are not the only staff who should be engaged in the school reform process. "Everyone in the building [who] comes in contact with children needs some level of training—the cafeteria staff, support staff, *and* the office staff," says Principal Miller. South Lexington sent 80% of its staff to training sessions when the school began its reform efforts with the Comer School Development Program, including cafeteria staff, support staff, and office staff. This approach allowed all of the adults in the building who have contact with children to understand the kind of transformation that was envisioned for the school. The training gave school employees time to relax and interact together outside the context of their busy school days and improved the school environment (J. Miller, personal communication, June 8, 2009).

The importance of engaging all staff in the school reform process became apparent later, when bus drivers who had not been involved in the training sessions used discipline tactics which differed from the approach that teachers used. Children tended to act out in response to the bus drivers' unfamiliar expectations, leading to more difficult transitions at the end of the long, tiring school day. On the basis of this previous experience, Principal Miller understood that it was important to include as many teachers and staff as possible in the FirstSchool learning community.

School Culture Affects Reform Efforts   Another key to successful school reform is the willingness of educators to step outside the traditional public school culture, which is heavily influenced by school accountability measures and high-stakes testing

(S. Ritchie, personal communication, June 3, 2009). Schools are under a great deal of pressure to focus on academic achievement to the exclusion of children's other needs. As a result of this pressure, "Schools tend to adhere to the culture of expediency," says Dr. Ritchie. Principals' willingness to adopt a new mind-set and provide leadership is essential to the FirstSchool process. Personnel must be motivated to engage in a process of reflection and inquiry, and that motivation begins with leadership from the principal. "You can't impose reform on schools. This has to be a voluntary process," says Dr. Ritchie.

Future Directions   Having learned these lessons, South Lexington will move forward with future FirstSchool reform efforts that will focus on improving parental involvement. Rather than asking parents to help with activities that benefit the school, such as asking them to chaperone field trips or participate in bake sales, the school will hold focus groups to learn about parents' expectations of the school and about their own experiences with school when they were youngsters. Focus groups will be facilitated by culturally matched facilitators in both English and Spanish. The goal of this effort is to foster positive relationships with parents so that they can support their children's education (J. Miller, personal communication, June 8, 2009).

South Lexington will also move toward a full-service school model, which the school hopes will support parent engagement. In summer 2008, the school opened its cafeteria and served lunch to entire families. The media center and library were also opened to families during that time so that they could watch videos or read books. The school planned to have the guidance counselor and school nurse work flexible schedules with later afternoon hours to make them more available to meet with parents. The school also planned to offer on-site access to mental health, public housing, medical, and dental services. These services are likely to increase parents' presence at the school. Because the town of Lexington has very limited public transportation, many parents who do not have cars are unable to travel to social service agencies to access services. Therefore, this new, full-service school model has great potential to benefit families (J. Miller, personal communication, June 8, 2009).

Conclusion   The FirstSchool model is a data-driven approach that addresses transition in multiple ways. It supports relationships both within the school building *and* with others in the community. As part of the FirstSchool process at South Lexington Elementary School, the principal, pre-K teachers, elementary school teachers, and other building staff worked together to address children's transitions during the school day and between grade levels. The FirstSchool learning community allows teachers at different grade levels to build relationships and improve the quality of their instructional practices through collaborative dialogue. As a result, children experience greater continuity with regard to classroom procedures and expectations as well as along the academic continuum.

FirstSchool at South Lexington also laid the groundwork for stronger relationships among the school, families, and community service providers. Increasing parent participation in the school facilitates children's transition from home to school, and the involvement of community service providers with the school increases families' access to needed services. These relationships allow the school to engage in a more coordinated, systematic approach to addressing children's needs by drawing on family and community resources. As a result, South Lexington embodies the concept of a ready school that has the systems in place to effectively address children's transitions.

Case Study—Keiraville Community Preschool
Transition To School Program
Romilla Karnati

Keiraville Community Preschool (KCPS) in Australia implements the Transition to School Program to support children and families during the children's move from preschool to primary school. The Transition to School Program employs a three-pronged approach to facilitating smooth transitions. First, it offers social networking opportunities for transitioning preschool children and their parents. Second, the program conducts events throughout the year to help children and families develop the skills, knowledge, and social competence that are needed to succeed in primary school. Third, educators at KCPS participate in the local Wollongong Transition to School Network, an initiative that fosters collaborative relationships among families, preschool teachers, and primary school educators. Together, these efforts have resulted in children and families who know what to expect in primary school, schools that are better equipped to address the needs of incoming students, and, consequently, smoother transitions for children.

Origins of the Keiraville Community Preschool's Transitions Efforts   KCPS was established in 1952 by three local mothers who recognized a need for early childhood education in Keiraville, a suburb of Wollongong on the South Coast of New South Wales. Over the years, many dedicated educators have worked with the children and implemented improvements to KCPS's program, including a comprehensive transition initiative that was introduced in 2001. The Transition to School Program consists of strategically timed events and activities to support children and families throughout the year that precedes school entry. Augmenting the preschool's own transition activities, KCPS educators joined with those from nearby communities in 2003 to form the Wollongong Transition to School Network.

Goals   The Transition to School Program reflects an understanding at KCPS that "ready schools" must take an active role in facilitating transitions—that while transitions necessarily demand flexibility on the part of children and families, schools must be flexible as well. KCPS encourages all stakeholders to participate in implementing a transition plan that is responsive to the needs of children, families, and schools, and works to establish and maintain positive relationships and mutual respect among all of the groups involved in the transition process. KCPS also seeks to honor individual children's development and learning throughout the transition process, operating with an understanding that children are capable learners with rich prior experience that should form the foundation for later learning as they enter preschool and move on to primary school.

   In addition to implementing transition plans that focus on children's movements from one setting to the next, KCPS supports its preschool educators with ongoing training and development, dedicating time and resources to the transition process. The Transition to School Program also conducts ongoing program evaluation to ensure that children, families, and educators are receiving the support they need. Ultimately, KCPS seeks to promote positive attitudes among children about beginning school, hoping to inspire enthusiasm and confidence in children and families about this important milestone in their lives (Dockett, Perry, & Howard, 2000; Keiraville Community Preschool, 2009).

Program Structure KCPS is a community-owned, nonprofit program that serves 106 children per week. Most of the children enrolled in KCPS come from middle-class urban homes, attend 2 days of preschool a week, and are between 4 and 5 years of age. The preschool is divided into four groups: The first two groups consist of children in the transition program, the third group consists of children who will return to preschool the following year, and the fourth group of children is a combination of children, including those who will be returning to preschool and those who will be leaving preschool in the following year. While there is a strong focus on transitions for the older children in the programs, the school also makes sure that preschoolers receive the attention they need. From their first day, all preschoolers at KCPS are building the attitudes and skills that underlie smooth transitions and a lifelong love of learning.

Implementation Working relationships between KCPS and primary schools ensure that schools are prepared for incoming students. In order to get schools ready for children, KCPS facilitates communication and relationships among children, families, and primary schools by using the three-pronged strategy described next.

Child Readiness Each year, KCPS graduates go on to enroll in as many as 18 different primary schools. To facilitate seamless transitions to such a variety of settings, KCPS pursues several year-round activities to prime children for the shift from preschool to primary school.

First, KCPS conducts a series of activities that are designed to help children develop social skills and build relationships with other children who will be attending the same primary school. Preschool educators use Playing and Learning to Socialize (PALS), an evidence-based program that incorporates stories, videos, puppets, songs, probe-questions, and role-play activities to help children cultivate positive social skills (Playing and Learning to Socialise, 2009). In addition to attempts to foster social development generally, Networking Morning Teas held at KCPS allow children who will be attending the same primary school to meet one another and develop relationships. Photographs of children who will be attending the same school are taken and included in each child's journal. Also, photographs of former preschool classmates in their present kindergarten are displayed in the preschool classroom to foster familiar links.

In addition to these socialization efforts, KCPS conducts activities to familiarize transitioning preschoolers with the expectations and routines that are characteristic of kindergarten classrooms. Throughout the third and fourth terms of the year prior to kindergarten entry, preschoolers spend an hour each day in a school-like setting. Spaces like KCPS's music room and courtyard are used for these sessions to accommodate larger group sizes approximating those of kindergarten classes. During these periods, children are expected to follow requests from educators, decide where they will spend their learning time, and participate in group activities. Exposure to this more structured environment, without the use of formal lessons, equips children with the learning skills that will help them succeed in school. Families are encouraged to join in during "school time" and actively participate. Therefore, in addition to preparing children for school, these mock kindergarten sessions provide families with a clearer sense of the environment that their children will encounter in primary school.

A third set of activities, including school visits and orientation days, promotes collaboration among families, children, KCPS, and public schools. KCPS preschoolers and families get the chance to travel in small groups to spend a morning at Keiraville Primary School. Before these visits, the children generate questions and send letters to the kindergarten teachers. Preschool educators also attend annual orientation days that are held at each of the primary schools children will be attending. At these orientation days, KCPS educators support the preschoolers, assist the primary classroom teacher, and help facilitate relationships among children, parents, and the primary school educators. Photos of the visit are used to form a record for ongoing reference (Keiraville Community Preschool, 2009).

Family Readiness   KCPS organizes information evenings for families and invites representatives from three local primary schools (including representatives from both Catholic and state schools) to attend the meetings. At these sessions, families receive information about their child's transition to primary school. Families also receive information about local schools, lists of children attending the various schools the following year, and a bimonthly newsletter on transition to school events. Furthermore, at the Networking Morning Teas, a parent mentor (one whose child is already attending primary school) is present to provide firsthand information to new families.

Families are invited to complete a survey on their thoughts and priorities in the transitions process, the results of which are distributed to all of the families of children in the preschool. Educators at KCPS also work with families to formulate individual transition-to-school plans for each child (Keiraville Community Preschool, 2009).

KCPS's Transition to School program has received positive reviews from families. Margaret Gleeson, Director of KCPS, shared the idea that "positive feedback gathered from families regarding their child's smooth transition to school confirms the effectiveness of Keiraville Community Preschool's transition program" (personal communication, September 2, 2009). One parent reported that "most valuable to us was the information evening regarding the program to let us know the way the program would help my child with their move to 'Big School'" (personal communication, September 2, 2009). In another sign of the program's success, families from KCPS actively participate in the Wollongong Transition to School Network events. According to Ms. Gleeson, families' enthusiasm for the transition process is a result of the transition efforts that have been undertaken at KCPS.

Primary School Readiness   KCPS connects with local primary schools to cultivate strong relationships between preschool and primary school teachers. Teachers exchange letters outlining the transition program, which encourages a two-way exchange of information. Teachers from primary schools are also invited to visit KCPS to meet the children, see the environment that they are coming from prior to primary school entry, and establish relationships with the preschool educators.

Perhaps the most meaningful vehicle for collaboration between schools is KCPS educators' active participation in the local Wollongong Transition to School Network. The network includes teachers from 30 preschool settings and 65 primary school settings who meet to exchange information and build relationships across school settings (K. Smith, personal communication, September 9, 2009). The network also provides professional development opportunities for educators in the Wollongong area, with up to 100 members attending some events.

Testimony from primary school teachers has been encouraging. Teachers indicate "that they can see a difference between those children who have attended KCPS and other school starters. These differences are exemplified by their enthusiasm for school, strong social skills, and comfort in a classroom situation" (M. Gleeson, personal communication, September 2, 2009).

Lessons Learned   The Transition to School Program has generated a variety of lessons for families, educators, and schools. KCPS's efforts to promote collaboration have demonstrated that relationships among all stakeholders need to be built over time and require an ongoing commitment. Opportunities such as participation in a local Transition to School Network can help build such relationships, break down barriers, and increase awareness of innovative practices to foster transitions. Given that it takes some time to build collaborative relationships, and that children's best interests are served by not rushing the process, the transition to school process cannot be left to the last weeks of the school; ideally, it should be integrated into the full-year curriculum.

Transition programs such as the one run by the KCPS have their challenges. Ms. Gleeson mentioned that while it is inspiring to see effective transition programs at other schools, it is difficult to replicate them due to each site's unique context. Issues such as staffing, available space, available resources, and the limitations of a daily routine all influence the type of program that can be implemented (personal communication, September 3, 2009). According to Ms. Gleeson, another challenge for KCPS was overcoming skepticism from representatives in primary schools who did not recognize the importance of promoting smooth transitions in early childhood (personal communication, July 26, 2009). These concerns are faced by many schools that are trying to develop effective transition programs.

Future Directions   Moving forward, KCPS's Transition to School Program hopes to get kindergarten children more involved in the transition activities. One new effort, for example, would have kindergartners visit the preschool and speak to the preschoolers about "Big School." In addition, KCPS plans to take a proactive approach to reducing practical and philosophical barriers between preschool and primary school teachers. For example, KCPS has a strong association with the University of Wollongong and has encouraged the University to include the importance of transition to school as part of its teacher training program.

Conclusion   KCPS's Transition to School Program is guided by a view that schools must actively respond to the needs of children and families. At KCPS, transition implies the need for ready schools as much as it does ready children. The program uses a three-pronged approach to ensure not only that children acquire the skills they will need in kindergarten but also that a network of supportive relationships is in place to help them adjust to new settings and expectations.

REFERENCES

Ahearn, C., Nalley, D., & Marsh, C. (Eds.). (2000). *School readiness in North Carolina: Strategies for defining, measuring, and promoting success for all children.* Report of the Ready for School Goal Team. Greensboro, NC: SERVE.

Barnett, W.S., Epstein, D.J., Friedman, A.H., Boyd, J.S., & Hustedt, J.T. (2008). *The state of preschool 2009: State preschool yearbook.* New Brunswick, NJ: Rutgers Graduate School of Education.

Berk, L., & Winsler, A. (1995). *Scaffolding children's learning: Vygotsky and early childhood education.* Washington, DC: NAEYC.

Bodrova, E., & Leong, D.J. (1996). *Tools of the mind: The Vygotskian approach to early childhood education.* Englewood Cliffs, NJ: Merrill.

Bogard, K., & Takanishi, R. (2005). PK–3: An aligned and coordinated approach to education for children 3 to 8 years old. *Social Policy Report, 19*(3). Society for Research in Child Development.

Burchinal, M., Howes, C., Pianta, R., Bryant, D., Early, D., Clifford, R., et al. (2008). Predicting child outcomes at the end of kindergarten from the quality of pre-kindergarten teacher–child interactions and
instruction. *Applied Developmental Science, 12*(3), 140–153.

Campbell, F.A., & Ramey, C.T. (1995). Cognitive and school outcomes for high-risk African-American
students at middle adolescence: Positive effects of early intervention. *American Educational Research
Journal, 32*(4), 743–772.

Carnegie Task Force on Meeting the Needs of Young Children. (1994). *Starting points: Meeting the needs
of our youngest children.* New York: Carnegie Corporation of New York.

Children's Defense Fund. (1991). *The state of America's children.* Washington, DC: Author.

Clifford, R.M., Early, D.M., & Hills, T. (1999). Almost a million children in school before kindergarten.
Young Children, 54(5), 38–51.

Cornell, E.H., Senechal, M., & Broda, L.S. (1988). Recall of picture books by 3-year-old children: Testing
and repetition effects in joint reading activities. *Journal of Educational Psychology, 80,* 537–542.

Crawford, G.M., Clifford, R.M., Early, D.M., & Reszka, S.S. (2009). Early education in the United States:
Converging systems, diverse perspectives. In R.M. Clifford & G.M. Crawford (Eds.), *Beginning School:
U.S. Policies in International Perspective* (pp. 1–12). New York: Teachers College Press.

Cunningham, W.G., & Cardiero, P.A. (2000). Educational administration: A problem-based approach.
Boston: Allyn & Bacon.

Darling-Hammond, L., & Bransford, J. (2005). *Preparing teachers for a changing world: What teachers
should learn and be able to do.* San Francisco: Jossey-Bass.

Deming, D., & Dynarski, S. (2008). The lengthening of childhood. *Journal of Economic Perspectives, 22,* 71–92.

Dockett, S., Perry, B., & Howard, P. (2000, January). *Guidelines for transition to school.* Paper presented at
the Australian Research in Early Childhood Education Annual Conference, Canberra, Australia.

Doyle, W., & Rutherford, B. (1984). Classroom research on matching learning and teaching styles. *Theory
into Practice, 23,* 20–25.

Early, D., Barbarin, O., Bryant, D., Burchinal, M., Chang, F., Clifford, R., et al. (2005). *Pre-kindergarten
in eleven states: NCEDL's Multi-state Study of Pre-kindergarten and Study of Statewide Early Education
Programs (SWEEP). Preliminary Descriptive Report* (NCEDL Working Paper). Chapel Hill: The
University of North Carolina at Chapel Hill. Retrieved from http://www.fpg.unc.edu/~ncedl/pdfs/
SWEEP_MS_summary_final.pdf

Early, D.M., Iruka, I.U., Ritchie, S., Barbarin, O.A., Winn, D.-M.C., Crawford, G.M., et al. How do pre-
kindergartners spend their time? Gender, ethnicity and income as predictors of experiences in pre-
kindergarten classrooms. *Early Childhood Research Quarterly, 5,* 2, 177–193.

FPG Child Development Institute. (2005, Spring). How is the preK day spent? *Early Developments, 9*(1),
22–27. Chapel Hill: The University of North Carolina at Chapel Hill.

Franklin, C., & Allen-Meares, P. (1997). School social workers are a critical part of the link. *Social Work
in Education, 19,* 131–135.

Henderson, N., & Milstein, M.M. (2003). *Resiliency in schools: Making it happen for students and educators.*
Thousand Oaks, CA: Corwin Press.

HighScope Educational Research Foundation. (2006). *Ready or Not? Schools' Readiness for Young Children.*
Ypsilanti, MI.

Hopkins, K.B., McGillicuddy-De Lisi, A.V., & De Lisi, R. (1997). Student gender and teaching methods
as source of variability in children's computational arithmetic performance. *The Journal of Genetic
Psychology, 158,* 333–345.

Keiraville Community Preschool. (2009). Transition to School Program 2008. Retrieved September 22,
2009, from http://www.transitiontoschool.com.au/pdf/KeiravilleCommunityPreschool.pdf

Lambert, L. (1998). *Building leadership capacity in schools.* Alexandria, VA: Association for Supervision &
Curriculum Development.

McKinsey & Company. (2009). *The economic impact of the achievement gap in America's schools. Summary
of findings.* Retrieved from http://www.mckinsey.com/App_Media/Images/Page_Images/Offices/
SocialSector/PDF/achievement_gap_report.pdf

National Center for Education Statistics. (2006). *Homeschooling in the United States: Statistical Analysis Report.*
Washington, DC: Author. Retrieved from http://nces.ed.gov/pubs2006/homeschool/TableDisplay.
asp?TablePath=TablesHTML/table_2.asp

National Commission on Children. (1991). *Children's hour: Report by the National Commission on
Children and John D. Rockefeller IV's efforts to promote legislation to protect children.* Washington, DC:
Author.

National Governors Association. (2005). *Building the foundation to bright futures: Final report of the NGA
Task Force on School Readiness.* Washington, DC: Author.

New, R., Palsha, S., & Ritchie, S. (2009). *Issues in Pre-K–3rd education: A FirstSchool framework for curriculum and instruction* (#7). Chapel Hill: The University of North Carolina at Chapel Hill & FPG Child Development Institute, FirstSchool.

Nieto, S. (1999). *The light in their eyes: Creating multicultural learning communities.* New York: Teachers College Press.

No Child Left Behind Act of 2001, PL 101-110, 115 Stat., 1425, 20 U.S.C. §§ *et seq.*

Pate-Bain, H., Achilles, C.M., & Boyd-Zaharias, J. (1992). Class size does make a difference. *Phi Delta Kappan, 74,* 253–256.

Peisner-Feinberg, E.S., Burchinal, M.R., Clifford, R.M., Culkin, M.L., Howes, C., Kagan, S.L., et al. (2000). *The children of the cost, quality and child outcomes study go to school.* Technical Report. Chapel Hill: University of North Carolina at Chapel Hill & FPG Child Development Institute.

Pianta, R.C. (2001). *STRS Student–Teacher Relationship Scale. Professional manual.* Odessa, FL: Psychological Assessment Resources.

Pianta, R.C., & Walsh, D.J. (1996). *High-risk children in schools.* New York: Routledge.

Playing and Learning to Socialise. (2009). PALS Social Skills Program. Retrieved December 2009. from http://www.palsprogram.com.au/

Ramey, C.T., & Campbell, F.A. (1991). Poverty, early childhood education, and academic competence: The Abecedarian experiment. In A.C. Huston (Ed.), *Children in poverty: Child development and public policy* (pp. 190–221). New York: Cambridge University Press.

Reynolds, A., Magnuson, K., & Ou, S.-R. (2006). *PK–3 education: Programs and practices that work in children's first decade.* New York: Foundation for Child Development.

Reynolds, A.J. (2003). The added value of continuing early interventions into the primary grades, *Early Childhood Programs for a New Century.* Washington, DC: Children's Welfare League of America Press.

Reynolds, A.J., & Temple, J.A. (2008). Cost-effective early childhood development programs from preschool to third grade. *Annual Review of Clinical Psychology, 4,* 109–139.

Ritchie, S., & Crawford, G. (2009). *Time is of the essence: Issues in PreK–3rd education* (#5). Chapel Hill, NC: The University of North Carolina at Chapel Hill & FPG Child Development Institute, FirstSchool.

Ritchie, S., Howes, C., Kraft-Sayre, M.E., & Weiser, B. (2001). *Emerging academics snapshot.* Los Angeles: University of California at Los Angeles. Unpublished manuscript.

Ritchie, S., Maxwell, K.L., & Bredekamp, S. (2009). Rethinking early schooling: Using developmental science to transform children's early school experiences. In O.A. Barbarin & B.H. Wasik (Eds.), *Handbook of child development and early education: Research to practice* (pp. 3–13). New York: Guilford.

Ritchie et al. (2010). *Ready or Not? Schools' Readiness for Young Children* (p113). Ypsilanti, MI; HighScope Press.

Schweinhart, L.J., Montie, J., Xiang, A., Barnett, W.S., Gelfield, C.R., & Nores, M. (2005). *Lifetime effects: The HighScope Perry preschool study through age 40.* Ypsilanti, MI: HighScope Educational Research Foundation.

Shonkoff, J.P., & Phillips, D.A. (Eds.). (2000). *From neurons to neighborhoods: The science of early childhood development.* Washington, DC: National Academies Press.

Shore, R. (1998). *Ready schools.* Washington, DC: National Education Goals Panel.

Shore, R. (2009). *The case for investing in PreK–3rd education: Challenging myths about school reform.* PreK–3rd Policy to Action Brief (No. 1). New York: Foundation for Child Development.

Smerdon, B.A., Burkam, D.T., & Lee, V.E. (1999). Access to constructivist and didactic teaching: Who gets it? Where is it practiced? *Teachers College Record, 101,* 5–34.

Snow, C.E., Burns, M.S., & Griffin, P. (1998). *Preventing reading difficulties in young children.* Washington, DC: National Academies Press.

Stuhlman, M.W., & Pianta, R.C. (2009). Profiles of educational quality in first grade. *Elementary School Journal, 109*(4), 323–342.

Ubben, G.C., Hughes, L.W., & Norris, C.J. (2001). *The principal: Creative leadership for effective schools* (4th edition). Needham Heights, MA: Allyn & Bacon/Longman.

Vygotsky, L.S. (1978). *Mind and society: The development of higher psychological processes.* Cambridge, MA: Harvard University Press.

Vygotsky, L. (1986). *Thought and language.* Cambridge, MA: The MIT Press.

10

Families and Transitions

Judy Langford

Families are the most important influence on their children's early development. Families are responsible for meeting the basic physical and emotional needs of their children and establishing the overall environment for their children's learning and development. They are the original case managers for their children's needs and the main agents of their education before they reach school age (Hepburn, 2004b). Entry into school signals the beginning of a major new influence on a child's development outside the familiar family environment; it formalizes a subtle shift in leadership from family to school in the child's education and socialization.

This change can be a challenge for both children and their families. There is a growing understanding that a high degree of continuity between the home and community environment, where the child's early experiences are formed, and the new environment of the school creates the best opportunity for a child's success in school. But for many schools—and many families— this alignment of intention and expectation seems out of reach. Understanding the family point of view about school transition is critical to designing and implementing more effective strategies that will help families and schools together guide children toward success from the beginning of their school years.

IN THE BEGINNING

Transitions are an integral and ongoing part of life from the very first day. As families welcome a baby into the world, they begin a long process of helping their child adjust to increasingly complex environments, beginning with the baby's first breath. The intricate dance between care-givers and infants as they manage these multiple transitions together shapes the child's growing sense of self, establishes his or her place in the family and community, and expands opportunities for learning. Transitions begin long before a child enters school and continue into the child's experience of school. The child's transition from home, preschool, or kindergarten into the formal education system is an important milestone in the life of the child and the family, one that is shaped significantly by the many experiences of transition that come before it. Transition to school does not start a few weeks before school begins, or even months before. Intentionally or not, the child and the family begin to prepare for the child's entry into school years before it happens—in the very first weeks of life.

Transitions in the Culture of the Family

Every transition that a young child experiences happens within the context of the family's child-rearing culture. One of the earliest transitions that infants make is the leap of learning to sleep through the night. They learn this habit primarily from the cues provided by the people in the household; they sense that the household quiets down after dark until it is very quiet and then gets more energetic when the light returns. In the course of their own development and with the reinforcement of their families, babies learn to expect the daily transition from day to night and slowly begin to align their behavior with the patterns of the household. Parents also work hard to ease the infant's transition into sleep, using a variety of strategies, including rocking and singing.

Many families allow (or encourage) toddlers to adopt a transitional object in the form of a favorite blanket or toy that helps the children learn to regulate emotions and actions. These objects are especially important when a child is in a new situation or with unfamiliar people. A first trip to the zoo, while very exciting, can also be disorienting, and a child may appreciate having something familiar to hold. A child may begin a group activity, like a music class or a storytelling session, by sitting quietly with a favorite blanket until he or she feels comfortable enough to participate in the group. Transitional objects are just one way that families can help children learn to comfort themselves independently, without the help of a parent or caregiver—an important aspect of transition.

The trusting relationships that families build with children provide a platform for the children's growing independence and a foundation from which to launch the many transitions that are an essential part of development. The transitions themselves offer rich opportunities for learning and for the social and emotional development that is fundamental to future success in school. Staying with a new caregiver for the first time, spending a night in a new place, or visiting relatives are all major learning events in a child's life. When parents and caregivers offer detailed explanations about where they are going, what will happen, and who will be involved, and when they take care to let children know when they will return, these efforts form important bridges into the new experience for the child. Such early experiences are the raw material of brain development, building the foundation of both social-emotional development and the cognitive processes that are essential to later academic success (Shonkoff & Phillips, 2002).

Navigating the Outside World

Transitioning into the world beyond the family presents other opportunities for a child's learning, and families both bridge and buffer children's experience in the broader society. The family's cultural or racial identity, religious practices, relations with extended family members, and network of relationships with neighbors and friends frame the world of the child outside the household. As the family integrates the child into this extended network, the child learns the social rules within the network and how to regulate his or her behavior accordingly. This network of close family and friends become the human relationships that are "the foundations upon which children build their future" (Pawl et al., 2000). The practices and traditions that are reinforced by family and friends create the parameters of the child's emerging world and signal the behaviors, language, and attributes that the larger society expects and values. These behaviors, language, and attributes may or may not be consistent with the ones that are expected by the school that a child will later attend.

In addition to the social networks that surround their family, most children experience a variety of services and opportunities that their families choose: medical care, recreation and learning opportunities, home-visiting programs, family resource centers, early care and education centers, or family child care. Parents help their children make sense of these new experiences in the larger world and link familiar patterns at home with patterns in the new environment. Parents play this same role at the time of their children's transition to school. Choices about service providers are shaped in large part by the availability of resources in the community and the affordability of services, considering the family's economic situation, but they are also strongly influenced by parents' own experiences and advice from peers about how their children will be received by particular service providers.

A child's preparation for health services, home visits, or a child care program reflects the family's perspectives about the child's entrance into society as a whole and about the service providers in particular. Parents who have experienced discrimination, disrespect, or humiliation in the past from teachers or service providers are likely to be especially cautious about exposing their children to similar experiences. They may take special care to warn their children about the possibility of feeling excluded and recommend ways to deal with those feelings (McAllister, Wilson, Green, & Baldwin, 2005). Other families expect that their children will have positive experiences and adapt easily to new situations and services, following the model of the parents' own experiences in school or in their communities. Still other parents who are new to the United States may not know exactly what to expect or how to help their children understand these new experiences if the services and opportunities differ greatly from their own experiences. Immigrant families with a strong allegiance to their original language and culture may resist exposing their young children to the dominant culture as long as possible out of fear that the children will lose their heritage in the process. The inclusive preschool or school may seem especially antithetical to some teachings and traditions of the home culture. Some families intentionally help their children learn how to switch back and forth from their home culture to other environments (Hepburn, 2004a).

ALIGNING FAMILY AND SCHOOL

When children reach school age, the circle of stakeholders in their lives expands in a new way. The needs and expectations of parents, extended family members, schools, community, and society differ, sometimes significantly. Communities of all kinds expect children to contribute to the well-being of the local area. They hope that children will grow up to be responsible citizens, leaders, workers for the next generation, and taxpayers who contribute economically to the society and benefit everyone. Schools are the institutional pathway toward achieving many of these goals. Schools' success is directly measured by how well children perform inside their walls and indirectly measured by how well their graduates meet the expectations of the wider society.

School personnel from superintendents to classroom teachers have a vested interest in their students' achievement and, specifically in recent years, in having their students perform well on standardized tests. When students begin school on track, with social skills, literacy, numeracy skills, and positive attitudes toward learning, the school's job is much easier. These skills come from the early learning environments that children have experienced and the family's own teaching. Aligning the school's needs and expectations with the realities and preferences of how families from diverse backgrounds shape the early learning experiences of young children, however, is an ongoing challenge (Pianta & Kraft-Sayre, 2003; Rouse, Brooks-Gunn, & McLanahan, 2005), even in countries where ethnic diversity is not as pronounced as it is in the United States (Corsaro & Molinari, 2006).

The Ready Families Paradigm

There is ample evidence that families play a big role in children's school success from the beginning (Henderson & Mapp, 2002; Reynolds, Magnuson, & Ou, 2006; Weiss, Caspe, & Lopez, 2006). There is also evidence of a big gap between children's early experiences and the skills that schools expect young children to have when they begin elementary school. As a result, increasing attention has been given to the multiple factors that influence children's readiness for school, as well as to how families and children manage the transition from home to school (Schorr, 2004).

In 2005, the National School Readiness Indicators Initiative, which is led by several distinguished national organizations and teams from 17 states, created a simple, useful expression to combine the components of improving school readiness across the nation (Rhode Island Kids Count, 2005). The School Readiness equation looks like this:

> Ready Families + Ready Communities + Ready Services + Ready Schools
> = Children Ready for School

The Ready Families part of the equation shows that families have foundational importance to their children's readiness to succeed. The question is how to define *readiness* in each component.

Risk Factors   A traditional understanding of family readiness has focused on risk factors, family characteristics are correlated with children's lower scores on readiness scales. These risk factors include family poverty, housing in unsafe conditions, reported child maltreatment, maternal depression, low educational level of parents, low maternal age, a primary language other than English spoken in the home, and other factors (Ounce of Prevention Fund, 2009; Rhode Island Kids Count, 2005). On the whole, family risk factors cannot be mitigated by interventions or special programs. In families with multiple risk factors, each additional factor reduces the likelihood that a child will experience a smooth transition to school.

Significant differences between children who are living in poverty and children who are not living in poverty that lead to diminished achievement are evident early (Annie E. Casey Foundation, 2007b; Heckman, 2008; National Center for Children in Poverty, 2007). For example, the number of different words that a child hears spoken in a low-income household may be only half as many words as children in affluent homes hear by age 3 (Hart & Risley, 1995).

Furthermore, the lack of high-quality early care and education experiences is profound for children in poverty. Nationally in 2008, 24% of all 4-year-olds and 4% of 3-year-olds were enrolled in publicly funded early childhood (i.e, state-sponsored prekindergarten) programs, but these numbers represent a wide variation in availability from state to state, from 90% of 4-year-olds enrolled in Oklahoma to less than 10% enrolled in some states. Head Start served an additional 11% of 4-year-olds and Early Head Start served an additional 8% of 3-year-olds, but these statistics are far below the total number of eligible children. Eighteen percent of 4-year-olds and forty-eight percent of 3-year-olds did not participate in any center-based program at all (Barnett, 2008).

There are also indications of significant racial gaps in children's readiness for school. Children of color, particularly African American and Latino children, come to school with significantly lower literacy and numeracy skills than do white children (Children's Defense Fund, 2008; Rhode Island Kids Count, 2005; Rouse et al., 2005). These gaps stem from myriad unequal opportunities in the children's early experiences, including inequities in children's health status, mothers' prenatal care, maternal depression, and highly stressed family situations that make learning stimulation difficult to provide (Annie E. Casey Foundation, 2007b). The same conditions also inhibit families' capacity to provide a stable, welcoming bridge to school.

Policy makers are concerned about mitigating family risk factors. Reducing risk raises the probability that children will arrive at school adequately prepared to take advantage of formal education. Because many of the same risk factors are related to other negative results—such as child abuse and neglect, chronic illness, and limited prospects for economic success—there are multiple (yet insufficient) efforts underway to eliminate poverty, decrease violence, reduce teen births, increase high school graduation rates, and screen for and treat maternal depression, among other goals. Most of these efforts, however, are not systematically connected to improving the school readiness of young children or easing their transition into school, even though the efforts may have an important impact on a child's early experiences.

Although it is important for policy makers to develop policy approaches and programs to reduce risk factors, schools, communities, and families need additional options to increase children's opportunity for success. Like most other families, the families with risk factors want their children to succeed in school from the very first day. Families with risk factors, however, are often stymied because they do not know how to support their children's development or they live in communities that lack sufficient child and family support services. Schools and community programs that wish to help families may also struggle to balance efforts that target a few families (usually those with multiple risk factors) with efforts to provide information and assistance to everyone. Many families find it difficult to enroll in programs that invite their participation on the basis of identified risk factors or programs that base eligibility on deficits. Community program developers are likewise skeptical of labeling their neighborhoods and stigmatizing the people in them by using deficits as the basis for the provision of services.

Protective Factors   An alternative approach to reducing risk factors relies on identifying and building on protective factors, which are family characteristics associated with optimal child development, increased family strengths, and reduced child maltreatment. Using these factors as a guide provides a strengths-based pathway for schools and communities to work alongside families to achieve ready families. This approach reduces risk factors without the stigma that is associated with deficit-based service models. Building on families' protective factors mitigates the impact of risk factors that cannot be changed, such as low maternal age or intergenerational poverty.

The Strengthening Families protective factors framework, which has been adopted by multidisciplinary teams in 30 states and by thousands of parent leaders and early childhood programs, identifies five protective factors that are related to a reduction in child maltreatment and an improvement in child development. These protective factors were identified through extensive literature reviews and a national panel of researchers and organizational leaders in early childhood, child abuse prevention, and health. The Center for the Study of Social Policy originally developed the framework, which has been widely adapted by other organizations, including the National Association for the Education of Young Children, Zero to Three, Parents as Teachers, the National Alliance of Children's Trust and Prevention Funds, and United Way of America (Center for the Study of Social Policy, 2008). Taken together, the protective factors form a comprehensive prescription for action by families, early childhood programs, service providers, and others who are working with families. The following protective factors constitute the framework:

- *Parental resilience.* Parents need to have the capacity to form positive relationships, including bonding with infants, to reach out for help as needed, and to feel confident about solving problems that arise in the normal course of family life.

- *Social connections.* Families need to have connections to extended family members, neighbors, and others who form a supportive network of mutual assistance and reciprocity.

- *Knowledge of parenting and child development.* Families require knowledge about patterns of children's development and need to have skills in managing and facilitating healthy development, including positive ways of dealing with children's challenging behavior and the knowledge to seek appropriate services (such as health care or literacy opportunities) for their children.

- *Concrete support in times of need.* Families need to have adequate economic resources to meet their basic needs, such as food, shelter, and clothing, and ways to access these resources in times of crisis. Families need access to competent treatment services for domestic violence, mental illness, or substance abuse, and access to special services for children with special needs.

- *Social and emotional competence of children.* Families need adequate capacity to facilitate their children's healthy social and emotional development, which in turn creates attachment and positive relationships with parents and other caregivers. Families need special assistance when their children's development is not on a typical trajectory and when special needs or developmental delays are identified.

Although all five of the protective factors are important for creating a family environment that is conducive to good parenting, nurturing, and stable child development, three of them in particular are related to school transition: the family's social connections, the family's knowledge of parenting and child development (Weiss et al., 2006), and the child's social and emotional competence (Pawl et al., 2000). Families' and children's capacity to form relationships are strong predictors of successful transitions to school, where initial success is measured by the child's progress making new friends, trusting the teachers, and feeling confident within the school culture. The positive relationships that parents form with teachers and school staff have a significant impact on their ability to help children adjust to school and begin to find success (Downer & Pianta, 2006; Fantuzzo, 2004; Henderson & Mapp, 2002; Ladd, Birch, & Buhs, 1999). Likewise, families' engagement in providing developmentally appropriate educational experiences for their children at home and in the community and in helping children gain self-regulation and appropriate social skills is strongly related to the children's later success in school (Weiss et al., 2006).

Although protective factors may be expressed differently in different cultures or communities, all services for children and families—including those provided by schools, churches, and other community organizations—can play a role in helping families build these fundamental protective factors. Families that have limited economic means, parents who are teenagers, high levels of stress, and multiple risk factors will need greater assistance from community resources and service providers to access the opportunities they need.

Culture and Perspective Gaps   Risk factors and protective factors in families help explain some of the differences in readiness and successful transition to school for young children. Another important part of the picture is the gap in perspective between schools and families. This gap plays out especially in the soft skills or general knowledge about behavior that children need to be successful in school. Although there is little uniformity among schools or teachers about expectations, there are some key situations in which families and schools may value different things when it comes to young children's social-emotional development. These differences can create conflict when the child begins school and needs to successfully fit into the classroom environment.

Kindergarten teachers regularly report a number of barriers to children's successful transition to school, starting with children's behavioral problems, such as an inability to get along with others, seek help, or regulate behavior (Heaviside & Farris, 1993; Rimm-Kaufman, Pianta, & Cox, 2000). Some of these differences in expected behaviors stem from differences in the cultural expectations at home or the lack of experience that children have in settings where the kinds of skills that teachers expect could be learned (Barbarin, 2002).

The family's ideas about what young children should know and be able to do when they arrive at school often differ significantly from the school's ideas or the individual teacher's ideas (Hepburn, 2004b). Many parents focus on skills such as counting to 20 or knowing colors and letters, while teachers believe that social-emotional skills are more important (Cowan, Powell, & Cowan, 1998; Heaviside & Farris, 1993). There are significant differences by parental culture, race, income, and education about expectations for young children's behavior and knowledge when they enter school (Bhattacharya, Olson, & Scharf, 2004). Non–English-speaking parents, for example, consider children's ability to communicate in English more important than teachers do. Parents who have a college degree tend to believe that rote skills, like knowing letters of the alphabet, are less important to school readiness than do parents with lower educational backgrounds (Ackerman & Barnett, 2005; Mashburn & Pianta, 2006; West, Geromino-Hausken, & Collins, 1995).

Families' beliefs about schools also influence their ability and motivation to help their children enter school with the attitudes and skills that children need to succeed. Some cultures consider school to be responsible for education, and parents in these cultures feel that their interference in school would be disrespectful. Other families believe that parents should not have any responsibility for helping their children learn because teachers and schools are being paid well to teach the children everything they need (Bhattacharya et al., 2004). Many parents are skeptical about the school's respect for their children and for them. Some express alienation and anger that teachers and administrators rarely seek out their opinions and appear to disregard their perspectives. These beliefs make it very hard for families to form effective partnerships with teachers around their children's needs or to pave the way for a smooth transition (Annie E. Casey Foundation, 2007b; McAllister et al., 2005).

Teachers and school personnel have a challenging task to understand the diversity of expectations that parents have about school and to respond to them in ways that will bridge the gaps and help children get off to a good start. Schools need to be ready to do their part to reach across these divisions. Because of these wide differences in perspectives, however, parents may need substantial help in understanding the school's expectations and their own roles in helping their children gain the skills and knowledge that they need to succeed. Without having a basic understanding of the school's expectations, parents are not likely to be able to support their children's entry into school and acclimation to the classroom. These gaps in understanding may be barriers to good transitions that are just as potent as the more readily understood barriers such as poverty and lack of opportunity (Barbarin, 2002; Bhattacharya et al., 2004).

Programs and Resources for Families

Most communities offer programs and opportunities that can help families guide their children into school on a positive note. The quality and quantity of these resources varies greatly from one neighborhood to another, however. Less affluent neighborhoods and those where fewer white people live, where families may need the most assistance, tend to have the fewest resources (Annie E. Casey Foundation, 2007b; Shulting, 2009). Family involvement in these early activities with their children increases the likelihood that the children will succeed later in school. These resources offer opportunities for families to build three different kinds of involvement, as described by the Harvard Family Research Project, that have been shown to improve academic outcomes for young children: 1) good parenting practices, 2) strong relationships with schools and other resource providers for children, and 3) significant "complementary learning" experiences that families provide for their children outside school (Weiss et al., 2006). Although specific research is lacking about how these dimensions of parental involvement are related to school transition, it is likely that they make a strong contribution to children's adjustment to school and early success there.

Early Care and Education Programs
The most effective avenue for aligning a child's early experiences with a positive transition and later school success (as well as for closing racial gaps in school achievement) continues to be enrollment in a high-quality early care and education program (Rouse et al., 2005). Enrollment in a high-quality program produces significant positive outcomes for both children and parents and many opportunities for families to gain both knowledge and skills to help them deal effectively with the later transition to the formal education system.

A high-quality program will provide a language-rich environment, opportunities for exploratory play and learning experiences, and consistent expectations for behavior in a group setting that are important to children's development. It may also provide an important boost to parents' capacity to become full partners with their childs school (Boethel, 2004). Most early care and education programs that showed substantial gains over many years include strong parent components that may have helped produce positive child outcomes (Reynolds et al., 2006). These programs helped families create learning environments at home that were more consistent with the school environments—one of the key elements in a successful transition to school. Evidence from the longitudinal study of the Chicago Parent Child Centers shows the value of family involvement beyond the educational achievement of children, such as a 52% reduction in the rate of substantiated child abuse cases (Reynolds et al., 2007). Studies of Early Head Start also showed significant improvements in parenting, including increased reading to children, support for language and learning, decreased spanking and increased alternative discipline strategies, and other measures of good parenting (Love et al., 2002). Several longitudinal studies and other evaluations show that early childhood programs can mitigate family risk factors, such as poverty, that may inhibit a child's development and later success in school (Karoly, Kilbourn, & Cannon, 2005; Ramey & Ramey, 2004).

Home-Visiting Programs and Doulas
Home-visiting programs also have been shown to counteract risk factors and improve parents' participation in their child's learning (Gomby, 2003; Harvard Family Research Project, n.d.). Most home-visiting programs target first-time mothers or other women who are identified as needing assistance in starting off right with their children. A parent's relationship with a parent educator (as the visitors from Parents as Teachers are called) or a registered nurse from the Nurse Family Partnership program has been shown to improve long-term outcomes for children and families. Other programs that use different strategies or curricula, such as Home Instruction for Parents of Preschoolers and Parents and Children Together, have also shown gains (National Governors Association, 2005). Some Early Head Start programs are home based or mix home visits with center-based activities. Many home-visiting programs are housed at family resource centers or within other programs for parents and young children, making it easier for parents to access a variety of resources at once.

Doula programs, another home-based service for young mothers, are gaining popularity in some areas. Doulas are birthing coaches who work with pregnant women, guide them through labor and delivery, and then follow up with home visits and coaching when the infant goes home. The special relationships that doulas create with their clients have shown great promise in helping teen mothers and other mothers with high-risk pregnancies or fragile infants. The bonding and attachment that doulas strive to promote lay the foundation for a child's social-emotional development—essential for successful transition to school—from the beginning. Most doulas are recruited from local neighborhoods, trained to be birth and early infancy coaches for women of similar education or ethnic background, and supervised as they carry out their work (Ounce of Prevention Fund, 2005).

The skills and relationships that families gain from home-visiting programs can be very helpful in promoting early literacy skills and preparing children for school. In the past, however, schools have rarely formed relationships with home-visiting programs or reached out to programs that target infants and toddlers. As additional federal funding expands the availability of home-visiting programs, local elementary schools will have new opportunities to work closely with those programs and their front-line workers, to align school expectations with the home-visiting experiences.

Family Resource Centers   Family resource centers offer a variety of opportunities to help families—especially new parents—build skills, knowledge, and social networks. Drop-in centers offer a convenient location that may house parent education materials, information about home-visiting programs, referrals to other family services, and a place for informal networking, staffed by workers who are trained to be welcoming and supportive. Some centers, like the settlement houses that preceded them, offer job training, GED classes, English language skills, and other ways to help families get ahead economically. Exemplary family resource programs often become social and information hubs for their neighborhoods and thus form an effective bridge between families and schools. Several states have developed sophisticated statewide networks of family resource centers with special attention given to disinvested neighborhoods that need extra resources for children. In many cases, family resource programs are linked or colocated with early care and education programs and sponsor a variety of community programs. In some cases, family resource centers are tightly connected with elementary schools or located inside school buildings, offering opportunities for families to connect with schools long before their children enroll.

Parent Education   Home-visiting programs and family resource programs offer parent education, but additional sources of information and skill building are available to families through classes and workshops. Curricula among these programs vary widely; programs help participants reach different goals and may target a certain group of families or children of a particular age. Some parent education programs focus on teaching skills such as communication and discipline, some provide basic child development or health care information, and still others teach leadership development and advocacy. Each of these areas of study contributes to the family's ability to support their children's development and to create and sustain an effective relationship with the school.

Community Programs that Support Literacy   Although there is no consensus about what parents need to know and do to help their children be ready for school, there is one aspect of school readiness about which everyone agrees: It is important for children to have the foundations for literacy when they enter school. A rich language environment within the family, including storytelling and regular reading to young children, is the place to start, because reading and listening are fundamental to daily life in the classroom. Learning to love stories and the imaginative play that they generate lays significant groundwork for ease and familiarity with behavior and activities that are valued in school.

Children who grow up in low-income families know thousands fewer words than more privileged children before they enter school, and this deficit creates a significant disadvantage that is difficult to make up (Ounce of Prevention Fund, 2009). Closing gaps in the foundations for literacy will help close the gap in school readiness as well. Children who are read to regularly by adults have a significant advantage once they arrive in school, because they gain both literacy skills and an understanding of how to engage adults as they read (Armbruster, 2002). Many studies point out that many young children don't have the regular experience of parents reading to them; among some cultural groups, fewer than half of the children have this experience (National Educational Goals Panel, 1997; Rhode Island Kids Count, 2005).

A number of programs encourage families to read to children daily as a way to promote literacy and love of reading, both of which are significant factors in making a successful transition into school. These programs address a number of factors that keep parents from reading: lack of access to a library or books (especially books in the primary language of the family if they are not English speakers), poor parental reading skills, and parental inexperience in reading with children. Some exemplary programs are Reach Out and Read, which is supported by pediatricians and other health care providers; Reading Is Fundamental (Reading Is Fundamental, n.d.); and Raising a Reader (Raising a Reader, n.d.). Ready to Learn local grants and the Even Start program that supports literacy for both parents and children are sources of federal funding for literacy enhancement action and often are provided in partnerships with schools and educational television. Each early literacy program offers outreach to encourage families to participate, raises public awareness, gives away free books, and provides an organized structure to increase the reading activity of families. Some programs are offered in conjunction with English as a Second Language courses, providing literacy activities for children while their parents learn English.

In many urban neighborhoods, the public library is the main consistent source for low-cost books and programs that encourage storytelling and reading among children and their parents. Library programs are often supplemented by literacy outreach activities that are funded by public television stations and linkages with other literacy programs, family resource centers, and early childhood programs. Some libraries have developed parenting programs and other activities for family child-care providers that are on site at the library and that emphasize school transition activities as well.

Opportunities for Connections

Families need multiple opportunities to connect with other parents, help their children build social skills, and begin to take leadership roles at home and in their communities. These opportunities also teach families about expectations for their children to be successful in school and help them to create active relationships with schools even before their children enroll. Formally organized programs like the ones previously described in this chapter, church programs, sports and recreation groups, family outings, and play groups can be important developmental opportunities for families as well as children (Weiss et al., 2006). Churches, parks, and recreation departments can play an important role in their communities by providing safe places for families to congregate, especially in neighborhoods where safety may be a concern (Bruner, Tirmizi, & Wright, 2007).

Accessible Information

Basic information about child development, ideas for how families can help the developmental process along, and suggestions for how they can prepare their children for school are available to families from a variety of sources, from public television and the Internet to books and pamphlets. Most states and communities have developed resources on child development and distributed them in many places that families already visit: health centers, government offices, schools, and child-care programs. A comprehensive resource guide provided by the Massachusetts Department of Early Education and Care in collaboration with the Department of Public Health, for example, provides extensive information about resources for services and supports that families can use, community activities that are widely available, and tips for families to help young children get ready for school starting at age 2 (Massachusetts Department of Early Education and Care & Massachusetts Department of Public Health, 2007). Other states have similar materials, along with outreach programs to disseminate them (National Governors Association, 2005). Born Learning child development materials are widely available through United Way of America's Success by 6 program (United Way, United Way Success by 6, & Civitas, 2005). In a number of states, United Way operates a central 211 telephone number that provides information for parents about a wide variety of topics and resources that are available to them, including advice on preparing children for school and asking the right questions of the school to ensure a healthy transition (United Way, 2009). A key challenge to providing accessible written materials is ensuring that the information appears in the multiple languages that families speak and at a literacy level that matches family capacity.

What Schools Can Do to Build Early Bridges to Families

Although community services and programs will boost a child's chances of healthy development in a number of ways and provide families with relationships and capacity building to ease their children's transition into the classroom, these programs are not always aligned with the expectations of schools. Many programs are not intentionally designed to help families understand what young children should know and be able to do when they arrive at school or to teach families how they can help their children adjust to a new environment and people. To remedy this deficiency, schools should reach out to the community resource providers and ensure that their materials provide the groundwork for later school success (Rhode Island Kids Count, 2005; Shulting, 2009). These efforts may help bridge the gap between schools' and families' perceptions about what children need to know when they enter school, especially when the suggestions focus on strengthening the relationships that are vital to children's success: relationships between parents and children, families and schools, and children and teachers (Ladd et al., 1999; Mashburn & Pianta, 2006).

When schools reach out to create partnerships with community resource providers and with families, they can provide information and skills and build relationships that will make the later transition to school easier for everyone (Mangione & Speth, 1998). One opportunity for schools to connect with families is through early care and education programs that are located within their school districts. Families often develop lasting relationships with child care providers, home visitors, preschool teachers, and others who care for and provide learning experiences for their children. These providers can play an important mediating role between schools and parents in transition. As part of their work, they offer both formal and informal information to families about what to expect from the school and how to prepare their children for school. Ongoing strong relationships with these providers are important opportunities for schools to provide accurate information about their programs and expectations to both the providers and parents of prospective students. The familiar setting of a child care program or a home visit can facilitate the handling of school logistics, such as registering for school, meeting health and legal requirements, and making transportation arrangements.

The most important opportunity provided by a strong relationship between schools and early childhood service providers is the opportunity to align the school's academic and behavioral expectations with the experiences that young children have in other programs. The providers of most early care and education, early literacy, health, and other programs for young children and their families welcome the opportunity to provide the children they serve with a better chance of success in school, by using input from the school (Weiss et al., 2006).

At the same time, early childhood providers can help bridge the gap between parents and school by providing the school with vital information about the values and perspectives of the families they serve. Language and cultural differences can be bridged more easily with the input of people who are familiar with the families and children who will be enrolling in school. When children or families have circumstances or needs that could affect the children's success in school, providers who have worked with these families in the past can provide support to the school by helping the school staff understand the needs of the families or helping the families access essential services long before the children are enrolled in the school.

In some communities, schools also have reached out to unregulated family, friend, and neighbor child care providers, including grandparents and neighbors, specifically to create relationships with the networks around the families that they will be serving in the future. Relationships between schools and family networks provide a vehicle for understanding expectations and opportunities well ahead of children's school enrollment. The development of an ongoing relationship is especially important in communities where the gap between school and families is wide because of cultural or language barriers, multiple risk factors, or a profound lack of resources for families.

SUCCESS IN SCHOOL

Once children enter school, the need for continuity between home and school does not end. The school may take a leadership role in providing learning experiences for children and guidance for their behavior for a substantial part of the day, but the ongoing support of families is critical to children's success (Downer & Pianta, 2006; Fantuzzo, 2004). Adjusting to the early days of school and learning the school's patterns of behavior and expectations are only the beginning. Achievement in analytic and language skills, the mastery of specific math and reading skills, and the building of friendships and other relationships are essential foundations for long-term success in school. When children enter school, families transition to a new relationship with the school and develop an urgent need to understand the school's expectations and know how they can best support their children's success.

Helping Families Foster Success

The National Education Goals Panel suggests that schools can start early to support children's transitions in several ways: providing familiar language or cultural bridges into school, creating links to the preschool experiences that children may have had, and ensuring that staff are well prepared to receive children from a variety of backgrounds (Shore, 1998). Schools that welcome every child with respect, pay attention to the child's individual transition, and follow through with excellent instruction that is designed to meet the needs of each child at a high level are likely to engage families at a high level too. Families continue to need communication and support as they shift into a partnership role with the school. There are three leading ways to continue to create alignment as children enter school.

First, the school's climate is critical to creating a welcoming backdrop that encourages both children and their families to have a positive relationship with the school. Schools have begun to understand the importance of ensuring that children can "see themselves" in the school from their first experience of it, starting with displays, books, and visual cues which tell children that the school is familiar and engaging and includes people who look like them. Families experience the school's attitude toward them from the moment they walk through the door, from subtle signs to interactions with school personnel. Schools are not always aware of the messages they are sending, particularly to parents who have negative feelings about school or who feel inadequately prepared to help their children. Respect is the most important starting point for a positive long-term relationship.

Second, schools need to continue to respond to the diversity of the families who are part of the school and encourage their leadership and involvement. Families as well as children are more likely to participate fully in the school when schools have provided materials in the multiple languages that various families speak at home and have trained teachers and other staff to welcome and respect the heritage of all of the students and their families. Listening carefully and consistently to parents is the most important way of showing respect and adapting the school environment to the needs of the children (McAllister et al., 2005). Resources and tools for helping schools engage and encourage families to be advocates for their children are increasingly available (Annie E. Casey Foundation, 2007c; Bhattacharya et al., 2004; Hepburn, 2004a).

Third, schools can take advantage of what health advocates have learned from widespread campaigns to reduce smoking and what marketers know when they target ads to children: What children learn in the classroom transfers to their homes (DePanfilis & Zuravin, 2002). Schools can take advantage of this fact by communicating with parents about what children are learning in school and encouraging parents to reinforce school lessons at home. The Second Step curriculum, which is used in many early childhood programs and elementary schools, originated as a classroom-focused violence prevention strategy that helps children learn social and emotional skills. Second Step provides a kit of well-designed materials for teachers, children, and parents. plus training for teachers about how to use it in their classrooms. Teachers and schools like the curriculum because it specifies and reinforces behaviors that children need to follow in order to promote a peaceful learning environment in the classroom and teaches them how to use positive ways of dealing with conflict, stated in simple terms that children can easily follow. Parents report that children bring the strategies home (Committee for Children, 2009).

Sustaining Difficult Partnerships

Even with the best of preparation, intentions, and outreach, some families will find it difficult to create a workable partnership with the school. The barriers to a positive partnership take many forms and include conditions such as substance abuse, illness or depression, disruptions to the family's circumstances such as moving or losing a job, embarrassment about not understanding the language or culture of the school, and a persistent suspicion of the school as a positive place for their child to be. Some families may stay away because they come from cultures in which they are not expected to participate in a child's schooling and they believe that parents are not supposed to interfere with teachers. Some of these barriers may be temporary conditions that resolve over time and permit the family to engage more productively, as long as they do not feel blamed or shut out because of their earlier lack of involvement.

Teachers should use persistent, creative efforts to engage reluctant parents. Effective programs working with hard-to-reach families report eventual success when families learn that the school, service provider, or home visitor is not going to give up on them no matter how many contacts it takes. Schools can learn effective strategies from family resource centers and home-visiting programs. Redoubling efforts to cross language or literacy barriers and communicate with families, engaging other school parents as peer outreach agents, and having teachers and other staff take time to understand the circumstances and cultures of families who are not in-clined to connect with the school are time-tested strategies for reaching across the barriers that reduce communication and participation (Boo, 2006).

Another strategy to engage families is by paying special attention to their children, espe-cially in the early days of school. The psychological and emotional aspects of transition for the children themselves are significant, not only in terms of academic and behavioral expectations. Providing a way for children to express and explore their own experiences of adjusting to a new environment and leaving their families behind is vital to their adjustment to new expectations, regardless of the family's level of participation. Children's perceptions of differences between home and school can also provide clues about how to engage their families.

The PassageWorks Institute has piloted a unique 16-week school transition curriculum for young children in several states. The curriculum focuses on helping children adjust to new circum-stances by analyzing what is new, reaching out for support from their families, and exploring the emotional dimensions of entering a new environment. One aspect of the program is a passage event focused on the children's celebration of their families and the role that they have played in help-ing them learn (Simpson & Kessler, 2007). Families sometimes become more engaged when their children invite them to see their successful adjustment and emerging achievement at school.

One red flag that may indicate a need for the school to reach out to a family more assertively in the early years of school is the child's pattern of chronic absence (missing more than 10% of school days). Chronic absence in kindergarten predicts lower academic achievement in first grade for all students, and it predicts the lowest levels of achievement by fifth grade for poor children. Families need more help to address this issue than letters sent home or messages left by telephone. Lack of resources or support, chronic health problems in children or adults, and high mobility are possible underlying reasons for the absences, and these problems may require additional assistance from other community resources. Schools need to review their attendance procedures and their communication and engagement with families to be sure that they are doing all they can to encourage attendance (Chang & Romero, 2008).

CONCLUSION

In spite of the significant challenges facing schools and families, education remains the primary pathway for ensuring success for the next generation, particularly in times of economic uncer-tainty. The new attention being focused on early childhood, new resources available for early childhood programs, and higher expectations for schools all mean that schools and families need new energy and new options to forge partnerships for children's success in a changing world. A smooth transition into formal school and the thrill of accomplishment in the early grades is the right beginning for every child's lifelong learning.

Case Study—The Family and Child Education Program (FACE)

A Program Fostering Transitions for American Indian Families from Home to School and the Workplace

Aleksandra Holod

The Family and Child Education Program (FACE) is an early childhood effort that helps American Indian parents and primary caregivers to be their children's first teacher. FACE is an integrated program of home visiting, early childhood education, and adult education that increases family literacy. The goals of the program are to 1) foster chil-dren's school readiness, 2) involve parents in their children's education, 3) increase high school completion rates among American Indian parents, and 4) support the cultural and linguistic heritage of the communities it serves. FACE strengthens connections among home, school, and community by locating services for participating families at the elementary school where the child will attend kindergarten. The FACE program promotes a family-oriented approach to transition by honoring parents' role in setting values and educational expectations for their children. It also facilitates children's transition from home-based services to center-based preschool and parents' transition into higher education and the workplace (Face Resources, nd).

The History of FACE   FACE was developed by the Office of Indian Education Programs, now the Bureau of Indian Education (BIE), within the Bureau of Indian Affairs in 1990. Initially called the Early Childhood/Parental Involvement program, it was implemented as a pilot program at six BIA-funded schools. Since the early 1990s, FACE has expanded to offer 44 programs in 11 of the 23 states where Bureau of Indian Education schools are located. The BIE collaborates with Parents as Teachers National Center (PATNC) and the National Center for Family Literacy (NCFL) to provide training and technical assistance for the program. FACE employs a two-pronged strategy, combining home- and center-based services to support families as children transition between home and school settings (Face Resources and Family and child education, 2009).

Home Visiting   Many FACE families begin their participation with home visiting, which serves families from pregnancy until age 3. Participating families receive weekly or biweekly personal visits from parent educators who are trained and certified in the Parents as Teachers Born to Learn® Curriculum. During home visits, the parent educator provides parent–child learning experiences that support the child's development, such as a book-sharing activity and a related activity to reinforce the lesson during the week. Parent educators also conduct regular developmental and health screenings with parents' help. If the screening identifies learning or health problems, the parent educator connects the family with community services to ensure that the child's needs are addressed.

In addition to receiving home visits, parents of young children are encouraged to attend a monthly family circle meeting at the school where the center-based FACE program takes place. The FACE program often provides transportation, food, and babysitting to make the meetings accessible for families. The meetings address topics of interest to parents, such as parenting practices, child development, native language and culture, and physical and mental health issues. Family circle meetings support transition by giving parents opportunities to connect with one another and receive support on child-rearing issues, thereby strengthening the protective factors that will translate into improved family participation in early education. These meetings also help parents build relationships with the staff who teach at the center-based FACE program and with the elementary school staff. The parent educators invite tribal agencies and special service providers from the community to give presentations at selected family circle meetings. These visits from service providers help families access needed services, especially when they live in isolated, rural areas (J. Power, personal communication, July 9, 2009).

When a child approaches 3 years of age, the child's family is incrementally transitioned from home-based to center-based FACE. The school offers transition days that introduce children to the new, center-based setting a few months before their third birthday. On these days, parents and children ride the school bus together to visit the FACE program. Children participate in a minilesson or small-group activity in the classroom, eat lunch, and then go back home. During the course of the day, children meet the bus driver, teacher, principal, and cafeteria staff. Center-based staff are familiar with participating families' needs prior to these visits because FACE home-visiting staff and center-based teachers participate in regular staff meetings together. The staff collaborate to develop individualized transition plans and document implementation of the plan for each family (J. Power, personal communication, July 9, 2009).

Center-Based Services   The center-based FACE program offers services for both children and their parents or caregivers, following a model that was developed by the NCFL. Many of the children who participate in home-based FACE go on to attend the center-based program. The program includes early childhood education, adult education, parent time, and time for children and parents to interact in the classroom. The early childhood education portion of the program is based on the *HighScope* curriculum and places a strong emphasis on parent involvement. The adult education program includes GED classes, job skills training, and career development. Parent time is a daily component during which parents discuss child rearing, family issues, and other topics of adult interest. Finally, Parent and Child Together Time (PACT) occurs daily in the early childhood classroom. During PACT, parents join their children in the early childhood classroom.

The center-based FACE program promotes child, parent, and family literacy simultaneously; the coordinated approach links the home and school environment, thereby easing children's transitions between settings. Parental involvement occurs through Parent and child together time (PACT). During PACT, parents join their children in the early childhood classroom and learn to engage their children in a variety of literacy activities. One lesson, for example, involves book reading. Each participating parent is taught to read to his or her child in a stimulating way by doing a book preview, asking the child questions about the book, and engaging the child in dialogue. This method of book reading, which is consistent with school-based book reading, is somewhat unfamiliar to many American Indian families, who have a strong tradition of oral storytelling but less experience with book reading. Circle time gives families an opportunity to reflect with each other and the teacher about their experiences with this new reading technique. Families then receive take-home activities to extend children's learning of the week's lesson. Parents also engage in adult literacy activities during the adult education portion of the day, such as reading about current events on the Internet or designing custom-made books for their children in both English and their native language.

FACE also facilitates parents' and caregivers' transition to the workplace. A quarter of all American Indians live below the federal poverty line (Bishaw & Semega, 2008) and only about half of them complete high school (Orfield, Losen, Wald, & Swanson, 2004). The FACE program addresses the challenges that face the American Indian community by helping parents earn GEDs and enroll in post-secondary education programs. With the support of the FACE program, some parents have earned degrees or the credentials they need to work in paraprofessional or technical careers. Parents also receive career counseling and job skills training, such as basic computer literacy, and participate in job shadowing to learn about different career options. Through its adult education and job training component, FACE addresses family risk factors, such as poverty and low parental education levels, that can be a barrier to children's school success.

Implementation   The BIE and its contractors work closely with FACE sites to implement and evaluate the program. FACE programs are provided with implementation guidelines, training, and technical assistance to ensure that the program model is implemented with fidelity. Evaluation information is also gathered to assess how the FACE program is benefiting children and their families.

Implementation Guidelines and Technical Assistance   Although the FACE program has been operating for 20 years, regular professional development and technical assistance are still offered to all FACE sites nationally. The BIE provides all necessary funding and program direction for the FACE model through a collaborative effort with PATNC and NCFL. An annual multiday conference for all program staff provides training and addresses implementation issues that are encountered in all aspects of the program, including the home-visiting, early childhood education, and parent education components. All FACE staff, including new staff and veterans, attend these conferences to strengthen their skills and learn about new approaches to their work. The BIE implements periodic teleconferences that allow staff and different sites to learn from each other and exchange ideas. PATNC and NCFL also conduct on-site technical assistance visits at least once a year for each site in concert with the BIE. During these technical assistance visits, programs brainstorm with providers about how to deal with implementation challenges, such as team coordination, team communication, and recruitment and retention of families.

The BIE developed implementation guidelines for the FACE program in 2004 and 2005 to ensure the fidelity of the program model at each site. The guidelines address admission criteria, required staff qualifications, roles and responsibilities, curriculum guidelines, health and safety standards, and other issues (Bureau of Indian Education, 2006). Program sites use them as a self-assessment tool to identify the strengths and weaknesses of their program in the context of the overall guidelines and to develop action plans to address challenges, with the help of the BIE and national technical assistance providers. Technical assistance is also based on program data in monthly administrative reports and information that is collected by program evaluators. For example, when administrative data suggested that attendance at family circle meetings could be improved, the BIE worked with the PATNC to develop materials that parent educators could use for outreach efforts and materials for kits that parents could take home after family circle meetings.

Evaluation Results   One of the most extensively evaluated programs funded by the BIE, FACE has demonstrated substantial benefits for children and families. The results are promising. It has been shown to narrow the gap on national school readiness benchmarks for American Indian children. Children who participate in FACE score higher on measures of number and letter recognition and verbal expression than do their American Indian peers who do not participate. Children with special needs are identified and receive services at higher rates and with greater intensity when they participate in the FACE program. Nearly 25% of children in the FACE preschool qualify for Early Childhood Special Education. American Indian children who receive Early Childhood Special Education services prior to kindergarten are half as likely to need special education in kindergarten if they participate in FACE. Families who participate in FACE have more books in their homes and read to their children more often. Significantly more FACE parents are involved in their children's elementary school. They attend parent–teacher conferences, school events, and parent meetings at higher rates, even in third grade—years after families complete the FACE program (Research & Training Associates, Inc., 2006).

Lessons Learned   Nationally and at the site level, partnerships are an important part of the FACE program. Over the years, PATNC and NCFL have realized how important it is for them to work together to support the FACE program, just as program staff work together on-site (K. Jacobs, personal communication, July 22, 2009). PATNC and NCFL meet annually for several days of planning prior to the national training conference, and representatives of the two organizations conduct all technical assistance visits jointly. To help sites foster better teamwork, PATNC and NCFL also have developed a series of team-building activities that foster dialogue and improve collaboration.

At the site level, programs have realized that parents may need incentives to stay engaged in the program (J. Power, personal communication, July 9, 2009). Some program sites have asked parents to sign contracts that state their commitment to supporting their child's education and their responsibilities as participants in the FACE program. Others offer incentive programs in which parents and children earn points for program attendance that can be used in the FACE store to purchase children's items such as flip flops, crayons, or bubbles; or essential personal care items such as laundry soap, diapers, or shampoo.

Future Directions   The FACE program model is well established and has shown significant results for children and families, but it continues to improve. The early childhood component at two FACE sites are NAEYC accredited, and components at two more sites are working toward accreditation. FACE administrators are providing support and technical assistance to sites that are motivated to achieve accreditation. Technical assistance providers are also examining ways to improve their services. For example, video conferences may make technical assistance more accessible and cheaper for programs. Home visitors may receive feedback on the basis of videotapes of their sessions with families. More frequent regional technical assistance meetings and conference calls will allow program staff to connect with one another and exchange ideas more often.

Conclusion   The FACE program recognizes the primacy of the parent as the child's first teacher and the importance of the home as the child's first school. Parent educators, preschool teachers, and adult educators work together as a team to provide a comprehensive, integrated set of family literacy services that address children's transitions from home to center-based preschool and elementary school. The program also facilitates parental transition to the workplace through GED completion classes and job skills training. FACE strengthens families' ability to support their children's education by connecting parents with one another and with community service providers. Because FACE programs are based in BIE schools, they help parents and children to form connections to the elementary school before the children even enroll in kindergarten. The FACE program also integrates families' native language and culture in home and classroom literacy activities. In total, FACE provides a comprehensive approach to family support that brings bringing the families and the school closer together and lessens the divide that children must navigate when they enter school.

Case Study—Turkey's Mother Child Education Program
Supporting Families During the Transition Years
Alejandra Cortazar

The Mother Child Education Program (MOCEP) is a home-based education program in Turkey that is designed to support mothers and their 5- and 6-year-old children who do not have access to preschool (Mother Child Education Foundation, n.d.). The program builds on families' protective factors, facilitating mothers' social connections and support among groups of their peers. The goal of MOCEP s to increase mothers' knowledge about parenting and child development and train them to promote their children's cognitive, social, and emotional development and competencies.

MOCEP is based on an ecological approach that emphasizes the importance of a child's interactions with the environment. The MOCEP training entails three components: 1) a Mother Support Program, 2) a Reproductive Health and Family Planning Program, and 3) a Cognitive Education Program (Bekman, 1998). During this training, each mother acquires new knowledge, skills, and attitudes that empower her as her child's first educator. This knowledge helps her to feel more confident in both her parental role and her ability to create stimulating environments that foster her child's holistic development (N. Çorapçi, personal communication, June 19, 2009). The group nature of the training creates a social and supportive environment for mothers.

Participants MOCEP engages mothers of 5- and 6-year-old children from economically disadvantaged families in 69 provinces in Turkey. The only eligibility requirement is maternal literacy, and the organization offers literacy training for mothers. Participation is voluntary and mothers do not receive any compensation for their participation (Bekman, 1998). Since the program began, MOCEP has reached over 237,000 mothers and children (N. Çorapçi, personal communication, June 19, 2009).

Origins The program began in 1982 as the home-based intervention in the Turkish Early Enrichment Project, a 4-year-long research project conducted by Drs. Çigdem Kagitçibasi, Sevda Bekman, and Diane Sunar. The research project evaluated the effectiveness of home-based early childhood intervention. The home-based program had a mother-enrichment component and a cognitive education program that was adapted from Home Instruction for Parents of Preschool Youngsters, a program developed by the Research Institute of Innovation in Education at Hebrew University, Jerusalem. After the home-based program was implemented, the study revealed that the program yielded positive benefits for children and families. Children whose mothers trained in this model surpassed children from the control group in all measures of cognitive, social, and emotional development. The most significant difference between mothers trained in this model and mothers in the control group was the quality of mother–child interactions. Mothers who participated in MOCEP were more responsive to their children, had higher expectations for them, and used higher levels of verbalization (Bekman, 1990).

To build on these promising results, the program model underwent some modification and was then expanded into a public program in 1991 called the Mother Child Education Program. The changes to the program included shortening the program from 60 weeks to 25 weeks and shifting the focus from 4- and 5-year-old children to 5- and 6-year-olds. A new cognitive training program was developed to replace the one that had been inspired by Home Instruction for Parents of Preschool Youngsters (Bekman, 1998), and a new component was added to address reproductive health and family planning (N. Çorapçi, personal communication, June 19, 2009).

Between 1991 and 1993, the Finance Foundation funded the program in collaboration with the United Nations Children's Fund and the Ministry of Education. Then, in 1993, the Finance Foundation established the Mother Child Education Foundation (ACEV) to oversee and support MOCEP (N. Çorapçi, personal communication, June 19, 2009). Also in 1993, MOCEP began providing services in adult education centers. A few years later, MOCEP was introduced as a free elective course at several universities throughout Turkey (Bekman, 1998). After being run collaboratively by ACEV and the Ministry of National Education for almost a decade, MOCEP was formally transferred to the Ministry of National Education in 2002 (Mother Child Education Foundation, n.d.). In the last decade, MOCEP has expanded beyond Turkey and has been implemented in Bahrain, Belgium, France, Germany, Holland, Jordan, and Saudi Arabia.

Program Structure   MOCEP is implemented as an education program of the General Directorate of Apprenticeship and Nonformal Education of the Ministry of National Education, with technical support from ACEV. It is an interesting example of collaboration between a nongovernmental organization (ACEV) and the national government of Turkey (Mother Child Education Foundation, n.d.).

The Ministry of Education employs the MOCEP staff of province coordinators and adult educators. Province coordinators supervise the implementation of services at the local level. Adult educators run the group meetings and conduct home visits to ensure that mothers are following the program. Most adult educators are permanent staff of the Public Education Centers where the programs are implemented. ACEV is responsible for training both province coordinators and adult educators. ACEV also provides advising and support during program implementation by holding regular meetings with province coordinators. A few programs are run with the support from the General Directorate of Social Welfare and Child Protection Agency in their community centers. These programs are led by social workers who are trained and supervised by ACEV (N. Çorapçi, personal communication, June 19, 2009).

Implementation   MOCEP brings together groups of 20 to 25 mothers for 3-hour sessions weekly for 25 weeks. Each session covers the three aforementioned components of the program. During the first part of the meeting, which lasts an hour and a half, the group covers a topic from the Mother Support Program. The women discuss the topic, share their experiences, and determine how to implement some of the ideas that they have learned in the session at home. Mothers' experiences putting these ideas into practice at home are reviewed in the next session. Conversations between mothers are intended to encourage the development of self-confidence, competence, and efficacy. The group format also provides mothers with a support group. Some of the topics discussed in the Mother Support Program include parenting roles, health and nutrition, communication, child development, mother–child interactions, and child-rearing practices.

The second part of the session lasts approximately 15 minutes and addresses the Reproductive Health and Family Planning program. This program contains 23 topics related to the female reproductive system, illness prevention, healthy pregnancy and motherhood, and family planning (Mother Child Education Foundation, n.d.).

The last hour of the session is devoted to the Cognitive Education Program. Working in groups of five or six women and using a role-playing strategy, mothers learn how to stimulate their children's cognitive development. Each week, mothers are taught about daily activities that they should do with their children. These activities are designed to take about 15–20 minutes (N. Çorapçi, personal communication, June 19, 2009). Worksheets and books promote the development of children's literacy and numeracy skills. Mothers learn how to provide scaffolding to their children and become their children's teachers, promoting their development throughout the day and facilitating them with a cognitively stimulating environment. Adult educators conduct home visits almost every month to help mothers implement these activities (Bekman, 1998; Mother Child Education Foundation, n.d.).

Highlights and Accomplishments   MOCEP has accomplished a great deal since it was first implemented more than 20 years ago. First, the program has had an impressive reach: It has helped more than 237,000 mothers and children from disadvantaged and low-income backgrounds make the transition from home to school. MOCEP has not only expanded throughout the country but also reached beyond Turkey's borders: Turkish migrant families in various European countries, including Holland, Germany, France, and Belgium, are participants. In addition to being available in Turkish and English, the program has been translated into Dutch and Arabic to be used with migrant families from other origins in Holland, Belgium, Bahrain, Jordan and Saudi Arabia. MOCEP has been an inspiration for other programs that cover literacy training, fathers' training, and education for mothers (such as an educational television show called "Will You Play with Me?") (N. Çorapçi, personal communication, June 19, 2009).

Several studies have assessed the impact of MOCEP. An experimental study found that children from mothers who were trained by MOCEP had significantly better outcomes on tests of preliteracy skills, prenumeracy skills, literacy skills, and numeric skills administered after the first year of school than did their peers, and the children of MOCEP-trained mothers earned higher final grades in first grade. Furthermore, teachers' rating of social and cognitive school readiness skills was also higher for program participants (Bekman, 1998). Children who were part of the program had also better attitudes toward school and remained in school longer than did nonparticipants (N. Çorapçi, personal communication, June 19, 2009).

The same study found that the mothers who participated in the training benefited, too. Compared with mothers who were not trained in the model, mothers who participated in the training sessions used fewer negative discipline methods and more positive behavior management, such as explaining and presenting rules. They also reported higher levels of confidence in their parenting roles and were assessed as having higher self-esteem. Trained mothers also appeared to be more interested in their children's experiences at school and in promoting their academic success. The positive effect of the program was also observable in the home environment. Mothers who had participated in the program provided their children with a more positive study environment at home and also engaged in better communication practices with their children and husbands (Bekman, 1998). Overall, the program has been effective in building on and promoting family protective factors that help program participants to become ready families, able to support their children in their transition to school and successfully negotiate other family transitions.

Challenges   An initial challenge of the program was to motivate parents to participate in the program. ACEV developed several strategies to promote the program, including advertisement through media and inviting mothers to visit the program. As the program expanded and became known and respected in communities, getting enough mothers to enroll ceased to be a concern. An ongoing challenge is high levels of attrition among participants: Some mothers drop out of the program because they lack child care during the training meetings. Finally, cuts in funding have compromised the amount of training and the number of supervision activities that can be offered. As a result, the training of adult educators had to be reduced from 4 to 2 weeks (N. Çorapçi, personal communication, June 19, 2009).

Lessons Learned   One lesson learned by program staff is the importance of targeting both the child and the mother. This approach enables the mothers to continue supporting their children beyond the preschool years (N. Çorapçi, personal communication, June 19, 2009).

The expansion of the program has led ACEV to reflect on the need to preserve quality. Nur Sucuka Çorapçi, program and project manager, states, "Quantity without quality is a waste of resources for the program; this is why solid program design and evaluation are essential" (personal communication, June 19, 2009). To sustain program quality, it is crucial for program administrators to monitor the implementation of the program. They accomplish monitoring by visiting the individual program sites and working with the province coordinators to keep track of the programs and maintain their quality. ACEV also has learned that reliable and valid evaluation tools are needed in order to be able to assess and ensure quality in a large-scale program.

Last, the positive collaboration with the Ministry of National Education has been crucial to the program's success. As a result of the collaboration, MOCEP has been able to capitalize on the government's infrastructure to deliver services to a large population in a cost-effective way (N. Çorapçi, personal communication, June 19, 2009).

Future Directions   MOCEP's future efforts will focus on extending its reach to support a greater number of families with young children. The content of MOCEP will be included in the national Parent Education Program developed by the Ministry of National Education. According to Nur Sucuka Çorapçi, ACEV will work to "come up with ways to include MOCEP (as a program) within this national program" (personal communication, June 19, 2009). ACEV also will continue to try to create awareness at all levels of society about the relevance of early childhood care and education. An example of this commitment is the "7 is Too Late" campaign initiated in 2007. The campaign involves publicity in public places, seminars, and meetings with policy makers. "7 is Too Late" aims to attain fundamental changes in education policies which will ensure that every child benefits from early childhood care and education and is ready to make a successful transition into primary school (N. Çorapçi, personal communication, June 19, 2009).

Conclusion   MOCEP has been effective in supporting children's transition from home to school by giving families and their children the information and support they need in order to enter school successfully. The program appreciates the crucial role that families play in their children's achievement and focuses on reinforcing the protective factors that families already possess to facilitate a smooth transition for their children to primary school.

REFERENCES

Ackerman, D., & Barnett, S.W. (2005). *Prepared for kindergarten: What does "readiness" mean?* New Brunswick, NJ: Rutgers University, National Institute for Early Educational Research.

Annie E. Casey Foundation. (2007a). *Making connections.* Baltimore: Author. Retrieved May 6, 2009, from http://www.aecf.org/MajorInitiatives/MakingConnections.aspx

Annie E. Casey Foundation. (2007b). *Race matters: Unequal opportunities for school readiness.* Baltimore: Author. Retrieved May 6, 2009, from http://www.aecf.org/upload/publicationfiles/fact_sheet2.pdf

Annie E. Casey Foundation. (2007c). *Strengthening families, Strengthening schools toolkit.* Retrieved May 6, 2009, from http://tarc.aecf.org/initiatives/mc/sf/index.htm

Armbruster, B.L. (2002). *Teaching our youngest: A guide for preschool teachers and child care and family providers.* Early Childhood Task Force. Washington, DC: U.S. Department of Education & U.S. Department of Health and Human Services.

Barbarin, O.A. (2002). Culture and ethnicity in social, emotional and academic development. In K.E.E. Exchange (Ed.), *Set for success: Building a strong foundation for school readiness based on the the social-emotional development of young children* (pp. 45–61). Kansas City, MO: Ewing Marion Kauffman Foundation.

Barnett, W.E. (2008). *2008 state preschool yearbook.* Rutgers, NJ: National Institute for Early Education Research.

Bekman, S. (1998). *A fair chance: An evaluation of the mother–child education program.* Istanbul, Turkey: Yapim Matbaasi.

Bekman, S. (1990). Alternative to the available: Home-based vs. center-based programs. *Early Child Development and Care, 58,* 109–119.

Bhattacharya, J., Olson, L., & Scharf, A. (2004). *Ready or not: A California Tomorrow think piece about school readiness and immigrant communities.* Retrieved May 8, 2009, from http://www.californiatomorrow.org/media/readyornot.pdf

Bishaw, A., & Semega, J. (2008). *Income, earnings, and poverty data from the 2007 American Community Survey* (Census Bureau Publication No. ACS-09). Washington, DC: U.S. Government Printing Office.

Boethel, M. (2004). *Readiness: School, family, and community connections. Annual synthesis 2004.* Retrieved May 8, 2009, from http://www.sedl.org/connections/resources/readiness-synthesis.pdf

Boo, K. (2006, February). Swamp nurse. *The New Yorker,* 54–65.

Bruner, C., Tirmizi, S.N., & Wright, M.S. (2007). *Village building and school readiness: Closing opportunity gaps in a diverse society.* Des Moines, IA: Child and Family Policy.

Bureau of Indian Education. (2006). Family and child education (FACE) guidelines, Washington, DC: Author

Center for the Study of Social Policy. (2008). *Strengthening families through early care and education.* Washington, DC: Center for the Study of Social Policy.

Chang, H., & Romero, M. (2008). *Present, engaged, and accounted for: The critical importance of addressing chronic absence in the early grades.* New York: National Center for Children in Poverty.

Children's Defense Fund. (2008). *State of America's children 2008.* Washington, DC: Author.

Committee for Children. (2009). *Second Step overview.* Retrieved May 22, 2009, from http://www.cfchildren.org/programs/ssp/overview/

Corsaro, W., & Molinari, L. (2006). *I compagni: Understanding children's transition from preschool to elementary school.* St. Paul, MN: Redleaf Press.

Cowan, P.A., Powell, D., & Cowan, C.P. (1998). Parenting interventions: A family systems perspective. In I.E. Sigel & K.A. Renninger. (Eds.), *Handbook of child psychology* (pp 3–72). New York: Wiley.

DePanfilis, D., &. Zuravin, S.J. (2002). The effect of services on the recurrence of child maltreatment. *Child Abuse and Neglect, 26,* 187–205.

Downer, J., & Pianta, R. (2006). Academic and cognitive functioning in first grade Associations with earlier home and child care predictors with concurrent home and classroom experiences. *School Psychology Review, 35*(1), 11–30.

Face Resources. (n.d.) Retrieved from http://faceresources.org

Family and child education. (2009). Chief Leschi Schools. Retrieved from http:www.leschischools.org/support/familyed.php.

Fantuzzo, J.M. (2004). Multiple dimensions of family involvement and their relations to behavioral and learning competencies for urban, low income children. *School Psychology Review, 33*(4), 467–480.

Gomby, D.E. (2003). *Building school readiness through home visitation.* Retrieved May 22, 2009, from http://www.ccfc.ca.gov/pdf/help/executivesummaryfinal.pdf

Hart, B., & Risley, T.R. (1995). *Meaningful differences in the everyday experience of young American children.* Baltimore: Paul H. Brookes Publishing Co.

Harvard Family Research Project. (n.d.). *Home visit forum.* Retrieved May 22, 2009, from http://www.hfrp.org/other-research-areas/home-visit-forum

Heaviside, S., & Farris, E. (1993). *Public school kindergarten teachers' views of children's readiness for school.* Washington, DC: Department of Education, National Center on Educational Statistics.

Heckman, J. (2008). *The economic case for investing in disadvantaged young children.* Chicago: University of Chicago Press.

Henderson, A.T., & Mapp, K. (2002). *A new wave of evidence: The impact of school, family, and community connections on student achievement. Annual synthesis 2002.* Austin, TX: Southwest Educational Development Laboratory.

Hepburn, K.S. (2004a). *Building culturally and linguistically competent services to support young children, their families, and school readiness.* Baltimore: Annie E. Casey Foundation.

Hepburn, K.S. (2004b). *Families as primary partners in their child's development and school readiness.* Baltimore: Annie E. Casey Foundation.

Karoly, L.A., Kilbourn, M.R., & Cannon, J.S. (2005). *Early childhood interventions: Proven results, future promise.* Santa Monica, CA: Rand Corporation.

Ladd, G.W., Birch, S.H., & Buhs, E.S. (1999). Children's social and scholastic life in kindergarten: Related spheres of influence? *Child Development, 70*(6), 1373–1400.

Love, J., Kisker, E.E., Ross, C.M., Schochet, P.Z., Brooks-Gunn, J., Paulsell, D., et al. (2002). *Making a difference in the lives of infants and toddlers and their families: The impacts of early Head Start.* Washington, DC: U.S. Department of Health and Human Services, Administration for Children and Families.

Mangione, P., & Speth, T. (1998). The transition to elementary school: A framework for creating early childhood continuity through home, school, and community partnerships. *The Elementary School Journal, 98*(4), 381–397.

Mashburn, A., & Pianta, R. (2006). Social relationships and school readiness. *Early Education & Development, 17*(1), 151–176.

Massachusetts Department of Early Education and Care & Massachusetts Department of Public Health. (2007). *Continuing the journey: A guide for families.* Boston: Massachusetts Department of Early Learning and Care.

McAllister, C., Wilson, P., Green, B., & Baldwin, J. (2005). "Come and take a walk": Listening to Early Head Start parents on school readiness as a matter of child, family, and community health. *American Journal of Public Health, 95*(4), 617–625.

Mother Child Education Foundation. (n.d.). Retrieved April 12, 2009, from http://www.acev.org/index.php?lang=en

National Center for Children in Poverty. (2007). *Promoting effective early learning: What every policymaker and educator should know.* New York: National Center for Children in Poverty.

National Educational Goals Panel. (1997). *Special early childhood report.* Washington, DC: Government Printing Office.

National Governors Association. (2005). *Building the foundation for bright futures: A governor's guide to school readiness.* Washington, DC: National Governors Association, Center for Best Practices.

Orfield, G., Losen, D., Wald, J., & Swanson, C. (2004). *Losing our future: How minority youth are being left behind by the graduation rate crisis.* Cambridge, MA: Harvard University, The Civil Rights Project.

Ounce of Prevention Fund. (2005). *The first days of life: Adding doulas to early childhood programs.* Chicago: Author.

Ounce of Prevention Fund. (2009). *It's possible: Closing the achievement gap in academic performance.* Chicago: Ounce of Prevention Fund.

Pawl, J.H, Ahern, C., Grandison, C., Johnston, K., St. John, M., & Waldstein, A. (2000). *Responding to infants and parents: Inclusive interaction in assessment, consultation and treatment in infant/family practice.* Washington, DC: Zero to Three.

Pianta, R.C., &.Kraft-Sayre, M. (2003). *Successful kindergarten transition: Your guide to connecting children, families, & schools.* Baltimore: Paul H. Brookes Publishing Co.

Raising a Reader. (n.d.). Raising a reader. Retrieved April 12, 2009, from http://www.raisingareader.org

Ramey, C., & Ramey, S.L. (2004). Early learning and school readiness: Can early intervention make a difference? *Merrill–Palmer Quarterly, 50*(4), 471–491.

Reading Is Fundamental. (n.d.). Reading is fundamental. Retrieved April 12, 2009, from http://www.rif.org

Research & Training Associates, Inc. (2006). *Family and Child Education (FACE) program: Impact study report.* Unpublished evaluation report.

Reynolds, A.J., Magnuson, K., & Ou, S. (2006). *PK–3 education: Programs and practices that work in children's first decade.* New York: Foundation for Child Development.

Reynolds, A.J., Temple, J.A., Ou, S., Robertson, D.L., Mersky, J.P., Topitzes, J.W., et al. (2007). Effects of a school-based, early childhood intervention on adult health and well-being: A 19-year follow-up of low-income families. *Archives of Pediatric and Adolescent Medicine, 161*(8), 730–739.

Rhode Island Kids Count. (2005, February). *Getting ready: Findings from the National School Readiness Indicators initiative.* Providence, RI: Author.

Rimm-Kaufman, S., Pianta, R., & Cox, M. (2000). Teachers' judgements of problems in the transition to kindergarten. *Early Childhood Research Quarterly, 15,* 147–166.

Rouse, C., Brooks-Gunn, J., & McLanahan, S. (2005). Introducing the issue: Closing racial and ethnic gaps in school readiness. *Future of Children, 15*(1), 5–14.

Schorr, L. (2004). *Pathways mapping initiative: School readiness pathway.* Washington, DC: Project on Effective Interventions at Harvard University.

Shonkoff, J., & Phillips, D. (2002). *From neurons to neighborhoods: The science of early childhood development.* Washington, DC: National Academies Press.

Shore, R. (1998). *Ready schools.* Washington, DC: The National Education Goals Panel.

Shulting, A. (2009). Promoting parent–school relationships during the transition to kindergarten. *Evaluation Exchange, 14*(1, 2).

Simpson, C., & Kessler, R. (2007). *First steps into elementary school.* Boulder, CO: PassageWorks Institute.

United Way. (2009). *211.* Retrieved from http://www.liveunited.org/211/

United Way, United Way Success by 6, & Civitas. (2005). *Born Learning Tools.* Retrieved May 6, 2009, from http://www.bornlearning.org/files/bornlearningtools.pdf

Weiss, H., Caspe, M., & Lopez, M.E. (2006, Spring). *Family involvement makes a difference: Evidence that family involvement promotes school success for every child of every age.* Boston: Harvard Family Research Project.

West, J., Geronimo-Hausken, E., & Collins, M. (1995). *Readiness for kindergarten: Parent and teacher beliefs* (Statistics in Brief). Washington, DC: National Center for Education Statistics.

11

The Neighborhoods Where Young Children Grow Up

Jeanne Brooks-Gunn

How is physical residence associated with young children's well-being? Does the location of children's homes influence the ways in which they experience life transitions such as their entry into preschool or kindergarten? Do some neighborhoods offer more of the basic services that support children's multiple transitions? To what extent do residential changes, which are more frequent in low-income neighborhoods, affect children generally and influence their ability to deal with other types of transitions? What is the intersection between neighborhood and family characteristics, vis-à-vis their contribution to child development and children's ability to navigate the many transitions that they encounter in their early years? These are some of the questions that are asked by those who study neighborhoods—scholars in the fields of economics, sociology, demography, psychology, and political science, as well as those in the applied fields of education, social work, and public health.

This chapter is divided into several sections. First, we outline the theoretical perspectives that have influenced neighborhood research. Second, we discuss the ways in which neighborhood characteristics have been measured and the research designs that have been used to disentangle the effects of the neighborhood from those of the family. Third, we document links between neighborhood characteristics and young children's well-being in terms of physical health, emotional health, and linguistic and cognitive outcomes. Fourth, we discuss the primary mechanisms through which neighborhoods might influence children's development, with a focus on the pathways that are most relevant to young children: environmental toxins, physical resources, institutions (availability of health care, child care, and preschool), and social and psychological neighborhood features. The final section of the chapter highlights efforts to track young children's development at a neighborhood level in order to determine what resources are needed in a particular community. Such efforts may target preschools and kindergartens as well

The research reported in this chapter was supported by the federal government (the National Institute of Child Health and Human Development, the National Science Foundation, the National Institute of Mental Health, the National Institute of Justice, and the U.S. Department of Housing and Urban Development) and by foundations (Spencer, Russell Sage, March of Dimes, MacArthur).

I wish to thank Rachel McKinnon and Erin Bumgarner for their invaluable assistance with the preparation of the manuscript for this chapter.

as neighborhoods, since educational institutions must be ready for the children in their community. In other words, if a neighborhood's children, on average, have difficulties with health, emotional regulation, or language, the local school ought to be prepared to respond to these needs. The final section of the chapter also considers the ways in which the neighborhood where children live might affect their responses to two common transitions: a family move and entry into preschool.

THEORETICAL PERSPECTIVES

The premise that neighborhoods influence child development has a long history. Neighborhood research has, in large part, been predicated on three lines of inquiry. First, an interest in the influence of spatial context and social mechanisms on behavior, particularly adolescent behavior, emerged at the beginning of the 1900s, a time when urban populations were increasing due to immigration, urbanization, and industrialization. Social workers focused on what seemed to be increases in juvenile delinquency in urban neighborhoods and largely ignored young children's transitions (although indirectly, they focused on the transition to parenting, which is compromised if youth are engaging in crime). Sociologists examined crime, delinquency, and disorder and found that they were more prevalent in certain neighborhoods. The University of Chicago's School of Sociology was responsible for much of this early work (Park, 1916; Shaw & McKay, 1942). Modern-day theories put forth by sociologist Robert Sampson and child psychiatrist Felton Earls are reminiscent of the Chicago School in that they focus on mechanisms underlying neighborhood-linked crime and delinquency like social cohesion, control, and networks. Recent research has applied notions of the social organization of neighborhoods to children, including preschoolers.

Just as this first tradition of neighborhood research explored demographic circumstances (e.g., unemployment, middle-class flight, segregation, job loss), a second line of inquiry explored the rapid rise in concentrated poverty in urban neighborhoods during the 1970s and 1980s. Sociologist William Julius Wilson (1987) outlined the reasons for the changes in economic status and their implications for families (e.g., lack of family routines, few opportunities for play, increased concerns about safety—all of which are relevant to young children). In highly concentrated urban poor neighborhoods, 30% or more of the residents are poor, and there are high rates of single parenthood as well as high numbers of unemployed and poorly educated adults. Poor African American and Hispanic American families are likely to reside in highly concentrated poor neighborhoods, often due to patterns of segregated housing, employment, and schools (Massey, 1990; Sampson & Morenoff, 1997). Poor white families are less likely to live in such neighborhoods; they tend to live in rural areas or in nonminority urban neighborhoods. Although the growth of these neighborhoods tapered off in the 2000s (O'Hare & Mather, 2003), about 15 million Americans still live in such circumstances.

The third tradition in research on neighborhoods came out of developmental psychology. Urie Bronfenbrenner (1979) championed the notion that children are embedded in a series of different contexts or ecologies, one of which is their neighborhood. He argued that although their families are important to children, so are schools, child care centers, parks, peer networks, parents' friendship networks, churches, and community organizations. He spurred many psychologists to consider neighborhoods a venue for development (Aber, Gephart, Brooks-Gunn, & Connell, 1997; Brooks-Gunn, Duncan, & Aber, 1997) and to examine the intersection between family and neighborhood influences on children (Brooks-Gunn, 1996). Of particular importance is Bronfenbrenner's insistence that contexts are nested—for example, that children are reared in families that are embedded in neighborhoods and that interactions occur among different cohorts (Leventhal & Brooks-Gunn, 2000).

MEASURING NEIGHBORHOOD EFFECTS

Whether any study of neighborhoods is successful (in terms of the ability to infer causality between neighborhood residence and outcome) depends on the adequacy of the design, the measures that are used, and the definition of *neighborhood* that is used. Almost 2 decades ago, social scientists began testing the premises underlying the Wilson and Bronfenbrenner perspectives. They started by appending U.S. census tract information to existing samples of children and families in order to estimate neighborhood effects that were occurring over and above family effects (Brooks-Gunn, Duncan, Klebanov, & Sealand, 1993; Brooks-Gunn et al., 1997). Often, scientists examined links between residence and outcomes in several data sets simultaneously to see whether trends were replicated. This work served the field well, although today these designs have been surpassed by methodologies that allow for better delineation between neighborhood and family influences.

Research Designs

It is very difficult to separate neighborhood from family influences. Families do have some choice about where they live (Tienda, 1991); therefore, part of the influence of neighborhood characteristics on children is likely due to the characteristics of the children's families. For example, one family might value education highly and thus decide to live in a smaller, cheaper apartment or house in a neighborhood with better schools, while another family with an equal income might choose a larger or more elegant residence in a neighborhood where the schools are not as good. Analyses of neighborhoods try to control as many family-level characteristics as possible in order to minimize the problem of selection bias (in this case, selection of families into particular neighborhoods). Scholars control for variables such as parental education, parental employment, parental age, family structure, number of persons in the household, and ethnicity. Even so, the study may not control for some characteristics that might be important—like the family's attitude toward education. Scholars have conducted analyses that take more psychological characteristics (e.g., parental mental health, parenting behavior, parenting knowledge) into consideration to reduce selection bias (Duncan, Connell, & Klebanov, 1997). In general, though, any analysis of neighborhood–child influences is subject to the criticism that some unmeasured characteristics of the family are responsible for these links.

Several techniques have been used to determine whether links are really causal. One method is to compare siblings who may live in different neighborhoods (Aaronson, 1997) or relocate at different ages (Duncan, Yeung, Brooks-Gunn, & Smith, 1998). For example, a family may move when one child is age 3 and another is age 8; the siblings' outcomes may then be compared, typically when the children are older so that outcomes such as high school completion, teenage parenthood, and criminal behavior can be measured (Duncan et al., 1998). Another within-family design used twins to study the effect of neighborhood on child outcomes (Caspi, Taylor, Moffitt, & Plomin, 2000).

Some studies have been designed to sample families within neighborhoods, using hierarchical linear modeling to separate out the effects on clusters of families living within the same or different neighborhoods (Sampson, 1997; Sampson, Raudenbush, & Earls, 1997; Sastry and Pebley, 2003). Two such studies have been conducted in the United States: the Project on Human Development in Chicago Neighborhoods and the Los Angeles Families and Neighborhood Study. (See Fauth & Brooks-Gunn, 2008, for a discussion of these designs.)

The most rigorous design is experimental. Natural experiments have been conducted on the basis of changes that occur in some, but not other, neighborhoods—changes that presumably do not influence where families reside. For example, one study examined child health before and after the Clean Air Act was passed (Currie & Neidell, 2005). Another interesting design compares young children's respiratory illnesses as a function of neighborhood residence in military families, which move regularly and do not have a choice about where they move (Lleras-Muney, in press).

Another type of study is a relocation experiment. In this design, families that are currently living in public housing are chosen by random selection to receive a voucher to move into private subsidized housing or into scattered-site public housing. The best known of these studies is Moving to Opportunity (MTO), which was conducted in five cities (Goering & Feins, 2003). Families that were living in public housing were assigned to three different conditions: stay in public housing, receive a Section 8 voucher (for use in private housing via a subsidy), or receive an MTO voucher (for use in private housing with the condition that the family had to move to a neighborhood where less than 10% of the residents were poor). Another design involved random assignment to stay in high-rise public housing in poor neighborhoods in Yonkers, New York, or to move into scattered-site public housing in middle-class neighborhoods in Yonkers (Briggs, Darden, & Aidala, 1999). Families with children and adolescents were followed in both studies. There were so few children ages 3 and 4 among the families that the impact of these moves on preschool transitions could not be studied. Instead, the study focused on how school-age children and youth were faring in their new schools.

Definitions of Neighborhood

The term *neighborhood* is being used to define a geographic entity. But neighborhoods are not always clearly demarcated. What is the size of a neighborhood? Is it an ecological area, defined generally by how individuals understand a place? In cities, neighborhoods are often defined by physical boundaries, both natural ones and those made by humans (rivers, parks, railroad tracks, highways), and by patterns of use (residential, mixed use, industrial, business). In most cities, these areas have been named (e.g., Manhattan's Harlem, Morningside Heights, Greenwich Village). But for studies of children, such areas are often too large to be meaningful units, considering that young children usually traverse a much smaller area and neighborhood schools serve more circumscribed populations. Often, research studies have used U.S. census tracts as a unit of analysis or have combined several census tracts on the basis of natural boundaries (e.g., the Project on Human Development in Chicago Neighborhoods). A census tract consists of 3,000 to 8,000 people; tracts have been formed with the use of local knowledge of boundaries and use patterns. Tract groups consist of two to three census tracts that are contiguous and similar in demographic characteristics (Sampson & Morenoff, 1997). Sometimes, smaller units such as block groups are used. Most census tracts contain about one to four block groups, each of which has between 600 and 3,000 residents.

Some scholars have asked residents to define their neighborhood themselves and have even had them draw maps. These psychological neighborhoods vary by the individual creator as well as by function. On the one hand, such variability within and across individuals makes it difficult to use the individual map-drawing procedure in large-scale studies. These findings illustrate how difficult it is to pinpoint exactly how individuals perceive their neighborhoods. On the other hand, in general, individuals' maps of physical neighborhoods resemble census tracts or tract groups (Coulton, Korbin, Chan, & Su, 2001; Sampson, 1997).

Neighborhood Characteristics

Characteristics of neighborhoods are often divided into two categories: structure and process. *Neighborhood structure* involves the sociodemographic characteristics of the neighborhood, whereas *neighborhood process* involves the resources, organization, and psychological features.

The census is used to portray a variety of neighborhood characteristics: median income, employment rate, educational level of adults, rate of single parenthood, stability of residences (length of time that a particular residence has had the same occupants), ethnicity, and immigrant status. All of these characteristics have been used in various studies (Jencks & Mayer, 1990; Leventhal & Brooks-Gunn, 2000). The most frequently used information is the socioeconomic status (SES) of a neighborhood. Other times, researchers use a composite measure termed *concentrated disadvantage* or *poverty*, which takes into account the percentage of poor residents, single-parent households, adults with less than a high school education, and adults who are unemployed (Aber et al., 1997). Sometimes, neighborhoods are classified in terms of both disadvantage and *affluence*, a measure that reflects the percentage of middle-income households, two-parent households, college-educated residents, and professional residents. Typically, these measures define three types of neighborhoods: low income, middle income, and high income. Along with other scholars, we have found that certain child outcomes are associated with residence in a disadvantaged neighborhood and others with residence in an advantaged neighborhood (Brooks-Gunn et al., 1993; Fauth, Leventhal, & Brooks-Gunn, 2007; Jencks & Mayer, 1990; Kohen, Brooks-Gunn, Leventhal, & Hertzman, 2002).

It is difficult, if not impossible, to disentangle these clusters of neighborhood characteristics (rates of poor residents, single-parent households, adults with low education, and adults who are unemployed within neighborhoods) because they are all highly correlated. Factor analyses—whether they are at the national, regional, or city level—find that these characteristics bundle together and cannot be examined separately. All analyses using neighborhood SES have to control for the same family-level characteristics (income, family structure, education, and employment) in order to account, in part, for the correlation between neighborhood and family conditions. For example, families in low-income neighborhoods are, by definition, more likely to be poor than those in middle-income neighborhoods; however, if a low-income neighborhood is defined as a neighborhood in which 30% or more of the adults are poor, that means that up to 70% of them are not poor.

Another dimension of neighborhoods that many studies examine and that is identified in factor analyses of census tract data citywide or nationwide is *residential instability* (the percentage of homeowners, residents who have moved in the past 5 years, and households that have lived in their current home for less than 10 years). Many analysts examine instability, SES disadvantage, and SES affluence in the same models to determine which dimensions of neighborhoods best predict certain outcomes (Brooks-Gunn et al., 1997; Leventhal & Brooks-Gunn, 2000; Leventhal, Dupéré, & Brooks-Gunn, in press; Sampson & Morenoff, 1997). Most analyses do not control for the moves that a particular family has made, even though they do control for SES characteristics at the family level (Brooks-Gunn, Johnson, & Leventhal, 2009).

Another dimension, or set of dimensions, involves the *racial integration* (the percentage of African Americans, Hispanic Americans, and whites) or *immigrant status* (the percentage of foreign-born individuals) of a neighborhood. The latter has become more important as a result of recent waves of immigration, particularly an influx of Hispanic Americans into large cities. Similar sociodemographic characteristics are used to describe families, and many studies include the racial/ethnic and immigration background at the family level in analyses of neighborhood influences.

Like family processes, neighborhood processes are more difficult to measure than are factors related to structure. Often, processes are divided into three groups: institutional resources, social organization, and psychological characteristics (although the last two categories overlap somewhat, depending on the theoretical perspective that the researchers take). Institutional resources include the presence and accessibility of services such as parks, grocery stores, health clinics, mental health service providers, schools, child care providers, recreational programs, and churches. Surprisingly few studies include such resources in their models; exceptions are the Project on Human Development in Chicago Neighborhoods and the Los Angeles Family and

Neighborhood Survey (Sampson, Morenoff, & Gannon-Rowley, 2002; Sampson & Raudenbush, 2004; Xue, Leventhal, Brooks-Gunn, & Earls, 2005). Such data are collected either from community surveys (which ideally are separate from the study of children in families), geocoded maps of the location of resources, scans of directories of services, or administrative records (Coulton & Korbin, 2007).

Measuring social organization processes has a long history. Measures include indicators of disorganization such as *physical disorder* (e.g., abandoned buildings, trash, graffiti) and *social disorder* (e.g., public drinking, fighting, drug use) (Ross & Jang, 2000; Sampson & Raudenbush, 1999). These types of disorder sometimes are measured by a community scan, performed by an observer who rates each block for the presence or absence of such conditions. For example, in the Project on Human Development in Chicago Neighborhoods, researchers videotaped thousands of city blocks from a van and then coded their levels of disorder (Sampson & Raudenbush); see also Burton, Price-Spratlen, & Spencer, 1997.

Social disorganization also includes more psychologically oriented dimensions, the most common being *social control* and *social cohesion*. Social control involves the monitoring of individuals' behavior within a neighborhood on the basis of societal norms. To measure it, members of a neighborhood are asked how likely neighbors would be to speak to a person (often a youth) who is fighting, being noisy, or defacing a building. Social cohesion is measured as connections and relationships within a neighborhood. Together, cohesion and control have been referred to as *collective efficacy* (Bandura, 1977; Elliot et al., 1996; Sampson et al., 2002).

NEIGHBORHOOD RESIDENCE AND CHILD WELL-BEING

What do we know about neighborhood residence and child well-being? Research has examined several aspects of young children's well-being. The best documented aspects are respiratory problems, lead poisoning, obesity, emotional regulation, and language or cognition. In older children and youth, researchers have measured levels of delinquency, crime, school achievement, and sexual behavior.

Respiratory Illnesses

It is believed that respiratory problems, including asthma, are linked to neighborhood residence, primarily due to variation in air quality and conditions within the home. Asthma affects 11%–12% of all children and is more prevalent among low-income children (Currie & Neidell, 2005). Its causes are believed to include secondhand smoke, household allergens (e.g., cockroaches, dust mites, cats), mold and mildew, and air pollution (Bukowski, Lewis, Gamble, Wojcik, & Laumbach, 2002; Currie & Neidell, 2005). Smoke, allergens, mold, and mildew are under the control of individual families (although it may be difficult to remove some allergens from the home in a building that is not properly maintained by the landlord). The last factor, air pollution, is related to geographic location.

Convincing links between neighborhood residence and respiratory illnesses have been revealed with the aid of natural experiments and by examining rates of infant mortality, early asthma, and preschooler hospitalizations (Chay & Greenstone, 2003). One study used the fact of repeated moves by military families, which are not under the control of the families themselves. The researchers reported an association between air pollution (especially ozone) and preschool children's hospitalizations (Lleras-Muney, in press). Another study examined levels of air pollution and infant mortality before and after the 1990 Clean Air Act Amendments, which significantly reduced air pollution. The analysis of pollution levels taken weekly by zip code found that a 1.1-unit decline in carbon monoxide over a decade saved 991 infants' lives (Currie & Neidell, 2005).

Somewhat surprisingly, relocation experiments generally have not reported a decrease in asthma when families move to less poor neighborhoods (see Fauth & Brooks-Gunn, 2008). It may be that air pollution levels experienced by families that relocated and by those that did not were not significantly different, since most of the families relocated to homes within 10 to 20 miles of the initial housing projects. In addition, household-based causes of asthma (e.g., second-hand smoke, pets, dust mites) probably moved with the families.

Obesity

Obesity is another health condition that is believed to be influenced by one's residence. With one third of children and two thirds of adults in the United States overweight or obese, the problem has rightly been called an epidemic (Anderson & Butcher, 2006; Sallis & Glanz, 2006). These trends are seen as early as age 3 (Kimbro, Brooks-Gunn, & McLanahan, 2007). Poor and minority children are more likely to be overweight (defined as being above the 85th percentile in weight for a certain height) or obese (being above the 95th percentile).

A recent analysis suggests that a child's status as overweight or obese is linked to maternal perceptions that the neighborhood is unsafe; due to the selection issue, a large number of family-level variables were controlled, including mothers' own weight (Kimbro, Brooks-Gunn, & McLanahan, 2009). To look at possible mediators of this link, Kimbro and colleagues examined the number of days that children played outside and the number of hours that they watched TV daily. Perceptions that the neighborhood was unsafe were associated with more TV time but not with reduced days of outside playtime. In fact, low-income 5-year-olds living in public housing played outside more days than did low-income children who were not living in public housing. We suspect that mothers in public housing have access to parks within their complexes, which makes it easier for them to take children outside.

Innovative work is being done on the influence of supermarkets, fast-food restaurants, and parks in neighborhoods, and some studies are beginning to link these aspects of the built environment to obesity in adults (Block, Scribner, & DeSalvo, 2004). More research is needed on the relationship between the built environment and young children's weight (Austin et al., 2005).

Lead Exposure

Lead exposure, even at what was once considered low levels, has negative effects on the well-being of children (Needleman, 1979, 1990; Needleman, Riess, Tobin, Biesecker, & Greenhouse, 1996). It is linked to deficits in attention, executive control, and other aspects of cognition (Bellinger, 2004). Young children seem to be at special risk because they absorb lead at higher rates (Bornschein et al., 1985). Gasoline emissions and house paint are the most frequent sources of lead, both of which are more common in urban neighborhoods, the first because of traffic and the second because of old housing.

The Clean Air Act mandated a reduction in gasoline lead levels that led to a 99% decrease of lead in gasoline over a 17-year period (U.S. Environmental Protection Agency, 2000). Lead levels in children have declined as well, as would be expected (Pirkle et al., 1994). Because no time-series data on young children's behavior problems, inattention, or low intelligence are available, it is not possible to determine whether behavioral changes occurred in tandem with the lead reductions. However, one interesting analysis examined changes in crime rates; childhood problems that are associated with high lead levels also are associated with adolescent delinquency and adult crime. When different birth cohorts were compared for crime rates and for lead exposure by year and by state, the two trends were found to have followed each other closely (Reyes, 2007).

Language and Cognition

Young children's language competence has been linked to neighborhood context. In general, residing in an affluent neighborhood (as opposed to a middle-income or low-income neighborhood) is associated with higher intelligence and vocabulary test scores. These links first appear at age 3 and continue through the preschool and kindergarten years. Indeed, the one study that assessed older children found that residence in affluent neighborhoods was still associated with better language skills.

Several hypotheses have been put forward to explain these links. One hypothesis relates to the quality of the home, another to the presence of neighborhood resources, and a third to the presence and quality of preschools (given that young children's educational experiences are nested within neighborhoods). The first two pathways have been studied: Cross-sectional work suggests that these links are mediated by the provision of linguistically and cognitively stimulating activities and materials by the mother in the home. Such activities are more likely to be presented when mothers reside in affluent neighborhoods, even controlling for family demographics and maternal linguistic ability (Chase-Lansdale, Gordon, Brooks-Gunn, & Klebanov, 1997; Klebanov, Brooks-Gunn, & Duncan, 1994; Klebanov, Brooks-Gunn, McCarton, & McCormick, 1998; Leventhal, Xue, & Brooks-Gunn, 2006). In addition, mothers in more affluent neighborhoods report taking their children out more frequently for educationally stimulating experiences (museums, libraries, and zoos).

These findings contrast with those from the relocation experiments, which focus on school-age children and adolescents and suggest that moving to less poor neighborhoods is not related to higher language or achievement test scores (Fauth, Leventhal, & Brooks-Gunn, 2008; Sanbonmatsu, Kling, Duncan, & Brooks-Gunn, 2006). The MTO analyses provide a partial answer to the disparate findings. The neighborhoods to which the relocated families moved were less poor than their original neighborhoods, but they were, in the vast majority of cases, not affluent. In the earlier studies, high test scores were related to residence in affluent neighborhoods, not middle-income or low-income neighborhoods. The relocation experiments typically have not moved families to such neighborhoods.

Emotional Distress and Regulation

In neighborhood research, traditional measures of mental health are used as indicators of emotional distress and regulation. These measures include depression and anxiety, aggression, and, to a lesser extent, impulse control (Fauth & Brooks-Gunn, 2008; Leventhal & Brooks-Gunn, 2000). Several studies have reported links between residence in certain types of neighborhoods and symptoms of depression and anxiety. In the MTO relocation experiment, elementary and high school girls who relocated to low-poverty areas had lower emotional distress scores than those who stayed in high-poverty areas in public housing (Orr et al., 2003). Mothers also showed less emotional stress after they moved. Interestingly, such effects were not seen among boys. It is hypothesized that these results are due to improved neighborhood safety.

In the Project on Human Development in Chicago Neighborhoods, Xue and colleagues (2005) examined similar symptoms in children ages 5 to 11. Children in poor neighborhoods were much more likely to be anxious and depressed (in terms of symptom ratings and severity ratings). These findings are particularly convincing because maternal depression and children's initial emotional distress scores were controlled. The same links were seen with the younger and the older children. Two cross-sectional studies of children ages 3–6 have also reported such links (Klebanov, Brooks-Gunn, Chase-Lansdale, & Gordon, 1997).

Two mediators seemed to be important in the most recent analysis. Residence in poor neighborhoods in large part was related to emotional distress because in these neighborhoods there were lower levels of collective efficacy, and collective efficacy is associated with reduced emotional distress. The existence of mental health services in the neighborhoods was also a mediator (Xue et al., 2005). These findings are especially convincing because the two mediated measures were based on a community survey, not on maternal report.

Similar findings have been reported for children's aggression, with collective efficacy mediating the effect of poor neighborhoods on children's aggression (Xue, Leventhal, Brooks-Gunn, & Earls, 2009). The links between both anxious/depressive and aggressive behaviors and neighborhood residence seem to appear in comparisons of low-income with middle-income and high-income neighborhoods, a somewhat different finding than what has been found for language and cognition.

MECHANISMS UNDERLYING LINKS BETWEEN NEIGHBORHOODS AND CHILDREN

The pathways through which neighborhood residence is linked to young children's outcomes include environmental toxins, the built environment, institutional resources, and social organization. Different mediators are thought to affect different outcomes. For example, environmental toxins are important to children's physical health (e.g., asthma) and possibly children's emotional health (e.g., aggression). Links with cognition and attention are also possible, but they have not been examined. (The new National Children's Study will allow for such analyses.) Aspects of the built environment are probably critical for obesity and its precursors: low levels of physical activity, high food intake, and sedentary pursuits. Institutional resources are likely to influence physical health (availability of health clinics; Brooks-Gunn, McCormick, Klebanov, & McCarton, 1998), emotional health (availability of mental health services; Xue et al., 2005), and cognition (e.g., availability of libraries, museums, and quality child care programs for preschoolers). Social organization might influence all aspects of children's well-being because concerns about safety might make mothers less likely to use parks, libraries, child care, preschools, and other neighborhood-based resources. Collective efficacy, which captures social control and cohesion of neighborhoods, is linked to emotional health measures. Furthermore, collective efficacy might influence how mothers interact with their children, although this effect has not been examined in studies of young children (see Browning, Burrington, Leventhal, & Brooks-Gunn, 2008, for an example of a study with adolescents).

The one mechanism that has not been tested in neighborhood studies of young children is child care and education. This is surprising because several strands of research have confirmed that preschool education is linked to school readiness. The first line of inquiry has shown that participation in preschool in the year preceding kindergarten is associated with better school achievement test scores, regardless of the preschool's quality (Magnuson, Ruhm, & Waldfogel, 2007a, 2007b; Magnuson & Waldfogel, 2005). The second line of inquiry uses randomized trials to demonstrate the efficacy of high-quality preschool at ages 2, 3, or 4, depending on the program (Barnett, 1995; Brooks-Gunn, 2004; Currie, 2006). The third type of research examines links between preschool quality and outcome in longitudinal, nonexperimental studies (National Institute of Child Health and Human Development Early Child Care Research

Network, 2000; Votruba-Druzl, Coley, & Chase-Lansdale, 2004). With regard to neighborhoods, then, the questions are whether children in certain neighborhoods (especially poor ones)
are less likely to receive preschool education at age 4 and whether the quality of preschools differs
by neighborhood.

Two lines of work address the issue of neighborhoods and the type of child care used. The
first type of research concerns the number of centers in various neighborhoods. In a California
study, about 3 times as many young children had access to preschool in affluent communities (defined by zip code, not census tract) than did children in poorer communities (Fuller, Coonerty,
Kipnis, & Choong, 1997). Another study found that both affluent and low-income communities
had more child care centers per capita than did middle-income communities (Loeb, Fuller, Kagan,
& Carrol, 2004). It is likely that the presence of Head Start and prekindergarten (pre-K) programs
accounts for the higher number of centers in poor neighborhoods than in middle-income ones.

The second line of research addresses the types of care that families use in different neighborhoods. Although differences in family characteristics as a function of enrollment in preschool
have been examined (Vandell, 2004), few studies have focused on neighborhoods. One study uses
data for the Project on Human Development in Chicago Neighborhoods (Burchinal, Nelson,
Carlson, & Brooks-Gunn, 2008) to examine the types of child care used by about 1,000 families
that were representative of preschool-age children in Chicago at the time. Four types of care were
identified: exclusive parental care, center care, care by nonrelatives, and care by relatives. When
family-level variables were controlled, neighborhood poverty was not seen to be related to the
type of care that families used. Even though neighborhood structure did not influence the type
of care used, neighborhood processes did affect the choice. In neighborhoods with high collective efficacy (controlling for neighborhood poverty), parents were more likely to use nonrelative
care (compared with parent or center care). It is likely that in neighborhoods with high social
cohesion and control, mothers feel more comfortable having their children cared for in other
families' homes. In neighborhoods with larger social networks, parents were more likely to have
their children cared for by relatives or by centers, perhaps because in the former case mothers had
relatives in the neighborhood and in the latter case mothers learned about child care centers via
social networks.

Research has also looked at the quality of care by neighborhood. In the Chicago study that
was just described, the quality of the child care centers was assessed with the Early Childhood
Environment Rating Scale, Revised Edition (ECERS-R). Public programs such as Head Start
were of higher quality than were community center programs by a large margin—about 1 point
on the ECERS-R. Neighborhood disadvantage was inversely related to quality of care for the
community programs. Interactions suggested that neighborhood poverty was associated with
low center quality for mothers with little education and little income (Burchinal et al., 2008).
These findings raise concerns about children in community preschool educational programs,
especially children who live in poor neighborhoods and whose families are poor. The findings
also underscore the importance of programs such as Head Start in poor communities: Without
such high-quality programs, even more children in poor neighborhoods would presumably be in
low-quality preschools.

NEIGHBORHOODS AND SCHOOL READINESS

The research we have reviewed has implications for school readiness. Indeed, all of the child
outcomes discussed in this chapter are indicators of school readiness. School readiness consists
not only of competence in academic skills such as language, reading, and math, but also is measured by physical health, emotional regulation, and relationships (Scott-Little, Kagan, & Frelow,

2006). Children's ability to learn is hampered by poor health and emotion regulation as well as linguistic and cognitive difficulties.

Neighborhoods are important if they influence the capabilities of the children who enter any given school. Not only do children need to be ready for school but also the schools need to be ready for the children who are entering them. How can schools and communities increase their readiness for young children entering school (with the emphasis on preschool and kindergarten, the two educational settings that are the first schooling experiences for the majority of children today)? Neighborhood-level analyses can provide some answers to this question. A notable example of such an analysis tracked early child development at the neighborhood level in British Columbia, Ontario, (Janus & Offord, 2007; Kershaw, Forer, Irwin, Hertzman, & Lapointe, 2007; Lloyd & Hertzman, 2009). The study is described in detail next because it is relevant to schooling transitions.

The Early Development Instrument (EDI) was developed in order to assess the skills and capabilities of young children who are entering school. The authors of this tool (Janus & Offord, 2007) take a comprehensive approach to school readiness; therefore, it includes physical, social, emotional, cognitive, and linguistic indicators of well-being. The focus is on the readiness of children within communities, not on the readiness of schools or teachers (although the EDI could be used as a planning tool by schools or other community institutions). Kindergarten teachers rate each child's readiness for school on five scales: physical health and well-being, social knowledge and competence, emotional health and maturity, language and cognitive development, and communication skills and knowledge. There are 104 questions that take a child about 20 minutes to complete. In several communities, every kindergarten teacher in both private and public schools has used the EDI, which generates a population-based portrait of kindergarten children in any given year.

The EDI was developed to 1) describe populations of young children within communities, 2) track changes in communities over time, and 3) provide a baseline from which to predict future school achievement within communities (Lloyd & Hertzman, 2009). It can be used to map children's well-being in aggregate—at the level of the neighborhood, individual school, school district, city, county, or province or state. The procedure is relatively simple to implement, and it provides information that can be used by local, state, or federal policy makers.

The work done in British Columbia highlights the usefulness of the EDI. The instrument was used to assess all of the kindergarten children in 93 school districts. Reports from the first four districts (almost 8,000 children in total) are available (Kershaw et al., 2007; Lloyd & Hertzman, 2009). The families of these children vary by ethnicity, family income, and parental education, and EDI scores vary by school district.

Children's EDI scores have been aggregated by neighborhood. The study includes 63 neighborhoods, each containing between 44 and 472 children; neighborhoods in the Vancouver school district have the most kindergarten children per neighborhood, while the other three school districts are bedroom suburban communities or semirural communities).

A figure from Lloyd and Hertzman (2009), reprinted here as Figure 11.1, illustrates EDI scores in the Vancouver School District. The background of each neighborhood is colored light gray to dark gray, according to the proportion of kindergarten children who were vulnerable on one or more scales of the EDI. (One-fourth of the children in the light gray neighborhood were of low vulnerability, and one-fourth of the children in the dark gray neighborhood were of high vulnerability.) In the foreground of each neighborhood, the left-hand semicircle represents the numeracy Community Index of Child Development (CICD) and the right-hand semicircle represents the reading CICD for the children who were in kindergarten while they lived in those neighborhoods. The size of each semicircle is proportional to the CICD. Thus, Figure 11.1 shows that, in general, the CICDs for numeracy and reading are larger

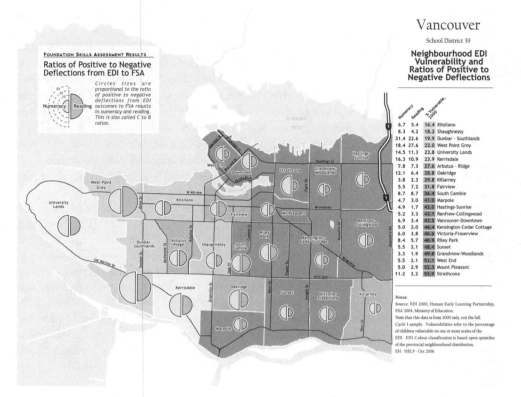

Figure 11.1. Numeracy and Reading Community Index of Child Development Scores, by neighborhood, for the Vancouver School District. (Reprinted from *Social Science & Medicine*, 68, Lloyd, J.E. & Dertzman, C., Kindergarten readiness to fourth-grade assessment; longtudinal analysis with linked population data, 118, [2009], with permission from Elsevier.)

in the lower vulnerability neighborhoods. In other words, Vancouver is a scenario of divergence, wherein children from more vulnerable neighborhoods start out behind and also tend to fall even further behind children from less vulnerable neighborhoods over the 4-year period examined (Lloyd & Hertzman, p. 118).

As we might expect, EDI scores were lower in neighborhoods whose residents had less education (and parents in these neighborhoods are also poorer). However, there is variation in EDI scores across the poorer neighborhoods, as in the Project for Human Development in Chicago Neighborhoods. In Chicago, variation within the poor neighborhoods was due to the psychological characteristics of the neighborhood (collective efficacy, social cohesion). Maps like those of Vancouver shown in Figure 11.1 can help policy makers pinpoint areas where, for example, child health or language capabilities are particularly low. It is very expensive to chart characteristics such as neighborhood collective efficacy, but it is relatively cost effective to use maps to identify neighborhoods where children are doing better than expected (on the basis of poverty rates). Such maps could be used for individual schools as well.

The EDI also can be used to track changes in neighborhoods or schools over time. For example, does the health of kindergartners in a particular neighborhood improve or deteriorate over time? Cohort comparisons can be used to chart overall changes as a function of specific interventions, such as the opening of new health clinics or the introduction of more preschool programs. But cohort comparisons are subject to bias because the composition of families in a particular neighborhood may change over time as different types of families move in and out. If programs are introduced and the population changes around the same time, it is difficult to know which factor accounted for the changes in EDI scores over cohorts. It is also difficult to examine factors in isolation from one another; a department of health makes decisions about where to locate new health clinics on the basis of need, rather than, for example, randomly selecting neighborhoods. The EDI can provide a method for tracking change, albeit imperfect. Of course, using census data and data on the families entering a school, researchers can determine how much a neighborhood's population of kindergartners changes over time, which helps them adjust for in- and out-migration from neighborhoods.

The EDI also can be used in conjunction with school achievement data. In British Columbia, researchers were able to link EDI scores for more than 85% of the 8,000 kindergarteners mentioned earlier with fourth grade achievement tests (Lloyd & Hertzman, 2009). One interesting analysis of these data involved dividing children into four groups on the basis of whether they were doing well on the EDI and on the fourth-grade test. Not doing well was defined by being at or below the 10th percentile on at least one of the five EDI scales at kindergarten and by not having passed the achievement test in fourth grade. The four groups were 1) students who did well at both test points (positive trajectory), 2) students who did well in kindergarten but not in fourth grade (negative deflection), 3) students who did not do well in kindergarten but did in fourth grade (positive deflection), and 4) students who did not do well at either test point (negative trajectory). Neighborhoods or schools that had a relatively high proportion of students with positive deflections are of particular interest, as these fourth graders are doing well despite having started kindergarten with either behavioral or academic challenges. If the practices that are leading to such positive outcomes can be identified, they may be instructive to other schools. For example, do the schools have more well-trained teachers, smaller classes, less grade retention, more pull-out services, more parent involvement, or more after-school programs than schools that have fewer children in the positive deflection group?

In sum, the map and track approach for the school readiness of young children is promising. It links neighborhood, family, and school information and can be used to track changes across cohorts of children or to track groups within a cohort of children. Communities and schools can implement such a system quite easily. The maps provide a way to display information on children's readiness, community characteristics, and community and school resources visually and simultaneously.

IMPLICATIONS FOR GENERATING KNOWLEDGE ABOUT NEIGHBORHOOD INFLUENCES

Although the research linking neighborhood residence with young children's well-being is accumulating, little work has been done directly on early transitions and neighborhoods. Several lines of work seem promising, however. The first type of research distinguishes between neighborhood residence and family moves, the second explores neighborhoods and the supply of child care, and the third examines child care settings as a venue for maximizing the social and psychological organization of neighborhoods. Each line of inquiry will be considered briefly. It should be noted that the second and third research lines have not considered how neighborhood residence directly influences child well-being.

First, neighborhood studies generally do not consider family moves; instead, they focus on a family's neighborhood of residence. One structural dimension of neighborhoods that we have already discussed involves instability. (The other two dimensions are socioeconomic status and residents' race, ethnicity, or immigration status.) In general, studies find that the socioeconomic status of neighborhoods, not their stability, is what matters for young children. The relocation experiments, in contrast, involve family moves to a new neighborhood. These studies confound neighborhood residence and the transition experience of moving. For this reason, the MTO program included three groups of families: families that stayed in public housing, families that received a Section 8 voucher to move (and that generally moved into the same neighborhood or same type of neighborhood as the public housing in which they resided prior to the experiment), and families that received a special voucher to move into a less poor neighborhood. The program compared all three groups, although often research reviews highlight only the differences between families that stayed and the MTO movers. It is important then, to note that the children who moved but did not move to a new type of neighborhood achieved test scores that were almost identical to those of the children who stayed in public housing. Thus, the move per se did not seem to alter outcomes; rather, it was the move to a less disadvantaged neighborhood that improved children's test scores.

Researchers are just starting to use nonexperimental studies to examine the possibly distinct effects of moving to a new neighborhood. Some work looks at movement patterns within a cohort in a city. Sampson and Sharkey (2008), for example, are finding that migration patterns are quite different for African American and Hispanic American families in the Chicago Project. The former are, for the most part, cycling among impoverished neighborhoods, while Hispanic Americans are dispersing into less poor neighborhoods. That is, segregation in poor neighborhoods is not being broken for most African American families. One analysis that took moving into account found that the percentage of time that school-age children spent in poor neighborhoods was highly related to lower verbal scores (Sampson, Sharkey, & Raudenbush, 2008). Another study, by Leventhal et al. (in press), examined changes in emotional distress and aggression over time in school-age children as a function of whether they stayed in their initial neighborhood or moved to a more or less advantaged neighborhood. In brief, more dynamic modeling of neighborhood conditions and moves is just beginning.

The second line of research examines the apparently sparse links between transitions into child care and education as a function of neighborhood residence. A fascinating analysis of the impact of state-level child care regulations on the supply of center-based and family-based care included information on local markets (Hotz & Xiao, 2009). The authors defined local markets by zip code and compared the effects of regulations on neighborhoods with higher and lower incomes (median split of all neighborhoods in the United States). The supply of child care was determined with data from the Census of Services Industries, which includes information on all child care centers in the United States, in 3 years (1987, 1992, and 1997). Two findings that are related to neighborhood income both suggest that regulations have negative impacts in lower income neighborhoods. First, more stringent state regulations are linked to a reduction in child care centers, but only in lower income markets. In addition, the quality of centers (judged by whether a center was accredited by the National Association of Education for Young Children) was higher when stricter state regulations existed, but this link was found only in the higher income markets. Thus, state regulations affected lower income markets by reducing their numbers without increasing the quality of the remaining centers.

The third line of research examines child care as a venue for social networks. Mario Small's ethnographic study (2009) examined how child care centers in New York City provide expanded social networks for mothers and how neighborhood and center characteristics influence the information and additional services that families receive from the centers that their children attend. Small found that some families gain a lot from these organizational connections but others do not; this variation is often related to the organization of child care centers, highlighting the role that institutions play in the perpetuation of inequality. Of particular interest for this chapter is the fact that child care centers in lower income neighborhoods had more ties to other services (both "formal referral" and "collaborative ties") than did centers in higher income neighborhoods. He provocatively suggests that low-income families that attend child care centers in higher income neighborhoods may not receive the mix of services that child care centers can broker. (See Brooks-Gunn et al.,1998, for a similar example for health care use in affluent and poor neighborhoods.)

CONCLUSION

Neighborhood residence is associated with both child and adolescent well-being. The literature base is more complete for the latter, in part because adolescents have been studied more extensively to determine why juvenile delinquency is more prevalent in some neighborhoods than others. Theorists disagree about whether neighborhood links are stronger for adolescents or children. On the one hand, adolescents have the opportunity to navigate neighborhoods on their own and to form friendships with less parental supervision, suggesting that the neighborhood would play a larger role for them. On the other hand, parents tend to manage the amount of input that their young children receive from the neighborhood. The transitions that young children make (residential moves, moves of individuals into and out of households, entrance into child care and preschool, and moves from one type of child care arrangement to another) are for the most part controlled by their parents. Parents themselves might be influenced by neighborhood residence in terms of the timing and number of transitions, the available resources in any given neighborhood, and the information that parents have about neighborhood resources. Also, the actual settings in which parents place their young children have organizational features that make it more or less likely that particular parents will learn about and receive services. Such features are probably more important for low-income families, because their resources (income, human capital, mental health, and parenting practices) are sometimes compromised (Brooks-Gunn & Markman, 2005). Another way to conceptualize differential neighborhood effects for lower and higher income parents is to suggest that the combined impact of neighborhood residence and family conditions is greater than the sum of their separate impacts. However, this notion has not been adequately investigated.

There are very few data that link neighborhood impact with transition for young children, even though the range of effects could be substantial. For example, greater familial mobility means more transitions for young children to new child care arrangements, churches, play groups, and other settings, and residency in low-income neighborhoods could exacerbate the difficulty of the transitions. An additional issue is related to children's transition to elementary school. Nothing is known about how children fare as a function of neighborhood (although the work by Hertzman and colleagues suggests that elementary school trajectories are a function of neighborhood residence; Janus & Offord, 2007; Kershaw et al., 2007; Lloyd & Hertzman, 2009). The importance of services to ease the transition into school, such as home-visiting programs for parents, alignment of preschool and elementary school curricula, integration of pre-K into elementary schools, and organizational ties between child care and early school institutions, is recognized and discussed in this volume. Whether such services are more beneficial to families living in low-income neighborhoods is not known.

Case Study—Transition and Alignment Through the Eyes of Spark

A Comprehensive Community-Based Strategy for Reform

Anthony Berkley and Kimber Bogard

In 2001, the W.K. Kellogg Foundation (WKKF) launched an ambitious national initiative linking ready kids to ready schools. The purpose of this initiative, Supporting Partnerships to Assure Ready Kids™ (SPARK), was to explore the role of community-based partnerships in improving education conditions for children. Given the limited focus at the federal level and the need to move from a federal to a community focus, the Kellogg board was interested in working on projects with a community focus and enthusiastically supported the effort. Lessons from this work illuminate the kinds of community leadership that are required to align preschool settings with the K–12 system, particularly for low-income children of color.

SPARK included 7-year commitments to eight sites across the country (in Florida, Georgia, Hawaii, Ohio, Mississippi, New Mexico, North Carolina, and Washington, D.C.). The purpose of the initiative was to promote permanent improvements in the systems that affect early learning, particularly among vulnerable children ages 3–8. It was predicated on the understanding that community-based strategies—strategies that are developed by community members and reliant on community resources—were necessary to effect change. Other foundations were funding broadly similar work; they included the Annie E. Casey Foundation, which funded Making Connections sites, and the William Casper Graustein Memorial Fund, which sponsored Discovery Communities.

Implementation

The SPARK Program Model   SPARK was designed with a rigorous evaluation plan and a clear intent to shape state policy. Grantees were charged with building local partnerships to better align existing programs and systems (Berkley, 2005). They developed innovative relationships across sectors with community organizations, including child care providers, child advocates, business leaders, and human service agencies. They also brought parents and schools into the mix. SPARK grantees developed numerous strategies to smooth children's transitions, align early education experiences, and improve quality in early childhood education and early elementary school settings.

Each SPARK site was unique, but the various communities' implementations of the vision followed similar paths. Grantees began their work by building relationships with preschool providers and helping them improve the quality of their programs. Grantees helped preschools attain National Association for the Education of Young Children accreditation and training in the program quality assessment to improve classroom quality. Children who were enrolled in SPARK preschool programs were given early screening and referrals, when needed, to speech therapy, family counseling, preventive dental work, and other needed services. At many sites, parents were trained to be their child's first teacher and learning advocate; at some sites, service coordinators took on the work of the learning advocate. As 3- and 4-year-olds age into kindergarten, many sites linked preschool with kindergarten by instituting early kindergarten enrollment, summer kindergarten camps, and individual learning plans. Each site drew on the full array of community resources to advance children's development during early childhood transitions.

Highlights and Accomplishments   The results of an evaluation of the initiative are good, according to a report from Walter R. McDonald & Associates, Inc. (2009), a third-party research firm. SPARK community coalitions can drive significant improvements in early education. During the 7 years that WKKF provided funding and support, grantees built a wealth of knowledge for positive change and directly helped vulnerable children and their communities. More than 8,000 children received much-needed early education services, and these services were shown to put them ahead of their non-SPARK counterparts at kindergarten entry. More than $100 million in additional funds were leveraged by SPARK grantees to sustain and spread their programs. By 2010, an additional 17,885 children will have benefited from the SPARK experience and will have entered kindergarten better prepared to succeed.

SPARK grantees appreciated the technical support that WKKF provided to build sustainable coalitions and communicate their work to a broad audience. Creating public will to improve education through outreach and communication activities was a necessary component of building a plan for sustainability that extended beyond foundation support. Leadership by grantees facilitated collaboration across agencies, which was essential to sustaining partnerships that were aimed at supporting high-quality, aligned learning experiences for children 3–8 years old Moreover, leadership at the state level was important for generating public funds to support partnerships that work to improve children's learning and development.

SPARK grantees succeeded in sustaining many of their early childhood programs and connecting to elementary schools. For example. the Georgia SPARK program initially worked with 12 elementary schools to establish school transition teams composed of parents, parent educators, early childhood education providers, and school staff. These teams worked together to create individual transition plans for children who would be entering kindergarten. The work of the Georgia SPARK program eventually extended to 46 schools. The United Way of Metropolitan Atlanta, the SPARK grantee, received additional private funding to replicate the SPARK model in 11 additional counties in the Atlanta area.

In Miami, the school district partnered with the Florida SPARK program and other key stakeholders. The comprehensive approach supported children's development and learning through partnerships that spanned pre-K–3. In collaboration with the Miami–Dade County Public Schools (M–DCPS), the Lastinger Center at the University of Florida is implementing a job-embedded master of arts program in schools and preschool centers to improve the quality of teaching in the early elementary school grades. The M–DCPS also launched a pre-K–3 demonstration school one summer to put alignment policies into practice. Many teachers from all over the district visited the school to learn how to connect pre-K–3. The work was scaled from the eight original SPARK elementary schools to all of the elementary schools in the district. The initial evaluation results are very promising.

Challenges   It is no secret that the early childhood education and K–12 fields operate within two different cultures. SPARK grantees were not able to affect the K–12 system in a deep and broad fashion. Overall, the culture of elementary schools receiving SPARK children was not transformed. Even though SPARK created quality improvements in early childhood education and in linking preschool to kindergarten, these efforts did not fundamentally change curriculum and instruction in the early years. This issue when the first cohort of SPARK kids entered kindergarten and experienced the great divide firsthand. It was clear that if they did not experience high-quality elementary education from kindergarten through at least third grade, then they risked losing much of the ground they had gained at 3 and 4 years old.

There are success stories about getting kids ready for school around the country, but it is not common for school readiness work to be linked with ready schools work. It is challenging to get kids ready for school and work with the fragmented early childhood education field (Goffin & Washington, 2007), but connecting high-quality early childhood learning experiences to the K–12 education system may be even more difficult. One issue is that preschool program quality is as variable as elementary school quality (Pianta, Belsky, Houts, Morrison, & the National Institute of Child Health and Human Development Early Child Care Research Network, 2007). So even if children attend a high-quality preschool, they are not guaranteed to have quality experiences in elementary school (Currie & Thomas, 2000). The result is what some evaluators have called *fade-out*. Conventional notions of fade-out suggest that even when children attend high-quality preschools and make significant gains compared with their counterparts who do not attend quality programs, they eventually fall into line with their peers when they enter elementary schools that lack resources.

Evaluation results showed that the SPARK initiative experienced three kinds of fade-out (Walter R. McDonald & Associates, Inc., 2009). First, SPARK confronted a fading out of data to tell the SPARK story. Research and evaluation were integral to the SPARK work, and data were collected on 1,000 children from each site. Being able to track children's experiences and outcomes across the years from preschool through third grade was an important component of determining the long-term effectiveness of the early childhood work. Although it was relatively easy to get data on children when they were in preschool settings, it became extremely difficult to track them into elementary schools. Most school districts did initially allow SPARK researchers to access child data, but the data that were available to tell the story dwindled appreciably as children advanced through elementary school. Seven of eight grantees had access to the data they needed to show the kindergarten readiness advantage of SPARK participants compared with a group of children from a similar background. By first grade, only three grantees had access to data on school success. By second grade, only one grantee had access to these data.

A second kind of fade-out was institutional; the commitment of the SPARK grantees to work with elementary schools decreased over time. Most SPARK grantees were child activists who were more comfortable working with children ages 0–5 than with children attending K–12. They created great transition programs to kindergarten and improved some classrooms in the early grades. But the intensity of SPARK interventions waned as the children advanced in school. Over time, SPARK grantees put less effort into aligning curricula, instruction, and assessment from the early childhood programs with those of the early elementary school grades.

The third and most conventional kind of fade-out concerned the individual academic achievement of SPARK kids compared with that of their peers from similar backgrounds. At this point we don't know enough to tell this story because of the lack of data described previously, but early indicators suggest that the differences between SPARK kids and their peers narrow over time. Anecdotal reports from teachers and parents suggest that SPARK kids are more likely than their peers to be viewed as classroom leaders and achievers, to advance to the next grade on time, and to be recommended for enrichment programs. WKKF is currently engaged in a longitudinal evaluation study to shed light on the school success story through first grade. With WKKF support, SPARK grantees are also engaged in collecting third-grade test scores.

Not all sites experienced this fade-out, however, preliminary results from the Ohio SPARK program indicate that strong academic abilities indicated by kindergarten readiness scores are sustained into third grade. The first cohort of SPARK children from Minerva, Ohio ($N = 39$) scored significantly higher on third-grade standardized achievement tests in reading and math than did their peers. Ohio achievement tests results for SPARK children showed an average reading score of 422.9, while the comparison group averaged 410.3. In math, the SPARK cohort averaged 435 points, 17.3 points higher than the comparison group. These differences are statistically significant with an effect size of .51 for reading and .61 for math. Although these results have not yet been subject to peer review, it is likely that the Ohio SPARK program is at least partly responsible for sustaining these outcomes through third grade.

Lessons Learned   Transition activities are not sufficient to maximize children's opportunities for long-term success. SPARK was more successful at easing children's transition than providing alignment (creating a continuum of education experiences) between grades. Transition typically focuses on activities that facilitate children's movement from pre-K to kindergarten. These activities rarely extend into third grade. In contrast, alignment is about systems change and bridging the divide between early childhood education and elementary school. Alignment entails mapping out a system of standards, assessments, instruction, and curricular materials that build on children's developmental capacities from one year to the next, from pre-K–3 (Bogard & Takanishi, 2005). For example, alignment could be facilitated by having teachers of different grades meet to discuss children's work, standards to reach learners, and strategies to support children's developmental needs. The SPARK evaluation results indicate that focusing on high-quality early childhood education and transition activities into kindergarten leads to successful outcomes through first grade. However, unless sustained follow-up efforts are made, the effects are likely to dissipate by the time children reach third grade if the children are in poorly run elementary schools. Alignment is necessary to maximize the gains that children make in high-quality early education settings.

Community-based partnerships have potential for sustaining aligned systems. In order to fully implement an aligned system that is sustained over time, partnerships that bridge the early childhood education and K–12 fields are necessary. Because many children receive pre-K education outside the public elementary school walls, it is imperative to develop relationships and sustain them over time. SPARK grantees laid the foundation for creating aligned systems by forming local partnerships of parents, child advocates, and systems leaders. These groups work to align systems and advance a set of proven strategies for empowering communities to take the lead in improving conditions. Creating systems of alignment for children 3–8 years old, or from pre-K–3, was a difficult task for SPARK grantees. But their successful partnerships with multiple stakeholders and the preparation of kids for school allowed many SPARK grantees to leverage WKKF grants to attract other public and private funds that they could use to expand their programs and sustain their investments in kids.

The current status of data systems limits informed education policy decision making. Good data that track children's learning experiences from pre-K through the end of their formal schooling are important for informing practice and policy decisions. Gathering data on the SPARK program in elementary schools was particularly challenging, which made it more difficult to identify why children's learning gains were not sustained into third grade or at what point one should intervene. A data system that links children, teachers, and schools can avoid this problem and can inform teaching and learning.

Many teachers use data on children's learning experiences to guide their instructional plans. Another use for school-based, linked data systems would be to inform professional development for principals and teachers. For example, data can point out strengths and weaknesses in student performance, which can lead to immediate school-based interventions in teaching. An integrated data system can be useful at the state level, too; data across school districts can inform certification standards and hence teacher preparation programs. At many different levels, a high-quality data system that links children, teachers, pre-K programs, and elementary schools can be used to improve teaching and learning.

Supportive leadership is needed for sustained educational alignment. Some SPARK grantees were fortunate to have strong leadership on their side, which allowed grantees to create public will for young children's early learning and development. For example, with the leadership of David Lawrence, Jr., President of the Early Childhood Initiative Foundation, Miami–Dade voters decided overwhelmingly to reauthorize a dedicated funding stream to support children's health, education, and development. Ohio Governor Ted Strickland has long been a champion of early childhood education, which increased the public will to improve early childhood education, facilitating the replication of SPARK across many Ohio communities. In contrast, Mississippi lacked a state-funded pre-K program, and the Mississippi SPARK program had to work hard on the early childhood education side. As a result, the alignment of early childhood education with the K–12 system was slow in that state. The Mississippi grantee scaled this obstacle by training learning advocates who went into homes to help families support their children's development and learning.

Future Directions   A lot of work remains to be done to bridge teaching and learning across ages 0–5 and grades K–12. Alignment of learning standards, teacher expectations, and curricula are essential, yet the divides between the two systems are deep. For example, 46 states have signed onto an effort led by the National Governors Association and Council of Chief State School Officers to establish a common core of voluntary, rigorous standards in mathematics and English language arts in Grades K–12 (McNeil, 2009). Even though most states support pre-K programs and have early learning standards, the effort to establish the standards did not include pre-K. As long as the world sees pre-K as a separate entity that is less important than K–12 education, the great divide will continue to exist and children will miss opportunities for learning.

SPARK has proven that positive change can happen as a result of community-based coalitions. WKKF is taking those community-driven practices and lessons to state-level policy makers to improve the teaching and learning that takes place in classrooms, schools, and communities. At the community level, WKKF will support community-based partnerships that have already created platforms for their work and that have achieved some level of success in early childhood education, health, and development. By supporting networks of practitioners who are already working together on behalf of children 0–8 years old, WKKF will facilitate the sustainability and expansion of models that can inform policy.

Conclusion   The SPARK initiative encouraged communities to engage in strategic planning with stakeholders from many different sectors, including elementary school principals, kindergarten teachers, preschool teachers, parents, and staff from community service agencies that work with young children. In the course of the planning process, each of the eight SPARK sites developed a transition model that had the support of local stakeholders *and* that drew on best practices. These pilot projects, many of which continue to be replicated and sustained in various communities, demonstrated the challenges and opportunities of community-level initiatives to improve transition. Their results suggest that the divide between early childhood education and elementary education can be bridged, in part, by bringing teachers and administrators together at the community level to build relationships and discuss expectations, teaching philosophies, and individual children's needs. Furthermore, SPARK home visitors and parent educators who are based in

community agencies connected families to a variety of services that they might not otherwise have accessed. The SPARK initiative addressed children's cognitive, physical, and
emotional development in a holistic manner that facilitated school readiness and eased
the transitions these children had to navigate from home to child care and kindergarten.

Case Study—East Africa Madrasa Program
A Community-Based Approach to Supporting Early Learning

Alejandra Cortazar

The Madrasa Early Childhood Development (ECD) program is a comprehensive, community-based strategy that promotes children's transitions. At the core of this effort are
community-owned and managed ECD preschools for disadvantaged urban, periurban,
and rural Muslim communities in Kenya, Uganda, and Tanzania (Aga Khan Foundation,
2008). The preschools bridge young children's home and school environments by providing a child-friendly and culturally relevant early education. The strategy is threefold: 1) the
curriculum integrates the *HighScope Preschool Curriculum* (see Chapter 8) and Muslim
culture; 2) instruction is delivered in children's mother tongue; and 3) the educational
environment and materials that children use are prepared by their parents to ensure that
the program is consistent with the children's home environment. The Madrasa program
also creates linkages between preschool and primary school teachers and works with the
local governments to facilitate pedagogical alignment between preschools and primary
schools (N. Rashic, personal communication, June 22, 2009). Madrasa resource centers train teachers and community members to teach and manage the preschool and
facilitate community engagement in children's early development.

Program Purpose   The Madrasa program's ultimate goal is to provide children with
the skills they need to succeed in a pluralistic society while simultaneously preserv-
ing their cultural identity. It seeks to facilitate awareness in the community of young
children's needs for early care and education and to promote families' participation in
community-based early childhood programs. It also aims to increase access to public
primary school and retention in school for children from marginalized Muslim communities. Finally, the Madrasa community-based approach aspires to be both replicable
and sustainable (Aga Khan Foundation, 2008; Issa & Evans, 2008).

Participants   The Madrasa program's reach is impressive. It supports ECD programs
in more than 200 marginalized communities in the three countries, serving over 3,000
households every year. Since 1986, the program has benefited 72,000 children and
has trained 4,500 teachers and 2,000 community members. Forty-nine percent of the
children attending the Madrasa programs are girls, and more than 12% are non-Muslim
children who come from other marginalized communities in the region (N. Rashid, personal communication, June 22, 2009).

Origins   The Madrasa program started in Kenya to meet the Muslim community's need
for early childhood education. In the 1980s, early childhood education was valued
in Kenya because preschools provided children with the skills that they needed to
succeed on the first-grade admission exam for the public schools. Muslim children
either did not attend early childhood programs or attended private Christian-based
programs. Children's access was limited because "parents were reluctant to send

their children to church preschools" (N. Rashid, personal communication, June 22, 2009) due to the discontinuity between the home and preschool culture.

In response to this problem, in 1982 Muslim leaders in Kenya asked His Highness the Aga Khan to find a solution for their children. In 1983, the dialogue between the Aga Khan Foundation in East Africa and the Islamic communities in Kenya began. A community assessment identified a need for affordable, culturally responsive early childhood programs. Of note, the assessment discovered that the resources were in place to provide ECD services: Villages had the infrastructure because space that was used for after-school programs was empty during the mornings, and there were school graduates in the village who could be trained as preschool teachers. After 3 years of study, in 1986 the first public preschool in the Coast Province of Kenya opened. The program opened in a mosque with four children and four adults. After 2 weeks of intense outreach, the preschool met its goal of enrolling 30 children (Aga Khan Foundation, 2008).

The Madrasa program expanded to Zanzibar in 1990 and to Uganda in 1993 (Issa & Evans, 2008). In 2002, the program extended its service model beyond early childhood education to include support for health and nutrition, parenting, and children's transition to primary education. Specifically, the Madrasa program began to include strategies to ease children's transition to primary school because children were observed to have difficulty adapting to the different pedagogical approach used in primary education settings and to the large class size in primary schools that resulted from free primary education policies (N. Rashid, personal communication, June 22, 2009). In 2008, an adaptation of the Madrasa preschool model was implemented in Egypt and Afghanistan, among other countries.

Program Structure   Madrasa preschool is run by a school management committee (SMC) that is composed of community members. Each committee has eight members, at least two of which must be women. The SMC addresses the community's needs related to early childhood, ensures the quality of early childhood programs, and encourages parents to get involved. The SMC is supported by a community resource team formed by the preschool lead teacher, the assistant teacher, and one additional community member (Aga Khan Foundation, 2008).

Teacher training, mentoring with regard to classroom practice, and support on program management are provided by Madrasa resource centers (MRCs). There are three MRCs: one in Kenya, one in Zanzibar, and one in Uganda. Each country's center has a project director, an assistant project director, a community development officer, trainers, and support staff. In addition to the MRC, each country has a national board formed by volunteer Muslim leaders, business people, and local educators. These boards oversee the work of the Madrasa resource centers (N. Rashid, personal communication, June 22, 2009).

The Madrasa program is also supported by a volunteer regional committee. Created by the Aga Khan Foundation, this committee oversees and advises the MRCs and links the three national boards. In addition, a regional office supports the coordination and collaboration of the three MRCs, facilitates sharing of best practices among the three countries, and works to optimize the efficiency of the overall project (Aga Khan Foundation, 2008).

Implementation   The implementation of a new Madrasa program occurs through a three-phase process, typically over the course of 6 years. First, the Madrasa program engages in *community sensitization and mobilization.* The needs of the community related to early childhood education are assessed, and a team of community members is created and charged with addressing those needs. During this phase, the community team selects the SMC, initiates school registration with the corresponding ministry, chooses a location for the program, starts selecting prospective teachers, and begins to enroll children in the ECD program.

The second phase includes *training, monitoring and evaluation, operations, and support.* Before a school can operate, the SMC and the Madrasa teachers receive training and the community resource team is developed. Teachers and community members participate in 2 years of training composed of three 3-week-long sessions each year. During this phase, programs undergo an assessment to see the extent to which the schools have satisfied the expected goals regarding community involvement, the teaching and learning environment, and school management. The schools graduate once they fulfill the goals of the Madrasa program.

The third and final phase focuses on *sustainability.* The Madrasa resource center must provide ongoing support to the SMC and the community resource team. In each country, preschool associations are formed as a vehicle for promoting sustainability (Aga Khan Foundation, 2008; Bartlett, 2003; Issa & Evans, 2008).

Services for Children   Madrasa preschools offer children early childhood education 5 mornings a week. The daily routine includes circle time, work time, a small-group religion lesson, directed activities, outdoor play, and a snack time. The materials, decoration, and toys, both in the classrooms and in the outdoor area, are made by the parents with local materials, many of which have been recycled (Aga Khan Foundation, 2008).

The preschools use a curriculum that integrates a child-friendly approach based on the HighScope Preschool Curriculum and Islamic culture and knowledge. In the words of a preschool graduate, "the teachers blended the learning of numbers and letters with Islam and the reality of life" (Aga Khan Foundation, 2008, p. 51). The program promotes children's moral and psychosocial development, nutrition, health, safety, and general well-being. The Madrasa preschools use children's mother tongue as the principal language of instruction and gradually incorporate the national official language and English, the language of instruction in primary school, into the curriculum (N. Rashid, personal communication, June 22, 2009).

Since 2002, the program has worked with primary teachers and government inspectors to bridge the gap between preschool and primary schools in East Africa by implementing strategies to facilitate children's transition to primary schools (N. Rashid, personal communication, June 22, 2009). The Madrasa resource centers have developed training activities for preschool teachers that address the transition from preschool into primary school, active learning methods, and classroom management strategies exclusively for primary school teachers in order to promote pedagogical continuity from preschool to primary school. The training activities teach preschool teachers how to support children's transition to the school system and primary school teachers how to prepare the school to receive the incoming students (N. Rashid, personal communication, September 4, 2009). The Madrasa program also invites primary school teachers to collaborate with Madrasa preschool teachers to create materials for their classrooms (Issa & Evans, 2008). The Madrasa resource centers also train community members of the SMC on strategies to involve parents in their children's transition from home to preschool and from preschool to primary school (N. Rashid, personal communication, September 4, 2009).

The Madrasa resource centers collaborate with local governments to implement transition workshops that facilitate collaboration between preschool and primary school teachers. Participants meet throughout the year to discuss transition issues and develop plans for curricular alignment (Aga Khan Foundation, 2008). The plans are implemented at the local level. Strategies to facilitate children's transitions are considered a central component of the program. Specifically, the effort encourages instructional continuity: Children attending preschool visit the primary school and the primary school teachers serve as "visiting teachers" in the preschool. The initiative also promotes communication with the families in the form of parent–teacher conferences and home visits by teachers. This work is currently being evaluated to determine its impact on child outcomes (N. Rashid, personal communication, June 22, 2009).

Highlights and Accomplishments   The Madrasa program began as one community preschool 25 years ago and has expanded throughout the three countries discussed. It has "been successful creating access for children" (N. Rashid, personal communication, June 22, 2009). Madrasa has not only helped communities to create ECD programs but has also facilitated the sustainability of such programs.

The Madrasa program has helped to remove social barriers to women's participation in education and community decision making. It also has facilitated parents' participation in their children's lives by increasing their understanding of their role and responsibility in their children's education (Aga Khan Foundation, 2008).

In addition to its work at the community level, the program has established partnerships with local governments, promoting public policies to improve children's holistic development and increase the continuity between preschool and primary education. Multiple organizations working in early childhood have taken an interest in the Madrasa model. In response to this interest, Madrasa is training more than 20 organizations across the region in its approach (N. Rashid, personal communication, June 22, 2009).

Several studies have evaluated the Madrasa program. The Madrasa Preschool Impact Study, conducted from 1999–2005, used a quasi-experimental design that compared children from the Madrasa program with children from non-Madrasa preschools and children who stayed at home. A total of 906 children were assessed in measures of cognitive development that were related to school readiness. The study found that Madrasa preschools had a significant and positive influence on children's cognitive development and readiness for primary school. Madrasa participants' outcomes exceeded those of the children from other preschools as well as those of children who stayed at home. The study found that, consistent with these findings, the quality of education in the Madrasa preschool was higher than the quality of education in the non-Madrasa preschools and that quality mediated children's cognitive development and school readiness (Aga Khan Foundation, 2008; Mwaura, Sylva, & Malmberg, 2008). Preliminary results of a new study launched in 2007 suggest that preschool experience facilitates children's enrollment in primary schools and helps to reduce grade retention (Aga Khan Foundation).

Challenges   An initial implementation challenge for the program was to establish trust and credibility among the different stakeholders. To build trust, Madrasa engaged community members who understood that the goal of the program was to prepare children for school and life success (Bartlett, 2003). A second challenge was convincing the community that early childhood education was important. After they realized the potential benefits of Madrasa, the initial community members "came on board and were very much up to anything and ready to start working for the program"

(N. Rashid, personal communication, June 22, 2009). A third challenge was creating appropriate settings for the preschools (Bartlett). Many programs were located in spaces such as mosques that were used for other purposes in the afternoon, so all materials, wall displays, and storage facilities needed to be assembled and disassembled routinely. Finally, the financial viability of the preschools was, and continues to be, a great challenge, especially since the Madrasa program works with marginalized poor communities. Each community is responsible for managing its own preschool, which includes making decisions regarding parents' fees and teachers' salaries. In many communities, teachers' wages are "as little as 20 dollars a month" (N. Rashid, personal communication), resulting in high rates of turnover as teachers get better offers from private schools.

Lessons Learned   Community ownership is critical for both community support and the sustainability of the program. The Madrasa program has found that achieving sustainability is a long-term goal that requires multiple partnerships, and that the most sustainable programs draw on available resources. Communities need to feel responsible and able to provide young children with a culturally relevant education. They "have to participate from the initiation of the process itself and acknowledge the work they do for the program" (N. Rashid, personal communication, June 22, 2009).

Children's smooth transition to primary school is possible only if there is pedagogical continuity between preschool and primary school and if schools and teachers are prepared to receive young children. Partnership with the government has been critical from the beginning in order to maintain the gains of the Madrasa program and to facilitate children's transition to secular primary schools. As Najma Rashid, the regional program director, states, "You can do all that you are doing in the early years, but if you do not ensure that the next level of learning environment is as cohesive as before, you lose it. The whole idea is to ensure progression, continuity that all the quality that you have added continues" (personal communication, June 22, 2009). The program staff realizes that it is not enough to prepare children and their families to enter schools. Schools and teachers also need to be prepared and ready to receive the children. To achieve this goal, preschool and primary-school teachers and leaders must work collaboratively.

Future Directions   The Madrasa program is working to expand to more communities in Tanzania, Uganda, and Kenya. It is also collaborating with other agencies and programs that are affiliated with the Aga Khan Foundation, both in East Africa and in other regions and countries. A partnership with the Aga Khan Agency for Microfinance, for example, is helping groups of parents get loans to generate disposable incomes to pay fees and teachers' salaries, facilitating program sustainability (N. Rashid, personal communication, June 22, 2009). The Madrasa program is also researching the impact of early childhood education and the importance of transitions. Finally, it is actively working with local governments to influence early childhood education policies in the region to ensure that children receive education that promotes their holistic development from preschool to primary school.

Conclusion   The Madrasa community preschools promote children's transition from home to school in four ways: 1) bridging young children's home and school environments by providing a child-friendly and culturally relevant early education, 2) promoting the skills that children need to enter and succeed in school, 3) creating linkages between preschool and primary-school teachers, and 4) advocating for pedagogical alignment between preschools and primary schools. Combined, these efforts engender a community that nurtures young children's development from birth through primary school.

REFERENCES

Aaronson, D. (1997). Sibling estimates of neighborhood effects. In J. Brooks-Gunn, G.J. Duncan, & J.L. Aber (Eds.), *Neighborhood poverty: Policy implications in studying neighborhoods* (Vol. 2, pp. 80–93). New York: Russell Sage Foundation Press.

Aber, J.L., Gephart, M., Brooks-Gunn, J., & Connell, J. (1997). Development in context: Implications for studying neighborhood effects. In J. Brooks-Gunn, G.J. Duncan, & J.L. Aber (Eds.), *Neighborhood poverty: Context and consequences for children* (Vol. 1, pp. 44–61). New York: Russell Sage Foundation Press.

Aga Khan Foundation. (2008). *The Madrasa Early Childhood Programme: 25 years of experience* (Aga Khan Development Network Series). Geneva: Judith Evans.

Anderson, P.M., & Butcher, K.F. (2006). Childhood obesity: Trends and potential causes. *Future of Children, 16*(1), 19–45.

Austin, S.B., Melly, S.J., Sanchez, B.A., Patel, A., Buka, S., & Gortmaker, S.L. (2005). Clustering of fast-food restaurants around schools: A novel application of spatial statistics to the study of food environments. *American Journal of Public Health, 95,* 1575–1581.

Bandura, A. (1977). Self-efficacy: Toward a unifying theory of behavioral change. *Psychological Review, 84,* 191–215.

Barnett, W.S. (1995). Long-term effects of early childhood programs on cognitive and school outcomes. *Future of Children, 5*(3), 25–50.

Bartlett, K. (2003). *The Madrasa Early Childhood Programme in East Africa.* Geneva: Aga Khan Foundation.

Bellinger, D.C. (2004). Lead. *Pediatrics, 113*(Suppl. 4), 1016–1022.

Berkley, T. (2005). SPARKing innovation. *The Evaluation Exchange, 11,* 22–24. Cambridge, MA: Harvard Family Research Project.

Block, J.P., Scribner, R.A., & DeSalvo, K.B. (2004). Fast food, race/ethnicity, and income: A geographic analysis. *American Journal of Preventative Medicine, 27,* 211–217.

Bogard, K., & Takanishi, R. (2005). PK–3: An aligned and coordinated approach to education for children 3 to 8 years old. *Social Policy Report, 19,* 1–24.

Bornschein, R.L., Succop, P., Dietrich, K.N., Clark, S.C., Hee, S.Q., & Hammond, P.B. (1985). The influence of social and environmental factors on dust lead, hand lead, and blood lead levels in young children. *Environmental Research, 38,* 108–118.

Briggs, X.S., Darden, J.T., & Aidala, A. (1999). In the wake of desegregation: Early impacts of the scattered-site public housing on neighborhoods in Yonkers, New York. *Journal of the American Planning Association, 65,* 27–49.

Bronfenbrenner, U. (1979). *The ecology of human development.* Cambridge, MA: Harvard University Press.

Brooks-Gunn, J. (1996). Unexpected opportunities: Confessions of an eclectic developmentalist. In M. Merrens & G. Brannigan (Eds.), *The developmental psychologists: Research adventures across the lifespan* (pp. 152–171). Boston: McGraw-Hill.

Brooks-Gunn, J. (2004). Intervention and policy as change agents for young children. In P.L. Chase-Lansdale, K. Kiernan, & R.J. Friedman (Eds.), *Human development across lives and generations: The potential for change* (pp. 293–340). New York: Cambridge University Press.

Brooks-Gunn, J., Duncan, G.J., & Aber, J.L. (1997). *Neighborhood poverty: Context and consequences for children* (Vol. 1). New York: Russell Sage Foundation Press.

Brooks-Gunn, J., Duncan, G.J., Klebanov, P.K., & Sealand, N. (1993). Do neighborhoods influence child and adolescent development? *American Journal of Sociology, 99,* 353–395.

Brooks-Gunn, J., Johnson, A., & Leventhal, T. (2009). Disorder, turbulence, and resources in children's homes and neighborhoods. In G.W. Evans & T.D. Wachs (Eds.), *Chaos and its influence on children's development: An ecological perspective.* Washington, DC: American Psychological Association.

Brooks-Gunn, J., & Markman, L. (2005). The contribution of parenting to ethnic and racial gaps in school readiness. *The Future of Children, 15*(1), 138–167.

Brooks-Gunn, J., McCormick, M.C., Klebanov, P.K., & McCarton, C. (1998). Health care use of 3-year-old low birth weight premature children: Effects of family and neighborhood poverty. *Journal of Pediatrics, 132,* 971–975.

Browning, C.R., Burrington, L., Leventhal, T., & Brooks-Gunn, J. (2008). Neighborhood structural inequality, collective efficacy, and sexual risk behavior among urban youth. *Journal of Health and Social Behavior, 49,* 269–285.

Bukowski, J.R., Lewis, J., Gamble, J.F., Wojcik, N.C., & Laumbach, R.J. (2002). Range-finding study of risk factors for childhood asthma development and national asthma prevalence. *Human and Ecological Risk Assessment, 8,* 735–765.

Burchinal, M., Nelson, L., Carlson, M., & Brooks-Gunn, J. (2008). Neighborhood characteristics, and child care type and quality. *Early Education and Development, 19,* 702–725.

Burton, L.M., Price-Spratlen, T., & Spencer, M.B. (1997). On ways of thinking about measuring neighborhoods: Implications for studying context and developmental outcomes for children. In J. Brooks-Gunn, G.J. Duncan, & J.L. Aber (Eds.), *Neighborhood poverty: Context and consequences for children* (Vol. 1). New York: Russell Sage Foundation Press.

Caspi, A., Taylor, A., Moffitt, T.E., & Plomin, R. (2000). Neighborhood deprivation affects children's mental health: Environmental risks identified in a genetic design. *Psychological Science, 11,* 338–342.

Chase-Lansdale, L., Gordon, R., Brooks-Gunn, J., & Klebanov, P.K. (1997). Neighborhood and family influences on the intellectual and behavioral competence of preschool and early school-age children. In J. Brooks-Gunn, G. Duncan, & J.L. Aber (Eds.), *Neighborhood poverty: Context and consequences for children* (Vol. 1, pp. 79–118). New York: Russell Sage Foundation Press.

Chay, K.Y., & Greenstone, M. (2003). The impact of air pollution on infant mortality: Evidence from geographic variation in pollution shocks induced by a recession. *Quarterly Journal of Economics, 118,* 1121–1167.

Coulton, C.J., & Korbin, J.E. (2007). Indicators of child well-being through a neighborhood lens. *Social Indicators Research, 84,* 349–361.

Coulton, C.J., Korbin, J., Chan, T., & Su, M. (2001). Mapping residents' perceptions of neighborhood boundaries: A methodological note. *American Journal of Community Psychology, 29,* 371–383.

Currie, J. (2006). *The invisible safety net: Protecting the nation's poor children and families.* Princeton, NJ: Princeton University Press.

Currie, J., & Neidell, M. (2005). Air pollution and infant health: What can we learn from California's recent experience? *Quarterly Journal of Economics, 120,* 1003–1030.

Currie, J., & Thomas, D. (2000). School quality and the long-term effects of Head Start. *Journal of Human Resources, 35,* 755–774.

Duncan, G.J., Connell, J.P., & Klebanov, P.K. (1997). Conceptual and methodological issues in estimating causal effects of neighborhood and family conditions on individual development. In J. Brooks-Gunn, G.J. Duncan, & J.L. Aber (Eds.), *Neighborhood poverty: Context and consequences for children* (Vol. 1, pp. 219–250). New York: Russell Sage Foundation Press.

Duncan, G.J., Yeung, W.J., Brooks-Gunn, J. & Smith, J.R. (1998). How much does childhood poverty affect the life chances of children? *American Sociological Review, 63,* 406–423.

Elliot, D.S., Wilson, W.J., Huizinga, D., Sampson, R.J., Elliot, A., & Rankin, B. (1996). The effects of neighborhood disadvantage on adolescent development. *Journal of Research in Crime and Delinquency, 33,* 389–426.

Fauth, R.C., & Brooks-Gunn, J. (2008). Are some neighborhoods better for child health than others? In R.F. Schoeni, J.S. House, G.A. Kaplan, & H. Pollack (Eds.), *Making Americans healthier: Social and economic policy as health policy* (pp. 334–376). New York: Russell Sage Foundation Press.

Fauth, R., Leventhal, T., & Brooks-Gunn, J. (2007). Welcome to the neighborhood? Long-term impacts on moving to low-poverty neighborhoods on poor children's and adolescents' outcomes. *Journal of Research on Adolescence, 17,* 249–284.

Fauth, R.C., Leventhal, T., & Brooks-Gunn, J. (2008). Seven years later: Effects of a neighborhood mobility program on poor Black and Latino adults' well-being. *Journal of Health and Social Behavior, 49,* 119–130.

Fuller, B., Coonerty, C., Kipnis, F., & Choong, Y. (1997). An unfair head start: California families face gaps in preschool and child care availability. Berkeley, CA: Berkeley–Stanford PACE Center, Yale University, and the California Child Care Resource and Referral Network.

Goering, J., & Feins, J.D. (Eds.). (2003). *Choosing a better life? Evaluating the Moving to Opportunity social experiment.* Washington, DC: Urban Institute Press.

Goffin, S.G., & Washington, V. (2007). *Ready or not: Leadership choices in early care and education*. New York: Teachers College Press.

Hotz, V.J., & Xiao, M. (2009). *The impact of regulations on the supply and quality of care in child care markets*. Manuscript under review, Duke University.

Issa, S., & Evans, J. (2008). Going to scale with effective ECD interventions: What is involved? A costing model of the Madrasa ECD Programme in East Africa. *Coordinators' Notebook, 30,* 41–45.

Janus, M., & Offord, D. (2007). Development and psychometric properties of the Early Development Instrument (EDI): A measure of children's school readiness. *Canadian Journal of Behavioural Science, 39,* 1–22.

Jencks, C., & Mayer, S. (1990). The social consequences of growing up in a poor neighborhood. In L. Lynn & M. McGeary (Eds.), *Inner-city poverty in the United States* (pp. 111–186). Washington, DC: National Academies Press.

Kershaw, P., Forer, B., Irwin, L., Hertzman, C., & Lapointe, V. (2007). Toward a social care program of research: A population-level study of neighborhood effects on child development. *Early Education and Development, 18,* 535–560.

Kimbro, R., Brooks-Gunn, J., & McLanahan, S. (2007). Racial and ethnic differentials in overweight and obesity among 3-year-old children. *American Journal of Public Health, 97,* 298–305.

Kimbro, R., Brooks-Gunn, J., & McLanahan, S. (2009). *Children's physical activity and maternal perceptions of neighborhood safety and collective efficacy*. Manuscript under review, Rice University.

Klebanov, P.K., Brooks-Gunn, J., Chase-Lansdale, L., & Gordon, R. (1997). Are neighborhood effects on young children mediated by features of the home environment? In J. Brooks-Gunn, G.J. Duncan, & J.L. Aber (Eds.), *Neighborhood poverty: Context and consequences for children* (Vol. 1, pp. 119–145). New York: Russell Sage Foundation Press.

Klebanov, P.K., Brooks-Gunn, J., & Duncan, G.J. (1994). Does neighborhood and family poverty affect mothers' parenting, mental health, and social support? *Journal of Marriage and the Family, 56,* 441–455.

Klebanov, P.K., Brooks-Gunn, J., McCarton, C., & McCormick, M.C. (1998). The contribution of neighborhood and family income to developmental test scores over the first three years of life. *Child Development, 69,* 1420–1436.

Kohen, D.E., Brooks-Gunn, J., Leventhal, T., & Hertzman, C. (2002). Neighborhood income and physical and social disorder in Canada: Associations with young children's competencies. *Child Development, 73,* 1844–1860.

Leventhal, T., & Brooks-Gunn, J. (2000). The neighborhoods they live in: The effects of neighborhood residence on child and adolescent outcomes. *Psychological Bulletin, 126,* 309–337.

Leventhal, T., Dupéré, V., & Brooks-Gunn, J. (in press). Neighborhood influences on adolescent development. In L. Steinberg & R. Lerner (Eds.), *Handbook of adolescent psychology* (Vol. 3). New York: Wiley.

Leventhal, T., Xue, Y., & Brooks-Gunn, J. (2006). Immigrant differences in school-age children's verbal trajectories: A look at four racial/ethnic groups. *Child Development, 77,* 1359–1374.

Lleras-Muney, A. (in press). The needs of the army: Using compulsory relocation in the military to estimate the effect of air pollutants on children's health. *Journal of Human Resources.*

Lloyd, J.E.V., & Hertzman, C. (2009). From kindergarten readiness to fourth-grade assessment: Longitudinal analysis with linked population data. *Social Science & Medicine, 68,* 111–123.

Loeb, S., Fuller, B., Kagan, S.L., & Carrol, B. (2004). Child care in poor communities: Early learning effects of type, quality, and stability. *Child Development, 75,* 47–65.

Magnuson, K.A., Ruhm, C., & Waldfogel, J. (2007a). Does prekindergarten improve school preparation and performance? *Economics of Education Review, 26,* 33–51.

Magnuson, K.A., Ruhm, C., & Waldfogel, J. (2007b). The persistence of preschool effects: Do subsequent classroom experiences matter? *Early Childhood Research Quarterly, 22,* 18–38.

Magnuson, K.A., & Waldfogel, J. (2005). Early childhood care and education: Effects on ethnic and racial gaps in school readiness. *The Future of Children, 15*(1), 169–196.

Massey, D.S. (1990). American apartheid: Segregation and the making of the underclass. *American Journal of Sociology, 96,* 326–358.

McNeil, M. (2009, June). *Forty-six states agree to common academic standards effort*. Retrieved from http://www.edweek.org/ew/articles/2009/06/01/33standards.h28.html?qs=461states

Mwaura, P., Sylva, K., & Malmberg, L.E. (2008). Evaluating the Madrasa preschool programme in East Africa: A quasi-experimental study. *International Journal of Early Years Education, 16*(3), 237–255.

National Institute of Child Health and Human Development Early Child Care Research Network. (2000). Characteristics and quality of child care for toddlers and preschoolers. *Applied Developmental Science, 4,* 116–135.

Needleman, H.L. (1979). Lead levels and children's psychologic performance. *New England Journal of Medicine, 103,* 163.

Needleman, H.L. (1990). The long-term effects of exposure to low doses of lead in childhood: An 11-year follow-up report. *New England Journal of Medicine, 322,* 83–88.

Needleman, H.L., Riess, J., Tobin, M., Biesecker, G., & Greenhouse, J. (1996) Bone lead levels and delinquent behavior. *Journal of the American Medical Association, 275*(5), 363–369.

O'Hare, W., & Mather, M. (2003). *The growing number of kids in severely distressed neighborhoods: Evidence from the 2000 census.* Washington DC: Annie E. Casey Foundation.

Orr, L., Feins, J.D., Jacob, R., Beecroft, E., Sanbonmatsu, L., Katz, L.F., et al. (2003). *Moving to Opportunity for fair housing demonstration interim impacts evaluation.* Washington, DC: U.S. Department of Housing and Urban Development, Office of Policy Research and Development.

Park, R. (1916). Suggestions for the investigations of human behavior in the urban environment. *American Journal of Sociology, 20,* 577–612.

Pianta, R.C., Belsky, J., Houts, R., Morrison, F., & the National Institute of Child Health and Human Development Early Child Care Research Network. (2007). Teaching: Opportunities to learn in America's elementary classrooms. *Science, 315,* 1795–1796.

Pirkle, J.L., Brody, D.J., Gunter, E.W., Kramer, R.A., Paschal, D.C., Flegal, K.M., et al. (1994). The decline in blood lead levels in the United States: The National Health and Nutrition Examination Survey (NHANES). *Journal of the American Medical Association, 272*(4), 284–291.

Reyes, J. (2007). Environmental policy as social policy? The impact of childhood lead exposure on crime. *National Bureau of Economic Research* (Working Paper No. 13097). Washington, DC: National Bureau of Economic Research.

Ross, C.E., & Jang, S.J. (2000). Neighborhood disorder, fear, and mistrust: The buffering role of social ties with neighbors. *American Journal of Community Psychology, 28,* 401–420.

Sallis, J.F., & Glanz, K. (2006). The role of built environments in physical activity, eating, and obesity in childhood. *Future of Children 16*(1), 89–108.

Sampson, R.J. (1997). Collective regulation of adolescent misbehavior: Validation results from eighty Chicago neighborhoods. *Journal of Adolescent Research, 12,* 227–244.

Sampson, R.J., & Morenoff, J.D. (1997). Ecological perspectives on the neighborhood context of urban poverty: Past and present. In J. Brooks-Gunn, G.J. Duncan, & J.L. Aber (Eds.), *Neighborhood poverty: Policy implications in studying neighborhoods* (Vol. 2, pp. 1–22). New York: Russell Sage Foundation Press.

Sampson, R.J., Morenoff, J.D., & Gannon-Rowley, T. (2002). Assessing "neighborhood effects": Social processes and new directions in research. *Annual Review of Sociology, 28,* 442–478.

Sampson, R.J., & Raudenbush, S.W. (1999). Systematic social observation of public spaces: A new look at disorder in urban neighborhoods. *American Journal of Sociology, 105,* 603–651.

Sampson, R.J., & Raudenbush, S.W. (2004). Seeing disorder: Neighborhood stigma and the social construction of "broken windows." *Social Psychology Quarterly, 67,* 319.

Sampson, R.J., Raudenbush, S.W., & Earls, F. (1997). Neighborhoods and violent crime: A multilevel study of collective efficacy. *Science, 277,* 918–924.

Sampson, R.J., & Sharkey, P. (2008). Neighborhood selection and the social reproduction of concentrated racial inequality. *Demography, 45,* 1–29.

Sampson, R.J., Sharkey, P., & Raudenbush, S.W. (2008). Durable effects of concentrated disadvantage on verbal ability of African-American children. *Proceedings of the National Academy of Science, 105,* 845–852.

Sanbonmatsu, L., Kling, J.R., Duncan, G.J., & Brooks-Gunn, J. (2006). Neighborhoods and academic achievement: Results from the Moving to Opportunity experiment. *Journal of Human Resource, 41,* 649–691.

Sastry, N., & Pebley, A.R. (2003). Neighborhood and family effects on children's health in Los Angeles (Working Paper DRU-240011-LAFANS). Santa Monica, CA: RAND Corporation.

Scott-Little, C., Kagan, S.L., & Frelow, V.S. (2006). Conceptualization of readiness and the content of early learning standards: The intersection of policy and research? *Early Childhood Research Quarterly, 21,* 153–173.

Shaw, C., & McKay, H. (1942). *Juvenile delinquency and urban areas.* Chicago: Chicago University Press.

Small, M.L. (2009). *Unanticipated gains: Origins of network inequality in everyday life.* New York: Oxford University Press.

Tienda, M. (1991). Poor people and poor places: Deciphering neighborhood effects on poverty outcomes. In J. Huber (Ed.), *Macro–micro linkages in sociology* (pp. 244–262). Thousand Oaks, CA: Sage Publication.

U.S. Environmental Protection Agency. (2000). *National air pollutant emissions trends, 1900–1998.* Research Triangle Park, NC: Office of Air Quality Planning and Standards.

Vandell, D.L. (2004). Early child care: The known and the unknown. *Merrill-Palmer Quarterly, 50,* 387–414.

Votruba-Drzal, E., Coley, R.L., & Chase-Lansdale, P.L. (2004). Child care and low-income children's development: Direct and moderated effects. *Child Development, 75,* 296–312.

Walter R. McDonald & Associates, Inc. (2009). *SPARK final evaluation report* (Technical Report). Washington, DC: Author.

Wilson, W.J. (1987). *The truly disadvantaged: The inner city, the underclass, and public policy.* Chicago: University of Chicago Press.

Xue, Y., Leventhal, T., Brooks-Gunn, J., & Earls, F. (2005). Neighborhood residence and mental health problems of 5- to 11-year-olds. *Archives of General Psychiatry, 62,* 1–10.

Xue, Y., Leventhal, T., Brooks-Gunn, J., & Earls, F. (2009). Changes in aggressive behavior from age 5 through age 17: Neighborhood influence. Manuscript in preparation, Columbia University.

IV

Policy Perspective

12

Governance and Transition

Sharon Lynn Kagan and Kristie Kauerz

Governance refers to how governments and organizations guide and manage their functions, whereas *transitions* conventionally relate to what young children and their families experience as they move from one locus to another. The former concept essentially deals with the decision making and management of collective goods and services; the latter is essentially a personal, if not private, matter. Governance is the purview of political scientists and organizational theorists, whereas transitions garner attention from experts in pedagogical theory and human and community development. Governance has barely been addressed in the early childhood literature, whereas transition (or the lack thereof) has been the subject of much investment and scholarship.

Although these two constructs are disparate, we suggest that they are indeed related and that their relationship is an important one. Contemporary governance approaches in early childhood education intend to create consistency, predictability, and continuity across programs and systems, just as efforts to address transitions intend to create consistency, predictability, and continuity for children and families as they move from one care and education setting to another. Done well, both governance and transition minimize problems related to the fragmentation and programmatic autonomy that exist in the early childhood field. We contend that without meaningful governance mechanisms, it will continue to be difficult to sustain consistent, effective transitions for young children and their families. Furthermore, unless attention is given to the various transitions that children experience throughout early childhood, effective governance will remain elusive.

In this chapter, we focus on the structural rationales for transitions by examining the ways in which governance can—and, in some places, does—meaningfully support effective transitions. Whether we consider governance from a domestic or an international perspective, two structural challenges affect transition: governance *within* the early care and education system spanning the time from birth to school entry and governance *between* the early care and education system (or nonsystem, as the case may be) and the primary education system.

We distinguish governance from other coordinative efforts by its properties of authority and accountability (Kagan & Kauerz, 2009). Furthermore, we discuss not only *structures* of governance—the agencies or entities that are organized to govern—but also specific *tools* of governance—the processes or instruments of action that are used to guide the management of various programs. Because knowledge of one aspect enhances knowledge of the other, we don both a domestic and an international lens to illuminate the relationship between governance and transitions.

We begin by reviewing the evolution of early childhood governance in the United States, highlighting how traditional approaches to governance have exacerbated transitions in early childhood education. We then turn to a discussion of more recent governance efforts, both in the United States and in other countries, that bring intentional focus to, and influence, issues of transition and from which the field may glean important insights.

THE UNITED STATES: TRADITIONAL APPROACHES TO GOVERNANCE

Although government is not the same as governance, the United States' national ethos toward the governance of early education is deeply embedded in historic ideas about the appropriate role of government in family life. Because they had escaped religious and governmental tyranny, American pioneers fervently respected the independence and privacy of the family. Antipathy toward a strong federal government and a preference for decentralized and privatized decision making constrained public engagement in services for normative populations of young children, as well as delayed the establishment of functional governance structures to oversee such services. Parents, who were seen as the foremost influencers of their children's development, were regarded as both rightful and effective consumers of a market-driven system, selecting whether and when they wished to enroll their children in early education programs. Parents governed choices for their children, and only limited governance external to the family was needed. Given this ethos, and the fact that, unlike the situation in primary and secondary schools, attendance was not compulsory in early childhood education programs, the programs grew in the private sector and remained inconspicuously remote from government purview.

Traditional Governance Structures: Siloed Programs

When efforts to govern early childhood education emerged, they took the form of program regulation and fiscal oversight of individual programs. Under these conditions, each program was *siloed*, with its own policy mechanisms, operational structures, policy tools, and decision-making processes.

The reasons for the establishment of siloed approaches to governance are best understood by examining the evolution of American early childhood public policy. Historically, significant programmatic involvement by the government took place during national crises—World War I, the Great Depression, and World War II—when embryonic systems of child care were established. These efforts were abolished after the crises ended, and they left a limited legacy. Another crisis, the War on Poverty, precipitated significant federal engagement in early education via the establishment of the nation's Head Start program. Authorized and appropriated by Congress, Head Start accorded parents an unprecedented role in the program's governance at the local level. Direct programmatic governance also is apparent in the large-scale publicly funded U.S. Armed Forces Child Care Program that was established to serve the needs of a specific population: military personnel and their families. Instilled with both strong authority and accountability, both programs are often regarded as closed systems in that they are quasi-contained, independently funded, and regulated efforts.

Meanwhile, state-funded prekindergarten (pre-K) programs proliferated rapidly, fueled in large part by the practical and political desires to improve children's school readiness and subsequent success in the K–12 system. The growth of pre-K programs is further evidence of the reliance on traditional approaches to governance whereby discrete or siloed programs have been and are being established. The vast majority of these pre-K programs are administered by state departments of education, and each one has its own staff, regulations, performance standards, monitoring mechanisms, and governance strategies. Furthermore, whether they are funded through the state school finance formula, an earmarked line item, or a special fund, the fiscal authority and accountability for these programs often resides separate from other funding streams and early education programs.

These forms of direct sponsorship of programs have not entirely ignored transition. Indeed, when we recall the history of Head Start and the research and demonstration efforts that are associated closely with it, we see a very strong commitment to transition and continuity. In fact, arguably the most significant transition work in the United States over the past 3 decades has been inspired by the national Head Start program. Despite this achievement, it is critical for us to underscore that most of the transition efforts sponsored by Head Start have addressed the linkages between Head Start and public schools, with the goal of easing children's transition to school, thereby sustaining gains made in Head Start. The linkages were designed to embrace the public schools; linkages with other early education programs, while they were not prohibited, were not the focus of the transition efforts. In other words, the focus was on establishing linkages *between* a single early childhood education program and the local elementary schools, not on establishing linkages *within* the system that were targeted to children from birth until their entry into school.

Within the military, the idea of transition took on another patina. Because military families tend to be highly mobile, transitions were regarded primarily as supports to children and families as they moved from one setting to another. A systematic approach links military families with family-run child care, child care centers, after-school programs, and resource and referral entities. Undergirded by a strong and well-enforced set of standards, within-military transitions have gained outstanding attention. Efforts also exist to support children and families as they transition from military to civilian life.

Despite those and other efforts to address transitions, traditional programmatic and siloed approaches to governance historically have not provided large-scale or systematic mechanisms for bridging a child's movement from one program to another. Thus, within the traditional structures of governance—individual mechanisms guiding and regulating the work of individual programs—the onus has been on the local program to create linkages with other early childhood care and education programs, as well as with local public schools. The result has been that issues of transition have been handled in isolation (e.g., an individual Head Start program creates a relationship with the local school district to assist the child in her transition from child care to public school).

Advancing Governance in the United States: An Increasing Attention to Transition

By any account, over the past 25 years the investment in early childhood education has dramatically increased, and there has been an unprecedented proliferation of programs. The combination of more public dollars flowing directly into early childhood programs from every level of government and the expansion of the role of the private sector has brought a growing recognition that siloed programs and independent services were not efficient in terms of their administration and financing. Nor were they effectively able to support the transitions that children and families must make. In response to this deficiency, the early childhood field used several diverse policy approaches that directly influenced how early childhood programs were funded, monitored, and administered. In effect, though not necessarily by intention, these approaches affected transitions in diverse ways that need to be understood as a prelude for discussing the contemporary transitions context.

In the first approach—the use of policy tools or instruments—the government used its authority to monitor and direct resource utilization, with effects on publicly funded programs and the vast array of early childhood services that exist in the public and private sectors. Although they are not necessarily new, these policy tools gained increasing currency as early childhood programs expanded. The second approach—the use of increasingly formalized forums for collaborative planning and decision making—differed in both genesis and range. The collaborative efforts were established primarily at state and local levels and sought to affect an array of early childhood programs. A third approach relied neither on tools nor on coordinating bodies, but on voluntary mechanisms that were focused largely on quality enhancements. Each of these approaches, in its own way, affected the conceptualization and implementation of transition. The approaches had both an individual impact and a tremendous collective impact on transitions. Taken together, the approaches shifted the zeitgeist from one that focused on transitions' creation of a dyadic relationship between two entities to one in which transitions are now regarded as far more complex, multifaceted interactions among diverse programs, institutions, and systems.

Policy Tools: A First Approach Governance and Transition

As early childhood services burgeoned, efforts to improve access and quality emerged in both the public and private sectors. Drawing on experiences in other fields, the government put some of its policy tools into play. Here we discuss three potent tools—regulatory oversight, subsidies, and tax credits—that had differential impacts on transition.

Regulatory Oversight   Because the vast majority of early education is not directly sponsored by government and is highly decentralized, government has influenced programs primarily through regulation and the establishment of rules and standards that specify expected behaviors or compliance benchmarks. In early childhood, such regulation provides a minimum set of criteria related to health, safety, program facilities, and staffing to which early education programs are expected to adhere in order to be licensed by the state or local authority. Examples in the early education field include the regulation of child care facilities, compulsory school attendance, and teacher certification requirements. Such regulation is problematic on several counts: It frequently falls short of quality standards and often legally exempts large numbers of programs, particularly programs that operate for only a few hours a day or that function in schools or religious facilities. All too often, regulations are not strictly monitored, and the reporting systems for tracking violations are insufficient, if not altogether absent. It is important to note that few, if any, regulations attend to issues that are related to transition. Even when they do focus on transition, the multiple layers of regulations—including regulations by federal, state, and local agencies and by various entities within each level of government—often contradict one another and add great complexity to the goals of efficiency and continuity. Because transitions are not seen as a crucial or manageable variable, they typically fall outside the purview of most federal, state, and local regulatory systems.

Subsidies to Individuals   In accordance with Americans' historical preference for making privatized, family-based decisions regarding young children, and in order to simultaneously try to meet the growing need of many families for safe child care arrangements, the federal government adopted a policy tool when it instituted the Child Care and Development Block Grant (CCDBG) in 1990. The CCDBG represents an effort by the federal government to address the social problem of families' growing need and demand for child care without establishing wholly new, independent programs. The CCDBG permits each state the flexibility to develop child care programs and policies that best meet the needs of its children and families. Furthermore, the CCDBG supports parental choice, empowering eligible working families to choose the child care arrangement that best suits their needs. The grant is a voucher-like policy tool that provides federal and state funds to indirectly support early childhood programs and directly support eligible families, vesting primary control in the hands of families rather than in any specific early care and education program. Although subsidies govern eligibility and payment levels, they do not directly govern the provision or quality of early care and education programs or services. Therefore, subsidization has done little to foster transitions among the programs or services for which the subsidies are used.

Subsidies inhibit families' ability to establish seamless early care and education for their young children. By design, subsidies are intended to make child care services more affordable to families. It is not surprising, then, that if a program raises its rates, parents often are forced to seek a less expensive child care option elsewhere that will be covered partly or entirely by the subsidy. As parents move from one program to another seeking more affordable care, the child's continuity of care is disrupted. In addition, subsidies are provided only for the period during which families are eligible to receive them and, in many states, eligibility lasts for only a short time. Furthermore, coordinating with other subsidy programs or other eligibility-based services (e.g., Head Start, state-funded pre-K) often becomes a burden, if not an outright barrier, for families.

As a tool of governance, subsidies hold little sway over the quality or performance of early childhood programs. By seating the decision about how and where the subsidy is used with families, subsidies can produce competitive environments that lower the costs and therefore the quality of services. In short, subsidies as a governing tool for early childhood education are inherently contradictory to the very ethos of transitions—to provide a predictable mechanism for continuity and stability of high quality care.

One potential exception to this is the emerging use of *conditional cash transfers* (CCTs), both domestically and internationally. Not automatic, CCTs are a form of subsidy in which funds are given to recipients conditional upon their changing their behavior in accordance with the policy's desired intent. Used when rapid change is sought and when individual behavior is deemed alterable, CCTs have demonstrated remarkable success and are gaining currency. They have proven to be an extremely effective tool to link diverse programs and to achieve programmatic and policy efficiencies (Levy, 2006), so they may hold promise for advancing transitions.

Tax Credits   Like subsidy policies and vouchers, tax credits emphasize the responsibility of families and the private sector to provide early childhood services. By using tax credits, the government can pursue its objectives of financing and supporting early childhood education—not by spending tax dollars directly, but by allowing individuals to keep and spend money that they otherwise would owe the government. In the realm of early childhood education, the federal Child and Dependent Care Tax Credit is the most prominent example of this policy tool. It serves as the second-largest source of federal child care assistance (National Center for Children in Poverty, n.d.). This tax credit reduces the amount of tax that working families with child care expenses are required to pay. Families at all income levels are eligible for the credit, but low-income families benefit the least because their incomes are typically too low for them to pay taxes.

The use of tax credits as a policy tool to finance and provide services offers government little to no influence or authority over the early care and education programs themselves. In turn, this means that tax credits have little to no influence over issues of transition. Because tax credits are claimed by individual families, there is virtually no way for government to systematically identify the early care and education programs that the families are gaining accessing to and, therefore, to instill an intentional focus on transitions. Furthermore, the Child and Dependent Care Tax Credit is claimed annually, so it does not guarantee long-term continuous support for families that are seeking care.

Emergence of Formalized Coordination: A Second Approach to Governance and Transition

In addition to the increased use of policy tools to influence and govern early childhood services, the past 2 decades have been characterized by an expansion of efforts to establish formal collaborative entities. The efforts were fueled by the need to establish more efficient and cost-effective coordination across programs and services and to improve effective transitions for individual children and families. The coordination efforts were intended to serve a convening function, providing a venue in which multiple programs—in some cases, exclusively within the public sector and, in other cases, across both public and private sectors—could work together to achieve common goals. Some of the collaborative bodies, including children's cabinets, partnerships, and advisory councils, were established within government, while others were convened and managed outside government.

Children's Cabinets Governors around the nation have convened children's cabinets to promote and formalize collaborative planning and action across state agencies and state-funded programs. Such cabinets include the ranking executives of multiple government agencies that are responsible for programs and services relating to young children. Most often, membership includes a state's secretaries of education, social or human services, health, and welfare; in some cases, leadership from economic development, labor, employment, and transportation agencies are also involved. In 2009, at least 22 states had children's cabinets or similar entities (Rennie Center for Education Research & Policy, 2009). The scope of effort, frequency of convening, and level of staff support vary widely, but typically children's cabinets address similar issues, including alignment of standards, allocation and streamlining of funding, and collaborative planning for program development and implementation. Children's cabinets also attend to issues of transition and continuity across programs. Despite the prestigious membership and collaborative goals of children's cabinets, however, most of them lack the authority and accountability to implement and enforce their recommendations.

Partnerships A partnership approach brings together representatives from government, business and industry, and the early childhood community to forge a vision and to plan for service delivery. In some cases, the work is directed toward the development and implementation of a new, often large-scale program or funding stream within a given state or community. Partnerships frequently are embedded in the legislation that funds the program and are not transitory entities. In general, one of the key goals of these partnerships is to provide a formal venue for already established programs to plan and work together to realize efficiencies, improve quality, and reach more children and families. In many cases, partnerships establish boards or councils at both state and local levels; these groups may hold the authority to develop standards and other policies that determine which local programs and services are eligible to receive funds and other technical resources from the partnership. Many partnerships' standards and funding plans place high priority on individual programs ensuring effective transitions for children and families. Such partnerships have multiple strengths. They engage a broad coalition of constituencies to advance early care and education; they provide meaningful planning and oversight of substantial funding sources; and they encourage and, in many cases, require the creation and sustenance of meaningful linkages among preschool programs in communities and between preschools and public schools. Partnerships' primary limitation is that they typically do not have authority over, and accountability for, all early childhood services within a state or locale. Thus, they are limited in their ability to govern or bring excellence and full cohesion to the array of early childhood efforts, including the early elementary grades.

Advisory Councils   Early childhood advisory councils blend qualities of children's cabinets and partnerships. Like children's cabinets, they often are convened or endorsed by government, and like partnerships, they include key stakeholders from both the public and private sectors among their members. Recent prominent examples of advisory councils include some of the coordinating bodies that were established by states to guide the Early Childhood Comprehensive System Grants funded by the Maternal and Child Health Bureau. Other examples include the multitude of special task forces and study commissions established by legislation or executive order each year. Although these councils may be effective in meeting short-term needs to advise a time-limited grant and/or to craft long-term strategic plans, in general they lack any authority to implement meaningful change and have not been durable.

Although advisory councils have long been called for in federal programs, with the advent of the Improving Head Start for School Readiness Act of 2007, there is a new optimism about both their longevity and their potential to effect meaningful change. Specifically, states are being called upon to establish collaborative bodies that foster linkages among, and transitions between, child-serving agencies, programs, and services. In so doing, formal state-level mechanisms to address transitions and linkages are being developed. Moreover, they are being regarded as durable entities that will improve the coordination and quality of programs and services for children from birth to the age at which they enter school.

In addition, the American Recovery and Reinvestment Act of 2009 will provide $100 million to support states' councils. The responsibility of the early childhood advisory council in each state is to lead the development of a high-quality comprehensive system of early childhood development and care for children from birth to age 5 that ensures statewide coordination and collaboration among the wide range of early childhood programs and services in the state. The federal legislation requires each state's council membership to include representatives from Head Start, state departments of health and education, local schools, and the Interagency Coordinating Council for Part C of the Individuals with Disabilities Education Improvement (IDEA) Act of 2004 (PL 108-446). The councils are intended to create a continuity of services for young children and to identify opportunities for, and barriers to, collaboration and coordination among programs and agencies.

The potential impact of these advisory councils on issues of transition is immense. They are asked to establish an integrated data collection infrastructure for public early childhood education and development programs and services throughout the state. In addition, the councils promote professional development for teachers and preparation of all early childhood programs by assessing the status of the early childhood workforce and the capacity of state institutions to train early childhood educators. Because the legislation has a defined scope of programs and services for children from birth to age 5, transitions within the early care and education system stand to gain the most. However, national organizations and some states themselves are planning to expand council priorities to define and embrace early childhood programs and services for children from birth through third grade (Satkowski, 2009). If the expansion of services occurs, states' early childhood advisory councils will be well positioned to profoundly affect both the transitions within the early care and education system and the transitions between early care and education and public schools.

Now that more comprehensive and formalized coordinating bodies have emerged, the construct of transitions is taking hold. Although programmatic boundaries are quite complex, understandings of and approaches to children's early development must transcend them. Children's cabinets, partnerships, and advisory councils are purposely designed to address transition and continuity, and, furthermore, are charged with visionary and planning functions that often are associated with governance.

Voluntary Cross-Sector Mechanisms: A Third Approach to Governance and Transition

In addition to policy tools and formalized coordination, the past 2 decades have seen increasingly prominent and sophisticated efforts to use voluntary mechanisms to influence the organization and management of early childhood programs and services. Such voluntary mechanisms have emerged in both the public and private sectors and have affected transitions in important ways. There are numerous examples, but arguably, foremost among them is the accreditation system that was developed in the private sector by the National Association for the Education of Young Children (NAEYC, 2008). Accreditation is a voluntary mechanism in which early childhood programs may engage to improve their program quality. Programs undergo a rigorous self-assessment and strive to improve their quality, followed by a visit from a third-party accreditator who verifies their quality. The programs that meet the high standards set by NAEYC receive accreditation. Although it is voluntary, the accreditation process demands that programs meet high standards, including a strong commitment to effective transitions. The idea that children need stable, supportive relationships to help them navigate their world permeates the early childhood program accreditation standards of the NAEYC; of its 10 standards, 3 are explicit about the need for transitions. The first standard focuses on relationships and requires early childhood programs to help children cultivate strong and stable relationships with others so that each child feels like a part of a larger community (NAEYC, 2008). The second and third accreditation standards that deal with transition focus on developing and maintaining "collaborative relationships with each child's family to foster children's development in all settings" and state that an effective early childhood program will "establish and maintain reciprocal relationships with agencies and institutions that can support it in achieving goals for...children's transitions" (NAEYC, p. 2). In the accreditation standards, transitions (both within early care and education and between early childhood education and K–12 systems) are substantively integrated as a critical component of the voluntary quality initiative.

Another example of a voluntary mechanism that urges attention to transition is state Quality Rating and Improvement Systems (QRISs). QRISs are voluntary in most states, and many of them include in their program standards the need for a comprehensive transition plan. For example, the standards on families and communities in Pennsylvania's QRIS require that programs focus on transitions in order to meet the quality standard (Pennsylvania Office of Child Development and Early Learning, 2009a). The extent to which the program must attend to transitions, however, varies at each tier of quality. It should also be noted that these programs are *voluntary*, thus reinforcing our earlier point that the traditional tools of governance have a limited reach.

In sum, the three approaches to new governance in the early childhood field—policy tools, formalized coordination, and voluntary mechanisms—have altered public management in rather fundamental ways. In particular, these endeavors have severed the financing of government action from the actual delivery of public services and have created complex relationships that merge the activities of federal, state, and local governments with public and private organizations in increasingly inventive ways (Salamon, 2002). Each approach to governance has influenced the transitions landscape in its own way.

LINKING GOVERNANCE AND TRANSITION IN THE UNITED STATES: 21st CENTURY STRUCTURES

With these three approaches serving as a platform, the contemporary governance landscape is rapidly changing, as are new approaches to transition. These new approaches to governance represent significant advances not only in their authority and accountability functions but also in their intentionality and comprehensiveness in keeping transitions front and center. We now discuss some of the new governance structures and analyze their effectiveness in fostering smooth transitions.

New Governance Structures

In order to increase their authority and accountability, a small number of states have undertaken a bold restructuring of government to integrate the administrative structures and functions of traditionally disparate agencies, funding streams, and programs. In general, states have embarked on three different structural approaches to administrative integration: 1) *stand-alone administrative integration,* wherein an altogether new state agency is created and given authority for early care and education 2) *blended administrative integration,* wherein a new entity is sanctioned by the governor and expected to work across existing agencies; and 3) *subsumed administrative integration,* wherein multiple programs and services are consolidated into a subunit of an existing state agency (e.g., a division or department). We will discuss each approach in more detail.

Stand-Alone Administrative Integration
The creation of an entirely new stand-alone state agency that is devoted solely to young children is perhaps the most dramatic new approach to governance that promotes transitions. The Massachusetts State Legislature established a stand-alone Department of Early Education and Care to oversea services for young children across settings. The department has the same level of authority as the Department of Elementory and Secondary Education.

A stand-alone state agency may be the most dramatic approach to reforming governance yet its effects on transition are mixed. On the one hand, a new agency can profoundly improve how transitions *within* the birth-to-school-entry system are viewed and addressed. Because there is a single governing board, the discontinuities among multiple programs, services, and standards can be more efficiently remedied. On the other hand, an entirely new and independent state agency devoted to early care and education may exacerbate discontinuities between early care and education and the K–12 system. At an extreme, especially when budgets are tight, the new agency and the K–12 agency must vie—often against one another—for limited state dollars and for prominence on political agendas. Despite these challenges, the creation of stand-alone early care and education agencies represents innovative and meaningful governance-based efforts to improve transitions among the array of programs and services that children experience in their earliest years.

Blended Administrative Integration
A second recent approach to governance is the creation of an office to lead and manage early childhood education efforts *across* state departments.

In this case, the office brings together management and staffing functions, but funding streams remain separate.

The most prominent example of blended administrative ntegration is The Pennsylvania Office of Child Development and Learning (see case study this chapter). Pennsylvanias approach to governance has provided an excellent platform for advancing linkages and transitions of many types, including common early leaning standards that are linked to the state's K–12 standards, common training and professional development experiences, common data systems, and common approaches to evaluation and monitoring across programs within the early childhood field. The office also works closely with the education, health, and welfare departments to promote continuity of experiences for children as they move into public schools or as they navigate diverse delivery systems. This blended administrative approach's effectiveness in fostering transitions is clear, as is its short-term governing effectiveness.

Subsumed Administrative Integration   A third recent approach to early childhood governance involves bringing together complementary programs, services, and initiatives, or subsuming them under a new or existing division within an existing state agency. The consolidated division or unit provides a unified staff to administer the variety of programs and often provides unified monitoring, regulatory, and enforcement authorities. Prominent examples of subsumed administrative administration integration can be found in Maryland and Washington D.C. The approach provides a consolidated platform from which to align and coordinate policies and practices related to transition. In Maryland, for example, it has facilitated the development of common approaches to assessment, accountability, and data management. A consolidated division or unit is often easier to implement than a stand-alone agency or one enacted through legislation, but it may be vulnerable over time to shifts in agency leadership or departmental priorities.

As our review suggests, although the importance of transitions has occupied a place on the practice agenda for quite some time, transitions have historically been given low priority on the governance agenda. Recent structural advances and policy tools are beginning to alter this stance and acknowledge the importance of transitions. In so doing, they may instantiate the importance of transitions and therein represent a significant advancement in the transition trajectory domestically. We now turn our attention to international matters.

GOVERNANCE AND TRANSITION IN OTHER COUNTRIES

As the United States continues on its path of envisioning and instituting bold new governance reforms in early childhood, an examination of how other countries support transition within early childhood programs and services provides a provocative perspective. Given the rich histories and experiences of other nations, the discussion will focus less on the policy structures and tools—though they will be addressed—and more on examples of governance efforts that promote different kinds of transitions.

Similarities and Differences

Unlike the United States, most other industrialized countries have long acknowledged the importance of early childhood education and have fostered government involvement in both the provision and administration of such services. Reflecting their national histories, particularly post–World War II, when pronatalist stances emerged, most European countries are unequivocal about the necessity of nurturing young children and have taken systemic approaches to early education. In so doing, they have created coherent regulatory, staffing, funding, and governance policies (Kamerman, 2000; Organization for Economic Co-operation and Development, 2001) that established aligned programs and services across the early years. Europe is distinct from the United States in that its commitment to the development and embedded continuity of services for young children is a durable component of national values and policies.

Despite their acknowledged commitments to young children, European countries vary in how they organize and carry out governance of early childhood services (United Nations Educational Scientific and Cultural Organization, 2006). There are two major approaches. In the first approach, services for young children are divided, generally on the basis of the children's age, between education and welfare systems. Preschool, serving children from 3 years to school entry, is handled by education ministries, while services for younger children are administered by social welfare or health ministries. Although there are efforts to establish linkages between the ministries, the dual administration of early childhood services often makes it challenging. This bifurcated structure is prevalent today in many countries, but it is giving way to the second and increasingly popular approach. That approach, like trends in the United States, lodges all services for young children in a single ministry so that administration is unified and a commitment to transition is embedded in the structure.

However, countries are moving to decentralize their authorities, allocating more decision-making power to local levels, thus rendering commitments to transitions potentially idiosyncratic. In some cases, national ministries are focusing on the development of broad parameters, leaving implementation to localities. Functions that are being carried out at the national level tend to include determination of age eligibility, regulation, financing, and quality assurance. Moreover, in some countries, there is an explicit commitment at the national level to collect data and to monitor and evaluate programs. The treatment of curricula and transition is often less clearly specified at the national level. Typically, and consonant with trends toward decentralization, national governments establish broad frameworks for local authorities to follow, including the specification of overall aims and objectives and staff qualifications. Where decentralization is prominent, the potency of a federal structure linking primary and preprimary education, usually under one ministry, becomes an important elixir of transition and continuity.

There are several major points related to transition and alignment in this context. First, although transition and alignment often are not mentioned as specific functions in most countries, the approaches they adopt indicate that fostering transitions for young children as they move into formal schooling is a primary concern. Such concern, as we have noted, is expressed in the structural alignments that have taken place at the ministerial level. Second, the movement toward decentralization, which follows decades of more centralized control, leaves an uncertain legacy for transition. Loosened central control has enabled local authorities to experiment with new approaches to administration and governance. Third, in some countries where international donors are active, international organizations are recognizing the importance of transitions and are working with ministries to inculcate programs and policies that promote transitions. In short, it is hard to generalize about the global state of transition and governance except to note that, as early education rises on the international agenda, it is likely to be accompanied by a focus on transition.

Transitions in Action Internationally

In addition to the direct governance approaches to transition that we have presented, there are important examples of indirect governance approaches that advance transitions. They are documented well elsewhere (Arnold, Bartlett, Gowani, & Merali, 2007; Neuman, 2002), and it is not our intent to chronicle such efforts here. Rather, we don the lens advanced in this volume and highlight some of the most germane international efforts that support pedagogical, programmatic, and policy alignment. In so doing, we will underscore the importance of the governance structure to all three forms of alignment. Moreover, we aim to provide some potentially transportable examples of effective governance strategies that might enrich both domestic and international transition practices in the areas of pedagogical, programmatic, and policy alignment.

Pedagogical Alignment   Numerous examples of pedagogical alignment exist around the world, and governments are taking seminal roles in advancing them. Accompanying the curriculum are learning materials, professional development materials, and information about children's development that span the ages and levels of education. In countries around the world, early learning standards are being developed for children from birth into primary school; in some cases these standards are accompanied by related curricula for children, parents, and teachers. Indeed, this strategy provides embedded alignment of the essential components of early childhood pedagogy. In such cases, governments are taking unified stances to promote transitions across ministries and agencies, fostering a continuity of experience for all of the children in the country.

In addition to pedagogical strategies that promote transitions directly for children, there are some important practices that do so indirectly, most frequently by educating the adults in children's lives about the importance of transition. One common strategy used internationally to promote pedagogical alignment occurs through the professional development opportunities that are afforded by governments to teachers; instructional staff; and, sometimes, parents. Governments do not stand alone as providers of professional development opportunities, however. The Step-by-Step program, which operates in countless countries, provides support to teachers as they adopt child-centered approaches to pedagogy using appropriate developmental theories and strategies. These efforts are designed to bridge the gap between preprimary and primary schools by providing continuous and aligned pedagogical approaches for the teachers of children from birth to age 8 (Cortazar, this volume). Step by Step is an example of a multinational approach to advancing the continuity of pedagogical knowledge and practice between preschool and primary schools, thereby facilitating transitions for children from one care and education setting to another. It also demonstrates that just as governance efforts can universalize a commitment to transition, nongovernmental efforts can inspire action at the pedagogical, programmatic, and, potentially, policy levels.

Programmatic Alignment   Transcending the alignment that needs to take place at the pedagogical level, transitions are best achieved when there is alignment among the home and family and among the multiple services that are needed or used by children and their parents. From a governance perspective, such efforts are often established and administered at the ministerial level, with local entities taking responsibility for implementation. Throughout Europe and other parts of the world, examples of programmatic alignment abound. The efforts, which take different forms, typically represent concerted outreach by early childhood programs to families; in addition, countries routinely provide for linkages among services.

Policy Alignment   International efforts provide some outstanding models for using policy to advance transitions. In part, their success results from the explicit attention they accord transition, but more often than not, it is a result of embedding policy efforts that promote transition in the implicit policy approaches that are used. Transition is not seen as an add-on to generic early childhood policy; it is part of it. Nations use diverse strategies to implement the policy. Some create ombudsmen or council offices for children that work to promote continuity and children's rights (Hodgkin & Newell, 1996). Others, such as Sweden and France, adopt more comprehensive strategies and provide patent examples of multiple types of alignment.

Sweden's governance system, described in the case study in this chapter, embeds a commitment to policy alignment that fully supports multiple types of transitions for children of various ages. Specifically, Sweden's Ministry of Education is responsible for the education of all children from ages 1 to 18 years. To that end, the ministry sets broad goals and benchmarks and monitors progress toward them; local municipalities are responsible for the implementation of these objectives and pay particular attention to the needs of children and families in their catchment areas. Despite the decentralized approach to governance, services for children are linked structurally across the age spectrum. In particular, these policy underpinnings permit the ministry and the municipalities to focus on alignment between preschool and primary school practices (Segal, case study, this chapter). At the preschool and primary school level, such alignment takes multiple forms that promote both pedagogical and programmatic transition: the preschool class, the national curriculum, workforce policies, and monitoring (Segal). The preschool class is a bridge for 6-year-olds from child care to primary school, attesting to Sweden's policy commitment to the holistic development of children and to their smooth transitions from one setting to another.

By contrast, in France, no single ministry is responsible for the age range that the ministry in Sweden supports. Instead, responsibility for children prior to the age of formal school entry is divided among three ministries: The Ministry of Education is responsible for 3- to 5-year-olds, and services for younger children are split between the Ministry of Health and Solidarity and the Ministry of Employment, Social Cohesion, and Housing (Newman, 2007). Although this structure poses a challenge to linkages across the full age spectrum, its limitations are recognized and there are policies in place to counteract the ministerial division. For example, France links policy by establishing the primary cycle that covers the latter years of preschool and the early years of formal schooling. Policies call for the development in the primary cycle of unified national objectives and expectations via a national curriculum and standards that span the age spectrum, therein promoting pedagogical alignment. Complementing the national primary school cycle, municipal early childhood coordinators focus on linking the early childhood programs to the primary school system and assisting families as they transition from child care to preschool, thereby advancing programmatic alignment (Tarrant, this volume). The point is that pedagogical and programmatic alignment can be fostered irrespective of ministerial structures by establishing polices that are based on sound developmental principles. In other countries, policy seems to have trumped structure up till now. The degree to which their system promotes embedded and durable approaches to transition and the degree to which such a stance would be germane to the United States is an open question.

CONCLUSION

As all the examples presented in this chapter demonstrate, the relationship between governance and transitions is a tricky one. Governance is intended to create durability, while transition is intended to allow for fluidity. One can certainly exist absent the other, but when governance and transitions exist as part and parcel of each other, children experience the best of both worlds. Although we have presented a range of examples in this chapter, governance structures, tools, and strategies are not easily transported to different contexts. Governance solutions rely heavily on countries' and states' macro sociopolitical contexts, fiscal structures,

and cultural norms. Nonetheless, the discussion of both domestic and international governance and transitions herein illuminates important lessons. This review suggests that states
and countries could learn much from one another regarding different policy approaches to,
and tools for, advancing transition.

There is not, nor will there ever be, a perfect governance solution, especially one that con-
clusively attends to transitions. Transitions will always occur in children's lives. Moving into unknown contexts and having the skill and disposition to thrive in the midst of change, indeed, is
an important part of growing up. Similarly, no matter how governance is operationalized, there
always will be discontinuities between institutions and organizations. A single set of authorities
and accountabilities will never encompass a child's entire journey through life. For these reasons,
transitions and governance are strange bedfellows. Transitions should be planned for, and can
take shape, irrespective of the governance structure that is employed.

Case Study—The Pennsylvania Office of Child Development and Early Learning

Innovative Governance to Create Continuity Across Programs

Jeanne L. Reid

The Pennsylvania Office of Child Development and Early Learning (OCDEL) provides an
innovative structural solution to overcome the fragmented nature of the early care and
education programs that are commonly administered and found in state governments.
Created during 2004–2006, OCDEL, a joint initiative of the Departments of Education
and Public Welfare, brings together the administration of programs that previously were
spread across multiple subunits of the two departments. A chief goal of OCDEL is to
create "a seamless system of quality early education from birth to age 5" (Pennsylvania
Office of Child Development and Early Learning, 2008a). With strong support from the
state governor, OCDEL has made substantial progress toward promoting effective transitions across the many early learning environments that children experience.

General Description   OCDEL serves more than 350,000 children and has a budget of
$1.36 billion (Pennsylvania Office of Child Development and Early Learning, 2008b).
The deputy secretary of OCDEL reports to the secretaries of both departments, and the
staff are organized and housed as a single team. Both the Departments of Education
and Public Welfare fund OCDEL, bear responsibility for its programs and services,
and share ownership of the results. Their collaboration applies a rational, systematic
approach to cohesive and fiscally responsible programming. OCDEL's funding comes
from the two departments, but the deputy secretary administers it as a single, unified
entity (H. Dichter, personal communication, July 16, 2009).

OCDEL oversees a substantial portfolio of programs, including Child Care Certification
(licensing), Child Care Works (subsidized child care), Community Engagement, Early
Intervention from birth to age 5, Family Support (Nurse Family Partnership, Children's
Trust Fund, and Parent–Child Home program), Full-Day Kindergarten, Head Start
Supplemental Assistance, Keystone STARS/Keys to Quality, Pennsylvania Pre-K Counts,
and Public–Private Partnerships (Pennsylvania Office of Child Development and Early
Learning, 2009a). With the governor's active support, OCDEL's programs have grown
substantially in recent years. The Keystone STARS program, for example, has grown

fivefold, from 898 programs in 2003 to 4,708 programs in 2008–2009 (Pennsylvania Office of Child Development and Learning, 2008a). The state Head Start program, which began in 2004, serves 5,610 children. Child Care Works serves 140,971 children, up 40% from 2002–2003. Pre-K Counts enrolls 12,000 children and is one of several areas in which OCDEL was able to establish a new funding stream and program to address a service gap (H. Dichter, personal communication, July 16, 2009).

Implementation   OCDEL has promoted continuity in its early education programs in four ways: 1) the creation of administrative coherence across programs and the leveraging of resources among them, 2) the alignment of early learning standards and assessments from birth through second grade 3) the collection of extensive data on all children in publicly funded programs, and 4) an emphasis on accountability at both the program and policy levels.

First, OCDEL brought administrative coherence and priority to programs that had been scattered in various subunits of the Education or Public Welfare departments. For example, before OCDEL, the Early Intervention program from birth to age 3 had resided in the Department of Public Welfare and the Early Intervention program from ages 3–5 had resided in the Department of Education. Today, OCDEL administers both programs. OCDEL also created a single, unified subsidy system to serve all families that are eligible for Child Care Works. Previously, this program had been managed jointly through the Welfare Department's Income Maintenance program office and its Children, Youth, and Family program office. The system resulted in families receiving their eligibility determinations and counseling from different parts of the agency and providers experiencing different payment policies and schedules (H. Dichter, personal communication, July 16, 2009). Now, a family eligible for a child care subsidy visits a single Child Care Works office to apply for the subsidy and providers have a uniform approach to payment. Moreover, OCDEL uses a uniform approach to provide information to parents: Each county now has one entity with expertise and knowledge about all of the OCDEL-funded options for families (H. Dichter, personal communication, July 16, 2009).

The joint administration of related programs has created opportunities to leverage the state's resources across them. For example, the state's QRIS, called Keystone STARS, offers incentives to disparate child care providers to participate in a quality-improvement program. Providers' quality is measured on a 4-star scale. One incentive for child care providers to participate is that OCDEL awards funds for program improvement (Support and Merit Awards), the pursuit of staff educational credentials (Education and Retention Awards), and the serving of low-income children who also participate in Child Care Works (a subsidy add-on rate) (H. Dichter, personal communication, July 16, 2009). Child care facilities that enroll children in early intervention programs or Child Care Works are able to "count" these children to meet the minimal enrollments they need to qualify for the Support and Merit Awards. In addition, the T.E.A.C.H. Early Childhood scholarship and voucher college reimbursement programs, which support the education and training of child care providers, are available only to individuals who work at Keystone STARS sites. Finally, Pre-K Counts is open on a competitive basis to school districts, Head Start, licensed nursery schools, and *only* child care centers that have earned 3 or 4 Keystone STARS. Thus, efforts to improve quality in one area of early education (child care) enhance the supply of quality programs in another area (pre-K).

Second, OCDEL promotes continuity across early education programs by aligning the content of their instruction. Consistent threads that run throughout OCDEL's early education programs are the early learning standards from birth through second grade and the child assessment tools that are used across programs. As in many states, the alignment of OCDEL's early learning standards, as well as their connection to the state's elementary school standards (beginning in third grade), was unclear. To address this problem, OCDEL intensively studied the alignment of its standards and of assessments from birth through third grade. The results of the analysis pointed out strengths in Pennsylvania's approach to early learning and weaknesses that it needed to address in order to improve the coherence of content in the multiple early education programs administered by OCDEL. A task force has been formed to reconsider the standards and assessment strategy in light of this analysis.

At the same time, OCDEL promotes the use of the Ounce Scale and Work Sampling System child assessment tools in all of its programs through both subsidies and state-sponsored trainings. OCDEL's decision to pursue the consistent use of the same assessment tools across programs accomplishes the twin goals of persistent quality improvement and continuity in data collection. OCDEL is phasing in a requirement for its programs to use the assessment tools and then the data to drive quality improvement in their care and education of young children (H. Dichter, personal communication, July 16, 2009).

The statewide use of the assessment tools also serves the third piece of OCDEL's effort to create a seamless system of quality programs: an ambitious, longitudinal database on children's learning, the Early Learning Network (ELN). A multiyear initiative, the ELN is a growing repository for assessment data on young children who are involved in state-sponsored early care and education programs. All children receive unique identification numbers that follow them through their careers in the Pennsylvania public school system. Beginning in 2009–2010, Dichter explained, most OCDEL programs were required to use the Ounce Scale and Work Sampling System and to report the results to the ELN. State-sponsored Head Start programs, child care centers with at least 3 Keystone STARS, and public school pre-K programs were required to send their data to the ELN in 2009–2010. Pre-K Counts and early intervention programs have been reporting their data since 2008–2009. Also in 2009–2010, Dichter said, OCDEL began linking the data with demographic information regarding children and their families. Finally, in 2010–2011, the Nurse Family Partnership, Parent–Child Home Program, Early Head Start, and family and group homes with at least three Keystone STARS will begin participating. Over time, OCDEL plans to include all children, such as those in Child Care Works or in programs that have earned fewer than three STARS, in all its programs (H. Dichter, personal communication, July 16, 2009).

This ambitious project has taken on challenges regarding technology, cost, and privacy concerns and will continue to address issues related to the validity, reliability, and control of the appropriate use of the data. The effort will provide OCDEL with an ability to know and understand the experience and progress of children in its programs both across the state and across time that will be unsurpassed in the nation. OCDEL will be able to analyze how program, family, and teacher elements interact and relate to child outcomes. The data will enable OCDEL to make informed, cogent policy decisions regarding multiple programs' promises.

All three of these efforts—administrative coherence, aligned early learning standards and assessments, and comprehensive data gathering—support OCDEL's emphasis on accountability at both the program and the policy level. At the level of OCDEL's multiple programs, the use of standards and assessments can nurture instructional adjustments to foster children's progress, inspire curriculum improvement and professional development, and promote overall program quality through the thoughtful use of assessment data to help answer the question, "How are we doing?" At the policy level, the ELN will inform decisions regarding resource allocation. Finally, it will allow OCDEL to build a case publicly that it effectively serves children and families in Pennsylvania with a system of programs that coherently addresses the complex needs of its constituents.

Lessons Learned   When OCDEL began, it was given the responsibility to oversee a maze of early childhood programs that had disparate auspices and missions. Strong support from the governor was a critical component of its ability to take measurable steps toward creating continuity for children across the multiple programs that serve children in different ways. Harriet Dichter, the deputy secretary at OCDEL, also credits OCDEL's ability to articulate its ambitious vision and generate a clear road map for achieving it:

> You cannot get what you don't ask for, which means that you can-
> not create a bigger tent, a continuum of services, get more money,
> uphold higher standards and expectations, and support quality
> implementation if you don't have the vision for these things, articu-
> late them, and then put plans into place to help everyone make
> movement and share ownership to getting it done (personal com-
> munication, July 24, 2009).

To sustain support for the ambitious scope of its goals, OCDEL also needed to call attention to its achievements, both big and small, along the way. Indeed, the ability to conceptualize the vision as both a bold initiative with wide impact and an orchestra-tion of small parts that work concurrently to support the whole was critical. Dichter suggests, "You cannot do everything at once. But to the extent that it is essential to get buy in, you cannot work on only one part of the system or one program at a time, as that is alienating to people whose leadership support and skills you need." In the complex and sometimes turbulent process of fundamentally changing the governance of multiple programs, Dichter explains that perfection is not the goal: "Phasing in work is just fine, but be mindful that it is important to keep going and to make progress, and not to let the perfect world stand in the way of progress" (personal communica-tion, July 24, 2009).

Future Directions   One of OCDEL's priorities continues to be the inclusion of more Child Care Works programs in the ELN and the pursuit of quality improvements in low-quality programs that have only one or two Keystone STARS. OCDEL certainly has faced bureaucratic challenges, technological obstacles, and an increasingly difficult fiscal climate, but it plans to pursue its mission of systematically supporting cohesive, high-quality programs with singular focus.

Conclusion   A seamless education system is within Pennsylvania's reach largely because of the innovative governance structure that is embodied by OCDEL. Recognizing the notoriously fragmented nature of early childhood programs, OCDEL applies a rational, unified approach to build a cohesive system of quality programs. The system undoubtedly produces important efficiencies, but more important are the benefits for children, who are more likely to experience continuity in the program set-tings that support their learning and development. The coherence in administration, instructional content, data collection, and accountability that OCDEL fosters across its many programs are foundational components of successful transitions for young children in Pennsylvania.

Case Study—Early Childhood Governance in Sweden
Caroline Segal

Sweden has long been a pioneer in early childhood education, implementing comprehensive policies and innovative programming that promote alignment and transition between the early years and compulsory schooling. A clear indicator of this alignment is that all education for children ages 1–18 falls under the same administrative unit, the Ministry of Education (Clifford & Crawford, 2009). Due to Sweden's historical tradition of strong child and family policy, the process of administrative integration has been well received and the government has been able to focus on aligning preschool and compulsory school practices (Martin-Korpi, 2007).

Origins of Sweden's Integrated Early Childhood Governance   The government assumed a major role in the provision of early childhood services in 1975 when the National Board of Health and Welfare issued the Preschool Act, which required all municipalities to provide at least 525 hours of preschool education to all 6-year-old children. Over the years that followed, the government became increasingly involved in expansion efforts. In 1985, the ministry proposed a bill to provide all children ages 1–6 years with a preschool education as long as their parents were working or studying (Martin-Korpi, 2007).

In 1995, the government issued a more comprehensive revision of the Preschool Act that enforced the municipalities to put the proposed legislation into action (Martin-Korpi, 2007). The growth in the number of children served is a testament to the success of the revised act. Between 1970 and 1998, the number of children in full–time care increased tenfold, from 71,000 to 720,000. At the end of 1998, 73% of young children were enrolled in preschools or family child care centers (Organization for Economic Co-operation and Development, 1999).

The responsibility for preschool education shifted from the Ministry of Health and Social Services to the Ministry of Education in 1996. The new minister shifted the focus of preschool from traditional notions of child care to an educational model focusing on the child's development and learning (Martin-Korpi, 2007).

Primary Functions   Four pillars of Sweden's governance system facilitate continuity: the preschool class, the national curriculum, workforce policies, and program monitoring. A core feature of Sweden's early childhood system is the Preschool Class, a recent initiative to transition from preschool to primary school. Historically, Swedish compulsory education began at age 7, with children ages 1–6 attending preschool programs or family-run child care. Some people contended that starting school at age 7 when other European countries began at age 6 made Sweden appear provincial, while others worried that an earlier start to education would take away an important part of childhood. In 1998, a compromise arose. A voluntary Preschool Class for 6-year-olds was established by the Swedish Parliament within the compulsory school system, along with the first preschool curriculum that set out pedagogical goals in a government document (Kaga, 2007; Martin-Korpi, 2007). This new focus on pedagogy gave preschool the status of education, but the class retained some of the development and learning activities of child care and preschool. The incorporation of both learning and care has been dubbed *educare*. The municipalities are now mandated to provide placement for all 6-year-old children who elect to enroll in the Preschool Class, and the initiative is funded by tax revenue, central government grants, and parental fees that are based on income level (Martin-Korpi). Ninety-six percent of 6-year-old children in Sweden attend the Preschool Class (Kaga).

This transitional year between preschool and compulsory school is an important time during which children are gradually introduced to structured educational activities. From ages 1–5, most children attend a full day of care with loosely structured activities and an emphasis on play and exploration. At age 6, children typically spend half of their day in the Preschool Class, where they engage in pedagogically based activities similar to what they will experience in compulsory schooling; then they spend the rest of their day in a leisure-time center. Leisure-time centers are child care centers that specifically provide care during after-school hours and holidays. Here, children can play freely as they did in preschool. By age 7, children spend more time in structured compulsory schooling and less time in leisure-time centers (Kaga, 2007).

As a result of this new view of the preschool class as a predominantly educational endeavor, a national curriculum was released in 1994. The Lpo 94 is shared by the Preschool Class, compulsory schools, and leisure-time centers and identifies general goals and guidelines that are set by the Ministry of Education and Research and that individual municipalities implement on their own terms (Ministry of Education and Research, 2008). The curriculum raises the legitimacy of preschool, putting it in sync with compulsory schooling. It also signifies an important commitment to continuity of education practices.

In order to align teacher education to the new curriculum, starting in 2001, preschool teachers, compulsory-school teachers, and after-school teachers were required to undergo a preparation program that is based on common coursework. The common qualifications equalize the professional status of these three types of teachers and promote collaboration among them. Professionals from each of these three specializations work closely together to design a plan for each child and communicate frequently about his or her progress (Kaga, 2007). The individualized plan for each student helps children to transition seamlessly from one program to the next (Neuman, 2007).

Although the goal of these alignment efforts is to develop a shared sense of respect and teamwork among educational staff, in practice some discrepancies still remain between preschool teachers and school teachers in terms of wages and level of respect (Kaga, 2007; Neuman, 2007). Nevertheless, the Ministry of Education's workforce policies engender pedagogical continuity between preschool and compulsory school.

The high level of administrative integration in Sweden also affects the monitoring of preschool and compulsory school programs. The Ministry of Education utilizes a common, formal, unified assessment to supervise the progress of reform efforts in all classes (Neuman, 2007).

Governance Structure   The Ministry of Education employs a decentralized system to govern early childhood services. Essentially, the central government is in charge of setting broad goals for early child care, whereas the municipalities have the responsibility to implement services and the power to interpret the Ministry of Education's policies. Although the central government allows municipalities to make many of their own decisions, it monitors them vigilantly. For example, the municipalities have power over staff employment, but the central government stays involved by providing the funds to pay staff salaries (Neuman, 2007). The municipalities also have the control to determine the fees paid by parents, but the central government set a maximum fee in 2002 to reduce disparities among different municipalities. The municipalities are allowed to control the private-sector provision of child care, but the government minimizes privatization by restricting subsidies to nonprofit private centers (Martin-Korpi, 2007). The policy has effectively reduced the number of preschools run by private organizations; in 2007, they accounted for only 5% of preschools (Kaga, 2007). Although the central government has delegated some decision-making power to local authorities, it supervises their work closely and lends a hand whenever possible.

Implementation   The Preshool Class in Sweden has developed considerably over the past couple of decades with the help of the national and municipal authorities. The program owes its success to a thorough and efficient method of implementation marked by government intervention, curricular alignment, and a genuine concern for the education system.

Highlights and Accomplishments   Sweden's system is innovative due to its high accessibility and steady financing through tax revenues and public grants (Martin-Korpi, 2007). Equal quality among preschools is one of the central government's highest priorities, and the government has taken actions to equalize opportunities for children across different municipalities, such as capping parent-paid fees for preschool (Neuman, 2007).

Sweden is also an exemplary model of alignment in transition efforts. Because all schooling from age 1–18 is organized under the same administration—the Ministry of Education—the ministry's education policies affect the entire education spectrum. The joint curriculum and unified teacher preparation system have been implemented to further align preschool and compulsory school and to encourage communication between teachers from both of these groups. Says Professor Inge Johansson of the Stockholm Institute of Education,

> "The preschool class is to use pedagogical approaches drawn from both preschool and school practices, keeping the child's holistic development as its overall aim. It is conceived as a bridge between the two distinct cultures . . . balancing their integration in an equal manner and enabling children to make a smooth transition from one educational stage to the next" (Kaga, 2007, p. 1).

Another major accomplishment of the Swedish system is the policy makers' awareness of educare. Under the auspices of the Ministry of Education, the Preschool Class became associated with the notion of education, and it became conceptually aligned with compulsory schooling (Martin-Korpi, 2007). An important element of Sweden's child care system is the integration of pedagogy and care, which encourages holistic development of children in a nation that attaches great importance to family values.

Implementation Challenges   Sweden has suffered from three main implementation challenges: economic setbacks, "overschoolification," and teacher shortages. The recession in the 1990s caused enormous difficulties during an important time in preschool reform (Martin-Korpi, 2007). To abide by the 1995 Act on Child Care, which called for the provision of child care for children ages 1–18, municipalities were forced to expand their services without sufficient funding (Neuman, 2007). Opening centers and hiring qualified teachers was expensive, so class sizes and teacher–child ratios increased. Parents were also forced to pay higher fees in a time that was already economically difficult. Making preschool available to young children was, by law, more important than making programs strong; preschool quality suffered as a result (Neuman, 2007).

Another difficulty for early childhood education in Sweden has been the apparent "overschoolification" of preschool. The original debate about starting 6-year-olds in preschool was whether taking an additional year away from childhood for the purpose of schooling was favorable. The goal of integrating preschool and compulsory school under one administration was to have preschool and compulsory school policies influence one another in an attempt to promote a smooth transition to lifelong learning (Taguchi & Munkammar, 2003). Evaluations carried out in recent years have shown, however, that the Preschool Class for 6-year-olds is structured more like an elementary school class than a preschool program (Neuman, 2007). Evaluations also show minimal improvements in classroom quality, except in schools where preschool teachers and compulsory school teachers have a history of collaboration (Taguchi & Munkammar). Preschool staff remark that although they collaborate with school teachers on the implementation of the shared curriculum and pedagogical planning for individual students, the primary-school teachers usually lead the discussion (Neuman).

On a similar note, preschool teachers have lower salaries than compulsory school teachers in spite of having had comparable training. Preschool teachers are therefore difficult to recruit because many teachers opt to teach older children. Decentralization of staff employment has given preschool teachers the ability to negotiate wages and jump from municipality to municipality in search of higher salaries, but the discrepancies between preschool and school teachers are still prevalent and problematic. The high teacher–child ratio caused by economic struggles has not yet been completely rectified, and more successful preschool teacher recruitment would likely increase the quality of preschool programs nationally (Martin-Korpi, 2007; Neuman, 2007).

Lessons Learned   According to a 2003 case study by the United Nations Educational, Scientific and Cultural Organization on Sweden's consolidation of education services under the Ministry of Education, a primary lesson learned is the importance of educare. Child care has historically faced opposition from families that believe care is the duty of the mother, and preschool has faced opposition from families that believe beginning a pedagogical life at such a young age takes away from childhood. Emphasizing the combination of education and care has become essential to winning favor from families, who want their children to have both experiences without one overpowering the other. As the case study report states, "The services need to be seen as something that families cannot entirely provide by themselves; that produce stimulating learning situations and friendships as well as democratic, collective nurturing." Educare appeals to Sweden's collectivist nature and its economic needs (Taguchi & Munkammar, 2003).

Another lesson learned, according to the United Nations study, is the power of combining centralization and decentralization to achieve national goals: "The Swedish approach to building a nation of knowledge and education revolves around strong central visions and goals, matched by an abiding trust in local responsibility and initiative." The study goes on to call this mixed-method system "perhaps the best approach in today's post-modern society" (Taguchi & Munkammar, 2003).

A final lesson speaks to the unconditional duty of Swedish municipalities to pro-vide voluntary preschool for all children. In the 1990s, unemployment rose and many children were denied a place in preschool or child care programs. The situation put additional pressures on parents to care for their children or find alternative care while the parents were trying to obtain jobs. Lack of child care possibly prolonged parents' unemployment. In 2001, the government realized the unfair and unproductive nature of these circumstances and guaranteed the children of unemployed parents a spot in preschool (Martin-Korpi, 2007). The importance of this lesson is that the Swedish gov-ernment detected an injustice in the system and took measures to correct it, uphold-ing the promise that has driven much of the reform in the past 30 years: preschool for all children, no exceptions.

Future Directions   The general goal for the future of Sweden's early childhood education is to continue to align preschool and compulsory schooling through the curriculum and teacher training program (Taguchi & Munkammar, 2003). Priorities include address-ing some of the aforementioned challenges, such as equalizing salaries for preschool and schoolteachers, encouraging people to accord young teachers more respect, and balancing "overschoolification" (Neuman, 2007). Preschool teachers have expressed interest in more communication with compulsory school teachers, but this concern is currently a low priority for schools (Neuman). The Swedish National Agency for Education has proposed "harmonisation of legislation on pre-schooling and schooling" and "implementation in relation to integration and the revised curriculum at the local level and in teacher education/training" in order to address this problem. Other mea-sures to foster fluidity of schooling include funding developmental projects to promote integration and conducting research on pedagogy (Taguchi & Munkammar).

Another main goal is to evaluate programs annually to investigate the quality of services, the achievement of national and curricular goals, and the effectiveness of school management. Resources are to be set aside specifically for this purpose. Other proposals from the National Agency for Education include in-service training for all staff, additional time devoted to collaboration between preschool and primary-school teachers, and continued integration of teacher approaches. An impressive amount of legislation to cultivate a path of lifelong learning in Sweden has passed within the past few years, but more work needs to be done (Taguchi & Munkammar, 2003). The coming years will be an important time to amend efforts as the results of program evaluations become clear. These assessments will be valuable to Sweden's local and central government systems to further streamline transition in schooling.

Conclusion   Sweden's Ministry of Education aims to facilitate a process of lifelong learn-ing and ensure a coherent and integrated education for all children, independently of their age or needs. For early childhood education, this governance structure bridges the pedagogical and administrative differences between preschool and primary school (Taguchi & Munkammar, 2003). By promoting consistency among different education levels, Sweden's governance structure facilitates children's transitions as they move from early care and education settings into compulsory school.

REFERENCES

American Recovery and Reinvestment Act of 2009, PL 111-5, 123 Stat.115.
Arnold, C., Bartlett, K., Gowani, S., & Merali, R. (2007). *Is everybody ready? Readiness, transition and con-tinuity: Reflections and moving forward* (Working Paper 41). The Netherlands: Bernard van Leer.

Clifford, R.M., & Crawford, G.M. (2009). Learning from one another. In R.M. Clifford and G.M. Crawford (Eds.), *Beginning school: U.S. policies in international perspective* (pp. 111–135). New York: Teachers College.

Hodgkin, R., & Newell, P. (1996). *Effective government structures for children*. London: Calouste Gulbenkian Foundation.

Improving Head Start for School Readiness Act of 2007, PL 110-134.

Individuals with Disabilities Education Improvement Act of 2004, PL 108-446, U.S.C. §§1400 *et seq.*

Kaga, Y. (2007). *Preschool class for 6-year-olds in Sweden: A bridge between early childhood and compulsory school* (Publication No. 38). Paris: UNESCO.

Kagan, S.L., & Kauerz, K. (2009). Governing American early care and education: Shifting from government to governance and from form to function. In S. Feeney, A. Galper, & C. Seefeldt (Eds.), *Continuing issues in early childhood education* (3rd edition, pp. 12–32). Upper Saddle River, NJ: Prentice Hall.

Kamerman, S.B. (2000). Early childhood education and care: An overview of developments in the OECD countries. *International Journal of Educational Research, 33,* 7–29.

Levy, S. (2006). *Progress against poverty: Sustaining Mexico's Progresa–Oportunidades program.* Washington, DC: Brookings Institution Press.

Martin-Korpi, B. (2007). *The politics of pre-school: Intentions and decisions underlying the emergence and growth of the Swedish pre-school* (3rd edition). Stockholm: Sweden Ministry of Education and Research.

Ministry of Education and Research (2008, March). The pre-school class. Retrieved from http://www.regeringen.se/sb/d/2098/a/72442

National Association for the Education of Young Children. (2008). Overview of NAEYC Early Childhood Program standards. Retrieved from http://www.naeyc.org/files/academy/file/OverviewStandards.pdf

National Center for Children in Poverty. (n.d.). Federal child and dependent care tax credit. Retrieved from http://www.nccp.org/profiles/extended_43.html

Neuman, M.J. (2002). The wider context: An international overview of transition issues. In H. Fabian & A.-W. Dunlop (Eds.), *Transitions in the early years: Debating continuity and progression for young children in early education* (pp. 8–22). New York: RoutledgeFalmer.

Neuman, M.J. (2007). *Governance of early care and education: Politics and policy in France and Sweden.* Unpublished doctoral dissertation, Columbia University, New York.

Organization for Economic Co-operation and Development. (2001). *Starting strong: Early childhood education and care* (Executive Summary). Retrieved from http://www.oecd.org/dataoecd/4/9/1897313.pdf

Pennsylvania Office of Child Development and Early Learning. (2008a). *Annual Report 2007–2008.* Harrisburg, PA: Departments of Education and Public Welfare.

Pennsylvania Office of Child Development and Early Learning. (2008b). *Executive Budget 2008–2009.* Harrisburg, PA: Departments of Education and Public Welfare.

Pennsylvania Office of Child Development and Early Learning. (2009a). *Executive Budget 2009–2010.* Harrisburg, PA: Departments of Education and Public Welfare. Retrieved from http://www.pde.state.pa.us/early_childhood/lib/early_childhood/OCDEL_budget_09-10final4-6-09.pdf

Pennsylvania Office of Child Development and Early Learning. (2009b). *Keystone STARS: Continuous quality improvement for learning programs. Center performance standards for FY 2009–2010* (p. 12). Harrisburg, PA: Author.

Rennie Center for Education Research & Policy. (2009). *Toward interagency collaboration: The role of children's cabinets.* Cambridge, MA: Author.

Salamon, L.M. (2002). The new governance and the tools of public action: An introduction. In L.M. Salamon (Ed.), *The tools of government: A guide to the new governance* (pp. 1–47). New York: Oxford University Press.

Satkowski, C. (2009). *The next step in systems-building: Early childhood advisory councils and federal efforts to promote policy alignment in early childhood.* Washington, DC: New America Foundation.

Taguchi, H.L., & Munkammar, I. (2003). *Consolidating governmental early childhood education and care services under the Ministry of Education and Science: A Swedish case study* (Early Childhood and Family Policy Series No. 6). Paris: UNESCO.

United Nations Educational Scientific and Cultural Organization. (2006). *Education for All Global Monitoring Report 2006—Strong Foundations: Early childhood care and education.* Paris: Author.

13

Accountability
Policies and Transitions

Thomas Schultz

This chapter will contribute to an understanding of children's transitions from early education programs to kindergarten and primary-grade classrooms by focusing on accountability policies. Delineating the divergent approaches to accountability that are applied to programs for children from birth through age 5 and on to elementary schools will illuminate a key influence on how teachers work with young children in early childhood education: school transitions. The tools of accountability—standards for children's learning and program quality, assessments, data collection, incentives, professional development, and technical assistance—can be used to support more intentional, coherent, and positive transition practices. Thus, viewing transitions through the lens of accountability policy helps to flesh out an understanding of the roots of current transition practices and to stimulate a more proactive approach to supporting children and families as they move from a variety of early childhood settings into elementary schools.

We live in an era of accountability. A Google search for references to "accountability" generates more than 29,400,000 items. Citizens are eager for evidence of responsiveness and responsibility from political leaders and public institutions, while consumers and investors hold similar expectations for private sector executives and corporations. Accurate, credible data on organizational effectiveness and outcomes are key to accountability and are increasingly in demand. In response to these expectations, the media are preoccupied with asking leaders and institutions "to account" for their behavior and performance.

Accountability is also a dominant theme in the management and oversight of public education and early childhood programs. The Government Performance and Results Act requires all federal agencies to establish outcomes-based performance targets for all programs and to report results on an annual basis. New federal accountability mandates have been applied to Head Start, child care, and early childhood special education programs. In 2002, President George W. Bush and the Congress transformed the Elementary and Secondary Education Act of 1965 (PL 89-10) from a funding stream for compensatory education to an astonishingly prescriptive education accountability initiative through the enactment of the No Child Left Behind (NCLB) Act of 2001 (PL 107-110) legislation. States are also mandating new accountability approaches for early childhood programs and public education.

Education accountability policies should be understood as a means to an end. They implement an interconnected system of standards, assessments, data collection, professional development, and technical assistance, with the goal of enhancing program credibility, improving program effectiveness, and maximizing child outcomes. Accountability systems enhance program credibility by publicly reporting objective evidence of the programs' performance. They seek to improve program effectiveness and results through the motivational power of outcomes-based incentives and by providing data-driven technical assistance and professional development.

Within this general theory of action, accountability policies also have a significant influence on the priorities of teachers and local administrators. Accordingly, in an ideal world, accountability mechanisms would support a "practices" approach to fostering positive early childhood transitions. For example, accountability policies could support coordination and consistency in early childhood and early elementary grade curricula, assessments, teaching strategies, parent engagement practices, and professional development initiatives. However, in the real world accountability mandates all too often hinder positive transitions by mandating conflicting priorities for early childhood and elementary school programs.

This chapter will examine the extent to which current accountability policies support or hinder efforts to promote more effective transitions for young children. I will provide a brief conceptualization of educational accountability and describe the current approaches to accountability for programs for children from birth to age 5 and from kindergarten to Grade 3. Then I will assess how well these current accountability approaches foster successful transitions for children and conclude with recommendations for improving transitions via more supportive accountability policies.

AN EDUCATIONAL ACCOUNTABILITY SYSTEM FRAMEWORK

Figure 13.1 outlines a four-stage framework of an accountability system for educational programs and institutions. This framework will guide the subsequent description and analysis of current accountability policies for early childhood programs and elementary schools. First, accountability systems involve the development of specific standards for program outcomes and quality. *Outcome standards* refer to desired results in children due to their participation in an early childhood program or school. Outcome standards may be framed in terms of goals in broad domains of child development (e.g., cognitive, physical, linguistic, social-emotional, approaches to learning), which is typical in early childhood programs, or in terms of grade-level achievement in reading, mathematics, science, and social studies, which is typical in elementary school. *Program quality standards* refer to desired program characteristics, practices, or levels of resources and include hygiene standards, class size, teacher–child ratios, levels of education for teachers, and teaching practices that are associated with positive outcomes for children.

Second, an accountability system includes the *assessment* of children and/or programs to determine levels of program performance in relation to outcome standards or program quality standards. Planning these assessments involves selecting or developing assessment tools, determining the timing and frequency of assessments, and establishing procedures to select, train, and oversee individuals who will administer the assessments. In addition, the decision must be made whether to assess entire populations of children, teachers, centers, or schools or to administer assessments to representative samples of these populations.

Third, an accountability system includes the management, analysis, and reporting of assessment *data* on the extent to which programs or schools have met or exceeded outcome or program quality standards. Data may be reported to audiences such as legislative bodies, the media, state and federal program managers, local early childhood programs, schools, teachers, and parents.

Fourth and finally, the data from standards-based assessments is used for *program improvement*. One way to use data is to provide incentives to reward programs that perform well and apply sanctions to motivate improvement in programs that perform less well. Other actions could include

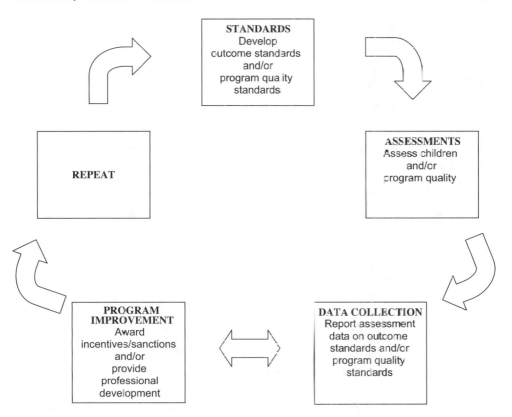

Figure 13.1. Education accountability system. A four-stage framework of an accountability system for educational programs and institutions.

targeting programs for technical assistance or providing professional development to staff members and managers to help them remedy deficiencies in performance and improve outcomes for children.

The ongoing cycle of performing standards-based assessments, analyzing the data that are gathered, and making program improvements is intended to increase program effectiveness and outcomes over time. Local education agencies and programs receive ongoing feedback on their performance and targeted assistance to help them capitalize on their strengths and remedy their weaknesses. In addition, by studying assessment data, state and federal managers can identify unusually high performing programs, schools, or school districts, study what distinguishes their approach to working with children, and incorporate their methods into technical assistance to improve weaker programs.

Accountability systems support or hinder the transition from early childhood education to school through the content of specific policies in the areas of standards, assessments, data analysis, and program improvement. It is possible to envision a set of policies that would be highly conducive to successful transitions for children. For instance, an optimal policy environment for promoting transitions would establish consistency, alignment, and coordination between accountability policies for early childhood and public education programs. In addition, accountability policies would focus attention and resources to promote optimal transition practices by teachers and program managers. Conversely, one can envision accountability policies that give low priority to transitions or that hinder the efforts of educators who are seeking to optimize the transitions process. As an introduction to my subsequent review of current accountability policies for early childhood programs and elementary schools, Table 13.1 delineates examples of such transition-supporting and transition-hindering accountability policies in the areas of standards, assessments, data analysis, and program improvement efforts.

Table 13.1.   Accountability policies and transitions

Policy element	Policies that hinder successful transitions	Policies that support transitions
Standards	Outcome standards and program quality standards for early childhood programs are inconsistent and/or misaligned with standards for elementary schools. Standards for program quality fail to incorporate attention to practices that are designed to promote successful transitions for children and their families.	Early childhood and early schooling outcome standards and program quality standards are aligned and integrated. Standards for program quality include explicit support for transition-enabling practices.
Assessments	Child assessment methods in early childhood programs are disconnected from assessment approaches in elementary schools. Assessments of program quality fail to examine transition practices or to document the degree of consistency in classroom practices and parent engagement efforts in early childhood programs and elementary schools.	Child assessment approaches and content reflect a carefully sequenced plan to document children's progress and accomplishments in all domains of development and learning in the early childhood and early school years. Assessments of program quality include data on transition practices and the consistency of classroom practices and parent engagement efforts in early childhood programs and elementary schools.
Data collection	Data on children's early childhood program experiences are housed in systems that are not connected with public education data systems. There are no mechanisms to share data from early childhood programs with elementary schools, nor for elementary schools to share data on children's progress with early education programs. Data do not include information on the implementation of recommended-approaches to transitions, or on the degree of consistency between early education/early elementary school classroom and parent engagement practices.	When children enroll in early childhood programs, they are assigned identification numbers that will also be used in the state's elementary and secondary education data system. Data from early childhood programs are shared with kindergarten and primary-grade teachers. Early education programs receive feedback on the progress of their children in kindergarten through grade 3. Data provide feedback on the degree of consistency between early education and early schooling classroom practices and parent engagement practices.
Program improvement	Professional development and technical assistance to elementary schools and early childhood programs are provided through separate, uncoordinated mechanisms and reflect differing priorities and conflicting approaches to working with children and their families. There are no specific professional development or technical assistance resources to promote optimal transition-enabling practices.	Early childhood and K–3 teachers participate in joint professional development on standards, curricula, pedagogy, and analysis and use of data on children's learning, classroom quality, student engagement and teacher–child interactions. Early childhood programs and schools receive joint, targeted professional development and technical assistance to improve support for transitions.

WORLDS APART: CURRENT EARLY CHILDHOOD AND EARLY ELEMENTARY ACCOUNTABILITY POLICIES

Policy leaders expect to hold early education programs, as well as public education for kindergarten and primary-grade students, accountable for their performance. However, an examination of our differing approaches to funding and governance of early education and elementary education suggests that current accountability policies do not provide optimal supports for successful transitions for young children. To document this contention, I will now highlight the salient characteristics of current accountability policies for programs serving children from birth through age 5 and for elementary schools.

Current Early Childhood Accountability Approaches

Programs for children birth through age 5 are funded by a variety of federal, state, and local agencies; parent fees; and other private-sector sources. The vast majority of public funding is provided by four major—and historically separate—categorical programs:

- Head Start and child care (managed by the U.S. Department of Health and Human Services)

- Early childhood special education (managed by the U.S. Department of Education)

- State-funded prekindergarten (managed by a variety of state agencies)

Accordingly, outcome and program quality standards, assessments, data analysis, and program improvement policies for early childhood programs are determined by decisions that are made in a variety of separate federal and state agencies and departments. There are three notable characteristics of accountability policies for programs serving children from birth through age 5. First, they are fragmented according to varied state and federal funding streams and program structures. Second, the dominant approach is based on standards, assessments, and guided improvement of metrics of program quality. Third, we live in an era of rapid change and innovation in this area of public policy. These characteristics shape the perspectives, priorities, and capacities of early childhood teachers and managers as they interact with elementary educators around transition issues.

Today's early childhood accountability and assessment efforts are fragmented and uncoordinated. Table 13.2 depicts how child care, Head Start, state prekindergarten, and early childhood special education programs are required to implement different outcome and program quality standards—as well as different systems for child and program assessment, data analysis, professional development, and technical assistance. This policy labyrinth generates a variety of complications and challenges. First, states are responsible for managing their varied systems and approaches (with the exception of Head Start, which operates through a federal-to-local management structure). They must ensure programs' compliance with multiple sets of standards and manage multiple systems of data on the performance of children and programs. Second, many local early childhood agencies receive funding from several sources and therefore struggle to implement multiple standards, assessments, and data requirements. Program managers are concerned about the difficulties of ensuring compliance with multiple standards and the costs of making separate reporting and monitoring efforts. Third, teachers may be required to administer several different (and often changing) assessments to their children. Simply understanding the content of multiple sets of voluminous standards documents is a daunting challenge. The difficulty of the task is important because the ultimate intention of these policy efforts is to have practitioners internalize the standards and use them to guide their work with children. In sum, teachers and program administrators must devote considerable time to navigating this

Table 13.2.   Current early childhood accountability policies

	Child care	Head start	State-funded prekindergarten	Special education
Program quality standards	State licensing standards (50 states) State QRIS assessments (13 states + 29 pilots)	Federal program performance standards	State program standards (39 states)	Federal IDEA regulations State program standards
Assessing local program quality	State licensing visits State QRIS assessments (13 states + 29 pilots)	Federal program monitoring	State program monitoring (30 states)	State program monitoring
Standards for children's learning	State early learning guidelines (49 states)	Federal child outcomes framework	State early learning guidelines (50 states)	Three functional goals (Federal)
Child assessments	No current requirements	Local agencies select and administer child assessment tools.	State pre-K assessments (17 states)	States report % of children in five categories on three goals
Research/program evaluations	Yes	Yes	Yes	Yes
Kindergarten-to-grade 3 standards, assessments, and data				

From PEW Charitable Trusts Task Force Members (2007). *Taking stock: Assessing and improv-ing early childhood learning and program quality* (p. 18). Washington, DC: PEW Charitable Trusts; adapted by permission.

conglomeration of policies, rather than using the feedback and resources that are generated by accountability systems to improve teaching and learning outcomes.

A second notable characteristic of early childhood accountability efforts is a long-standing tradition of holding programs accountable for compliance to program quality standards, includ-ing metrics in the areas of program inputs, practices, staffing, and services. From their inception, child care, Head Start, state prekindergarten (pre-K), and early childhood special education pro-grams were established with legislative mandates and regulations that were related to program quality standards. Assessments of the implementation of program quality standards have also been in place in all 50 states for decades, in the form of child care licensing visits, federal monitor-ing of local Head Start programs, the use of standardized observational rating scales to document the quality of pre-K programs, and other systems of on-site review. Accordingly, early childhood program managers are experienced in preparing for reviews of program quality and are comfort-able understanding and using data from assessments of program quality. By contrast, the move to establish outcome standards for the preschool years is relatively recent, and only about one third of all states are currently gathering data on the learning progress and accomplishments of children prior to kindergarten entry (Scott-Little & Martella, 2006). Early childhood program managers have relatively little experience in implementing outcome standards, using large-scale accountability-related child assessment initiatives, or understanding and using child assess-ment data as a resource for program improvement. In fact, the use of child assessment data in early childhood accountability systems is a highly contentious issue (National Early Childhood Accountability Task Force, 2007; Snow & Van Hemel, 2008).

A third characteristic of the accountability policy context for early childhood programs is innovation and change. In the last 5 years alone, the early childhood field has seen new state early learning guidelines, rapid growth of quality rating and improvement systems (QRISs) to assess and improve child care program quality (Mitchell, 2005), new evaluation studies of state pre-K programs (Barnett, Lamy, & Jung, 2005; Early et al., 2005; Gilliam & Zigler, 2004), and a major new national child-assessment initiative in early childhood special education programs. During this same period, Head Start initiated a large-scale assessment of more than 400,000 4- and 5-year-olds, although it was subsequently terminated by congressional action. Also during this time, the nation's largest early childhood professional organization, the National Association for the Education of Young Children, restructured its voluntary program accreditation system. Thus, early childhood professionals face not only the challenge of implementing multiple accountability mandates but also the imperative to absorb new initiatives and changes in existing systems and policies, one right after the other.

In sum, as early childhood educators work with elementary school teachers and principals to optimize transitions for children, they contend with the complexities and burdens of implementing multiple systems of standards, assessments, data analysis, and program improvement, as well as absorbing a variety of new accountability initiatives. Moreover, they are strongly oriented toward a conception of accountability that is based on program quality standards and assessments rather than on outcome standards for children.

Current Early Elementary Accountability Approaches

Early childhood accountability policy has a fragmented structure, a dominant focus on program inputs, practices, and quality, and an environment of rapid innovation. In contrast, the accountability context for elementary school teachers and classrooms follows a single policy approach, emphasizes student test scores as the core measure of school performance, and has been relatively stable.

Because they are based on our national system for funding and governance of public education, local schools and districts face a more unified accountability framework than do early childhood programs. Whereas school districts may administer a variety of categorical programs, they implement a single dominant accountability strategy that is derived from the joint efforts of the U.S. Department of Education, state boards of education, and state departments of education.

The dominant paradigm for accountability in elementary and secondary education is an outcomes-based strategy to assess and improve student achievement in core academic subject areas. The federal government's NCLB program is the most recent example of this approach and links student assessment data to a variety of incentives and sanctions for schools and school districts. NCLB requires that all students in Grades 3 through 8 be assessed annually on core academic skills, that test scores be disaggregated for multiple subgroups of students, and that schools be accountable for moving all students toward grade-level proficiency and for improving students' performance for each of these subgroups. In response to these requirements, each state has developed a set of grade-level outcome standards and assessments, systems to analyze and report achievement test scores, and improvement initiatives to strengthen or reconstitute low-performing schools.

Within this context, it is noteworthy that accountability mandates for kindergarten and primary-grade students and teachers are somewhat less prescriptive than are requirements for higher grade levels. As we have noted, annual NCLB-mandated assessments apply to students in Grades 3 through 8, not to children in kindergarten through Grade 2. A recent review of state learning standards and assessments reveals that only 36 of the 50 states have grade-specific standards for kindergarten, first, and second grade; only 5 states administer statewide assessments to all first graders, and only 8 states assess all second graders (Kauerz, 2006). However, anecdotal evidence indicates that many school districts require kindergarten and primary-grade teachers to administer standardized assessments and review results in order to improve student outcomes and reduce achievement disparities in anticipation of the NCLB-mandated assessments at the end of third grade. Clearly, kindergarten and primary-grade teachers work in an atmosphere in which preparing students to perform well on standardized tests and the varied NCLB performance metrics is a high priority.

A final contrast between early childhood and elementary education accountability efforts is the relatively stable context of accountability policy for elementary and secondary educators. The implementation requirements of NCLB are challenging and voluminous, but this central approach to accountability has been in place since 2003 and was preceded in many states by analogous reform initiatives that drove student improvement through outcome standards, testing, incentives, and school improvement.

Implications of Current Accountability Policies for Early Childhood Transitions

In sum, current accountability policies complicate efforts to promote successful transitions to school for young children in two ways. First, divergent paradigms for accountability in early childhood and elementary school programs make it difficult to mount cooperative transition initiatives across these institutions. Although early childhood and elementary school teachers are jointly responsible for fostering young children's healthy development and early school success, they work in different worlds in terms of the dominant methods and metrics for assessing their work. Local programs serving preschool children are oriented toward compliance with standards for program quality while kindergarten and primary-grade programs focus on promoting student achievement on standardized tests. The problem of conflicting paradigms also appears in differing approaches to defining outcome standards. As we noted earlier, the dominant approach to creating outcome standards for early childhood programs is based on broad domains of child development. Alternatively, outcome standards for elementary education are heavily focused on reading, mathematics, science, and other subject areas and rarely include objectives in the domains of social-emotional development, physical development, or approaches to learning. Thus, when early childhood and elementary educators convene around transition issues, they are oriented to different images of desired outcomes and lack a common vocabulary for discussing issues as basic as standards.

The second policy barrier to improving early childhood transitions is structural. It is extremely challenging to mesh the efforts of elementary schools and teachers with the scores of diverse early childhood education programs and their staff members. The fragmented set of state and federal accountability mandates for early childhood programs exacerbates these challenges. For example, data on the characteristics of young children and their experiences in local early childhood programs could be a major asset in planning effective transitions as children enroll in kindergarten programs. Information on children's patterns of progress in early learning, along with a record of the early childhood programs that they have attended (and the curriculum, teaching, and parent engagement practices and levels of quality in these programs) could help inform transition planning in kindergarten and primary-grade classrooms. It is difficult, however, for elementary schools to obtain this information from the many different local early childhood programs, and it is even more difficult for them to understand and use data generated by different assessment tools in relation to varied outcome and program quality standards.

RESHAPING ACCOUNTABILITY POLICIES
TO OPTIMIZE TRANSITIONS FOR YOUNG CHILDREN

Using this overview of current accountability policies for early childhood programs and kindergarten-to-Grade-3 schooling, can we chart a pathway to a more unified strategy that builds supports for and removes barriers to positive transitions for children and families? I will argue that, in order to promote smoother and more positive transitions to school, we will need to reconcile divergent accountability paradigms for early education programs and elementary schools; build more explicit attention to transition practices and relationships into standards, data collection, and other accountability system elements; and create new forums to convene early childhood and early elementary-grade teachers and administrators to use data from accountability systems.

Step 1—Reframe Accountability
to Encompass Child Outcomes *and* Program Quality

A first step in reframing accountability policies to support transitions is to build a unified system of early-childhood-through-primary-grade standards, assessments, and data analysis to document and guide improvement in children's learning and development *as well as* in program quality, teaching practices, and learning opportunities. This approach can promote a richer, more balanced, and more nuanced understanding of the workings, quality, and effectiveness of early childhood and early elementary programs—and a stronger basis for improvement efforts—compared with accountability systems that focus solely on learning outcomes or program quality. If adopted, this approach would improve prospects for successful transitions by providing a shared framework of goals for early childhood programs and elementary schools and a common vocabulary for teachers to use when they plan and work together.

Reframing accountability in this way would provide multiple benefits for early childhood and elementary education leaders and programs. Generating data on the performance of programs and schools on both quality and child outcome metrics would help answer difficult policy questions. Legislators, parents, and the media are interested in data on the extent to which children are progressing toward age-appropriate benchmarks for learning and development as well as information on how well early childhood programs and schools are meeting standards for high-quality services and learning opportunities.

For the early childhood education community, expanding accountability efforts to incorporate data on children's progress and accomplishments would help sharpen awareness of achievement disparities for disadvantaged children and highlight the need to enrich and intensify learning opportunities for children with multiple risk factors. Building data systems that include program quality and child outcome data would deepen our understanding of how different subgroups of children progress as they participate in different combinations of early childhood programs with different levels of quality, curricula, and approaches to teaching and parent engagement. For the public education sector, building a database on the quality of teaching and learning opportunities (along with child assessment data) could generate valuable insights to inform program improvement efforts. For example, if some combinations of early childhood education and early elementary school programming can be shown to generate higher-than-expected rates of progress for children, data on the quality of teaching and other aspects of these settings could inform technical assistance efforts to strengthen weaker programs.

Movement in this direction will require substantial technical work to develop new systems of standards, assessments, and data analysis. The key tasks in the early childhood sector are building standards-based child assessment mechanisms, data systems to manage and report data from child assessments, and support systems to help educators and managers understand and use child assessment data to improve their daily work with children. The key tasks in the elementary school sector are building a framework of research-based standards for program quality and teaching practices in kindergarten and primary-grade classes and the related assessment, data analysis, and professional development components to implement such an approach.

Fortunately, state and federal agencies can draw on models, tools, and lessons from current accountability initiatives as they tackle this sizeable agenda. That is, early childhood program quality standards and models of large-scale program quality assessment systems (including, for example, standardized observational rating scales to assess the quality of classroom environments and teaching practices) can be adapted to jump-start an expansion of elementary school accountability systems to incorporate data on program quality. In addition, lessons and models from several decades of federal and state outcomes-based education reform strategies can inform the expansion of early childhood accountability systems to incorporate child assessment data.

Step 2—Align and Integrate Early Childhood and Early Elementary Outcome and Program Quality Standards and Assessments

A second step in promoting transitions would be to improve the coherence and consistency of the expectations that are embedded in early childhood and elementary education standards and assessments. As discussed in Chapter 7 in this volume, this work would begin with careful analysis and adjustments to ensure vertical alignment of outcome standards across the early childhood and early elementary years. Vertical alignment of these standards would improve the continuity of expectations for children's learning and development as they move from infant–toddler programs to preschool, from preschool to kindergarten, from kindergarten to first grade, and so forth. This exercise would create the opportunity to resolve the current differences between the developmental-domain–based orientation of early childhood outcome standards and the curriculum-subject–based early elementary outcome standards.

An obvious challenge is the need to reconcile disparate standards across different early education programs and funding streams. Such unification was recommended in a recent effort to design a more inclusive, unified accountability system for all forms of publicly funded early childhood services (National Early Childhood Accountability Task Force, 2007). As a beginning step, states can map the relationships among current standards for early childhood outcomes and program quality, noting areas of agreement and disparities. In many cases, states may see opportunities to move toward a single set of outcome or program quality standards for all forms of early childhood services. However, in some cases, it may not be possible to reconcile differing standards because they derive from legislative mandates or reflect substantial disparities in levels of funding for different forms of early care and education. Another possible solution, exemplified in many state QRISs, is to use a tiered approach to standards when one set of standards is higher, more challenging, or more detailed than those promulgated by a different funding source.

During this process, states could also develop a common set of program quality standards in the area of transition practices to be applied to both early childhood programs and elementary schools. These standards could include outreach by schools to entering parents and children; meetings among early childhood, kindergarten, and primary-grade teachers to exchange information on expectations for children and classroom practices; transfer of data from early childhood programs to local elementary schools; and collaborative efforts to align curricula and provide professional development to teachers.

Step 3—Share Data on Children, Families, Teachers, Program Quality, and Practices Across Early Childhood and Early Elementary Programs

Once standards and assessments are aligned, states can take a third bold step to promote transitions by building a comprehensive, common, and easily accessible database on children, teachers, program characteristics, and program quality across the early childhood and early schooling years. Such a repository should contain, in one place, information on

- *Children* from birth through Grade 3, including their demographic characteristics, the early childhood programs in which they participate, and information assessing their skills or development

- *Programs* (early childhood education and elementary school), including funding sources and results of reviews of program quality

- *Workforce* (for teachers of children birth through third grade) including levels of education, credentials, and experience

A key aspect of building such a data management and reporting system is assigning unique identification numbers to children when they enter early childhood programs and linking the numbers to the student identification numbers that are assigned by public school districts. This feature would enable states and local communities to connect data from children's early childhood years to public education data systems that track their later education. It would allow children's progress to be followed over time as they move among programs, schools, and communities. Elementary school teachers would be able to view and use information on children's progress and experiences in various early childhood programs. Early education programs would be able to get feedback on how their graduates progress when they enter school.

A shared data system would highlight important elements of the early-childhood-to-early-schooling transition experience. Local schools and early childhood programs could be directed to collect and report data on the key features of their approaches to transitions, as well as key characteristics of their approaches to teaching and serving children and families. An analysis of this information would draw attention to the degree to which early childhood and early elementary school classrooms are similar or different, to wit:

- How do teachers allocate time to address different curricular goals, and how do they use differing instructional strategies (e.g., whole group, small group, or individualized learning; teacher-directed vs. child-directed activities)?

- What approaches do teachers use to enhance student engagement, and what are rates of student engagement in different types of learning opportunities?

- What is the nature and quality of teacher–child relationships?

- How are parents and families engaged and supported?

Step 4—Build Early Childhood and Early Elementary Teams to Study and Use Assessment Data to Improve Transitions for Young Children

Accountability policies could enhance transitions by generating new opportunities for early childhood and elementary school educators to review assessment data and use the findings to strengthen teaching, learning, and professional development. Vertical teams of early childhood and elementary school teachers and administrators could review assessment information that was related to the trajectories of children's progress, as well as information on teaching strategies and learning opportunities across the early childhood and early elementary years. They could use this information to adjust, enrich, and add to their curriculum to offer new forms of learning experiences and teaching strategies that would ease transitions and support children's continuous progress.

In order to build effective teams for planning to improve children's transitions, the participants must be sensitive to differences in status, credentials, and compensation between early childhood and public school educators. Even as these differences are acknowledged, partnerships can unleash new ways for practitioners to teach and learn from each other. For example, teams composed of pre-K, Head Start, child care, early childhood special education, and K–3 teachers could work together to examine all available information on the progress of English-language learners throughout early childhood, as well as curricula, teaching practices, and family engagement efforts that are relevant to this group. They can use the data to develop collective plans to improve learning opportunities and outcomes across early childhood and early elementary grade classrooms—as well as using it in joint professional development efforts. Sustained collaborative review of child assessment data should also foster a stronger sense of shared responsibility among all teachers for children's success across the early learning years.

CONCLUSION

Rethinking and reforming accountability policies can contribute to an overall campaign to improve transitions from early childhood programs to kindergarten classrooms and beyond. Current accountability approaches create a context in which heroic special efforts are required to establish a strong system of transition-supportive practices in early childhood centers and elementary schools. If we reform the disconnected and contradictory accountability systems in the right manner, we can make it easy for teachers and program managers to do the right things to foster successful transitions. Reframing early childhood and early elementary accountability standards, assessments, data analysis, and program improvement policies will enable educators who work with children from birth through the early school years to transform how they think about and enable successful transitions to school.

Fortunately, we are at a significant turning point in early childhood and school reform policy. A new presidential administration and Congress are providing substantial resources for public education and early childhood programs and launching new reform initiatives. These efforts will provide novel opportunities to build a more coherent and systemic approach to oversight and improvement of all early childhood programs. Initiatives such as State Early Childhood Advisory Councils and the proposed Early Learning Challenge Fund initiative provide substantial support to improve outcome and program quality standards, assessments, data systems, and professional development. There also are substantial new funds and federal leadership to build longitudinal education data systems that would span and link early childhood, elementary, secondary, and postsecondary education. Finally, the new Race to the Top fund and, in particular, the Elementary and Secondary Education Act (the reauthorization of which is pending) will provide opportunities to build new models and reform policies to create public education accountability. The time is right to use these opportunities to transform early childhood transitions from a problem to an asset in our early-childhood to-postsecondary-education pipeline.

Case Study—The Maryland Model for School Readiness

The Development of a Comprehensive Approach to Early Childhood Assessment

Jeanne L. Reid

The Maryland Model for School Readiness (MMSR) is a framework that is being used in preschool and kindergarten classrooms to help prepare young children for success in kindergarten and elementary school. Conceived as a complement to the state's K–12 accountability system, the MMSR is a statewide, low-stakes accountability system that is designed to improve instruction in early childhood programs. It is aligned with state standards and uses developmentally appropriate assessments. The MMSR is supported by an extensive professional development program offered to teachers in all public schools, child care programs, and Head Start programs. One major project of the MMSR is its kindergarten assessment. Teachers collect data on children's skills and behaviors in the fall of kindergarten and use the data to inform instruction in ways that are aligned with those of Maryland's public elementary schools. The MMSR has become an integral component of the state's efforts to promote continuity and successful transitions between early childhood programs and elementary schools in Maryland.

General Description   In 1990, the National Education Goals Panel recommended that the nation strive to have all children enter school ready to learn by the year 2000. In response, the Maryland State Department of Education (MSDE)[1] developed a definition of school readiness and piloted the use of an assessment tool called the Work Sampling System (WSS) in the kindergarten programs of several local school systems. According to Rolf Grafwallner (2005), the assistant state superintendent in the division of early childhood development, a major question for the schools that participated was, "How does the statewide project relate to the existing process of teaching and learning at the participating local school districts, namely the curriculum, assessment, grading protocols, and report cards?" Recognizing the need for a more comprehensive approach, the department reconfigured the pilot program to foster the aligned use of curricula, instructional strategies, and assessments and to incorporate family communication, extensive professional development and mentoring at the local level (R. Grafwallner, personal communication, July 10, 2009). In 1997, this multifaceted initiative was named the Maryland Model for School Readiness (Maryland State Department of Education, 2009a).

The MMSR was conceived as an extension of the state's K–12 accountability system. Yet the distinctive structure and nature of early care and education programs posed unique challenges to creating accountability measures that would be aligned with those in elementary school. A large obstacle was the gap in professional culture and training that had long divided preschool and elementary school educators:

> When we defined 'school readiness' in 1994, it was driven by what schools wanted children to know and be able to do when they arrive at

---

[1] Since 2005, when all early childhood programs were consolidated within MSDE, the project was led by the Division of Early Childhood Development.

school. But how would programs with different perspectives—child care, nursery school, Head Start, pre-K—all fit under this tent? How would a Head Start director and a public school pre-K director feel equally responsible for getting a child ready for kindergarten? (R. Grafwallner, personal communication, July 10, 2009)

In this context, two aspects of the WSS appealed to Maryland policy makers. First, it offered assessment guidelines for each age from preschool to Grade 5. The guidance on assessing children across the early years of learning supported the state's focus on continuity between preschool programs and elementary schools. "We needed a hook to attach our elementary assessments to kindergarten, and the WSS gave us that instrument," said Grafwallner. Second, the Work Sampling assessment was structured around developmental domains, the common framework for preschool educators. At the same time, the WSS used some of the nomenclature that was associated with learning theory and that was more familiar to elementary school educators, such as language/literacy and mathematical thinking instead of cognition—a concept more at home in developmental theory. "We had two different professions using two different languages. We needed something to bring them together," and again, WSS was a useful tool (R. Grafwallner, personal communication, July 10, 2009).

At first, the MSDE focused the MMSR on public pre-K and kindergarten teachers by providing them annually with 5 full days of professional development modules in 12 districts. The goal of the trainings was to foster the use of the Work Sampling assessment and its alignment with the local district's curriculum on several dimensions: the determination of learner outcomes, application of instructional strategies, instructional planning, portfolio assessment, effective communication between teachers and parents regarding children's progress, and "transition practices that included the articulation of assessment information from pre-K to kindergarten," according to Grafwallner. Staff from MSDE also helped local school systems revise their pre-K and kindergarten report cards to reflect the WSS indicators, which would demonstrate to parents the continuity in their children's education. In 1999, the Department of Education sponsored an evaluation of the initiative and found that the integrated approach of the MMSR had "honed teachers' ability to differentiate instruction, to become better observers of learning, and to refine the documentation for student referrals" (2005). These were the beginnings of an integrated approach to pedagogy across the early years of learning.

In 2000, pressure from the state legislature accelerated the development of the MMSR. A bipartisan Joint Committee on Children, Youth, and Families told the agency heads, "School readiness is a priority, and before we put any money into early education, you need to tell us how we are doing" (R. Grafwallner, personal communication, July 10, 2009). The legislature made it clear that enrollment numbers would no longer suffice as evidence of how well the state was serving its young children. "We had the concept of MMSR and the WSS, so we decided to build on that," said Grafwallner.

The department began by defining a dual purpose for the readiness assessment. The first goal was to advance teaching and learning, and specifically, to inform early childhood teachers' instruction (Grafwallner, 2005). The second goal was to inform policy makers about "the learning status of groups of children." The objective was explicit that it was *not* to use the data for high-stakes program accountability, which might lead to the defunding of individual programs. That type of program accountability was not an option for two reasons: 1) Lacking attendance data for individual programs, the state had no way to account for whether a child had been in a preschool program for a month or a year, and 2) lacking preschool assessment data, the state had no way to evaluate a child's growth during preschool (R. Grafwallner, personal communication, July 10, 2009). Convincing early educators that the data would not be used for high-stakes accountability, however, was not easy. To overcome their resistance, Grafwallner said, "We had to do a lot of outreach and demystify it."

After the purpose of the assessment had been clearly defined, the Department decided to adapt its prior use of WSS to provide a set of indicators of learning that reflected the state's school readiness definition. The Department had to decide how to bridge the gaps between preschool and elementary school educators. Grafwallner (2005) explained, "The design team preferred an assessment that would give equal weight to the essential learning domains, but it also wanted information that would clearly articulate the skill levels with which entering kindergartners begin their school year."

To serve these two interests, the team chose 28 Readiness Indicators from the 66 WSS indicators for kindergarten. The indicators fell across the seven domains of learning defined in the WSS—Personal & Social Development, Language & Literacy, Mathematical Thinking, Scientific Thinking, Social Studies, the Arts, and Physical Development—with four indicators per domain. After a pilot phase in 2000–2001, the MSDE added two indicators in the Language & Literacy domain for a total of 30. Each year, when the MSDE receives the results of the assessments, it uses indicator scores for each child to generate individual scores that fall into one of three levels: Proficient, In Process, or Needs Development. The results are then aggregated and analyzed by subgroups. The terms used for the group scores are "full," "approaching," or "developing readiness."

The piece that was missing from the MMSR was content standards that would be aligned horizontally with the assessment and vertically with the elementary-grade standards. In 2000, the state developed pre-K–to–Grade-8 content standards. The intent was to foster a common "understanding of what it takes to get children to the point of a successful transition to kindergarten." When the Department received feedback from educators that the standards were too broad and were not being used consistently for instruction, the state's education policy leaders responded by developing a voluntary state curriculum. The voluntary curriculum articulates specific learning objectives and defines learning outcomes for each grade level, including pre-K and kindergarten. Grafwallner explained, "That gave us all the components we needed—assessment, curriculum, and standards"—to create a framework for pedagogical continuity in the early years of learning (personal communication, July 10, 2009).

Implementation   The aggregated data, which now cover approximately 58,000 children, appear in an annual report that is categorized by demographic subgroups of children such as gender, race or ethnicity, status as English language learner, and qualification for free or reduced-price lunch (Maryland State Department of Education, 2009b). The data are analyzed along with additional demographic information about children, such as their care arrangements before kindergarten. The state, which has an annual budget of $1.7 million, offers free professional development to participants.

The aggregated kindergarten data provide feedback to early educators on how well they are preparing children for kindergarten and what areas of learning need to be addressed. For example, a Head Start director could look at county-level data to see how well Head Start programs in the area are meeting the state's readiness objectives. The aggregated data also inform policy decisions and strategic planning at the Division of Early Childhood Development and among other early childhood stakeholder groups. Perhaps most important, the data are used in the classroom to alter instruction in ways that will foster seamless transitions for children between the preschool and kindergarten years. Whether data are collected solely in the fall of kindergarten or at one or more of the voluntary data points in pre-K and the spring of kindergarten, teachers can interpret the data to reflect on their own practices, use the data for report cards, and identify children who need particular support. For example, a teacher could ask how well children are developing phonemic awareness or specific aspects of their self-regulation (R. Grafwallner, personal communication, July 10, 2009).

Indeed, the MSDE actively promotes the use of the data to align pedagogy between preschool and kindergarten and thus improve instruction. For example, the state helps to fund statewide efforts to distribute the data locally and to provide multiple, sequenced trainings on translating the data into parenting practices, instructional strategies, and curriculum decisions that promote children's readiness for school (Corwin, Rohde, & Andrews, personal communication, July 27, 2009; Ready at Five, 2009).

Lessons Learned   When MSDE was searching for an assessment tool and strategy, it realized that there might be a conflict between appropriate assessment practices for children enrolled in early childhood education programs and standardized testing. Although standardized testing instruments meet national psychometric quality standards, conventional assessment practices for that age group call for valid documentation of young children's learning and behavior and use of the information for instructional purposes. In order to be successful, the assessment and the accountability system need to be valid, reliable, and aligned to inform practice. The developer of the assessment design felt that teachers who conduct classroom observations and formulate their own well-honed system of documentation are in the best position to assess children's growth.

When teachers use portfolio assessment techniques to evaluate children's skill levels, the teachers must be careful to be objective in their evaluations. They must be thoroughly trained not only in techniques to conduct the assessment but also in the standard for proficiency in a given skill after the first quarter of the kindergarten year. To address this challenge, MSDE developed a systematic format for scoring children's learning. The state offers so-called exemplars that connect the voluntary state curriculum standards, indicators, and WSS indicators and provide descriptions of typical student skills and behaviors that a teacher can use when he or she is assessing a child on the WSS indicator (Maryland Division of Early Childhood Development, 2007). Exemplars provide descriptions of how a child might demonstrate the given skill in ways that may be judged as *Proficient*, *In Process*, or *Needs Development* related to specific learning objectives. Figure 13.2 provides a sample page from the MMSR to illustrate the structure and layout of the standards. Grafwallner said that the assessment process "had to be standardized. Otherwise, a teacher in one county and a teacher in another county might define proficiency differently because they have different backgrounds or different types of students" (personal communication, July 10, 2009).

Prekindergarten

MMSR Exemplars

Fall   (Spring)

Content Area: Language and Literacy - **6.0** Listening

WSS Indicator: **II A2** Follows two- or three-step directions

MMSR/VSC: **6A 2** Comprehend & analyze what is heard

Objective:	Proficient	In Process	Needs Development
Follow a set of two- or three-step directions	Student is able to consistently follow two- and three-step verbal directions that have been modeled by an adult. (May rely on signs, symbols, or visual cues.)	Student is able to consistently follow two-step verbal directions that have been modeled by an adult. (May rely on signs, symbols, or visual cues.)	Student occasionally follows two-step verbal directions that have been modeled by an adult. (May rely on signs, symbols, or visual cues.)

Figure 13.2. Maryland Model for School Readiness sample page illustrating the structure and layouts of standards. (From MMSR Exemplars, Language and Literacy [2007]. *Maryland Model for School Readiness: Pre-Kindergarten Expanded Exemplars Spring Exit* [5th ed., p. 26]. Maryland State Department of Education; adapted by permission.

Another significant lesson learned was the importance of making the fall kindergarten assessment mandatory. Although use of the WSS is voluntary in preschool and the spring of kindergarten, kindergarten teachers must *by law* submit the assessment results of all children after the first quarter reporting period to MSDE. Mandating the fall kindergarten assessment was critical to making its use comprehensive. Initially, local school districts feared that the associated assessment results of incoming kindergartners would rest with the schools and not the early childhood programs from which they had transitioned. In an effort to assuage these concerns, MSDE and a number of early childhood stakeholders clarified the purpose of the assessment and justified the regulatory requirement as an effort to improve the learning opportunities for children before they come to kindergarten (R. Grafwallner, personal communication, July 10, 2009).

Several factors are critical to the success of the MMSR (Grafwallner, 2005). First, it creates the framework for aligning early learning in preschool with instruction in the primary grades. It also establishes an infrastructure of accountability for the early childhood community, which focuses work with children on essential early learning outcomes and continued improvement. Furthermore, this concept informs practice in numerous ways: by integrating early childhood assessment with a comprehensive strategy for improving teaching and learning, by using the assessment for instructional accountability rather than high-stakes accountability, by establishing broad-based support for the assessment and the process of improving early learning opportunities for all children, and by allowing this system to develop over time. As federal policies changed and as the state fiscal climate shifted and outreach initiatives provided feedback, MSDE refined the early learning standards, assessment guidelines, professional development modules, and dissemination of project materials. Such adaptability in an unavoidably turbulent landscape strengthened the complex and ambitious MMSR.

Future Directions   Since the 2000–2001 school year, the state's annual reports (titled *Children Entering School Ready to Learn*) have documented a steady improvement in children's preparedness for kindergarten. The state attributes this success, at least in part, to the implementation of the MMSR in combination with strategic approaches to improve the entire early care and education system (Maryland State Department of Education, 2009b). Yet challenges remain, including the enduring need to convince thousands of child care providers across the state to follow the systematic use of standards, curriculum, and assessment. The Division also feels that the exchange of assessment data between pre-K and kindergarten teachers as a means of smoothing transitions is not occurring often enough, so it is trying to nurture collaborations to facilitate this component of effective transitions between pre-K, kindergarten, and first grade (Grafwallner, 2005).

Conclusion   The MMSR is an ambitious effort to align early learning programs with elementary schooling that is founded on the use of assessment tools. The focus on assessment is not for the program's own sake; rather, the state has implemented a comprehensive strategy to use the assessment results to alter curricula and instruction in ways that foster connections between a child's experiences in preschool programs with those that begin in kindergarten and the elementary grades.

Perhaps most important, this MMSR has prompted a remarkable degree of participation from both preschool and kindergarten teachers:

We figured this would go for a year and die. And then suddenly, the initial resistance turned into an enormously positive reception. The early childhood community became very eager to get the information each year, and the data became a springboard for other action. You have to hope that people come on board, learn about it, and become companions in the effort. The training had something to do with it, but it also filled a void. The field was fragmented and people were not talking to each other. The MMSR got everyone talking and made them see how it really is all about the kids, and then people even started feeling proud of it. (R. Grafwallner, personal communication, July 10, 2009)

REFERENCES

Barnett, W.S., Lamy, C., & Jung, K. (2005). *The effects of state prekindergarten programs on young children's school readiness in five states.* Retrieved from http://www.nieer.org/resources/research/multistate/fullreport.pdf

Early, D., Barbarin, O., Bryant, D., Burchinal, M., Chang, F., Clifford, D., et al. (2005). *Pre-kindergarten in eleven states; NCEDL's multi-state study of pre-kindergarten & study of state-wide early education programs* (SWEEP) (NCEDL Working Paper). University of North Carolina–Chapel Hill.

Gilliam, W.S., & Zigler, E.F. (2004). *State efforts to evaluate the effects of prekindergarten: 1977 to 2003.* Retrieved from http://www.nieer.org/resources/research/StateEfforts.pdf

Grafwallner, R. (2005). *Maryland Model for School Readiness (MMSR) kindergarten assessment: A large-scale childhood assessment project to establish a statewide instructional accountability system.* Paper prepared for the National Early Childhood Accountability Task Force, Pew Charitable Trusts, Philadelphia.

Kauerz, K. (2006). *K–2 standards and assessments: A 50-state review.* The National Early Childhood Accountability Task Force. Retrieved from http://www.pewtrusts.org/uploadedFiles/wwwpewtrustsorg/Reports/Pre-k_education/kauerz%20K_2%20Paper_TSformatted_12Jun06.pdf

Maryland Division of Early Childhood Development. (2007). *Maryland Model of School Readiness (MMSR): Kindergarten expanded exemplars, fall/entry.* Baltimore: Author. Retrieved from http://mdk12.org/instruction/mmsrexemplars/pdf/ExamplarsKindergarten_Fall.pdf

Maryland State Department of Education. (2009a). *School Improvement in Maryland: Maryland Model of School Readiness (MMSR).* Baltimore: Author. Retrieved from http://mdk12.org/instruction/ensure/MMSR/index.html

Maryland State Department of Education. (2009b). *2008–2009 Maryland school readiness report: Children entering school ready to learn.* Baltimore: Author. Retrieved from http://www.marylandpublicschools.org/NR/rdonlyres/BCFF0F0E-33E5-48DA-8F11-28CF333316C2/19574/MMSR_ReadytoLearn_200809.pdf

Mitchell, A.W. (2005). *Stair steps to quality: A guide for states and communities developing quality rating systems for early care and education.* Alexandria, VA: United Way Success By 6. Retrieved from http://www.unitedwaywb.org/Community_Resources/Untitled/Success_by_Six/ResourcesSS/UWA_Stair_Steps_To_Quality.pdf

PEW Charitable Trusts Task Force Members, (2007). *Taking stock: Assessing and improving early childhood learning and program quality.* Philadelphia: PEW Charitable Trusts.

Ready at Five. (2009). *Getting Ready.* Retrieved from http://www.readyatfive.org/facts/documents/GettingReady_Statewide09.pdf

Schultz et al. (2007). Taking stock: *Assessing and improving early childhood learning and program quality.* Washington, DC: National Early Childhood Accountability Task Force.

Scott-Little, C., & Marsella, J. (2006, April). *Standards-based education, child assessment and evaluation in early childhood programs: A national survey to document state-level policies and practices.* Paper presented at the annual meeting of the American Educational Research Association, San Francisco.

Snow, C.E., & Van Hemel, S.B. (Eds.) (2008). *Early childhood assessment: Why, what, and how.* Committee on Developmental Outcomes and Assessments for Young Children, Board on Children, Youth and Families, Board on Testing and Assessment, Division of Behavioral and Social Sciences and Education. Washington, DC: The National Academies Press.

14

Transitions in Early Childhood

The Case for a Consistent, Competent, and Stable Workforce

Susan D. Russell and Carol Brunson Day

Workforce continuity is an important aspect of early childhood programs that can bring real benefits to children. Consider the example of early childhood teacher Patricia (Pat) Holman, who has been at the same center in Chapel Hill, North Carolina, for more than 20 years, having been promoted from an assistant teacher to the master teacher in the toddler Early Head Start classroom. Her many years of experience allow her to serve as a mentor to new teachers, helping them develop their skills. In addition, because Pat has lived and worked in the community for many years, she is connected to many of the families she serves. Anna Mercer-McLean, the center's director, described how Pat's working style makes her one of the center's best teachers.

> Pat knows how to attend to the social-emotional development of young children, to work and support families, and encourage the development and use of language. She manages transitions with children well, whether it is a transition with mom into the classroom or moving between inside and outside activities or leaving her classroom to go to the new classroom when the child is ready. Pat takes personal care with each child, whether with words, a hug, or holding them at the window to say goodbye. She helps children use words to express themselves, and gives them words when they don't have them. She walks and talks children through the process when they are unsure of what to do. She helps guide and support friendships when a new child comes to the class and doesn't know anyone. She uses songs and games to help transition from daily routines, and she smiles and laughs with her children to show how much she cares. She enjoys her children and they can count on her to be there for them.

INTRODUCTION

Young children need and deserve to have families and communities which provide opportunities that foster the best possible chance for their productive lives and bright futures. Over the past 30 years, this goal has become much more feasible as the field of early care and education (ECE) has expanded dramatically. Growth has occurred in response to mounting evidence that underscores the vital importance of early life experiences to ensure favorable outcomes. From new revelations about early brain development (Shonkoff & Phillips, 2000) to emerging confirmation about the lifelong benefits of early intervention (Schweinhart et al., 2005), there is every indication that increased participation in quality early education will bring benefits to the children who are involved and to their society.

With growth comes the responsibility of ECE to build systems of services that address the dramatic changes in young childrens experiances. During most of the 20th century, young children made one significant transition from home to school when they entered kindergarten or first grade. But today's young children often experience multiple transitions before they even reach kindergarten. As women have increased their participation in the labor force, more children have transitioned from the home, to infant care, to preschool care and then on to school. The greater use of infant care and prekindergarten programs means that children may now make two or three transitions between early care and education settings before they transition to school.

Transitions for young children can take place 1) between home and an early childhood program, 2) between programs as children move from an infant–toddler program to a prekindergarten (pre-K) program or from a pre-K program to kindergarten, 3) within programs as children change classrooms or 4) within children's homes as a result of changes in economic or housing circumstances, separation and/or divorce of the parents, birth or adoption of siblings, or the serious illness or death of a family member. Such situations require children to adjust to differences in people, environments, expectations, routines, and perhaps cultures and languages.

As we examine the diverse transitions that children make, we must pay particular attention to the role that adults play in facilitating children's transitions. Children have many relationships with the people around them: adult family members, peers, siblings, and teachers. In this chapter we address the role of teachers in assisting children as they navigate diverse settings and situations. We focus on teachers for several reasons. First, after immediate family members, teachers arguably have the largest influence on the developing child. Second, contemporary early childhood teachers face multiple challenges and multiple transitions; they, too, must cope with the increasing number of transitions that children make as more children enroll in infant and toddler care, and they must deal with the transitions occasioned by rampant workforce turnover in American early care and education programs. Moreover, teachers must be sensitive to the demographic changes in the racial and cultural composition of the child population and must embrace their responsibility to create culturally supportive environments. Finally, as critical influences in the developmental trajectory of young children, early childhood teachers must commit themselves to helping children have meaningful, useful, and stable early experiences.

Specifically, this chapter addresses how the early childhood education workforce must cope with the transitions facing young children, the field of childhood education, and its own profession. We begin with an overview of contemporary issues that create the need for effective transitions in children's lives. Then we discuss the early childhood workforce and its ability to address transitions given the myriad other challenges it also faces. Policies that support the improvement of the workforce are presented as recommendations and are intended to enhance the early childhood workforce's capacity to address the transition needs of young children and their families.

BACKGROUND: TRANSITION ISSUES FACING YOUNG CHILDREN

A more diverse, stable, and skilled workforce is fundamental to bridging children's home and school environments. The need for a high-quality workforce is particularly acute because of several recent trends in the demographic characteristics of young children: increased diversity, higher poverty rates, and greater use of infant and toddler care.

Increased Diversity of Families with Young Children

Although the United States has a long history of ethnic and racial diversity in its population, diversity has increased dramatically in recent decades, a trend that is expected to continue (Child Trends Data Bank, 2003). From 1980 to 2000, the percentage of non-Hispanic white children of all ages fell from 74% to 62%, and it is projected to decline to 53% by 2020. The Hispanic child population, on the other hand, increased from 9% to 19% between 1980 and 2004 and is expected to rise to 24% by 2020. Non-Hispanic Asian and Pacific Islander children increased from 2% to 4% of the population between 1980 and 2000 and are expected to increase to 5% by 2020. Meanwhile, non-Hispanic black children have remained relatively constant at about 15% of the population since 1980 and are expected to remain at that level in 2020. Note, however, that race categorization has changed slightly, so estimates that are calculated after 2000 are not directly comparable with earlier ones.

When we look at specific age groups of children, we see that school-age youngsters (ages 5–17) are more culturally diverse than ever before, largely due to growth in immigrant populations. There are 9.7 million school-age children of immigrants in the United States, and they account for 18.3% of the total school-age population. The children of immigrants represent such a large percentage of the school-age population because a high portion of immigrant women are in their childbearing years, and immigrants tend to have more children than natives. The effect of immigration on public schools will continue to grow, because 19.3% of children approaching school age have immigrant mothers (Camarota, 2002).

As stand-alone facts, these data are remarkable even more impressive, however, are the changes that they will bring to early childhood programs. Early childhood teachers will need to be sensitive to the culture and language of the home, so they will need to be more culturally and linguistically competent than ever before. Moreover, policy and practices regarding staff recruitment and training will need to be more sensitive and responsive to cultural diversity in order to ensure continuity in children's development.

Higher Rates of Families with Children in Poverty

Another factor influencing the need for increased attention to transitions is the increasing number of families and children who are living in poverty. In 2008, 19% of U.S. children lived in families with incomes that were below the federal poverty line. The poverty rate is even higher among the nation's youngest children: Of those under age 6, 21.3% come from poor families (U.S. Census Bureau, 2009). The poverty rate is particularly profound among immigrants and their U.S.-born children under age 18. Immigrants and their minor children now account for almost 1 in 4 individuals living in poverty. Competent teachers are crucial for these young children who are facing the dual challenges of poverty and cultural or linguistic marginalization.

Economic downturns exacerbate poverty. According to the Foundation for Child Development (2009), the consequences of a significant decrease in family economic well-being will precipitate negative effects across other dimensions of child well-being. For example, although the rate of residential mobility for children normally decreases during a recession, severe housing crises increase the mobility of low-income families. They may lose their housing and either move or become homeless—two forms of mobility that are detrimental to children's neighborhood-based social relationships. The loss of the parents' employment or of the home can also disrupt children's participation in early care and education. Moreover, economic downturns have differential impacts on children; low-income African American and Latino children are generally more vulnerable to the consequences of economic fluctuations. When the economy is doing well, gains in their well-being are more dramatic; when the economy slumps, they are harder hit than their white counterparts because more African American and Latino children live in poverty to begin with (Foundation for Child Development, 2009). In sum, whenever family life is disrupted—by mobility, joblessness, or any other specific circumstances that often accompany poverty—the instability that children experience at home and in their neighborhoods magnifies the need for workforce continuity in their care arrangements. Indeed, the early childhood workforce plays a critical role in ameliorating the negative impact of poverty, disruption, and cultural alienation. Teacher stability and continuity is essential in order to provide a consistent context for children.

Increased Use of Early Care and Education for Infants and Toddlers

A third circumstance that requires us to pay greater attention to transition and continuity is the growing number of infants and toddlers in out-of-home care. More than half of mothers with infants return to work by the time their babies are 6 months old (U.S. Census Bureau, 2008). Forty-five percent of requests made to child care resource and referral agencies nationally are for referrals for infant or toddler care (National Association of Child Care Resource & Referral Agencies, 2008). During the work week, these very young children often spend more waking hours with their early childhood teachers than with their parents. Therefore, it is critical for the teachers and ECE settings to provide those very young children with the essential ingredients they need for maximum development in all domains. Babies need adults who are consistently present and responsive and who ensure that their needs for safety and security are met. When the environment is predictable, a young child is ready to explore and develop. When the environment is unpredictable and neglectful, however, children's stress levels increase, affecting their ability to learn (Parlakian & Seibel, 2002).

For some infants and toddlers, early care and education can be the inoculation that is needed to balance the negative effects of family poverty and stress. Parents who are preoccupied with a daily struggle to ensure that their children have enough to eat and are safe from harm may not have the resources, information, or time to provide the stimulating experiences that foster optimal brain development. Infants and children who are rarely spoken to, who are exposed to few toys, and who have little opportunity to explore and experiment with their environment may fail to fully develop the neural connections and pathways that facilitate later learning (Hawley, 2000). Children in these extremely disadvantaged circumstances can benefit greatly from exposure to rich early learning settings and competent teachers who effectively bridge children's home and school environments. Indeed, while the importance of transitions has long characterized the early childhood field, the new and highly significant trends we have just discussed accelerate the need to pay attention to transition in new ways.

THE ECE WORKFORCE: RESPONDING TO TRANSITIONS

High-quality early childhood programs recognize that supporting key transitions in a child's life requires highly competent teachers to give children and families the special attention they need. Programs also must have access to necessary resources so that their staff can effectively manage and support both the expected and unexpected transitions that children experience. Several major operational and structural conditions that characterize the early childhood workforce pose serious challenges to its overall ability to address transitions, particularly in light of the changing demographics presented earlier. Among the most inhibiting factors are 1) low teacher education standards, 2) teachers' limited access to higher education, and 3) high rates of teacher turnover.

Low Teacher Education Standards

"No ECE program can succeed without teachers who can establish warm and caring relationships with children, light the fires of children's curiosity and love of learning, and foster their development and readiness for school" (Whitebook, Gomby, Bellm, Sakai, & Kipnis, 2009, p. 1). Yet despite the amply demonstrated connection between teachers' skills and children's experiences, the standards for teacher education in child care settings are extremely low. Only 4 states require lead teachers in regulated child care centers to have a Child Development Associate (CDA) credential or an associate's degree; in 20 states, the standard is less than a high school diploma, and in 22 states, the standard is a high school diploma or a GED (National Association of Child Care Resource & Referral Agencies, 2009). In one study, Herzenberg, Price, and Bradley (2005) found that only about 19% of center-based teachers had a 4-year college degree and about 39% had some college.

Teacher education standards are generally higher in state-funded prekindergarten programs, 54% of which require teachers to have bachelor's degrees (Barnett, Epstein, Friedman, Boyd, & Hustedt, 2008). Head Start program standards increasingly are requiring teachers to have a bachelor's degree in early childhood education. Across all types of ECE programs, however, few standards address education and training with respect to children from diverse cultural and linguistic backgrounds or children whose families are in crisis. Teachers are not being given the skills they need to effectively facilitate smooth transitions.

Teachers' Limited Access to Higher Education

The ECE workforce has lacked, and continues to lack, access to the higher education system. In one large statewide study of the workforce, researchers found that 49% of teachers and assistant teachers and 45% of family child care providers who were not enrolled in college wanted to take college courses (Child Care Services Association, 2003). A number of personal and systemic barriers affect their decisions about attending college. On a personal level, barriers include the high cost of tuition and books, the need to balance work with family time, a lack of support from family or spouse, poor previous school performance, fear of admissions testing, fear of stringent requirements associated with general education coursework (e.g., math, English as a second language), and a lack of familial precedence in attending college. Systemic factors also limit access to college. College can be intimidating to people who have never been on a college campus. The application, admissions, placement testing, and financial aid processes can be daunting, and it is not easy for a working teacher to transition into the role of student and adult learner. The prerequisite courses that ECE teachers need to take may be unavailable or may not count toward a credential or degree. The days and times when classes are held and their locations may be inconvenient or inaccessible. Completing courses or a degree online is not always an option, and some states do not have a wide dispersion of colleges that offer early childhood degrees, so in those cases access to college may be limited by geography. For financial or family reasons, some students may need to learn part time, which extends the time they need to earn a degree. Field or practicum courses may require students to leave their work sites to teach in a practicum site, causing them to lose crucial income. Some students may be unaware that they need to complete previous learning and coursework prior to taking some classes, resulting in repetition of courses and later completion of a degree. Finally, compensation levels in the field do not adequately reward those who make sacrifices to pursue higher education.

High Rates of Teacher Turnover

In addition to having limited access to education and training, teachers experience working conditions in early care and education settings—job stress, little professional recognition and support, low salaries, and few benefits—that fuel teacher turnover. In turn, high rates of turnover produce conditions that are extremely disruptive to children's experiences. Nationally, teacher turnover in child care ranges from 30% to 40% annually (Whitebook, Sakai, Gerber, & Howes, 2001). This rate is significantly higher than the annual 16.8% turnover in public schools (National Commission on Teaching and America's Future, 2007), and it is a significantly more complex issue because of its unpredictability. Unlike turnover in elementary schools, which typically occurs between school years when children are transitioning to a new class anyway, turnover in child care happens throughout the year. As a result, children experience unpredictable transitions all year long, as well as the more predictable transitions that occur at the beginning of each year. Because infants and toddlers are particularly dependent on their caregivers, teacher turnover can have a significant impact on their daily routines and feelings of security and trust. Squires compared the high turnover in child care to the emotional trauma that children experience with divorce: "Children must repeatedly say goodbye to people they may have just learned to trust and love—a process that statistics tell us will happen again and again. In this loss crisis there are no visitation rights or joint custody" (2004, p. 74).

High turnover is largely related to the poor compensation within the early care and education workforce. Low salaries, lack of health insurance and retirement benefits, and little or no paid sick or annual leave are prevalent in the child care system. Within Head Start, salaries and benefits are better, but they do not reach parity with the public schools. As we noted earlier, standards differ among child care, Head Start, and pre-K programs, and so does teacher compensation. Thus, not only do teachers leave the field looking for better jobs but they also jump from one early education system to another looking for better compensation (Whitebook et al., 2001, 2009).

For young children who already experience numerous transitions in their lives, the instability associated with teacher turnover creates another fissure in their care. Improving workforce quality and stability, therefore, is crucial to minimizing the number of transitions that young children experience and helping them navigate the transitions that they do encounter.

POLICIES AND PRACTICES TO SUPPORT EARLY CARE AND EDUCATION WORKFORCE QUALITY AND STABILITY

Children are more likely to successfully weather transitions when they are enrolled in high-quality programs with competent teachers who are supported and adequately compensated and who make a long-term commitment to the teaching profession. Howes and Hamilton (1993) found that 4-year-olds in settings with high staff turnover rates expressed more aggressive behaviors than their peers. In another study, children who felt secure in their relationships with their teachers had more positive relationships (Howes, Whitebook, & Phillips, 1992). Skilled, consistent teachers in high-quality programs engage in practices to help children enter the early care and education setting smoothly and then successfully adjust to a new pre-K or kindergarten setting. Such teachers do not contribute to the stress of children and families by having the children undergo inappropriate transitions within their own programs or between programs. In order to stave off teacher turnover and, in turn, enhance the continuity that young children need, a number of issues need to be addressed: 1) sufficient resources for ECE programs, 2) standards that promote excellent early education and directly speak to transitions, 3) content that addresses transition in training and higher education coursework, 4) alignment between ECE and K–12 schools, 5) access to higher education for teachers, and 6) increased recognition and compensation for the ECE workforce.

Sufficient Resources

A strong and steady supply of highly trained ECE teachers who enter the workforce and remain there would be a major aspect of stable care that fosters children's development. Yet creating this condition would require a major increase in investments, because so many of the conditions that contribute to the transient character of the workforce stem from structural inadequacies within the broad early care and education system. Most states rely solely on federal funding from the Child Care and Development Fund to address structural problems within their child care systems; only a few states add a large or sustained commitment of state resources. The small proportion of available funds for ECE to support compensation efforts does not approach the amount needed to fill the gap between what families can afford to pay and what it would cost to have a degreed workforce with adequate compensation. Head Start, for example, has raised the education standards for its workforce without proportionally increasing its investments. It is encouraging that pre-K investments have dramatically increased in the past few years, with state investments almost doubling from fiscal year FY 2002 to FY 2008. During economic downturns, however, states may pull back on the investments they have made in child care, Head Start, and prekindergarten programs. Such withdrawals will cause the loss of the infrastructure for quality and staffing that has taken years to establish.

Raising Program Standards

It is critically important for children to be in high-quality settings that are governed by standards for ensuring excellence in the child care environment, the adult–child interactions that occur there, teacher education and compensation, and policies and practices that support children as they deal with multiple transitions in their lives. The expansion of pre-K programs has helped to raise the quality of early care and education in many states. Because pre-K is offered in child care settings in many states, its more rigorous standards can improve the overall quality of early care and education in those settings. Pre-K Now (n.d.) suggests that state-funded pre-K programs have contributed to an increase in funding for the child care system, increased job opportunities and salaries for early childhood teachers, and better support for transitions to public school.

The National Institute for Early Education Research identified 10 standards for pre-K programs and measured 50 state-funded programs against those standards in FY2008. While 46 of the state-funded programs met the standards for class size, 45 met the standards for teacher–children ratio, and most of them also met the standards for early learning, developmental screenings, and referral, far fewer programs met the standards for education and professional development. Only 37 state programs required teachers to have specialized training in early childhood education, and only 12 required assistant teachers to have at least a CDA credential. None of the 10 standards speaks directly to policies and practices around transitions.

Quality Rating and Improvement Systems (QRISs) that establish program standards are helping states improve the overall quality of child care. Standards for measuring quality often include an assessment of the overall classroom environment, the education and/or training of teachers, group size and ratio, the use of curriculum and assessment, and/or -national accreditation. Within high-quality settings, there is a greater chance that directors and teachers will have the expertise to implement policies and practices that support smooth transitions for young children.

The potential for QRIS to support the work force is seen in North Carolina, one of the few states have embedded their QRISs within the state's licensing structure, which means that all children in licensed child care programs are governed by this system. Since 1999, all licensed programs in the state have been rated on a 5-star system, with 1 star representing the minimum licensing requirements. In addition, substantial technical assistance and financial resources have been invested in helping teachers improve their educational levels and in helping programs meet higher QRIS standards. Tiered reimbursement rates for children in the subsidized child care system are tied to the number of stars a program has received.

The results for workforce quality and stability in North Carolina are promising. In 2004, about 37% of children enrolled in licensed homes and centers across the state were in 4- or 5-star programs; by 2009 that number had increased to 54%. In some counties, 1- and 2-star programs no longer exist. Data from an early childhood workforce study (Russell, Lutton, & Smith, 2009) found that the statewide turnover rate in centers had dropped from 42% in 1993 to 24% a decade later. The technical and financial resources (including funding to improve the education, compensation, and retention of the workforce) that accompany QRISs thus contribute to significant gains in program quality and reductions in systemic turnover.

The North Carolina example illustrates what can be accomplished with increased resources, higher standards, increased access by teachers to higher education, and major investments in the workforce compensation. Yet even within this well-developed system there is no mandate that early childhood programs address transitions for young children. Transitions are a neglected area in our standards across the nation, one that needs attention to ensure that young children have the support they need. Because children experience so many types of transitions (e.g., within the family, between home and early childhood programs, between one class or program and another), polices must take a broad view of the role that teachers and programs play.

Improving the Content and Quality of Education and Training

One belief that the ECE field holds steadfastly is that teacher qualifications affect the quality of children's classroom experiences (Early et al., 2007). Although ECE workforce qualifications remain uneven and low, a great deal of effort has gone into establishing standards for the content and quality of ECE teachers' professional preparation and the development of policies and practices that institutionalize these standards.

Over the past 20 years, progress has been made in developing and refining personnel preparation standards for the CDA entry-level credential (Council for Professional Recognition, 2006; Day, 2004) and for early childhood coursework at 2- and 4-year colleges (Hyson, 2003). Although content standards address the skills and competencies for managing transitions in children's lives and in the lives of families, they tend not to designate transitions as a separate skill area. For example, teacher standards for family engagement include supporting families that are under stress due to various reasons (e.g., relocation, death of a family member, or other kinds of trauma). Standards that are geared toward children's social-emotional development include supporting children who are entering school or changing schools. Among the CDA competencies, none of the 13 functional skill areas specifically requires candidates to demonstrate the ability. One specific indicator example does encompass helping families with transitions in the area of "Self" and requires CDA candidates to demonstrate skill to support social and emotional development and to provide positive guidance. From a content standpoint, standards, competencies, and coursework that focus on strategies for helping children and families through periods of stress, separation, and transitions are still weak.

State policy is beginning to establish professional preparation content standards, address the lack of cross-sector systems of professional development for early educators, and advance program administration (LeMoine, 2008). Progress is being made in defining the content of professional preparation and ongoing development for various roles in ECE as states delineate career pathway policies that align content. In some states, alignment appears in statute: New Hampshire has established a state-issued credential for child care, preschool, and Head Start personnel with specified education and training requirements. In other states, alignment occurs in nonstatutory ways: Colorado's Office of Professional Development has issued a standards guide that describes the development of common core knowledge and a mechanism for standardizing professional requirements and training. Career development policies provide an opportunity to raise teachers' awareness of the importance of transitions and improve their understanding of approaches to providing continuity. Such policies also can encourage the use of teaching strategies that support children's developmental levels, helping personnel to be prepared to serve a range of children as they develop over time. These skills and knowledge are at the heart of fostering effective transitions.

Although the content of professional development vis-à-vis transitions raises concerns, the structure of the training and higher education systems is perhaps even more problematic. As we noted earlier, removing obstacles to higher education would help ECE teachers attain credentials or degrees. But such obstacles are hardly the only challenge. Training and formal education systems need to be far better coordinated and to provide continuity for adults. Promising practices organize the informal training delivery so that it complies with the eligibility training requirements for the national CDA credential or links with other formal systems of professional development. Training systems such as the ones organized by the network of resource and referral agencies often set up registries for child care providers to keep track of their informal training experiences, provide advice and counseling about where to find education and training that leads to credentials or degrees, and secure continuing education credits for participants.

When structural continuity is missing, opportunities for ongoing professional development are lost, contributing to the disintegration of a skilled personnel pool. LeMoine (2008) also suggested that professional standards should align and create coherent career pathways for ECE professionals, making the case that state policy should support the continuous progress of individuals. Examples of states that have created such pathways are Connecticut, where multiple agencies created a statewide coordinated child care and early education training system (with scholarship assistance, career counseling, and training), and Pennsylvania, where a statewide Quality Career Lattice outlines eight levels of educational qualifications (LeMoine).

Last, collaborations of many types can yield systemic arrangements to help teachers enroll in comprehensive coursework to build a body of competence and substantive skill in practice. Multiple states have articulation agreements between 2- and 4-year colleges, including Oklahoma, Connecticut, California, North Carolina, New York, and New Jersey (Coffman, 2005; LeMoine, 2008). Although these agreements vary greatly, collectively their intent is to improve the content, quality, and consistency of the education and training for the ECE workforce.

Decreasing the Tensions Between Early Care and Education and K–12 Schools

Vast differences between teacher preparation standards and qualifications are evident between early care and education and K–12 public education systems, differences that contribute to a variety of discontinuities among the workforce. As we previously noted, K–12 systems require a 4-year degree, whereas child care requires far less formal education. In addition, the jurisdiction of the regulatory bodies governing each level of education remains separate. In general, state departments of education are responsible for primary-grade teacher qualifications and state departments of human and social services are responsible for establishing personnel qualifications within their governance of child care programs.

The structural discontinuities between the two segments of the early childhood workforce are substantial. The youngest children experience teachers for whom the requirements are lowest, who have the lowest status, and who participate in the highest turnover. Policy that aligns the two systems would help reduce the discontinuities and improve the services that young children receive.

Whitebook et al. (2009) made a case for aligning teacher preparation and professional development for K–12 and early childhood teachers. Alignment starts with a healthy understanding of the differences and similarities between ECE and K–12 among delivery systems, standards and educational requirements; teacher evaluation, certification, and career pathways; fieldwork; induction mentoring and professional development; and teachers' work environments. To move away from a silo view with K–12 as one world and ECE as another, we must understand the two sectors, work toward shared terminology, and build collaborative research agendas that will enable both arenas to learn from one another.

This theme is echoed by the National Association for the Education of Young Children (NAEYC) in a recently published set of policy recommendations for the workforce (LeMoine, 2008). The organization recommends that state policies create an integrated system of professional development that crosses the early childhood sectors—child care, Head Start, pre-K public schools, early intervention, and special education services. Such policies would intentionally promote the building and support of efficient cross-sector systems (or at least encourage alignment between them) to decrease duplication of efforts and increase sustainability. For example, policies should be embedded in or linked to the following state implementation strategies:

- QRISs
- Unified data systems
- Coordinating bodies or efforts for higher education
- Early learning councils
- Early childhood comprehensive systems planning work

NAEYC also addresses professional standards for teacher preparation and ongoing development and recommends that the standards be integrated with existing teacher licensing, state-based credentials, Head Start, and pre-K standards. In addition, the organization recommends that credentials, degree programs, and certifications be recognized across all sectors, including the licensing/regulatory sector, the higher education sector (departments of education or early childhood), and the program sector made up of agencies requiring standards that are specific to children's ages, development, or roles (such as Head Start programs). There are two additional recommendations to promote cross-sector integration of professional preparation and development systems. The first recommendation is articulation policies that connect institutions of higher education to one another and to community-based training; such policies ensure that advisory structures of organizations and initiatives include representatives from all early childhood education sectors. The second recommendation is to coordinate federal, state, and private funding sources for professional development system needs. Those recommended policies have the potential to minimize major discrepancies between teacher qualifications across ECE settings.

Increasing Access to Higher Education to Promote a Diverse Workforce

It is critical that early childhood teachers understand the cultural and linguistic backgrounds of the children in their classrooms so that they can minimize the discontinuity between children's home and school environments. It is also critical that we increase access to higher education for prospective teachers whose cultural and linguistic backgrounds match those of the students they teach. This access is essential to giving teachers the core knowledge they need concerning child development, cultural diversity, and the role of teachers in helping young children make successful transitions.

Community colleges are increasing their efforts to make education more accessible. Data from an unpublished study of 289 early childhood departments at community colleges in 16 states found that 73% of them offer ECE courses online, 89% offer ECE courses in the evening, and 39% offer ECE courses on Saturdays (Russell et al., 2009). More than three quarters of these community colleges (77%) had articulation agreements with 4-year institutions, averaging about two agreements per community college. New Mexico has set the standard for a well-articulated early childhood higher education system. The state created common course catalogues for 2- and 4-year institutions with clearly defined articulation of both early childhood and general education credits (Haggard, 2002a).

In the study of community colleges just cited, Russell et al. (2009) found that only 6% of the 289 community colleges they investigated offered courses in Spanish; the Milwaukee Area Technical College was one of them. Under the leadership of Dr. Wilma Bonaparte (Locke, Whitebook, Kipnis, Bonaparte, & Miller, 2009), the College has created a bilingual early childhood associate's degree program that expanded from 12 graduates in 2002 to 97 graduates in 2008. The program includes community outreach, flexible course schedules, and bilingual advisors, instructors, and tutors. The program has had 76 Hispanic graduates since it was fully implemented, and in the program overall some participants have attained grade point averages over 3.4. Many colleges and universities struggle with bilingual education because their states have prohibitions against teaching in languages other than English. Yet in Milwaukee, students are learning English as they complete their associate's degrees, and they are working within the increasing Hispanic community, using what they have learned to support young children and their families. Programs like the one in Milwaukee equip teachers with the linguistic and cultural competence to facilitate home-to-school transitions for linguistically and culturally diverse young children.

Comprehensive scholarships that address the needs of the working early childhood teacher have also facilitated access to higher education for many in the workforce. In FY 2008, 21 states invested $28.3 million of federal and/or state funds to support T.E.A.C.H. Early Childhood®

scholarships (Child Care Services Association, 2008). Scholarship participants completed almost 130,000 credit hours during the year. About 65% of participants were taking coursework leading to an associate's degree at one of 393 different community colleges; 7.4% were working toward baccalaureate degrees in child development or early childhood education. Scholarships were awarded to a diverse population of participants (46% were of color and 9% of Hispanic origin), helping to increase the knowledge and competence of a culturally and linguistically diverse workforce. For T.E.A.C.H. recipients who were working at the same time as they earned their degrees, overall compensation for their child care work increased and annual average turnover was less than 10%.

Another promising approach to helping first-generation college students, as well as bilingual learners, is the use of a cohort model to keep and support students together as they take required courses. In a 5-year longitudinal study, Whitebook et al. (2008) followed 120 students who were working to complete their bachelor degrees in early childhood education while simultaneously working in early childhood settings. The students were placed in cohorts of 6–30 attending a variety of higher education institutions in California. Almost all of them reported that the cohorts helped create learning communities and were a support system.

All of the strategies we have cited strive to increase access to and earning of early childhood degrees for a diverse and often excluded population of teachers. The diversity among teachers closely mirrors the increasing diversity of children in ECE settings and can be very effective in bridging home and school cultures and languages if the teachers are given opportunities to understand the basic principles and best practices of early childhood education.

Raising Compensation and Recognition

To ensure workforce stability and inhibit teachers' transitions in and out of programs, we need policies and funding that recognize and adequately compensate ECE teachers. *The Child Care and Development Fund Report of State and Territory Plans FY2008–2009* indicates that 10 states used its funds to provide wage enhancements for the early childhood workforce. Many of those efforts are modeled after the Child Care WAGE$® Project, which has been operating in North Carolina for 15 years and has a large repository of data on participants and their professional outcomes. In that model, teachers working in child care, Head Start, or prekindergarten settings are eligible to receive periodic wage supplements. The amount of the wage supplements varies according the level of college coursework that participants complete. Supplement amounts also vary on the basis of geography, ranging from $3,000 to $6,250 per year for teachers with a bachelor's degree in early childhood education. In North Carolina, the annual turnover rate among 8,753 recipients of the wage supplement was 16% in FY2008; the turnover rate was even lower for teachers with degrees. ECE teachers who were in geographic areas that offered larger supplements were more likely to obtain additional education and had lower turnover rates. More than 50% of the participants were individuals of color. There was no disparity between whites and people of color in terms of educational attainment: An equal proportion of both populations had 2- or 4-year degrees (Child Care Services Association, 2009). The Child Care WAGE model is a promising strategy to raise teacher compensation, stem high turnover rates, and provide children with more stable ECE arrangements.

Growth in state-funded pre-K programs has also given many teachers hope of earning fair wages and benefits. In the last 6 years, the number of 4-year-olds in pre-K has grown by 73%. Unfortunately, this growth has led to additional transitions for young children as their teachers migrate from child care into better paying pre-K programs. Ensuring that teachers in all programs are fairly and equitably compensated can help reduce the likelihood that children will experience burdensome transitions resulting from teacher turnover. Looking at compensation requirements, the National Institute for Early Education Research found that of the 50 state-funded programs, only 12 required all teachers to be paid on the public salary scale, 25 required teachers in public but not private settings to be paid on the public scale, and 13 did not require teachers in either setting to be paid on the public scale (Barnett et al., 2008). Salaries and benefits have improved in some states, but disparity still exists for child care, Head Start, and prekindergarten teachers, depending on where they work.

Most states require certification or licensure for teachers working in the public education system; this is not true in child care settings. However, a number of states have or are working on developing professional registries that collect and house information about the early care and education workforce. Registries often are the first step in documenting and recognizing the professional qualifications of personnel. In most states participation in the registries is voluntary, although in a few states it is mandatory. North Carolina is working toward a certification system for its entire early care and education workforce.

CONCLUSION

The early childhood workforce plays a key role in supporting young children as they make multiple transitions. Although we may look back and romanticize the way in which children were cared for in the past, gone are the days when tight-knit family and community networks provided stable informal care arrangements for young children. In an era of family mobility, single-parent households, and climbing rates of women in the workforce, romantic notions of early childhood have largely been replaced by a reliance on institutional care that requires a large-scale orchestration of policy and practice. Hope for the future of young children and of early childhood education rests with our ability to establish sound policies and practices. Such policies must promote adequate compensation for teachers, provide articulation between ECE levels of preparation, and create workplace supports to ensure the stability of recruitment, preparation, and retention of a consistent, competent, and stable workforce. In the end, we want to make it possible for every child to have a teacher like Pat, whose story, described in our opening and closing scenarios, is real and expresses the benefits we want to make available to all children and families.

Workforce continuity doesn't just happen. Pat Holman, the teacher who was described in this chapter's opening vignette, was supported by her center and by a financed professional development system. Her promotions occurred because Pat took advantage of T.E.A.C.H. Early Childhood® scholarships to earn both her associate's degree in early childhood education and her bachelor's degree in child development—while working full-time and rearing three children of her own. The scholarship helped her afford tuition, books, and travel; provided her with paid release time to study or attend classes; and ensured increases in compensation. It took Pat about 11 years to complete both degrees. In addition, Pat received a Child Care WAGE$® salary supplement every 6 months for about 5 years to encourage her to stay in her center. Because Pat continued to work in the same center and had completed her bachelor's degree, her earnings dramatically increased. Pat is no longer eligible for a salary supplement because her salary now exceeds $19 per hour. The Community School for People Under Six where Pat works and the children with whom she has worked have benefited from policies that support a well-educated, compensated workforce. The center serves a high proportion of children from low-income families. It meets the highest state standards with a 5-star license, is accredited by the National Association for the Education of Young Children, and meets standards for both Early Head Start and the state pre-K program. Indeed, highly competent and stable teachers working in high quality programs represent our greatest opportunity for supporting young children's transitions.

Case Study—New Mexico's Professional Development Initiative

Workforce Policy that
Promotes Alignment

Jocelyn Friedlander and Kate Tarrant

New Mexico's Office of Child Development (OCD) has developed The Early Care, Education, and Family Support Professional Development System (PDS), a workforce policy premised on alignment. It includes: a career lattice and corresponding credentialing system for all early childhood teachers, administrators, home visitors, and early interventionists that transcends early childhood settings and specific age levels. The PDS sets common core competencies and related training and licensure requirements for early childhood practitioners in New Mexico, thereby facilitating alignment of providers' knowledge and practices within these programs and across the age spectrum through third grade.

General Description The OCD was created by statute in 1989, was funded in July 1990, and became operational in November 1990. One of its primary statutory responsibilities was to establish a professional development system. Guided by the early childhood Higher Education Task Force, composed of faculty from the early childhood programs at New Mexico's institutions of higher education and of midlevel managers of early childhood programs within state government, the OCD established the PDS to build a competent and stable early childhood education workforce.

The central feature of the PDS is a career lattice structured with six levels of increasingly advanced competence and corresponding certification and licensure. It is designed as a developmental progression leading to the comprehensive early childhood education teacher license. In 2009, more than 3,500 individuals held the license, which is required for teachers in the state-funded prekindergarten program and is optional otherwise. (J. Fifield, personal communication, June 2, 2009).

The career lattice is linked to the state's certification mechanisms. OCD issues certificates for individuals who complete the requirements for the 45-hour entry-level course, the 1-year vocational certificate, the Associate of Arts or Science degree, and the 45-hour entry-level course facilitator training. To license early childhood providers, the PDS establishes requirements and the Public Education Department administers the license.

Implementation The PDS allows individuals to move seamlessly within and between early childhood credentialing programs and the various systems serving young children. It represents a major improvement from the situation in 1993, when the Higher Education Task Force convened for the first time. The committee's original members were faced with a highly "fragmented and inconsistent" approach to professional development across the state: There was no unifying philosophy, relationships between 2- and 4-year institutions were tenuous at best, and some institutions lacked coherent early childhood programs altogether (Turner, 2002). From its inception, then, the Task Force has worked to foster inclusiveness and consistency at multiple levels of the system.

The Task Force developed core competencies and a common course of study to be offered in public institutions across New Mexico. Common courses use universally accepted titles and syllabi. This work significantly streamlined the process of transferring credits, making it possible for individuals to progress smoothly along the career lattice regardless of where or when they did so. For example, common courses taken online are accepted at institutions statewide. Furthermore, because the system includes all teachers working with children from birth through third grade and is recognized by all programs serving young children, it grants a similar degree of flexibility to practitioners. As the Task Force puts it, the PDS facilitates horizontal, vertical, and diagonal movement within and across systems (Haggard, 2002). Of course, the ultimate hope is that building a workforce with comprehensive and universal training will translate to consistency for children as they transition among early care and education settings.

Implementing such an ambitious agenda has been challenging on many levels. Perhaps the most fundamental challenge has been overcoming conventional misconceptions about the very mission of early childhood education and, related to this, the need for a professionalized workforce. Judy Fifield, director of Early Childhood Professional Development, explained,

> Sometimes individuals don't understand what we're trying to do. They don't think of early childhood education as education; they think of it as babysitting. So the process of trying to provide information about the importance of early childhood education is a continuing struggle. We have to convey the importance of having people teaching young children who have that specialized education. (J. Fifield, personal communication, June 2, 2009)

Over the years, the OCD has reached out to individual principals and human resources personnel from elementary schools to emphasize the need for quality early childhood education and to increase support for the PDS. Although attracting support takes work, New Mexico has been fortunate to have leaders at the state level who have prioritized services for children. In particular, Governor Bruce King, under whose leadership the cabinet-level Children, Youth, and Families Department was created in 1992, set a precedent for state investment in young children (Paiz & Maes, 2002).

Beyond the very basic challenge of altering attitudes toward early childhood education, the Higher Education Task Force confronted conceptual challenges in determining the structure of the degree program. In particular, members strove to balance an imperative for inclusiveness with opportunities for specialization. A degree program with a single career path is in place, but a revised system with three pathways has been approved for implementation. As Director Fifield explains,

> We have been criticized for the current early childhood teacher training program because it is from birth to age 8, and people felt that that was too large of a developmental span, or age span. And because we were preparing teachers for early elementary grades, there was criticism that our competencies didn't focus as much as individuals thought they should on content areas like math and reading (personal communication, June 2, 2009).

Although it is still built around a common core, the new system will include specialized associate's- and bachelor's-level programs leading to credentials and licensure in three areas, all under the umbrella of Early Childhood Education: Early Childhood Teacher Preparation, Early Childhood Program Administration, and Family Infant Toddler Specialist. Core courses at the associate's level articulate to those at the bachelor's level, complemented at each stage by coursework in a field of specialization.

In addition, to address concerns regarding the age span for the existing early childhood license, the new Early Childhood Teachers Preparation pathway will allow for specialization in one of two age groupings: birth through age 4, and age 3 through grade 3. At the bachelor's level, both licensure and nonlicensure options will be available for the birth-to-4 concentration, and the age-3-to-grade-3 concentration will dedicate more focus to content areas than does the current program (J. Fifield, personal communication, June 2, 2009). Implementing a more complicated system does raise a host of logistical challenges, particularly the question of whether all new courses can be offered statewide. So as it revises the credentialing system, the Higher Education Task Force has tried to address conceptual and logistical challenges without sacrificing its original mission to foster consistency and inclusiveness.

Lessons Learned   New Mexico's Professional Development System is a unique effort that has generated valuable lessons for the rest of the country. Perhaps the most important lesson is that *a degree in early childhood education makes a difference in the classroom.* To teach kindergarten through third grade in the public schools, individuals must obtain either the current early childhood education license or an elementary education license—two pathways that, according to some, ultimately produce different kinds of teachers. Fifield explains:

> What we're finding as we've had this in place now for so long is that principals at elementary schools or human resource people at elementary schools prefer, and try to hire, individuals that have that early childhood license rather than an elementary education license. It makes a difference when they've done a specialized teacher preparation degree program. (personal communication, June 2, 2009)

According to Higher Education Task Force Co-Chair Erica Volkers, more public school administrators know and appreciate early childhood expertise. They say, "I want someone who is trained in early childhood" (personal communication, June 23, 2009). So teacher preparation in early childhood really does seem to translate into meaningful differences in practice.

Other lessons from the work accomplished in New Mexico relate to practical issues in designing and implementing a fundamentally new system. Crucial among these issues is recognizing that it takes time to build relationships. At the heart of the PDS has been the Early Childhood Higher Education Task Force, a group of faculty from around the state that has met consistently, typically monthly, for over a decade. To plan a new program, "getting a group together like the Early Childhood Higher Education Task Force is a place to start. It takes a while to establish that and build those relationships—to feel comfortable with each other" (J. Fifield, personal communication, June 2, 2009). The members of the Task Force are notable for their camaraderie and level of commitment to the initiative.

Another lesson from New Mexico is that relationships and commitments among individuals must be supported by investments at the state level. The Early Childhood Higher Education Task Force began from the ground up; without state backing,;individual members shouldered the burden of the group's operating costs (Turner, 2002). Although this was commendable, the arrangement eventually proved to be unsustainable. "There needs to be support at the state level like we have with the Child Development Board and the Office of Child Development supporting the work of the Task Force" (J. Fifield, personal communication, June 2, 2009).

A final lesson has been to focus on the capacity of the higher education system. Now that a fully articulated system is offered throughout the state, each institution has to devote resources to offering the necessary courses for students to achieve higher levels within the career lattice. Now that three pathways are being offered, institutions need capacity to sustain the courses for each specialization (J. Fifield, personal communication, June 2, 2009). In the words of Erica Volkers, "You can't demand a level of education without the capacity and incentives to support them in reaching that level" (personal communication, June 23, 2009). In this regard, the professional development system requires an ongoing dedication from the higher education community.

Future Directions   Following the implementation of the three new degree pathways, New Mexico's PDS will serve as a starting point for reform to other components of the state's early childhood system. For example, it will be possible to link the new career lattice with the state's quality rating system. "We're always looking at the quality rating system and what that should look like and what the requirements should be . . . . It will be interesting to see how that evolves over time" (J. Fifield, personal communication, June 2, 2009). In its current form, the quality rating system does not differentiate among levels of teacher preparation. Because it does not acknowledge the difference between an entry-level certificate and a bachelor's degree, the quality rating system provides few incentives for teachers outside the public schools—where licensure is not required—to pursue higher levels of certification. Linking the quality rating system to the early childhood career lattice would make for more meaningful distinctions between programs and create an incentive for teachers working with the state's youngest children to pursue licensure. This is just one of the ways in which this comprehensive professional development system might serve as a basis for further reform.

An ongoing effort for the Higher Education Task Force and the PDS is to advocate for compensation parity between early childhood teachers in elementary schools and their counterparts in private preschools (E. Volkers, personal communication, June 23, 2009). The higher pay offered by the public schools is a powerful incentive for teachers to leave preschool programs once they get licensed. Integrating teacher qualifications into the state's quality rating system is one strategy to reward licensed preschool teachers and encourage them to stay in their programs.

Conclusion   Led by the Higher Education Task Force, New Mexico's OCD has established an early childhood credentialing system with alignment as its guiding principle. A career lattice allows for both flexibility and continuity as individuals progress in their training and practice. The statewide availability of professional development courses and the articulation between levels of competence have streamlined the licensure process. And because the early childhood certifications are universally recognized by programs that serve young children, teachers can move within and across systems as they pursue higher levels of competence. Perhaps most importantly, these features of the PDS ensure that children will experience continuity as they transition among early care and education settings.

Case Study—Sweden's Integrated Teaching Degree

Alejandra Cortazar

Sweden's Integrated Teaching Degree is a government-mandated teacher preparation program for all preschool, primary school, and after-school (also called *leisure-time*) teachers (Ministry of Education and Research, 2000). It requires all teachers to have at least 3 years of training, including 1 1/2 years dedicated to a common core module that is relevant to teachers at all levels and the remainder of the time devoted to subject area or age-group specializations (Linde, 2003). By providing teachers with a shared knowledge of the full spectrum of child development, the degree program ensures that teachers understand the knowledge and competencies of their students as they pass through preschool and primary schools. This approach aligns teachers' expectations and therefore eases children's transitions from one grade level to the next. The integrated degree policy is one of the key strategies of the Ministry of Education and Research to provide children with continuous and coherent lifelong learning (Ministry of Education and Research, 2000).

Program Purpose   The unified approach of the integrated teaching degree provides all of Sweden's teachers, from preschool through adult education, with a common understanding of pedagogy. The teacher preparation program trains teachers to identify the goals of preschool, primary school, and adult education and to develop activities that are aligned with the national regulations and curricular guidelines (Linde, 2003). It builds a shared professional knowledge base and identity for teachers that encourages teamwork across grade levels.

The program is guided by goals stated in the System of Qualifications in the Higher Education Ordinance that teacher candidates should be able to meet upon graduation. The goals address the importance of sound pedagogical strategies, such as using assessment to inform practice, collaborating with colleagues in developing course content, communicating with families, and using technology in teaching. The goals also assert teachers' role in promoting students' appreciation of social values, human issues, and ecological and global conditions (Linde, 2003).

Participants   The integrated teaching degree is geared toward all prospective teachers, including those working in preschool, compulsory primary school, and after-school programs. More than 36,000 full-time students and 3,500 teacher trainers participate in Sweden's teacher preparation system. The integrated degree is offered at 26 universities and university colleges in Sweden, approximately half of all the universities in the country (Swedish Government Official Reports, 2008).

Origins   Early childhood teacher preparation in Sweden has evolved over the last 25 years, incrementally moving toward an integrated system. Historically, early childhood teachers were prepared at training academies and through a special course offered by upper secondary institutions. The system was completely separate from the training of primary and secondary school teachers. In 1977, greater attention to program quality fueled the integration of training for preschool and after-school teachers into the higher education system (Linde, 2003). Although separate degrees existed for the different levels of education, one set of institutions prepared the teaching workforce.

Further integration occurred in the early 1990s, in the wake of several studies that criticized teacher preparation for presenting teacher candidates with an incomplete and disjointed understanding of education. The integration coincided with other national efforts to build a unified early childhood system for Sweden's young children. In 1991, the Ministry of Education and Research added a flexible entry policy allowing parents to enroll their 6-year-old children in primary schools. Teachers from primary schools, preschools, and after-school programs were often involved in creating the curriculum for this age (Lohmander, 2004). Research highlighted the need for all teachers, regardless of the grade level or setting in which they taught, to have a common vocabulary and shared perspective on children's development (Pramling & Mauritzon, 1997). The government continued to work to bring preschool and primary schools together, and in 1996 administrative responsibility for preschool shifted from the Ministry of Social Health and Welfare to the Ministry of Education and Research in order to better bridge the two levels of education. The movement for the integration of preschool and primary education systems had clear implications for teacher education (Lohmander).

Following the reforms in the systemic revisions of early care and education, increased attention to accountability tilted attention toward teacher quality. In 2000, the Swedish government presented a bill to Parliament suggesting teacher education reform in the form of a single teacher preparation degree for all teachers. After Parliament approved the bill in 2001, the new integrated teaching degree replaced the early childhood degree and eight other teaching degrees (Linde, 2003).

Implementation The Ministry of Education and Research is responsible for administering all levels of education in Sweden, from preschool to graduate studies. In the case of teacher preparation programs, the government sets specific requirements that teacher candidates need to satisfy in order to graduate (International Review of Curriculum and Assessment Frameworks, n.d.). Higher education institutions then offer and operate the integrated teaching programs in a way that is consistent with the policies and the education law of the Ministry of Education and Research. These institutions also make decisions regarding students' admission, determine the exact content of the program, and choose the instructional and assessment methods that are used to prepare teachers for the classroom. Programs across universities can vary which allows can give students to choose a program or focus depending on their own interests (Linde, 2003).

Although there is some variation among the programs, they share a common structure based on the allocation of course credits. The integrated teaching degree consists of 180 to 330 credits and takes 3 to 5 1/2 years of full-time study, depending on the degree. (A year equals 60 credits.) Teachers of vocational subjects in upper secondary school must complete 180 credits to graduate, preschool and after-school teachers must complete 210 credits to graduate, primary-school teachers are expected to complete between 210 and 240 credits, and the degree for secondary teachers requires 270 credits. The exact number of credits depends on the subjects and specializations that are chosen by the teachers. Despite the differences in the duration of the degree program, all teachers must complete 90 core credits in general education.

The teacher training program is divided into three areas: general education, subject area knowledge, and specialization. General education covers topics that are relevant to teachers of all subjects and age groups, such as theory of teaching and learning, child and youth development, special needs education, interdisciplinary subject studies, and common national values of Swedish society (Kallos, 2003; Ministry of Education and Research, 2000). At least 15 of these credits must be completed through fieldwork in educational settings (Kallos). The flexible design of the program acknowledges that although all teachers need to have a shared common knowledge of education, knowledge in particular content areas is also important to quality teaching. Hence, the integrated degree requires teachers to take additional coursework in specific subject areas and specializations.

Students take at least 60 credits of courses related to an area of their interest to complete the subject area knowledge requirement. Students can choose a traditional subject such as language, English, or mathematics, or they may choose to learn about interdisciplinary studies or subject-related pedagogies (International Review of Curriculum and Assessment Frameworks, n.d.).

The last area of the degree entails a specialization in a particular age group or in a non-subject-related supplementary specialization. Depending on the specialization, the number of credits that students take varies, with a minimum of 30. At the end of the program, all students must complete a thesis or final project (5 or 30 credits) (International Review of Curriculum and Assessment Frameworks, n.d.; Ministry of Education and Research, 2000). By requiring prospective teachers to participate in fieldwork at the different stages of the teaching program, the integrated degree facilitates teachers' collaboration, not only among teachers of the same age group but also among teachers who share similar specializations and areas of interests.

Teachers who are already in service can access some general education and specialization courses either at the institution of higher education or through distance learning, thus strengthening the links between preservice and in-service teacher education. The integrated teaching degree puts additional emphasis on creating a research-based teaching cadre. Building research into the degree program supports teachers' development into reflective practitioners who have the skills and research methods to enhance their knowledge base (Kallos, 2003). It creates the continuum of lifelong learning for teachers and opens avenues for those who want to pursue postgraduate studies.

Since the implementation of the new teaching degree, several problems with the integration of certification of teachers across multiple grade levels have emerged (P. Klingbjer, personal communication, August 26, 2009). The cohesive policy design has not translated into cohesive practice. Indeed evaluations of the degree suggest that the program is highly fragmented and lacks consistency in its delivery (Åstrand, 2006). In addition, many experts perceive that the program places low demands on students because the general education core is too broad and vague. The flexibility of the program gave students options to finish their degrees without taking courses that were related to teaching and education. Some universities also created systems in which the core knowledge was not compulsory and graduates did not have the basic skills to teach initial reading and writing. This application of the program had direct implications for teachers' employability after graduation (Åstrand). As a result of these problems, enrollment in the teaching degree decreased and dropouts from the program increased (Swedish Government Official Reports, 2008). In order to face these challenges, the government engaged an inquiry chair to study the possibility of modifying the teaching degree. The government is developing a proposal to present to the Parliament at the end of 2009 (P. Klingbjer, personal communication, August 26, 2009).

Future Directions   The Ministry of Education and Research s reviewing the integrated teaching degree and considering several changes to it. The inquiry chair has presented a report titled *Sustainable Teacher Education* that includes proposals for modifying teacher education. Notably, the report proposes to divide the current integrated teaching degree into two degrees: one degree for preschool and primary-school teachers and one degree for secondary-school teachers. The preschool and primary-school teachers' degree would offer grade-level specialization for teachers and would take up to 4 years to complete. The secondary-school degree would offer grade-level specialization for compulsory education teachers as well as specializations in adult education, vocational subjects, and practical and artistic subjects (Swedish Government Official Reports, 2008).

In order to further professionalize teaching and attract more applicants, the new system will provide students with both a professional and a general degree. Thus, students who do not finish the professional specializations still receive the general degree (Swedish Government Official Reports, 2008). With this strategy, the government hopes to reduce attrition and ensure students' commitment to the program.

The inquiry chair's new proposal elaborates the core knowledge that all teachers need to share in eight domains:

> The organization of education and its conditions; foundations of democracy; curriculum theory and didactics; theory of science, research methods and statistics; development and learning; special needs education; social relations, conflict management and leadership; assessment and grading and; evaluation and development work. (Swedish Government Official Reports, 2008, p. 27)

The inquiry chair believes that all teachers, independent of their specialization or age group they teach, should share this knowledge and skill-set.

Conclusion   The integrated early childhood degree for all teachers within Sweden's Ministry of Education and Research provides the structural foundation for smooth transitions between preschool and primary school. Indeed, the integrated teaching degree was designed to promote pedagogical continuity across the different levels of schooling by fostering in teachers a shared understanding of appropriate practices for children at each developmental stage. It is important to note that teacher education policies are evolving to meet the needs of Sweden's young children and the teachers responsible for their education. Informed by research and the report of an inquiry chair, government officials are now finessing the system to further develop a workforce that is both unified and effective.

REFERENCES

Åstrand, B. (2006). Aspects of recent reforms of teacher education in Sweden. In *Posodobitev pedagoskih studijskih programov v mednarodnem kontekstu* (pp. 72–84). Retrieved from http://www.see-educoop.net/education_in/pdf/workshop/tesee/dokumenti/monografija/Astrand.pdf

Barnett, W., Epstein, D., Friedman, A., Boyd, J., & Hustedt, J. (2008). *The state of preschool: 2008 state preschool yearbook.* New Brunswick, NJ: The National Institute for Early Education Research.

Camarota, S. (2002). *Immigrants in the United States—2002: A snapshot of America's foreign-born population*. Washington, DC: Center for Immigration Studies.

Child Care Services Association. (2003). *Working in child care in North Carolina: The North Carolina child care workforce survey 2003*. Chapel Hill, NC: Author.

Child Care Services Association. (2008). *The T.E.A.C.H. Early Childhood® & Child Care WAGE$® Projects annual program report 2007–2008*. Chapel Hill, NC: Author.

Child Care Services Association. (2009). *The Child Care WAGE$ annual report for North Carolina*. Chapel Hill, NC: Author.

Child Trends Data Bank. (2003). *Racial and ethnic composition of the child population*. Washington, DC: Author.

Coffman, J. (2005). *Articulating success: A case study of successful early childhood education articulation in New Jersey*. Retrieved from http://www.acnj.org/main.asp?uri=1003&di=477&dt=8&chi=2

Council for Professional Recognition. (2006). *The Child Development Associate Assessment System and Competency Standards* (2nd edition). Washington, DC: Author.

Day, C.B. (Ed.). (2004). *Essentials for child development associates working with young children*. Washington, DC: Council for Professional Recognition.

Early, D.M., Maxwell, K.L., Burchinal, M., Alva, S., Bender, R.H., Bryant, D., et al. (2007). Teachers' education, classroom quality, and young children's academic skills: Results from seven studies of preschool programs. *Child Development, 78*(2), 558–580.

Foundation for Child Development. (2009). *The 2009 Foundation for Child Development Child and Youth Well-Being Index (CWI) report*. New York: Author.

Haggard, D. (2002a). Articulation, common catalogue of courses, and prior learning assessments. In P. Turner (Ed.), *La Ristra: New Mexico's comprehensive professional development system in early care and education, and family support* (pp. 83–90). Albuquerque, NM: Higher Education Early Childhood Task Force, Office of Child Development in the Children, Youth and Families Department, & the Center for Family and Community Partnerships at the University of New Mexico. Retrieved from http://www.newmexicokids.org/Resource/Library/LaRistra.pdf

Haggard, D. (2002b). Foundational decisions. In P. Turner (Ed.), *La Ristra: New Mexico's comprehensive professional development system in early care and education, and family support* (pp. 21–27). Albuquerque, NM: Higher Education Early Childhood Task Force, Office of Child Development in the Children, Youth and Families Department, and The Center for Family and Community Partnerships at the University of New Mexico. Retrieved from http://www.newmexicokids.org/Resource/Library/LaRistra.pdf

Hawley, T. (2000). *Starting smart: How early experiences affect brain development*. Chicago: Zero to Three and Ounce of Prevention Fund.

Herzenberg, S., Price, M., & Bradley, D. (2005). *Losing ground in early childhood education: Declining workforce qualifications in an expanding industry, 1979–2004*. Washington, DC: Economic Policy Institute.

Howes, C., & Hamilton, C.E. (1993). The changing experience of child care: Changes in teachers and in teacher–child relationships and children's social competence with peers. *Early Childhood Research Quarterly, 8*(1), 15–32.

Howes, C., Whitebook, M., & Phillips, D. (1992). Thresholds of quality: Implications for the social development of children in center-based child care. *Child Development, 63,* 449–460.

Hyson, M. (Ed.). (2003). *Preparing early childhood professionals: NAEYC's standards for programs*. Washington, DC: National Association for the Education of Young Children.

International Review of Curriculum and Assessment Frameworks. (n.d.). Retrieved from http://www.inca.org.uk/723.html

LeMoine, S. (2008). *Workforce designs: A policy blueprint for state early childhood professional development systems*. *NAEYC Public Policy Report*. Washington, DC: National Association for the Education of Young Children.

Linde, G. (2003). The meaning of a teacher education reform: National story-telling and global trends in Sweden. *European Journal of Teacher Education, 26*(1), 109–122.

Locke, E., Whitebook, M., Kipnis, F., Bonaparte, W., & Miller, A. (2009, June). *Increasing the diversity and success of early childhood teachers in higher education: Scholarships, cohorts, coursework and compensation*. Presented at the National Association for the Education of Young Children National Institute for Early Childhood Professional Development Conference, Charlotte, NC.

Lohmander, M. (2004). The fading of a teaching profession? Reforms of early childhood teacher education in Sweden. *Early Years, 24*(1), 23–34.

Ministry of Education and Research. (2000). *A new system of teacher education* (Government Bill 1999/2000:135, Fact sheet) Retrieved from http://www.unesco.org/education/uie/pdf/country/Sweden_app8.pdf

National Association of Child Care Resource and Referral Agencies. (2008). *Child care in America: 2008 state fact sheets*. Arlington, VA: Author.

National Association of Child Care Resource and Referral Agencies. (2009). *We can do better: 2009 update. NACCRRA's ranking of state child care center regulation and oversight*. Arlington, VA: Author.

National Child Care Information and Technical Assistance Center. (n.d.). *Child Care and Development Fund Report of State and Territory Plans FY 2008–2009*. Retrieved from http://nccic.acf.hhs.gov/pubs/stateplan2008-09/index.html

National Commission on Teaching and America's Future. (2007). *Policy brief: The high cost of teacher turnover*. Washington, DC: Author.

Parlakian, P., & Seibel, N.L. (2002). *Building strong foundations: Practical guidance for promoting the social-emotional development of infants and toddlers*. Washington, DC: Zero to Three Press.

Piaz, J, & Maes, J. (2002). Partners in change: The past is prologue. In P. Turner, (Ed.), *La Ristra: New Mexico's comprehensive professional development system in early care and education, and family support* (pp. 1–20). Albuquerque, NM: Higher Education Early Childhood Task Force, Office of Child Development in the Children, Youth and Families Department, and The Center for Family and Community Partnerships at the University of New Mexico. Retrieved from http://www.newmexicokids.org/Resource/Library/LaRistra.pdf

Pramling, S., & Mauritzon, U. (1997). Att lära som sexåring. *Skolverkets monografiserie*. Stockholm: Skolverket.

Pre-K Now. (n.d.). *Community-based pre-K providers*. Retrieved from http://www.preknow.org/educators/providers.cfm.

Russell, S., Lutton, A., & Smith, E.S. (2009, April). *Elements of a responsive early childhood community college system*. Presentation at the National T.E.A.C.H. Early Childhood® and Child Care WAGE$® Conference, Chapel Hill, NC

Schweinhart, L.J., Montie, J., Xiang, Z., Barnett, W.S., Belfield, C.R., & Nores, M. (2005). Lifetime effects: The HighScope Perry Preschool Study through age 40. *Monographs of the HighScope Educational Research Foundation, 14*. Ypsilanti, MI: HighScope Press.

Shonkoff, J.P., & Phillips, D.A. (2000). *From neurons to neighborhoods: The science of early childhood development*. Washington, DC: National Academies Press.

Squires, J.H. (2004). America's other divorce crisis. *Young Children, 59*(3), 74–76.

Swedish Government Official Reports. (2008). En hållbar lärarutbildning. Stockholm: Statens Offentliga Utredningar. Retrieved from http://www.regeringen.se/content/1/c6/11/67/37/b4b3b355.pdf

Turner, P. (2002). The higher education early childhood articulation task force. In P. Turner (Ed.), *La Ristra: New Mexico's comprehensive professional development system in early care and education, and family support* (pp. 27–41). Albuquerque, NM: Higher Education Early Childhood Task Force, Office of Child Development in the Children, Youth and Families Department, & the Center for Family and Community Partnerships at the University of New Mexico. Retrieved from http://www.newmexicokids.org/Resource/Library/LaRistra.pdf

U.S. Census Bureau. (2008). *Maternity leave and employment patterns of first-time mothers: 1961–2003*. Retrieved from http://www.census.gov/prod/2008pubs/p70-113.pdf

U.S. Census Bureau. (2009). *Income, poverty, and health insurance coverage in the United States: 2008*. Retrieved from http://www.census.gov/prod/2009pubs/p60-236.pdf

Whitebook, M., Gomby, D., Bellm, D., Sakai, L., & Kipnis, F. (2009). *Preparing teachers of young children: The current state of knowledge, and a blueprint for the future. Executive summary*. Berkeley University of California, Institute for Research on Labor and Employment, Center for the Study of Child Care Employment.

Whitebook, M., Sakai, L., Gerber, E., & Howes, C. (2001). *Then and now: Changes in child care staffing, 1994–2000*. Washington, DC: Center for the Child Care Workforce.

Whitebook, M., Sakai, L., Kipnis, F., Almaraz, M., Suarez, E., & Bellm, D. (2008). *Learning together: A study of six B.A. completion cohort programs in early care and education. Year I report*. Berkeley University of California, Institute for Research on Labor and Employment, Center for the Study of Child Care Employment.

V

Integrating Pedagogy, Programs, and Policy

15

Integrating Pedagogy, Practice, and Policy
A Transitions Agenda

Kate Tarrant and Sharon Lynn Kagan

As this volume has testified time and time again, early childhood represents a unique developmental phase during which children face many important changes. The way that children experience these changes—as important learning opportunities or as harmful disruptions in their growth—has implications for their development, their families' well-being, their schools' effectiveness, and their communities' success. For this reason, and as we share throughout the volume, families, schools, and communities all play important roles in ensuring that children thrive during periods of change and adjustment.

The need to focus on transitions is particularly pressing today because children are moving into early childhood settings at younger ages and are being faced with more academically demanding environments. In such a context, we contend, children need a different kind of education to prepare them for a world of unprecedented change: an education that is built on a foundation of continuity and structural alignment during the first 8 years of life.

This final chapter advances a transitions agenda that is guided by an ethos of integration to ensure consistency during children's early years. Our three-pronged model gives equal weight to pedagogy, programs, and policy. We integrate our framework with practical examples because, we contend, a conceptual framework alone cannot durably align young children's experiences. Finally, we integrate international and U.S.-based research and highlight exemplary efforts to spur cross-national dialogue and spark innovative strategies to address transitions and alignment.

We begin this chapter with a discussion of contemporary challenges which indicate that we need to pay greater attention to transitions. Then we highlight promising efforts that are underway to address transitions, emphasizing policies that target structural alignment. From that platform for change, we proffer pedagogy-, program-, and policy-oriented recommendations for an aligned early childhood system which ensures that children's transitions are smooth and that they promote healthy development.

CONTEMPORARY TRANSITION CHALLENGES

Although each chapter in this volume tackles transitions from a unique perspective, two cross-cutting themes frame contemporary considerations of transitions. First, the demographic composition of the population of young children who are eligible to attend early childhood programs is changing. Second, the institutional composition of early childhood efforts is changing. Each condition is in dramatic flux and each represents a real opportunity for strengthening alignment to ensure that young children have a successful start in life and in school.

Demographic Changes

Demographic changes are continually affecting the world's population, with fluctuations in mobility within and across countries. In the United States, for example, the population of children from immigrant families grew by 8.1 million from 1990 to 2007 while the native-born child population grew by just 2.1 million (Fortunay & Chaudry, 2009). Of children under age 6, 22% have at least one foreign-born parent and 93% of those children are born in the United States (Urban Institute, 2006). Far from being a monolithic group, these children are diverse in national origin, with 40% coming from Mexico while the rest hail from around the world (Hernandez, Denton, & Macartney, 2007). The vast majority of these children are, at some point in their lives, dual-language learners. Such shifts in populations are not unique to the United States but occur throughout the world. They thrust an unprecedented number of children into new linguistic and cultural settings, often settings that do not represent the traditions of their homes. Such juxtapositions at an early age make continuity in children's lives very important. If they are handled well, transitions can ease the negative effects of mobility and provide an opportunity for families and schools to forge positive relationships.

Mobility is not the only source of demographic changes. As society's appreciation of the importance of the early years grows, young children command more attention and services. New efforts to screen children for disabilities are increasing the number of children with recorded disabilities around the world. Again, using the United States as an example, the National Center for Education Statistics (2009) notes that the number and percentage of children receiving special education services consistently increased from the inception of the Elementory and Secondary Education Act of 1965 (PL 89-10) until the Individuals with Disabilities Education Improvement Act (IDEA) of 2004 (PL 108-446). The number of children and youth ages 3–21 who were served under the legislation jumped from approximately 3.7 million (5% of the total) in 1966–1967 to 6.7 million (9% of the total) in 2006–2007. Chapter 5 of this volume documents how children with disabilities need special supports as they encounter multiple transitions among an array of professionals. Because transitions are a daily reality for these young children, they constitute another population for whom greater focus on transitions is essential.

In the majority world, young children's needs have always been extreme.* The devastation that is created by natural disasters, armed conflict, and global epidemics combined with deep problems associated with persistent poverty are raising the ante for interventions to support young children's development. The data are stark. According to the United Nations Children's Fund (2009a), approximately 200 million children under the age of 5 suffer stunted growth as a

---

*Consistent with Chapter 4, we use the term *majority world* in preference to terms such as developing world, Third World, least developed countries, and global South due to the disparaging, outdated, or inaccurate connotations that are associated with those terms. In this chapter, the term *minority world* refers to wealthier nations, many of which participate in the Organization for Economic Co-operation and Development. These countries are home to a minority of the world's population; they are sometimes referred to as the global North or as developed, advanced industrialized, or First World countries.

result of extreme malnutrition. The HIV/AIDS epidemic alone has orphaned approximately 15 million children, and data indicate that these children are less likely to attend school than their nonorphaned peers (Joint United Nations Programme on AIDS, 2006). In fact, poor school attendance is a problem throughout the majority world. The United Nations Children's Fund (2009b) estimates that in 2007, 101 million school-age children were not enrolled in school; nearly two thirds of them live in conflict-affected countries or territories. Early childhood programs hold the potential to help overcome the specific challenges of low school enrollment and poor academic achievement, as well as the broader social challenges that face children and families in majority world nations (United Nations Educational, Scientific and Cultural Organization, 2007). Great care must be taken in designing and implementing early childhood services for children whose basic needs are compromised to bridge the home and school environments so that the care they receive is culturally relevant and sensitive to their needs.

Institutional Composition of Early Childhood Efforts

In addition to being affected by major demographic changes, young children are experiencing changes in the nature of the services that they receive. At the most basic level, throughout the world, heightened awareness of and attention to early childhood development has led to increased numbers of early childhood programs. New programs that serve children in formal centers, in homes, in community centers, and even under trees in small rural villages are burgeoning. Services to support families as their children's first educators are also being created. For young children worldwide, the advent of these services represents a key transition from the life of the home to that of a more formal setting. Recognizing the challenges that such transitions can pose at the entry to a formal program, many programs have established effective linkages between the culture of the home and early childhood services. Africa's Madrasa initiative and the W.K. Kellogg Foundation's SPARK initiative, described in Chapter 11's case studies, are examples of community-based approaches to bridging children's home and school environments.

Transitions for young children need to be supported not only at children's entry into a program but also during the program itself. As early childhood has tilted its orientation toward school readiness, the academic expectations placed on young children have increased. In the United States, for example, the advent of the No Child Left Behind (NCLB) Act of 2001 (PL 107-110) brought with it standards, assessments, and accountability for young children, raising the stakes for preschool education. In response to this legislation and the increasing demands of primary schooling, services for young children were forced to increasingly attend to children's transitions to the primary grades and prepare children to meet the expectations of those grades.

Policy changes in other countries also can increase the need to attend to young children's transitions. In Kenya, for example, the establishment of free primary education in 2003 boosted enrollment in the primary grades but compromised early childhood programs. Many families chose not to enroll their children in private early childhood programs because primary education was free; without the support of family fees, early childhood programs cut back on the quality of their services or closed entirely, thereby breaking the link that early childhood programs had been providing between home and primary school (United Nations Educational, Scientific and Cultural Organization, 2006). NCLB and the Kenya experience highlight the importance of attending to transitions when establishing education policy that will affect young children. Creating smooth transitions, then, becomes increasingly important as educators, administrators, and policy makers work to ensure a continuity of experience and expectations for young children.

Finally, as the number of early childhood programs increases, often with little or no systematic planning, multiple arrangements emerge, creating a need for institutional linkages among settings. For example, in the United States, many children experience multiple care arrangements, including home-based care, center-based care, and prekindergarten (pre-K) programs, sometimes even on a daily basis (Morrissey, 2009). Working parents, in particular, are often forced to piece together multiple arrangements to provide a full day of services for their children. As a result, a child may have to adjust to different settings, different expectations, different teaching styles, and different demands in the course of a single day. Recognizing this multiple-provider reality, early childhood institutions are making strong efforts to communicate with one another, to participate in collaborative efforts, and to improve the quality of their programs, irrespective of sponsorship or the label on the door.

CURRENT POLICIES AND THEIR FOCUS ON TRANSITIONS

Demographic changes and changes in the nature of services that young children receive make it readily apparent that we need to pay increased attention to transition. What is less apparent, however, is the attention that transition has been accorded in policy. Promising examples of policy focused on structural alignment appear throughout this volume. Here, we share U.S.-based and international efforts that create the policy context for attention to transition and pave the way for a future transitions agenda.

U.S. Federal Policy and Its Focus on Early Childhood Transitions

Applying a domestic lens in this section, we review four major pieces of federal legislation that provide early care and education—Head Start, IDEA, NCLB, and the Child Care and Development Block Grant (CCDBG)—to discern the degree to which they do and do not attend to transitions.

Head Start   Since its inception in 1965, Head Start has provided comprehensive child development services and has accorded special attention to bridging children's experiences with their homes, early childhood programs, and elementary schools. One of its founding goals is "establishing patterns and expectations of success for the child that will create a climate of confidence for future learning efforts" (B. Allen, personal communication, November 3, 2008). This goal placed Head Start on children's developmental pathway between home and elementary school. Recent policy changes, both in statute and regulations, place a new emphasis on transitions, specifically in the domains of ready schools and ready families. Head Start must now address transitions using a variety of strategies as it strives to model effective transitions through pedagogical, programmatic, and policy approaches.

Pedagogically, the Head Start Act mandates the alignment of curricular objectives and the coordination of teaching with other early childhood programs. Specifically, the law urges educators to link the curricula that Head Start programs use, the Head Start Outcomes Framework, and state early learning standards (Head Start Act, 2007). When state standards address the full birth–to–age-8 spectrum, as we saw in Chapter 7's case study of the model early learning standards in Wisconsin, Head Start curricular objectives are integrated into a common set of developmental expectations for young children. Alignment between Head Start and elementary school pedagogy is reinforced through joint training for school and Head Start staff.

Programmatically, the recent Head Start Act (2007) calls on grantees to 1) develop transition policies and procedures in collaboration with local educational agencies, 2) develop family outreach and support programs in collaboration with schools and other related entities, and 3) assist parents, especially parents with limited English proficiency, to understand the services that schools provide and the importance of parental involvement. The 2007 statute encourages Head Start programs to collaborate with public early childhood programs by sharing information, transportation, and facilities. It calls for joint staff training as well. Head Start's Performance Standards reinforce the Head Start Act's attention to transitions. For example, the Head Start Performance Standards (2007a) call on programs to assist parents in becoming their children's advocates when children make the transition into Early Head Start or Head Start and later into elementary school, a Title I preschool program, or a child care setting. Finally, Head Start Program Performance Standards (2007b) provide guidance to programs regarding transitions for children with disabilities.

From a policy perspective, Head Start's attention to transitions and alignment is multifaceted. Most directly, the aforementioned pedagogical and programmatic strategies are instantiated in legislation and regulation. As a part of their federal mandate, all Head Start grantees are expected to implement transitions strategies. Head Start legislation has other dimensions to facilitate alignment within the early childhood system. Specifically, the 2007 reauthorization called for states to designate advisory councils on early childhood education and care with representatives from the agency responsible for early childhood under IDEA, state education agencies, and local education agencies. The councils' many responsibilities include identifying opportunities for collaboration and coordination among entities that carry out federally funded and state-funded child development, child care, and early childhood education programs. Thus, Head Start policy reinforces structural alignment for this foundational component of an early childhood system.

Together, the Head Start Act and its associated program performance standards set the bar for alignment on multiple dimensions. There is still work to be done, however, to further align Head Start with elementary school systems. Workforce policies such as professional development requirements and compensation levels remain inconsistent. Furthermore, there is a need to determine the extent to which Head Start's policy requirements affect transitions in practice. Nevertheless, Head Start policy lays important groundwork for an early childhood system built on alignment.

IDEA   IDEA includes extensive language regarding transition. Chapter 5 discussed the implications of this law for pedagogical, programmatic, and policy alignment. IDEA guides services for children with disabilities: early intervention (Part C) for children birth to age 3 and preschool special education (Part B) for children ages 3–5. Early intervention providers work with the family to develop individualized family service plans (IFSPs) to meet the needs of younger children and individualized education programs (IEPs) to meet those of older children. Transitions and the relationships among service providers are integral components of both IFSPs and IEPs. Pedagogically, collaboration among therapists, teachers, and families ensures that what children learn aligns across all settings. From a programmatic perspective, the law states that parents, Part C service coordinators, and the local education agency must be involved in transition planning. Finally, the policy component requires states to promote collaboration among Early Head Start programs, early education and child care programs, and services under Part C. States also must train personnel to coordinate transition services for infants and toddlers who are served under Part C (IDEA, 2004). Like Head Start, transitions and alignment are high priorities within IDEA, shaping pedagogy, program practices, and public policy.

More Federal Early Childhood Education Policy: NCLB and CCDBG   Although Head Start and IDEA legislation make great strides for transitions, they are only two among multiple programs and myriad policies guiding the provision of early childhood education.

Indeed, both NCLB and CCDBG, the two other major federal early childhood policies, should accord transitions and alignment much greater attention. NCLB indicates that a schoolwide Title I program shall include "plans for assisting preschool children in the transition from early childhood programs, such as Head Start, Even Start, Reading First, or a State-run preschool program, to local elementary school programs" (No Child Left Behind Act, 2001). Title I funds may be used to fund a number of components of an early education program that may or may not address children's transitions. Funds may also be used for developmental screenings or comprehensive health, nutrition, and social services if these services are not otherwise available. Few states or districts, however, are implementing transition activities as delineated in the legislation. One explanation for the limited implementation of transition activities mentioned in NCLB is that not enough Title 1 funding is actually allocated to early education services because states and school districts direct these resources to other strategies to improve outcomes for children who are at risk of poor academic achievement (Ewen & Matthews, 2007).

Finally, the CCDBG, which supports a substantial portion of early childhood education in the United States, makes no explicit mention of transitions. Indeed, the CCDBG's focus on parental employment may even undermine continuity in young children's lives, because eligibility for this service changes with parents' employment status and families must regularly document their eligibility, which is an impediment to maintaining financial support for child care (Adams, Snyder, & Banghart, 2008). CCDBG's quality set-aside may be used to promote linkages between child care and other early childhood settings, yet transitions and alignment are not explicit dimensions of this policy.

In sum, we see that U.S. early childhood policy presents mixed approaches to transition, with some policies giving it noteworthy attention and others according it very low priority. This piecemeal approach to transitions at the policy level is antithetical to the kind of structural alignment that is needed to ensure continuity in young children's lives. Not only should all policies accord transitions and alignment significant weight but also they should provide the accountability and monitoring that will put alignment into practice. For that reason, we advance a transition agenda that integrates pedagogical, programmatic, and policy objectives in concert.

Transitions in International Policy

Throughout the world, public policy directed at young children and families tends to reflect each country's unique circumstances. Early childhood policies in the United States, for instance, reflect an ethos that favors the privacy and primacy of the family and that has left a legacy of diverse and highly idiosyncratic policies. In contrast, many other minority world countries, such as Sweden and France, have national policies that conceptualize early childhood education as an entitlement. In this context, transition policies include structural adjustments to foster horizontal alignment across programs and administrative entities and vertical alignment spanning grade levels. In the majority world context, policies that attend to transitions are emerging from a rights-based framework that is focused on the whole child.

In nations that have national early childhood policies, the establishment of an integrated governance structure has been a powerful step in bringing coherence to early childhood and primary school services. Sweden, for example, transferred the governance of preschool from the Ministry of Health and Human Services to the Ministry of Education in 1996, at the same time that it made preschool available to all children ages 1–6 years. This shift was detailed in the case study in Chapter 12. Reconceptualizing early childhood as part of the larger education system, with corresponding consolidation at the governance level, paved the way for a variety of policies—the preschool class, integrated teaching degrees, joint curricula, and program monitoring—that create structural alignment as children move through the education system. In France, responsibility for preschool similarly falls with the Ministry of Education, as described in the case study for Chapter 7. The arrangement has made possible the development of a national curriculum and a primary school cycle that transcends the preschool and primary years. The primary school cycle has served as the basis for aligned assessments and programmatic policies regarding teacher collaboration and parent involvement around transition plans for individual children. Although integration of early childhood services into the education administration is prevalent in Europe, several majority world nations, such as Brazil, Kazakhstan, South Africa, and Vietnam also have made strides to align early childhood and primary school service (United Nations Educational, Scientific and Cultural Organization, 2007). In these countries, a centralized approach to early childhood governance has created opportunities for pedagogical and programmatic alignment.

In many majority world countries, the challenge facing those in early childhood is not forging transitions among fragmented policies but creating policies where few exist. In such a context, structural alignment and developmental continuity can be built into the very fabric of early childhood policy development. Early learning and development standards are increasingly used as the starting point for developing integrated systems for young children. In countries like Tajikistan and Macedonia, for example, recently developed standards for what children should know and be able to do at various ages offer a base for future policy, programmatic, and pedagogical initiatives that create smooth transitions for children.

Nongovernmental organizations that work on early childhood education, including the United Nations, and its partners such as the World Bank, play a major role in early childhood education by incubating services and by collaborating with governments to expand efforts. The United Nations' Millennium Development Goals and the United Nations Educational, Scientific and Cultural Organization's Education for All Goal 1—to expand and improve early childhood care and education, especially for the most vulnerable and disadvantaged children—highlight the potential of early childhood services to mitigate poor outcomes for young children. Thanks to resources from nongovernmental organizations that are dedicated to achieving these goals, exemplary transition efforts are being promulgated throughout the world, such as the Step by Step program described in Chapter 8 that is supported by the Open Society Institute. These international examples demonstrate some of the ways in which transitions accommodate existing early childhood administrative, policy, and programmatic structures. Indeed, transition policy efforts reflect each country's political economy and sociocultural heritage.

A TRANSITIONS AGENDA: PEDAGOGY, PROGRAMS, AND POLICY

This volume is dedicated to renewing and strengthening a commitment to continuity in young children's lives. It does so by offering a new conceptual framework for understanding transitions. We contend that structural alignment along three dimensions—pedagogical, programmatic, and policy—is required to ease children's transitions during the early years. We believe that focusing on these three types of alignment will mitigate the divides that have characterized the field for decades, thereby easing the flow of services for young children. To ensure that meaningful and sustained improvements occur in the transition ecology, we offer several recommendations that correspond to each dimension of the structural transitions framework.

The recommendations that follow are designed to be applicable in majority and minority countries. Having noted that, we also are aware that countries differ on every measurable variable associated with early childhood development, including investment amounts, coverage and access, governance, and the nature of regulations and accreditation, to mention only a few. Some of the recommendations, therefore, will be more relevant in some contexts than in others. There is no way to address such variation in a single chapter, so, for the purposes of simplicity, we focus our recommendations at the state or nation-state level for several reasons. First, states and nation-states act with similar authority in early education and in primary education policy development. Second, as new policies unfold domestically and internationally, it is increasingly clear that the role of states or nation-states, rather than of municipalities, will be critical in advancing the transitions agenda. Finally, and pertinent to the U.S. context, states are the central actors that move the early childhood agenda: With the exception of Head Start, state agencies administer and monitor all public, federal early childhood programs. For these reasons, and fully recognizing that not all recommendations will apply to all contexts, we use the terms *states* and *nation-states* in the discussion that follows.

Area 1: Pedagogical Recommendations

Pedagogical alignment is central to high-quality early childhood education. It is the alignment of our expectations for what and how young children learn and for how teachers learn and teach. Development during the first 8 years of life is highly episodic and occurs just as children are experiencing some of the most significant transitions of their lives: moving from home to early childhood settings, and later, to elementary school. Far too often, however, major institutional fissures characterize young children's experiences. The child-centered constructivist instructional approach typically found in high-quality early childhood settings often runs up against a standards-driven, teacher-directed instructional approach in kindergarten through third grade. Neither teachers nor children thrive in that oppositional climate. Fortunately, as this volume has demonstrated, there are beacons of light showing a renewed commitment to the alignment of early childhood content, assessment, and curriculum. The case study in Chapter 12 described the work that the state of Pennsylvania commissioned to ensure vertical and horizontal alignment of pedagogical content. In Minnesota, New Jersey's Red Bank, and France, intentional linkages between early childhood and elementary school content have laid the groundwork for smooth transitions. Scaling up and replicating successful efforts like these are important to achieving pedagogical alignment based on sound principles of child development. The following recommendations lay out the important steps for doing so.

Recommendation 1.1: Align Standards   It is essential that the standards that govern what children are expected to know and be able to do are aligned across age periods. Although these early learning and development standards or guidelines will not be the same for children from birth through age 8, it is imperative to vertically align the domains and subdomains of the standards. It is also imperative that the standards represent the full range of children's development and that the expectations be developmentally sequenced. To implement this recommendation, states and nation-states should

- Review their standards for children from birth to age 8 to ensure that there is continuity in expectations and that all domains of development are addressed at each age level. Such a review process should be undertaken by teachers and academics from diverse disciplines every 3–5 years to incorporate research advancements.

- Allocate human, technical, and financial resources to complete the standards review and alignment process. Once the standards have been reviewed, any discontinuities should be rectified.

Recommendation 1.2: Align Content and Assessments   Just as the standards for young children's learning should be aligned from birth to age 8, so should the content of their

learning (often expressed as curriculum) and the assessments of their progress. Both horizontal and vertical alignment should be undertaken. Horizontal alignment creates consistency in early learning standards, curricular content, and assessment at each age level, exposing children to learning opportunities that comport with the expectations for their learning. Vertical alignment addresses the degree to which the standards and the assessments are age appropriate across the age spectrum from birth to age 8 and ensures that they are sequenced to avoid redundancies. To implement this recommendation, states and nation-states should

- Conduct horizontal and vertical analyses of their standards, content, and assessments to ensure that material is age-appropriate and properly sequenced

- Provide the human, technical, and fiscal resources to carry out such analyses

Recommendation 1.3: Support Teacher Preparation and Development

In order to cement continuity in young children's experiences, caregivers and teachers need to understand the stages of child development and be familiar with developmentally appropriate instructional and assessment strategies. In particular, it is essential for early childhood personnel to appreciate and clearly understand the development and the educational experiences that children have prior to and following their contact with early childhood staff. To implement this recommendation, states and nation-states should

- Review teacher certification standards to ensure that teachers across the early childhood continuum have the critical prerequisites to teach young children with a special eye toward transitions

- Review the content requirements of all teacher professional development efforts—formal and informal—to discern the degree to which they address transitions. Where transition is not addressed, correct preservice offerings and consider altering the requirements

- Provide and incentivize the joint training of preschool and school personnel to familiarize them with typical stages of child development, appropriate behavior for children of different ages, diverse instructional strategies, and parent engagement strategies

- Provide and encourage elementary school administrators to participate in professional development in early childhood education to ensure that they understand and support developmentally appropriate early childhood instruction

Recommendation 1.4: Provide Quality Enhancement

Greater attention to child development has fueled the development of many quality enhancement efforts. At this critical juncture, all of these efforts should be reviewed to discern the degree to which they address transition. The review should encompass efforts such as Quality Rating and Improvement Systems in the United States, program accreditation, and data system development. Internationally, the emerging bevy of policy documents should also be reviewed to discern their attention to transition. To implement this recommendation, states and nation-states should

- Review all existing efforts and documents that seek to promote quality in direct services for young children, with an eye toward discerning their commitment to transition. Such efforts should include a review of the ways in which early childhood programs and school quality, along with transitions, is defined and evaluated.

- Provide financial incentives for quality enhancement efforts that focus on transitions.

Recommendation 1.5: Support Dual-Language Learners and Children with Disabilities As this volume clearly demonstrates, transitions are important for all young children and their families, but they are particularly important and are too often overlooked for children who are learning a new language and children with disabilities. Each of the recommendations in this section has to be considered in light of the unique needs of those populations and the needs of the individual children therein. To implement this recommendation, states and nation-states should

- Require school districts and statewide early childhood programs that serve dual-language learners to develop individualized transition plans. Like IEPs and IFSPs for children with disabilities, transition plans for dual-language learner students should be coconstructed with their families. Such plans should delineate the steps that families and the program should take to support children as they make vertical and horizontal transitions.

- Evaluate the impact of transition efforts for children with disabilities on their developmental outcomes, using the results to improve the effectiveness and efficiency of transitions practices. Evaluations should consider the full array of informal and formal transitions that children with disabilities experience in their daily lives.

- Review existing curricula, assessments, regulations, and requirements to ensure that children's home cultures and backgrounds, as well as their physical and emotional needs, are accounted for in all transitions.

Area 2: Programmatic Recommendations

Programmatic alignment refers to continuity in the circle of services that children and their families experience. Such alignment aims to link the many programs and disciplines that serve young children, with the goal of fostering continuity in practice across these efforts. Programmatic alignment transcends the classroom and encompasses the efforts that happen in all elements of the programs, including the ways in which programs reach out to families, provide comprehensive services, and link to schools and other community institutions. Strategies to bridge disparate programs, such as the community-based strategy of the W.K. Kellogg Foundation's SPARK initiative, which was described in the case study for Chapter 11, bring continuity to early childhood education. Programs whose purpose is to minimize divides among families, early childhood settings, and elementary schools—like the Bureau of Indian Affairs' FACE initiative and Turkey's Mother Child Education Program, described in the case studies for Chapter 10—also fall within this category of alignment. Although there exist solid examples of programmatic alignment, we recommend scaling up existing efforts so that they will become normative for all programs.

Recommendation 2.1: Promote Ready Families Families are young children's first and most important teachers. Irrespective of intention, families teach children by modeling, demonstrating, and communicating attitudes, values, and expectations. It is especially important for the families of young children to generally understand the importance of the early years, and specifically appreciate the importance of transitions, to their children's healthy development. Informal and formal programs have the capacity and responsibility to acquaint parents with the implications of effective transitions and strategies to promote them. To implement this recommendation, states and nation-states should

- Provide information to all parents regarding the health and well-being of young children and the available services to achieve these ends

- Develop a voluntary child passport which chronicles the services that young children receive prior to their entry to school. Parents would safeguard such a passport and present it as their children receive services. The document would enable providers to know what services the child had received and would provide a means for coordination of such services.

- Provide universal parenting education on a voluntary basis to all families. This process should forge partnerships between families and schools and should take special care to support families as their children make essential transitions.

Recommendation 2.2: Promote Ready Schools

There is a great deal of outstanding literature about ready schools, and a bevy of wonderful models exist. We should build on these approaches and extend them to all schools, in particular ensuring that a key component of any ready schools initiative concentrates efforts on vertical, horizontal, and structural transitions. To implement this recommendation, states and nation-states should

- Review their ready schools efforts across the state to determine the degree to which such efforts incorporate a transitions component

- Create flagship schools informed by the FirstSchool model described in Chapter 9 that can serve as training centers for other schools. A flagship would receive stipends for collaborating with ready schools satellite efforts. This turnkey approach would reward existing ready schools for their accomplishments at the same time that they export the concept to other schools.

Recommendation 2.3: Ready Communities

Families and schools do not exist in a vacuum as they seek to ease transitions for young children. Communities need to adopt a transitions agenda that will engage them in the process. To implement this recommendation, states and nation-states should

- Provide incentives to a select number of communities or villages to delineate the services that they offer to young children and their families throughout the community. This mapping exercise would indicate the range of available services, agencies of sponsorship, and the population eligible for the services.

- In the communities where comprehensive service maps have been developed and where it is technically feasible to do so, fund the development of an electronic file that contains the mapped information. All child-serving agencies should be able to use and distribute the file; the goal is to make all community providers aware of the array of services that is already offered.

- Create community children's cabinets or other administrative entities within the executive branch of government to foster linkages among community services for children

Area 3: Policy Recommendations

Alignment in policy targets the infrastructure that supports historically disparate services—health services, early education and elementary school services, and welfare services. As we have noted earlier in this volume, historically the policies relating to early childhood at the federal, state, and local levels instantiated and even exacerbated fissures among the home, early childhood education facilities, and elementary schools. In most states, for instance, major differences in teacher qualifications for child care, Head Start, state-funded pre-K programs, and elementary schools reinforce the different expectations for the type of care that children receive in each setting. Both in Sweden and in New Mexico, the unified professional development frameworks for all teachers provide practical guidance for minimizing differences within the workforce. Yet deep inequity in teachers' compensation and work environments across settings persists in the United States and in many countries throughout the world. Much work remains to be done to develop and implement policies that will render true compensation parity for early childhood professionals and continuity for children. We offer the following policy-oriented recommendations to move the early childhood system toward structural alignment.

Recommendation 3.1: Improve Conditions for the Workforce   At the heart of any transition effort are the teachers whose well-being and working conditions affect the lives of the children whom they serve daily. Severe inequities persist that divide teachers who serve children of various ages. To resolve these inequities and to create a platform for transition, states and nation-states should

- Examine and rectify compensation disparities among teachers of preschool-age children and teachers of older children who have equal training, experience, and credentials. These factors, rather than where an individual teaches or the ages of the children who are taught, should guide teachers' salaries and benefits.

- Encourage the development of national guidelines for rigorous early childhood credentials. Consistent high standards would ensure that teacher credentials would transfer across settings and ages of children served and would attest to the competence of the early childhood provider. In addition to supporting the development of such credentials, states should encourage teachers to acquire credentials that meet these guidelines by paying for the teachers to complete their schooling, in return for 2 years of guaranteed teaching in the state. Such a credential would acknowledge the importance of transition to the educative enterprise.

Recommendation 3.2: Improve Funding   Throughout the world, per-child public expenditures vary dramatically for preschool-age children and their school-age counterparts. Resource inequities fuel inequities among services and hinder the capacity of institutions to deliver comparable transition efforts. To make funding more equitable, states and nation-states should

- Examine and rectify the state's per-child funding formula to reimburse services for preschool-age children on a regular and ongoing basis at the same rate per child as for elementary children. Such a reimbursement formula would elevate the quality, consistency, and continuity of early childhood services.

- Increase funding to support early childhood services; whether the funding is provided by governments or by nongovernmental organizations, new early childhood services should link with local primary schools

Recommendation 3.3: Establish Accountability   Increasingly, states and nation-states are establishing accountability and data systems that will enable the routine collection of data on school-age children. The overall goal of such accountability efforts is to improve services and outcomes for students. Because the achievement of young children is of equal concern, a provision for data collection and accountability monitoring for them should be considered. Unlike accountability for older children, such efforts must accommodate the unique learning approaches, episodic learning patterns, and individual development of young children. In addition, such efforts should be linked with those of primary and secondary education to ensure maximum utility of data processing and use of the data to improve children's education. To implement this recommendation, states and nation-states should

- Review their existing approaches to accountability to discern how best to create and link data systems for children across the age spectrum

- Fund the development and maintenance of a unified accountability system that uses a unique child identifier and begins at birth. Informed by the data from the accountability system, create continuous learning opportunities for children from birth through age 8.

Recommendation 3.4: Unify Governance   As we have noted throughout this volume, the governance and administration of early childhood services is highly idiosyncratic and varies with the funding stream, regulations, and governance mechanisms. To rectify the discontinuity that results from a fragmented policy context, states and nation-states should

- Consider creating a unified governance entity for programs and services for children who are below the age of formal school entry. Such an entity should be imbued with authority and accountability for the management of early childhood services. It should link officially with the primary and secondary school governance entity to ensure that pedagogical, programmatic, and policy alignment occurs.

- Require the early childhood governance entity to establish a transition oversight group. The focus of the group's work would be to prepare a transition plan documenting and delineating the status and nature of transition efforts in the state. The transition plan would include annual goals, strategies to accomplish these goals, and a method for monitoring the achievement of the goals.

Recommendation 3.5: Improve Transition Research and Evaluation   Although there has been considerable research on transition efforts, the new paradigm fostered in this volume suggests that the time is ripe to accelerate our research and evaluation efforts. We hope that new approaches to transitions will be undertaken as a result of the work of the volume's contributors. Such approaches should be carried out in contexts throughout the world and should be rigorously studied and evaluated. In some cases, the evaluations will necessitate the development of new instruments and new approaches to collective accountability. These efforts should be accommodated. To implement this recommendation, states and nation-states should

- Fund, perhaps as a part of the governance entity, efforts to evaluate transition practices with the goal of using the data to improve children's transitions

- Collaborate with one another to chronicle and evaluate their transition efforts

CONCLUSION

By definition, the work of transitions does not happen in a vacuum. It occurs in a dynamic landscape with changing demographic contexts and a shifting policy environment, which demand flexibility and adaptability of transitions policy reforms. It occurs because the very nature of early childhood education is characterized by temporal, disciplinary, institutional, and contextual variability. Given this perpetual state of flux, we present a conceptual framework of structural alignment to serve as an anchor for the early childhood system.

We conjecture that the documented failure of transition efforts to date lies in pedagogical, programmatic, and policy fissures that define early childhood education. These fissures are so deep that they cannot be bridged with one-time idiosyncratic efforts. They demand the construction of strategies that align the structural underpinnings of early childhood: pedagogy, programs, and policy. By adding structural alignment to the vertical and horizontal alignment that has historically characterized transition efforts, we hope to advance a way of thinking that accepts transitions as the norm. Now that we have examined early childhood through the transitions prism that embraces pedagogical, programmatic, and policy alignment, it is our hope and conviction that the research, knowledge, and recommendations embedded in this volume can catalyze reform.

REFERENCES

Adams, G., Snyder, K., & Banghart, P. (2008). *Designing subsidy systems to meet the needs of families: An overview of policy research findings*. Retrieved from http://www.urban.org/publications/411611.html

Ewen, D., & Matthews, H. (2007, October). *Title I and early childhood programs: A look at investments in the NCLB era* (Child Care and Early Education Series, Paper No. 2). Washington, DC: Center for Law and Social Policy.

Fortunay, K., & Chaudry, A. (2009). Children of immigrants: Immigration trends (Fact Sheet 1). Retrieved from http://www.urban.org/UploadedPDF/901292_immigrationtrends.pdf

Head Start Act, 42 U.S.C. § 9837 (2007).

Head Start Performance Standards, 45 CFR § 1304.40 (2007a).

Head Start Performance Standards, 45 CFR § 1308.21 (2007b).

Hernandez, D.J., Denton, N.A., &. Macartney, S.E. (2007). *Children in immigrant families–The U.S. and 50 states: National origins, language, and early education (2007–11)*. Retrieved from Child Trends website: http://www.childtrends.org/Files//Child_Trends-2007_04_01_RB_ChildrenImmigrant.pdf

Individuals with Disabilities Education Improvement Act (IDEA) of 2004, PL 108-446, 20 U.S.C. §§ 1400 *et seq*.

Joint United Nations Programme on HIV/AIDS. (2006). *2006 Report on the global AIDS epidemic*. Retrieved from http://www.unaids.org/en/KnowledgeCentre/HIVData/GlobalReport/2006/default.asp

Morrissey, T. (2009). Multiple child-care arrangements and young children's behavioral outcomes. *Child Development, 80*(1), 59–76.

National Center for Education Statistics. (2009). *Participation in education: Children and youth with disabilities (Indicator 9)*. Retrieved from http://nces.ed.gov/programs/coe/2009/section1/indicator09.asp

No Child Left Behind Act of 2001, PL 107-110, 115 Stat, 1425, 20 U.S.C. §§ 6301 *et seq*.

United Nations Children's Fund. (2009a). *Tracking progress on child and maternal nutrition: A survival and development priority*. Retrieved from http://www.unicef.org/media/files/Tracking_Progress_on_Child_and_Maternal_Nutrition_EN_110309.pdf

United Nations Children's Fund. (2009b). *All children, everywhere: A strategy for basic education and gender equality*. Retrieved from http://www.unicef.org/publications/files/All_Children_Everywhere_EN_072409.pdf

United Nations Educational, Scientific and Cultural Organization. (2006). *Impact of free primary education on early childhood development in Kenya. UNESCO policy brief on early childhood*. Retrieved from http://unesdoc.unesco.org/images/0014/001433/143320E.pdf

United Nations Educational, Scientific and Cultural Organization. (2007). Strong foundations: Early childhood care and education. Education for all: Global monitoring report. Retrieved from http://unesdoc.unesco.org/images/0014/001477/147794e.pdf

Urban Institute. (2006). *Children of immigrants: Facts and figures*. Retrieved from http://www.urban.org/UploadedPDF/900955_Children_of_Immigrants.pdf

Index

Tables and figures are indicated by *t* and *f* respectively.